W9-DAE-605

DECISIONS on the RULES OF GOLF

Official Rulings on over 1,000 Golf Situations

By the
United States Golf Association®
and
The Royal and Ancient Golf Club
of St. Andrews, Scotland

For more information on the USGA®, contact:

United States Golf Association®
Golf House
Far Hills, New Jersey 07931
(908) 234-2300

Printed in the United States of America

CONTENTS

Relief Situations and Procedure

Other Forms of Play

Administration

INTRODUCTION

Each year, the United States Golf Association and the Royal and Ancient Golf Club of St. Andrews, Scotland receive thousands of phone calls and letters regarding clarification of the Rules of Golf. In order to help millions of golfers around the world better understand how these detailed Rules are applied and interpreted, the USGA and R&A developed the comprehensive *Decisions on the Rules of Golf*. The topics of Etiquette, Definitions, and the Rules of Play are discussed at length. The format is geared towards questions and answers and is designed to be used as a reference at home, or right on the golf course.

Since 1951 the USGA and R&A have been meeting regularly in order to establish a uniform code of Rules. *Decisions on the Rules of Golf* is the result of these meetings. However, each year brings about a whole new round of questions not specifically addressed in the *Rules of Golf*. Committees meet from both organizations to discuss these new questions — anything from water hazards, and points of relief, to how to play a ball near a dead elk — and arrive at a decision with which both the USGA and R&A agree. *Decisions on the Rules of Golf* is amended every two years in order to keep up on the ever evolving game of golf.

The partnership of the USGA and the R&A has worked to further the understanding and enjoyment of the game of golf. With their official expertise, golf enthusiasts can rest assured that even the most unusual situation can be addressed. Whether it's a question of casual water, loose impediments, or line of play, no answer is out of bounds.

INDEX

AGREEMENT TO WAIVE RULES

ANTS

AREA OF INTENDED SWING

CADDIE (Continued)

CLAIMS AND DISPUTES (Continued)

CLUBS

COMMITTEE

LOOSE IMPEDIMENTS (Continued)

LOST BALL — See also "BALL: Identifying"

LOST BALL (Continued)

MARKER

MATCH PLAY

OUT OF BOUNDS (Continued)

OUTSIDE AGENCY

PLAYING FROM WRONG PLACE (Continued)

ROAD OR PATH (Continued)

ROUGH

RULE(S)

SAND — See also "HAZARD"

WRONG TEEING GROUND

THE RULES OF GOLF

Section I
ETIQUETTE

Courtesy on the Course

Safety

Prior to playing a *stroke* or making a practice swing, the player should ensure that no one is standing close by or in a position to be hit by the club, the ball or any stones, pebbles, twigs or the like which may be moved by the *stroke* or swing.

Consideration for Other Players

The player who has the *honor* should be allowed to play before his opponent or *fellow-competitor* tees his ball.

No one should move, talk or stand close to or directly behind the ball or the *hole* when a player is *addressing the ball* or making a *stroke.*

No player should play until the players in front are out of range.

Pace of Play

In the interest of all, players should play without delay.

If a player believes his ball may be *lost* outside a *water hazard* or *out of bounds,* to save time, he should play a *provisional ball.*

Players searching for a ball should signal the players behind them to pass as soon as it becomes apparent that the ball will not easily be found. They should not search for five minutes before doing so. They should not continue play until the players following them have passed and are out of range.

When the play of a hole has been completed, players should immediately leave the *putting green.*

If a match fails to keep its place on the *course* and loses more than one clear hole on the players in front, it should invite the match following to pass.

Priority on the Course

In the absence of special rules, two-ball *matches* should have precedence over and be entitled to pass any three-

or four-ball *match*, which should invite them through.

A single player has no standing and should give way to a *match* of any kind.

Any *match* playing a whole round is entitled to pass a *match* playing a shorter round.

Care of the Course

Holes in Bunkers

Before leaving a *bunker*, a player should carefully fill up and smooth over all holes and footprints made by him.

Repair Divots, Ball-Marks and Damage by Spikes

A player should ensure that any divot hole made by him and any damage to the *putting green* made by a ball is carefully repaired. On completion of the hole by all players in the group, damage to the *putting green* caused by golf shoe spikes should be repaired.

Damage to Greens — Flagsticks, Bags, etc.

Players should ensure that, when putting down bags or the *flagstick*, no damage is done to the *putting green* and that neither they nor their *caddies* damage the *hole* by standing close to it, in handling the *flagstick* or in removing the ball from the *hole*. The *flagstick* should be properly replaced in the *hole* before the players leave the *putting green*. Players should not damage the *putting green* by leaning on their putters, particularly when removing the ball from the *hole*.

Golf Carts

Local notices regulating the movement of golf carts should be strictly observed.

Damage Through Practice Swings

In taking practice swings, players should avoid causing damage to the *course*, particularly the tees, by removing divots.

Section II
DEFINITIONS

Abnormal Ground Conditions

An *"abnormal ground condition"* is any *casual water, ground under repair* or hole, cast or runway on the course made by a *burrowing animal,* a reptile or a bird.

Addressing the Ball

A player has *"addressed the ball"* when he has taken his stance and has also grounded his club, except that in a *hazard* a player has *addressed the ball* when he has taken his *stance.*

Advice

"Advice" is any counsel or suggestion which could influence a player in determining his play, the choice of a club or the method of making a *stroke.*

Information on the *Rules* or on matters of public information, such as the position of *hazards* or the *flagstick* on the *putting green,* is not *advice.*

Ball Deemed to Move

See *"Move or Moved."*

Ball Holed

See *"Holed."*

Ball Lost

See *"Lost Ball."*

Ball in Play

A ball is *"in play"* as soon as the player has made a *stroke* on the *teeing ground.* It remains *in play* until *holed* out, except when it is *lost, out of bounds* or lifted, or another ball has been substituted whether or not such substitution is permitted; a ball so substituted becomes the *ball in play.*

Bunker

A *"bunker"* is a *hazard* consisting of a prepared area of ground, often a hollow, from which turf or soil has been removed and replaced with sand or the like. Grass-covered ground bordering or within a *bunker* is not part of the *bunker.* The margin of a *bunker* extends vertically downwards, but not upwards. A ball is in a *bunker* when it lies in or any part of it touches the *bunker.*

Burrowing Animals

A *"burrowing animal"* is an animal that makes a hole for habitation or shelter, such as a rabbit, mole, ground hog, gopher or salamander.

Note: A hole made by a non-burrowing animal, such as a dog, is not an *abnormal ground condition* unless marked or declared as *ground under repair.*

Caddie

A *"caddie"* is one who carries or handles a player's clubs during play and otherwise assists him in accordance with the *Rules.*

When one *caddie* is employed by more than one player, he is always deemed to be the *caddie* of the player whose ball is involved, and *equipment* carried by him is deemed to be that player's *equipment,* except when the *caddie* acts upon specific directions of another player, in which case he is considered to be that other player's *caddie.*

Casual Water

"Casual water" is any temporary accumulation of water on the *course* which is visible before or after the player takes his *stance* and is not in a *water hazard.* Snow and natural ice, other than frost, are either *casual water* or *loose impediments,* at the option of the player. Manufactured ice is an *obstruction.* Dew and frost are not casual water. A ball is in *casual water* when it lies in or any part of it touches the *casual water.*

Committee

The *"Committee"* is the committee in charge of the competition or, if the matter does not arise in a competition, the committee in charge of the *course.*

Competitor

A *"competitor"* is a player in a stroke competition. A *"fellow-competitor"* is any person with whom the *competitor* plays. Neither is *partner* of the other.

In stroke play foursome and four-ball competitions, where the context so admits, the word "competitor" or "fellow-competitor" includes his partner.

Course

The *"course"* is the whole area within which play is

permitted (see Rule 33-2).

Equipment

"Equipment" is anything used, worn or carried by or for the player except any ball he has played at the hole being played and any small object, such as a coin or a tee, when used to mark the position of a ball or the extent of an area in which a ball is to be dropped. *Equipment* includes a golf cart, whether or not motorized. If such a cart is shared by two or more players, the cart and everything in it are deemed to be the *equipment* of the player whose ball is involved except that, when the cart is being moved by one of the players sharing it, the cart and everything in it are deemed to be that player's *equipment.*

Note: A ball played at the hole being played is *equipment* when it has been lifted and not put back into play.

Fellow-Competitor

See *"Competitor."*

Flagstick

The *"flagstick"* is a movable straight indicator, with or without bunting or other material attached, centered in the *hole* to show its position. It shall be circular in cross-section.

Forecaddie

A *"forecaddie"* is one who is employed by the *Committee* to indicate to players the position of balls during play. He is an *outside agency.*

Ground Under Repair

"Ground under repair" is any part of the *course* so marked by order of the *Committee* or so declared by its authorized representative. It includes material piled for removal and a hole made by a greenkeeper, even if not so marked.

All ground and any grass, bush, tree or other growing thing within the *ground under repair* is part of the *ground under repair.* The margin of ground under repair extends vertically downwards, but not upwards. Stakes and lines defining *ground under repair* are in such ground. Such stakes are *obstructions.* A ball is in *ground under repair* when it lies in or any part of it touches the *ground under repair.*

Note 1: Grass cuttings and other material left on the *course* which have been abandoned and are not intended to be removed are not *ground under repair* unless so marked.

Note 2: The *Committee* may make a Local Rule prohibiting play from *ground under repair* or an environmentally-sensitive area which has been defined as *ground under repair*.

Hazards

A *"hazard"* is any *bunker* or *water hazard*.

Hole

The *"hole"* shall be 4¼ inches (108mm) in diameter and at least 4 inches (100mm) deep. If a lining is used, it shall be sunk at least 1 inch (25mm) below the *putting green* surface unless the nature of the soil makes it impracticable to do so; its outer diameter shall not exceed 4¼ inches (108mm).

Holed

A ball is *"holed"* when it is at rest within the circumference of the *hole* and all of it is below the level of the lip of the *hole*.

Honor

The player who is to play first from the *teeing ground* is said to have the *"honor."*

Lateral Water Hazard

A *"lateral water hazard"* is a *water hazard* or that part of a *water hazard* so situated that it is not possible or is deemed by the *Committee* to be impracticable to drop a ball behind the *water hazard* in accordance with Rule 26-1b.

That part of a *water hazard* to be played as a *lateral water hazard* should be distinctively marked. A ball is in a *lateral water hazard* when it lies in or any part of it touches the *lateral water hazard*.

Note 1: *Lateral water hazards* should be defined by red stakes or lines.

Note 2: The *Committee* may make a Local Rule prohibiting play from an environmentally-sensitive area which has been defined as a *lateral water hazard*.

Note 3: The *Committee* may define a *lateral water hazard* as a *water hazard*.

Line of Play

The *"line of play"* is the direction which the player wishes his ball to take after a *stroke*, plus a reasonable distance on either side of the intended direction. The *line of play* extends vertically upwards from the ground, but does not extend beyond the *hole*.

Line of Putt

The *"line of putt"* is the line which the player wishes his ball to take after a *stroke* on the *putting green*. Except with respect to Rule 16-1e, the *line of putt* includes a reasonable distance on either side of the intended line. The *line of putt* does not extend beyond the *hole*.

Loose Impediments

"Loose impediments" are natural objects such as stones, leaves, twigs, branches and the like, dung, worms and insects and casts or heaps made by them, provided they are not fixed or growing, are not solidly embedded and do not adhere to the ball.

Sand and loose soil are *loose impediments* on the *putting green*, but not elsewhere.

Snow and natural ice, other than frost, are either *casual water* or *loose impediments*, at the option of the player. Manufactured ice is an *obstruction*.

Dew and frost are not *loose impediments*.

Lost Ball

A ball is *"lost"* if:

a. It is not found or identified as his by the player within five minutes after the player's *side* or his or their *caddies* have begun to search for it; or

b. The player has put another ball into play under the *Rules*, even though he may not have searched for the original ball; or

c. The player has played any *stroke* with a *provisional ball* from the place where the original ball is likely to be or from a point nearer the *hole* than that place, whereupon the *provisional ball* becomes the *ball in play*.

Time spent in playing a *wrong ball* is not counted in the five-minute period allowed for search.

Marker

A *"marker"* is one who is appointed by the *Committee* to record a *competitor's* score in stroke play. He may be a *fellow-competitor*. He is not a *referee*.

Matches

See *"Sides and Matches."*

Move or Moved

A ball is deemed to have *"moved"* if it leaves its position and comes to rest in any other place.

Nearest Point of Relief

The *"nearest point of relief"* is the reference point for taking relief without penalty from interference by an immovable *obstruction* (Rule 24-2), an *abnormal ground condition* (Rule 25-1) or a *wrong putting green* (Rule 25-3).

It is the point on the *course* nearest to where the ball lies, which is not nearer the *hole* and at which, if the ball were so positioned, no interference (as defined) would exist.

Note: The player should determine his *nearest point of relief* by using the club with which he expects to play his next *stroke* to simulate the *address* position and swing for such *stroke*.

Observer

An *"observer"* is one who is appointed by the *Committee* to assist a *referee* to decide questions of fact and to report to him any breach of a *Rule*. An *observer* should not attend the *flagstick*, stand at or mark the position of the *hole*, or lift the ball or mark its position.

Obstructions

An *"obstruction"* is anything artificial, including the artificial surfaces and sides of roads and paths and manufactured ice, except:

a. Objects defining *out of bounds*, such as walls, fences, stakes and railings;

b. Any part of an immovable artificial object which is *out of bounds*; and

c. Any construction declared by the *Committee* to be an integral part of the course.

An *obstruction* is a movable *obstruction* if it may be moved without unreasonable effort, without unduly delaying play and without causing damage. Otherwise it is an immovable *obstruction*.

Note: The *Committee* may make a Local Rule declaring

a movable *obstruction* to be an immovable *obstruction*.

Out of Bounds

"Out of bounds" is beyond the boundaries of the *course* or any part of the course so marked by the Committee.

When *out of bounds* is defined by reference to stakes or a fence or as being beyond stakes or a fence, the *out of bounds* line is determined by the nearest inside points of the stakes or fence posts at ground level excluding angled supports.

Objects defining *out of bounds* such as walls, fences, stakes and railings, are not *obstructions* and are deemed to be fixed.

When *out of bounds* is defined by a line on the ground, the line itself is *out of bounds*.

The *out of bounds* line extends vertically upwards and downwards.

A ball is *out of bounds* when all of it lies *out of bounds*.

A player may stand *out of bounds* to play a ball lying within bounds.

Outside Agency

An *"outside agency"* is any agency not part of the match or, in stroke play, not part of the *competitor's side*, and includes a *referee*, a *marker*, an *observer* and a *forecaddie*. Neither wind nor water is an *outside agency*.

Partner

A *"partner"* is a player associated with another player on the same side.

In a threesome, foursome, best-ball or four-ball match, where the context so admits, the word "player" includes his *partner* or *partners*.

Penalty Stroke

A *"penalty stroke"* is one added to the score of a player or side under certain Rules. In a threesome or foursome, *penalty strokes* do not affect the order of play.

Provisional Ball

A *"provisional ball"* is a ball played under Rule 27-2 for a ball which may be lost outside a *water hazard* or may be *out of bounds*.

Putting Green

The *"putting green"* is all ground of the hole being

played which is specially prepared for putting or otherwise defined as such by the *Committee.* A ball is on the *putting green* when any part of it touches the *putting green.*

Referee

A *"referee"* is one who is appointed by the *Committee* to accompany players to decide questions of fact and apply the *Rules.* He shall act on any breach of a Rule which he observes or is reported to him.

A *referee* should not attend the *flagstick,* stand at or mark the position of the *hole,* or lift the ball or mark its position.

Rub of the Green

A *"rub of the green"* occurs when a ball in motion is accidentally deflected or stopped by any *outside agency* (see Rule 19-1).

Rule

The term "Rule" includes:

a. The Rules of Golf;

b. Any Local Rules made by the *Committee* under Rule 33-8a and Appendix I; and

c. The specifications on clubs and the ball in Appendices II and III.

Sides and Matches

Side: A player, or two or more players who are *partners.*

Single: A match in which one plays against another.

Threesome: A match in which one plays against two, and each *side* plays one ball.

Foursome: A match in which two play against two, and each *side* plays one ball.

Three-Ball: A match play competition in which three play against one another, each playing his own ball. Each player is playing two distinct *matches.*

Best-Ball: A match in which one plays against the better ball of two or the best ball of three players.

Four-Ball: A match in which two play their better ball against the better ball of two other players.

Stance

Taking the *"stance"* consists in a player placing his feet

in position for and preparatory to making a *stroke.*

Stipulated Round

The *"stipulated round"* consists of playing the holes of the *course* in their correct sequence unless otherwise authorized by the *Committee.* The number of holes in a *stipulated round* is 18 unless a smaller number is authorized by the *Committee.* As to extension of *stipulated round* in match play, see Rule 2-3.

Stroke

A *"stroke"* is the forward movement of the club made with the intention of fairly striking at and moving the ball, but if a player checks his downswing voluntarily before the clubhead reaches the ball he is deemed not to have made a *stroke.*

Teeing Ground

The *"teeing ground"* is the starting place for the hole to be played. It is a rectangular area two club-lengths in depth, the front and the sides of which are defined by the outside limits of two tee-markers. A ball is outside the *teeing ground* when all of it lies outside the *teeing ground.*

Through the Green

"Through the green" is the whole area of the *course* except:

a. The *teeing ground* and *putting green* of the hole being played; and

b. All *hazards* on the *course.*

Water Hazard

A *"water hazard"* is any sea, lake, pond, river, ditch, surface drainage ditch or other open water course (whether or not containing water) and anything of a similar nature.

All ground or water within the margin of a *water hazard* is part of the *water hazard.* The margin of a *water hazard* extends vertically upwards and downwards. Stakes and lines defining the margins of *water hazards* are in the *hazards.* Such stakes are obstructions. A ball is in a water hazard when it lies in or any part of it touches the *water hazard.*

Note 1: *Water hazards* (other than *lateral water hazards*) should be defined by yellow stakes or lines.

Note 2: The *Committee* may make a Local Rule prohibiting play from an environmentally-sensitive area which has been defined as a *water hazard.*

Wrong Ball

A *"wrong ball"* is any ball other than the player's:

a. *Ball in play,*

b. *Provisional ball,* or

c. Second ball played under Rule 3-3 or Rule 20-7b in stroke play.

Note: *Ball in play* includes a ball substituted for the *ball in play* whether or not such substitution is permitted.

Wrong Putting Green

A *"wrong putting green"* is any *putting green* other than that of the hole being played. Unless otherwise prescribed by the *Committee,* this term includes a practice *putting green* or pitching green on the *course.*

Section III
THE RULES OF PLAY

THE GAME

Rule 1. The Game

1-1. General

The Game of Golf consists in playing a ball from the *teeing ground* into the *hole* by a *stroke* or successive *strokes* in accordance with the *Rules.*

1-2. Exerting Influence on Ball

No player or *caddie* shall take any action to influence the position or the movement of a ball except in accordance with the *Rules.*

(Removal of movable obstruction — see Rule 24-1.)

PENALTY FOR BREACH OF RULE 1-2:

Match play — Loss of hole;
Stroke play — Two strokes.

Note: In the case of a serious breach of Rule 1-2, the *Committee* may impose a penalty of disqualification.

1-3. Agreement to Waive Rules

Players shall not agree to exclude the operation of any *Rule* or to waive any penalty incurred.

PENALTY FOR BREACH OF RULE 1-3:

Match play — Disqualification of both sides;
Stroke play — Disqualification of competitors concerned.

(Agreeing to play out of turn in stroke play — see Rule 10-2c.)

1-4. Points Not Covered by Rules

If any point in dispute is not covered by the *Rules,* the decision shall be made in accordance with equity.

1-1/1 Two Balls in Play Simultaneously at Different Holes

Q. Two players on the 8th hole play their approach shots to the 8th green. They agree to tee off at the 9th hole and then putt out on the 8th green. This is to avoid having to walk back up a hill to the 9th tee and to save time. What is the ruling?

A. In match play, the players are disqualified under Rule 1-3 for excluding the operation of Rule 2-3 by failing to play the stipulated round.

In stroke play, the competitors are disqualified under Rule 3-2 for failing to hole out.

1-1/2 Player Unaware He Has Holed Out Puts Another Ball into Play

Q. A player, unable to find his ball, puts another ball into play. He then discovers that his original ball is in the hole. What is the ruling?

A. The score with the original ball counts. The play of the hole was completed when the player holed that ball.

1-1/3 Player Discovers Original Ball in Hole After Searching Five Minutes and Then Continuing Play with Provisional Ball

Q. At a par-3 hole, a player, believing his original ball may be lost, plays a provisional ball. He searches five minutes for the original ball and then plays the provisional ball onto the green. At that point, the original ball is found in the hole. What is the ruling?

A. The player's score is 1. The play of the hole was completed when the player holed the original ball (Rule 1-1).

1-1/4 Player Discovers Own Ball Is in Hole After Playing Wrong Ball

Q. A player played to a blind green and putted what he thought was his ball. He then discovered that his own ball was in the hole and that the ball he had putted was a wrong ball. What is the ruling?

A. Since the play of the hole was completed when the original ball was holed (Rule 1-1), the player was not in breach of Rule 15 for subsequently playing a wrong ball.

Player Discovers Own Ball in Hole After Playing Wrong Ball; Opponent Claims Hole and Claim Not Disputed — See 2-5/5.

Player with Lost Ball Concedes Hole; Ball Then Found in Hole — See 2-4/11.

1-2/1 Line of Putt Altered Purposely by Opponent or Fellow-Competitor by Stepping on It

Q. An opponent or a fellow-competitor purposely steps on the player's line of putt with the intention either of improving the line (e.g., by pressing down a raised tuft of grass) or of damaging it (e.g., by making spike marks). What is the ruling?

A. In either case, the opponent or the fellow-competitor was in breach of Rule 1-2. The penalty is loss of hole in match play or two strokes in stroke play, unless the Committee decides to impose a penalty of disqualification — See Note under Rule 1-2.

In stroke play if the line of putt has been damaged, the player, in equity (Rule 1-4) may restore the line of putt to its previous condition. A player is entitled to the lie and line of putt he had when his ball came to rest. The line of putt may be restored by anyone. (Revised)

Competitor Sanctions Repair of Spike Damage on His Line of Putt by Fellow-Competitor — See 13-2/36.

Loose Impediments Brushed Along Line of Putt Rather Than to Side — See 16-1a/10.

Line of Putt Stepped on Accidentally by Opponent or Fellow-Competitor — See 16-1a/13.

Ball Lifted on Putting Green Placed Ahead of Ball-Marker and Then Moved Back to Original Position — See 16-1a/17.

Ball Mark in Position to Assist Opponent Repaired by Player — See 16-1c/2.

Placing Object Marking Position of Ball in Front of Ball — See 20-1/19.

1-2/2 Shielding Line of Putt from Wind

Q. May a player lay his golf bag parallel to the line of putt to shield the line from the wind?

A. No. Such procedure would be a breach of Rule 1-2.

1-2/3 Flagstick Lying on Putting Green Removed by Player to Prevent Another Player's Ball from Striking It

Q. B removes the flagstick, places it on the putting green behind the hole and putts. A, believing that B's ball will strike the flagstick, picks up the flagstick, allowing B's ball to roll beyond where the flagstick had been placed. What is the ruling?

A. In match play, A loses the hole for removing an obstruction which might influence the movement of the ball while the player's ball was in motion — Rule 1-2 or 24-1.

In stroke play, A incurs a penalty of two strokes — Rule 1-2 or 24-1.

B incurs no penalty.

Adjustment of Flagstick; Player's Rights — See 17/4.

Opponent or Fellow-Competitor Attending Flagstick for Player Deliberately Fails to Remove It; Player's Ball Strikes Flagstick — See 17-3/2.

Ball Deliberately Deflected or Stopped on Putting Green by Fellow-Competitor — See 19-1/5.

Removal of Loose Impediments Affecting Player's Play — See 23-1/10.

Opponent or Fellow-Competitor Removes Obstruction Affecting Player's Play — See 24/16.

1-2/3.5 Player Repairs Hole After Holing Out But Before Opponent, Fellow-Competitor or Partner Holes Out

Q. After holing out, a player observes that the edge of the hole is ragged. He pats the ragged edge with his hand and smooths it. Does the player incur a penalty under Rule 1-2 if his opponent, fellow-competitor or partner has not holed out?

A. If the player smoothed the edge of the hole as a courtesy to following players, which seems likely, there is no penalty under Rule 1-2. However, he incurs a penalty under Rule 1-2 if he smoothed the edge of the hole for the express purpose of influencing the movement of the opponent's, fellow-competitor's or partner's ball.

Since the player had holed out, he is not subject to penalty under Rule 16-1a.

If a four-ball competition was involved and the player's partner had not completed the hole, the partner is subject to penalty under Rule 16-1a — See Definition of "Partner."

1-2/4 Player Jumps Close to Hole to Cause Ball to Drop

Q. A ball overhangs the lip of the hole. The player jumps close to the hole in the hope of jarring the earth and causing the ball to fall into the hole, which it does. Is this permissible?

A. No.

If the ball was still moving when the player jumped, the player took action to influence the movement of the ball in breach of Rule 1-2. In match play, he lost the hole. In stroke play, he incurred a penalty of two strokes, and the ball was holed.

If the ball was at rest when the player jumped, it should be assumed that the player caused the ball to move, and he incurred a penalty of one stroke in both match and stroke play under Rule 18-2a and was required to replace the ball.

If it is not possible to determine whether the ball was still moving, it should be presumed to be moving unless it was deemed to be at rest under Rule 16-2.

1-2/4.5 Player Leaves Putt Short and Instinctively Throws Putter at Ball

Q. A player putts and the ball comes to rest just short of the hole. The player then instinctively throws his putter toward the ball, but misses. Should the player incur a penalty for a breach of Rule 1-2 which prohibits taking action to influence the position of a ball?

A. No. See Decision 14/6 which deals with a similar case.

If the putter had moved the ball, the player would have incurred a penalty stroke under Rule 18-2a, and would be required to replace the ball.

1-2/5 Player Putts with One Hand and Catches Ball in Hole with Other Hand

Q. A player whose ball is on the lip of the hole putts with one hand and catches the ball with his other hand after the ball is below the level of the lip of the hole. What is the ruling?

A. The player purposely stopped his moving ball.

In match play, he lost the hole — Rule 1-2.

In stroke play, he incurred a penalty of two strokes and was required to place his ball on the lip of the hole and hole out — Rule 1-2. If he did not do so, he was disqualified under Rule 3-2 for failing to hole out.

In order for a ball to be holed (see Definition of "Holed"), it must be at rest within the circumference of the hole.

Ball Popped Up Swung at in Disgust — See 14/6.

Ball Overhanging Hole Knocked Away by Opponent Before Player Determines Status — See 16-2/2.

Casting Shadow on Ball Overhanging Hole — See 16-2/3.

1-2/6 Player Removes Loose Impediment Affecting Opponent's Lie in Hazard

Q. As a gesture of sportsmanship, a player removes a loose impediment in a hazard, thus improving the lie of his opponent's ball in the hazard. The player's ball was not in the hazard. What is the ruling?

A. Under Rule 1-2, the player incurs a penalty of loss of hole.

Other Decisions relating to Rule 1-2:

Caddie Holds Back Tree Branch to Prevent Branch from Deflecting Dropped Ball — See 20-2a/5.

Caddie Stops Dropped Ball Before It Comes to Rest; When Penalty Incurred — See 20-2c/4.

1-3/1 Players Agree Not to Tee Off in Prescribed Order to Save Time

Q. In match play, a player wins a hole. On his way to the next tee, the player returns to retrieve a club left at the last green and suggests that the opponent play first to save time. The opponent does so. Are the players in breach of Rule 1-3?

A. Yes, because they agreed to exclude the operation of Rule 10-1a. However, in these particular circumstances, the Committee would be justified in waiving the disqualification penalty under Rule 33-7. If the players subsequently agreed to exclude the operation of Rule 10-1a, they should be disqualified.

Competitors in Stroke Play Agree to Play Out of Turn But Not for Purpose of Giving One of Them an Advantage — See 10-2c/2.

1-3/2 Agreement to Concede Short Putts

Q. In a match, the two players agree in advance to concede all putts within a specified length. Is this contrary to Rule 1-3?

A. Yes. The players agreed to exclude the operation of Rule 1-1 and should be disqualified under Rule 1-3. Under Rule 2-4, the only stroke which may be conceded is the "next stroke" and it cannot be conceded in advance.

1-3/3 Player and Opponent or Fellow-Competitor Agree to Repair Spike Marks on One Another's Line of Putt

Q. A player and his opponent or fellow-competitor agree that they will repair spike marks on one another's line of putt. Is this a breach of Rule 1-3?

A. Yes. Both would be subject to disqualification for agreeing to waive Rule 16-1a (Touching Line of Putt).

1-3/4 Failure of Players to Apply Known Penalty

Q. In a match, a player discovers at the 2nd hole that he has 15 clubs in his bag contrary to Rule 4-4a, but his opponent refuses to apply the penalty. The extra club is declared out of play and the match continues. The Committee disqualifies both players. Is this correct?

A. Yes. Since the players agreed to waive the penalty, they should be disqualified under Rule 1-3.

1-3/5 Players Unaware Penalty Incurred

Q. In a match, A incurred a penalty stroke under Rule 12-2 for lifting his ball for identification without announcing his intention to B, his opponent. A did not penalize himself and B did not make a claim because neither A nor B was aware a penalty had been incurred. Should the Committee disqualify A and B under Rule 1-3 for agreeing to waive a penalty?

A. No. Since the players were not aware a penalty had been incurred, there could have been no agreement between them to waive the penalty.

Players Unable to Resolve Rules Problem Agree to Consider Hole Halved — See 2-1/1.

Disregarding Breach of Rules by Opponent — See 2-5/1.

1-3/6 Marker Attests Wrong Score Knowingly and Competitor Aware Score Wrong

Q. In stroke play, B failed to hole out at a hole. A few holes later he realized he had erred. A, B's marker and fellow-competitor, was aware both that B had infringed the Rules and that B knew this, but nevertheless he signed B's card. B was disqualified under Rule 3-2 (Failure to Hole Out). Should A, who knowingly overlooked the breach, be penalized?

A. A should have been disqualified for a breach of Rule 1-3.

Marker Attests Wrong Score Knowingly But Competitor Unaware Score Wrong — See 6-6a/5.

Competitor Seeks Help from Fellow-Competitor to Avoid Penalty — See 33-7/7.

1-3/7 Agreement That Side Losing After 18 Holes of 36-Hole Match Will Concede Match

Q. Prior to a 36-hole match, the players agree that they will play only 18 holes and whoever is behind at that point will concede the match. Is this permissible?

A. No. Both players should be disqualified under Rule 1-3 for agreeing to exclude the operation of a condition of the competition (Rule 33-1).

Wrong Form of Play Used in Match Play Event — See 6-1/1.

Match Decided by Wrong Form of Play by Agreement — See 33-1/4.

[1-3/8 Reserved]

Other Decisions relating to Rule 1-3:

Players Agree to Consider Hole Halved During Play of Hole — See 2-1/1.5

Two Holes Purposely Omitted in Match — See 2-3/3.

Handicap Stroke Given at Incorrect Hole in Error — See 6-2a/2.

Discontinued Match Replayed Instead of Being Resumed from Where Play Stopped — See 2-3/5.

Competitor Requests That Ball in Position to Assist Him Should Not Be Lifted — See 22/6.

Competitor Refuses to Lift Ball Assisting Play — See 22/7.

Player Who Has Reached Third Round of Match Play Disqualified for Agreeing to Waive Rules in First-Round Match — See 34-1a/1.

1-4/1 Player Distracted by Ball Dropped by Another Player Mis-Hits Ball

Q. As A was making his backswing, B accidentally dropped a ball, which rolled within six inches of A's ball. The appearance of the dropped ball startled A, causing him to top his shot. In equity, should A be permitted to replay his stroke?

A. No. Distractions are a common occurrence which players must accept.

1-4/2 Ball Adhering to Face of Club After Stroke

Q. A player plays a stroke from wet sand or soil and the ball adheres to the face of the club. What is the ruling?

A. In equity (Rule 1-4), the ball should be dropped, without penalty, as near as possible to the spot where the club was when the ball stuck to it. But see also Decision 14-4/1.

1-4/3 Flagstick Stuck into Green Some Distance from Hole by Practical Joker

Q. A practical joker removes the flagstick from the hole and sticks it into the putting green some distance from the hole. The players approaching the green are unaware of this action and they play towards the flagstick and not the hole. Do the players have the option to replay?

A. No. In equity (Rule 1-4), the players must accept the resultant advantage or disadvantage.

Other Decisions relating to Rule 1-4:

Player Lifts Ball in Mistaken Belief That Next Stroke Conceded — See 2-4/3.

Putting Out After Concession of Stroke Assists Partner — See 2-4/6.

Player Concedes Opponent's Next Stroke and Plays Before Opponent Has Opportunity to Lift Ball — See 2-4/8.

Ball-Marker Moved by Opponent's Caddie Accidentally — See 20-1/7.

Player Plays Away from Hole to Assist Partner — See 30-3f/6.

1-4/4 In Anger Player Strikes Ball Played by Player in Following Group

Q. A is nearly struck by a ball played by a player in the following group. In anger, A hits the ball back towards the group. Has A played a practice stroke or a wrong ball?

A. No. However, in equity (Rule 1-4), A should incur the general penalty of loss of hole in match play or two strokes in stroke play.

1-4/5 Removal of Obstruction in Hazard Would Move Loose Impediment

Q. In a hazard, a player's ball lies against a movable obstruction. A loose impediment lies on top of the obstruction in such a position that the player cannot remove the obstruction without also moving the loose impediment. Under Rule 24, the player is entitled to remove the movable obstruction, but under Rule 23 is not entitled to move the loose impediment. What is the procedure?

A. The player may remove the obstruction as authorized by Rule 24-1. If the loose impediment is incidentally moved in the process, in equity (Rule 1-4) the player incurs no penalty and he must place the loose impediment as nearly as possible at the spot where it originally lay.

1-4/6 Two Balls Lie Together in Hazard and Neither Is Identifiable

Q. Two balls lie together in a hazard. Both balls are playable. The ball nearer the hole would interfere with a stroke at the other ball, and vice versa. It appears likely that one of the balls is the player's ball. However, neither ball is identifiable because the markings on both balls are obscured by mud. What is the proper procedure if the other ball is (a) probably the ball of an opponent or a fellow-competitor or (b) an abandoned ball?

A. The Rules of Golf do not contemplate such a situation. In equity (Rule 1-4), the player may lift the ball farther from the hole following the procedure prescribed in Rule 12-2, and clean it to the extent necessary for identification.

In situation (a), if the lifted ball is a ball in play, it must be replaced. Before playing, the owner of the ball which had been lifted would be entitled to have the other ball lifted by its prospective owner under Rule 22.

In situation (b), if the lifted ball is an abandoned ball, the player may discard it and play the other ball.

Other Decisions relating to Rule 1-4:

Ball in Bunker Moves Closer to Hole When Obstruction Removed and Ball Will Not Remain at Rest When Replaced; All Other Parts of Bunker Are Nearer Hole — See 20-3d/2.

Loose Impediment Affecting Lie Moved When Ball Lifted — See 23-1/7.

Loose Impediment Affecting Lie Removed While Ball Lifted — See 23-1/8.

1-4/7 Ball Lost in Either Water Hazard or Casual Water Overflowing Hazard

Q. A ball is lost. It is either in a water hazard or in casual water overflowing the hazard. What is the proper procedure?

A. In equity (Rule 1-4), the player must proceed under the water hazard Rule.

1-4/8 Nearest Point of Relief from Cart Path Is in Casual Water; Nearest Point of Relief from Casual Water Is Back on Cart Path

Q. A player's ball lies on a paved cart path from which he wishes to take relief under Rule 24-2b(i). It appears that the nearest point of relief will be in a large area of casual water which adjoins the cart path and the nearest point of relief from the casual water under Rule 25-1b(i) would be back on the cart path. What are the player's options?

A. The player may proceed in accordance with Rule 24-2 and then, if applicable, Rule 25-1. He is not entitled to take relief from both the immovable obstruction and the casual water in a single procedure, unless after proceeding under these Rules, the player is essentially back where he started and it is evident that such a procedure is necessary to obtain relief from both conditions.

Therefore, the player should proceed as follows:

(1) He may lift and drop the ball in accordance with Rule 24-2b(i) in the casual water.

(2) He may play the ball as it lies or take relief from the casual water, in which case he would lift and drop the ball in accordance with Rule 25-1b(i).

(3) If the ball when dropped comes to rest in such a position that there is interference by the cart path, he may play the ball as it lies or proceed in accordance with Rule 24-2b(i). If the nearest point of relief is in the casual water, as an additional option, the player may, in equity (Rule 1-4) obtain relief without penalty as follows: Using the new position of the ball on the cart path, the nearest point of relief from both the cart path and the casual water shall be determined which is not in a hazard or on a putting green. The player shall lift the ball and drop it within one club-length of and not nearer the hole than the nearest point of relief, on a part of the course which avoids interference by the cart path and the casual water and is not in a hazard or on a putting green.

If the dropped ball rolls into a position where there is interference by either the cart path or the casual water, Rule 20-2c applies.

The same principle would apply if there was interference from any two conditions, i.e., casual water, a hole made by a burrowing animal, an immovable obstruction, from which relief without penalty was available and in taking relief from one condition it resulted in interference from the second condition. (Revised)

1-4/9 Bird's Nest Interfering with Stroke

Q. A player's ball came to rest in a bird's nest or so close to the nest that he could not play a stroke without damaging it. Is he entitled to relief without penalty?

A. Yes. In equity (Rule 1-4), the player may, without penalty, drop the ball at the nearest spot not nearer the hole which would allow him to make his stroke without damaging the nest. If the ball lies in a hazard, it must be dropped in the hazard.

Other Decisions relating to Rule 1-4:

Lie or Line of Play Affected by Pitch-Mark Made by Partner's, Opponent's or Fellow-Competitor's Ball — See 13-2/8.

Player's Lie Affected by Sand from Partner's, Opponent's or Fellow-Competitor's Stroke from Bunker — See 13-2/8.5.

Extension of Line of Play Affected When Opponent or Fellow-Competitor Creates Footprints in Bunker — See 13-2/29.5.

Partner's, Opponent's or Fellow-Competitor's Divot Comes to Rest Near Player's Ball in Bunker — See 13-4/18.

Lie in Bunker Changed by Another Player Taking His Stance — See 20-3b/2.

Lie Changed by Removal of Gallery-Control Stake — See 20-3b/3.

1-4/10 Dangerous Situation; Rattlesnake or Bees Interfere with Play

Q. A player's ball comes to rest in a situation dangerous to the player, *e.g.*, near a live rattlesnake or a bees' nest. Does the player have any options in addition to playing the ball as it lies or, if applicable, proceeding under Rule 26 or 28?

A. Yes. It is unreasonable to expect the player to play from such a dangerous situation and unfair to require the player to incur a penalty under Rule 26 (Water Hazards) or Rule 28 (Ball Unplayable).

In equity (Rule 1-4), as an additional option the player should be permitted, without penalty, to drop a ball on the nearest spot not nearer the hole which is not dangerous.

If the ball lay in a hazard, it should be dropped, if possible, in the same hazard and, if not, in a similar nearby hazard, but in either case not nearer the hole. If it is not possible for the player to drop the ball in a hazard, he may drop it, under penalty of one stroke, outside the hazard, keeping the point where the original ball lay between the hole and the spot on which the ball is dropped.

If it is clearly unreasonable for the player to play a stroke because of interference by anything other than the dangerous situation he may not take relief as prescribed above, but he is not precluded from proceeding under Rule 26 or 28.

Danger from Fire-Ants — See 33-8/22.

1-4/11 Meaning of "Dangerous Situation"

Q. According to Decision 1-4/10, a ball lying near a live rattlesnake or bees' nest is a "dangerous situation" and relief should be granted in equity.

If a player's ball comes to rest in or near an area of plants such as poison ivy, cacti or stinging nettles, should the provisions of Decision 1-4/10 apply?

A. No. The player must either play the ball as it lies or, if applicable, proceed under Rule 26 (Water Hazards) or Rule 28 (Ball Unplayable).

Decision 1-4/10 contemplates a situation which is unrelated to conditions normally encountered on the course. Unpleasant lies are a common occurrence which players must accept.

Other Decisions relating to Rule 1-4:

Player Lifts Opponent's Ball-Marker — See 2-4/5.

Procedure if Both Original and Second Balls Dropped in Wrong Place and Played — See 3-3/5.5.

Playing Characteristics of Club Changed While Play Suspended; Error Discovered Before Play Resumed — See 4-2/2.

Match Discontinued by Agreement Cannot Be Resumed Until Three Days Later; One Player Wishes to Play on Competition Course Prior to Resumption — See 7-2/10.

Match Discontinued by Agreement on 13th Tee Cannot be Resumed Until Following Day; May Players Play First Twelve Holes Prior to Resuming Match — See 7-2/11.

Player's Team Mate in Gallery Hits Ball to Green to Show Player Whether Green Will Hold — See 8-1/23.

Advice Given by Team Coach or Captain — See 8-1/24.

Player Places Mark to Indicate Distance for Pitch Shot — See 8-2a/3.

Determination of Honor at Hole Following Disputed Hole — See 10-1a/2.

Competitors Estimate Area of Teeing Ground When One Tee-Marker Missing — See 11-4b/2.

Divots Replaced and Pressed Down in Area in Which Ball Is to Be Dropped — See 13-2/4.5.

Flying Insect in Water Hazard — See 13-4/16.5.

Ball Thrown into Bounds by Outside Agency and Played; Neither Player Nor Caddie Aware of Action of Outside Agency — See 15/10.

Hole at Which Wrong Ball Played Unknown — See 15-1/3.

Opponent or Fellow-Competitor Attending Flagstick for Player Fails to Remove It; Player's Ball Strikes Flagstick — See 17-3/2.

Ball Stolen by Outside Agency from Unknown Spot — See 18-1/5.

Ball Lodged in Tree Knocked Down by Outside Agency — See 18-1/9.

Ball Dislodged from Tree; Replacement of Ball Not Possible — See 18-2a/29.

Ball Moved by Fellow-Competitor's Ball, Neither Competitor Nor Fellow-Competitor Aware of Movement Until After Completion of Hole — See 18-5/3.

Ball Deliberately Deflected or Stopped on Putting Green by Spectator — See 19-1/4.

Ball Deliberately Deflected or Stopped Through the Green by Spectator — See 19-1/4.1.

Ball Deliberately Deflected or Stopped on Putting Green by Fellow-Competitor — See 19-1/5.

Ball Deflected by Player's Golf Cart Being Pulled by Opponent or Fellow-Competitor Without Player's Knowledge — See 19-2/6.

Ball Moved in Measuring to Determine If Re-Drop Required — See 20-2c/6.

Interference by Immovable Obstruction Within Teeing Ground — See 24-2a/3.

Lifting Ball to Determine Whether It Lies in Burrowing Animal Hole — See 25/21.

Ball Dropped from Casual Water in Bunker at Point of Maximum Relief Rolls Elsewhere — See 25-1b/6.

Dropped Ball Embeds; Procedure If Ball Again Embeds When Re-Dropped — See 25-2/2.5.

Lifting Ball to Determine Whether It Is Embedded — See 25-2/7.

Provisional Ball Not Distinguishable from Original Ball — See 27/11.

Gate in Boundary Fence — See 27/18.

Caddie Shared by Opponents' Side in Four-Ball Match Moves Player's Ball — See 30/2.

Player Who Has Reached Third Round of Match Play Disqualified for Agreeing to Waive Rules in First-Round Match — See 34-1a/1.

Player Who Has Advanced in Match Play Is Disqualified for Wrong Score in Qualifying Round — See 34-1b/8.

Rule 2. Match Play

2-1. Winner of Hole; Reckoning of Holes

In match play the game is played by holes.

Except as otherwise provided in the *Rules,* a hole is won by the *side* which *holes* its ball in the fewer *strokes.* In a handicap match the lower net score wins the hole.

The reckoning of holes is kept by the terms: so many "holes up" or "all square," and so many "to play."

A *side* is "dormie" when it is as many holes up as there are holes remaining to be played.

2-2. Halved Hole

A hole is halved if each *side holes* out in the same number of *strokes.*

When a player has *holed* out and his opponent has been left with a *stroke* for the half, if the player thereafter incurs a penalty, the hole is halved.

2-3. Winner of Match

A match (which consists of a *stipulated round,* unless otherwise decreed by the *Committee*) is won by the *side* which is leading by a number of holes greater than the number of holes remaining to be played.

The *Committee* may, for the purpose of settling a tie, extend the *stipulated round* to as many holes as are required for a match to be won.

2-4. Concession of Next Stroke, Hole or Match

When the opponent's ball is at rest or is deemed to be at rest under Rule 16-2, the player may concede the opponent to have *holed* out with his next *stroke* and the ball may be removed by either *side* with a club or otherwise.

A player may concede a hole or a match at any time prior to the conclusion of the hole or the match.

Concession of a *stroke,* hole or match may not be declined or withdrawn.

2-5. Claims

In match play, if a doubt or dispute arises between the players and no duly authorized representative of the *Committee* is available within a reasonable time, the players shall continue the match without delay. Any claim, if it is to be considered by the *Committee,* must be made before any player in the match plays from the next *teeing ground* or, in the case of the last hole of the match, before all players in the match leave the *putting green.*

No later claim shall be considered unless it is based on facts previously unknown to the player making the claim and the player making the claim had been given wrong information (Rules 6-2a and 9) by an opponent. In any case, no later claim shall be considered after the result of the match has been officially announced, unless the *Committee* is satisfied that the opponent knew he was giving wrong information.

2-6. General Penalty

The penalty for a breach of a *Rule* in match play is loss of hole except when otherwise provided.

2/1 Players in Singles Match Accompanied by Third Party

Q. Prior to a singles match between A and B, A stated to B that a third player, C, would be playing with them. B played the match under protest and lost. What ruling should the Committee give?

A. A single is a match in which one plays against another. Since B made a timely claim, the Committee should have awarded the match to B. If B had not protested, *i.e.*, had agreed that C accompany the match, the result of the match would stand as played.

Wrong Form of Play Used in Match Play Event — See 6-1/1.

Match Decided by Wrong Form of Play by Agreement — See 33-1/4.

2-1/1 Players Unable to Resolve Rules Problem Agree to Consider Hole Halved

Q. In a match, A putted to within three inches of the hole and then knocked his ball away. B, the opponent, objected. He stated that he wanted A's ball left by the hole. A and B were uncertain how to resolve the matter, so they agreed to consider the hole halved. Should A and B be disqualified under Rule 1-3?

A. No. There was no agreement to waive the Rules. Rather, the players were ignorant of the Rules.

2-1/1.5 Players Agree to Consider Hole Halved During Play of Hole

Q. In a match, a player and his opponent play their second shots on a par-5 hole. Unexpectedly, neither ball can be found. Rather than proceeding under Rule 27-1, both players agree to a half. Is this permitted?

A. Yes. An agreement to halve a hole being played does not of itself constitute an agreement to waive the Rules.

However, if the players agree to consider a particularly difficult hole halved without either player making a stroke, they should be disqualified under Rule 1-3 for agreeing to exclude the operation of Rule 2-3 by failing to play the stipulated round.

Hole Not Completed by Either Player — See 2-5/3.

2-1/2 Minus or Zero Net Score

Q. In a handicap match, a player entitled to two handicap strokes at a par-3 hole scores a 2 or a hole-in-one. What would be his net score in each case?

A. The player's net score would be zero (0) if he scored a 2 or minus one (-1) if he had a hole-in-one.

The same would be true in a four-ball stroke play or Stableford competition since scores are calculated on a hole-by-hole basis. (Revised)

Determination of Honor in Handicap Match — See 10-1a/1.

2-2/1 Player Putting for Half Is Given Advice by Opponent

The following is an example of the application of the second paragraph of Rule 2-2:

> In a match, A has holed out. As B, A's opponent, is preparing to putt for a half, A gives B advice as to his line of putt. A would normally lose the hole for a breach of Rule 8-1, but Rule 2-2 becomes operative in these circumstances and the hole is halved.

Player Reporting Wrong Score Causes Opponent with Chance for Half to Pick Up — See 9-2/6.

Player Incorrectly Believing He Has Won a Hole Lifts Opponent's Ball-Marker; Opponent Had Putt for Half — See 2-4/5.

2-3/1 Players Under Impression Match Is Over Later Realize It Was All Square

Q. In a match, A and B left the 18th green under the impression that A had won. They later realized that in fact the match was all square. The matter was referred to the Committee. What is the ruling?

A. Since there was no indication that wrong information had been given, the match stands as played, with A the winner.

Players Mistakenly Believing Match Is All Square After 18 Holes Play Extra Hole Without Claim Being Made — See 2-5/6.

Rightful Winner of Match Makes No Claim and Agrees to Play Extra Holes — See 2-5/7.

Match Play Finalists Both Disqualified — See 33/3.

True State of Match Not Determinable — See 34-3/5.

2-3/2 Hole Inadvertently Omitted in Match; Error Discovered After Match Concluded

Q. The players in a match inadvertently omitted playing a hole. The error was discovered after the match had been played to a conclusion. What is the ruling?

A. The result should stand.

2-3/3 Two Holes Purposely Omitted in Match

Q. The players in a match agreed to omit two holes, *i.e.*, agreed to settle the match over 16 holes. Is this permitted?

A. No. The players should be disqualified under Rule 1-3 for excluding the operation of Rule 2-3 by failing to play the stipulated round.

2-3/4 Three Holes Played Out of Sequence in Match

Q. In an 18-hole match, the players by mistake play three holes out of sequence. The error is discovered before the match concludes. What is the ruling?

A. The holes played out of sequence should be disregarded and the match resumed at the proper hole. However, if such procedure would delay the competition, both players should be disqualified unless one of them concedes the match to the other.

2-3/5 Replaying Match When Play Discontinued Instead of Resuming from Where Play Stopped

Q. A match which was all square after 16 holes was discontinued by agreement due to darkness. The match should have been resumed at the 17th hole. However, the players, thinking it was in accordance with the Rules, replayed the match starting at the 1st tee. The result was posted. At that point the Committee became aware of the improper procedure. What is the ruling?

A. The result of the match as replayed should stand. The players were not subject to disqualification under Rule 1-3 because they were unaware that their procedure was contrary to the Rules.

2-4/1 Player Concedes Opponent's Next Stroke and Then Knocks Opponent's Ball into Hole

Q. A player conceded his opponent's next stroke and then, in attempting to knock the opponent's ball back to him, he inadvertently knocked the ball into the hole. The opponent, who had played three strokes prior to the concession, claimed a 3 for the hole. Was the claim valid?

A. No. The player conceded the opponent a 4 for the hole and, at that point, the opponent had completed the hole. It is irrelevant that the player subsequently knocked the opponent's ball into the hole, whether he did so inadvertently or otherwise.

Opponent's Ball Knocked Away by Player After Concession Moves Player's Ball — See 18-2a/18.

2-4/2 Ball Falls into Hole After Concession of Next Stroke

Q. A player's ball overhung the edge of the hole. After elapse of the time allowed in Rule 16-2, the opponent conceded the player's next stroke for a 5, after which the player's ball fell into the hole. What was the player's score for the hole?

A. The player's score was 5. It is immaterial that the player's ball fell into the hole after the opponent had conceded the player's next stroke. If the opponent had not conceded the next stroke, the player's score would also be 5 because in those circumstances the player would be deemed to have holed out with his last stroke and he would incur a penalty stroke — Rule 16-2.

Ball Overhanging Hole Knocked Away by Opponent Before Player Determines Status — See 16-2/2.

2-4/3 Player Lifts Ball in Mistaken Belief That Next Stroke Conceded

Q. In a match between A and B, B made a statement which A interpreted to mean that his (A's) next stroke was conceded. Accordingly, A lifted his ball. B then said that he had not conceded A's next stroke. What is the ruling?

A. If B's statement could reasonably have led A to think his next stroke had been conceded, in equity (Rule 1-4) A should replace his ball as near as possible to where it lay, without penalty.

Otherwise, A would incur a penalty stroke for lifting his ball without marking its position — Rule 20-1 — and he must replace his ball as near as possible to where it lay.

In Four-Ball Match Player with Putt for Half Picks Up in Error at Suggestion of Opponent Based on Misunderstanding — See 30/5.

2-4/4 Whether Picking Up Opponent's Ball Is Concession of Next Stroke

Q. In match play, A holes a putt and, thinking he has won the match, picks up B's ball. B then advises A that he (B) had a putt to win the hole. Did A concede B's next stroke when he picked up B's ball?

A. No. A incurred a penalty stroke under Rule 18-3b; B must replace his ball and now has two putts to win the hole.

2-4/5 Whether Lifting Opponent's Ball-Marker Is Concession of Next Stroke

Q. In a match, A, believing he has won a hole, picks up the coin marking the position of his opponent B's ball. In fact B had a putt to halve the hole. Should the picking up of B's ball-marker be considered a concession of B's next stroke?

A. No. In equity (Rule 1-4), A should be penalized one stroke. Therefore, under the second paragraph of Rule 2-2 the hole is automatically halved.

2-4/6 Putting Out After Concession of Stroke

Rule 2-4 does not cover the question of whether a player may putt out after his next stroke has been conceded. A player incurs no penalty for holing out in such circumstances. However, if the act would be of assistance to a partner in a four-ball or best-ball match, the partner is, in equity (Rule 1-4), disqualified for the hole.

Agreement to Concede Short Putts — See 1-3/2.

2-4/7 Concession of Stroke Refused by Player and Withdrawn by Opponent; Player Then Putts and Misses

Q. In a match between A and B, A putts and his ball comes to rest near the hole. B concedes A's next stroke. A says: "No. I haven't holed out yet." B says: "OK. Go ahead and putt." A putts and misses. In such circumstances, is the concession invalidated?

A. No. When B conceded A's next stroke, A had completed the hole. Concession of a stroke may not be declined or withdrawn — see Rule 2-4.

2-4/8 Player Concedes Opponent's Next Stroke and Plays Before Opponent Has Opportunity to Lift Ball

Q. In a match between A and B, A chips and his ball comes to rest about one foot from the hole. B concedes A's next stroke. A states that he wishes to lift his ball. However, B proceeds to play his next stroke before A has an opportunity to lift his ball and B's ball strikes A's ball. What is the ruling?

A. B deprived A of his right to lift his ball after his next stroke was conceded. In equity (Rule 1-4), B lost the hole, whether or not his ball struck A's ball.

Ball Resting Against Flagstick; Putt Conceded and Ball Removed Before Player Can Remove Flagstick — See 17-4/2.

2-4/9 Player Concedes Hole After Which It Is Discovered Opponent Had Played Wrong Ball

Q. In a match between A and B, A has played two strokes and the ball with which he played his second stroke out of the rough is on the green. B, having played five, concedes the hole to A. A then discovers that he has played a wrong ball to the green. What is the ruling?

A. Since A did not play the wrong ball from a hazard, he lost the hole (Rule 15-2) before B conceded it to him. Therefore, B's concession was irrelevant.

2-4/9.5 Player Concedes Hole After Which It Is Discovered Opponent's Last Stroke Was Played with a Wrong Ball from a Hazard

Q. In a match between A and B, B has played four strokes and his ball lies three feet from the hole. A, who has played two strokes, plays a stroke out of a bunker to the edge of the hole. B concedes the hole.

A and B pick their balls up, whereupon A discovers that he has played a wrong ball from the bunker, but has incurred no penalty for doing so (Rule 15-2, second paragraph).

What is the ruling?

A. The concession stands — see Rule 2-4.

2-4/10 Player Concedes Hole After Which Opponent Plays Wrong Ball

Q. In a three-ball match, A loses his ball and concedes the hole to B and C. Subsequently, B plays a wrong ball. Is A's concession to B binding?

A. Yes.

Player Concluding He Played Wrong Ball When Opponent Misread Number on Player's Ball Concedes Hole — See 9-2/11.

2-4/11 Player with Lost Ball Concedes Hole; Ball Then Found in Hole

Q. In a match, A played his second shot towards the green but he could not find his ball. He conceded the hole to B, whose second shot was on the green. The following players then found A's ball in the hole. What is the ruling?

A. Since a player may not concede a hole after conclusion of the hole — Rule 2-4 — A holed out in two strokes and won the hole if he made a claim before B played from the next teeing ground (Rule 2-5). If A did not do so, he lost the hole.

2-4/12 Player Concedes Hole on Basis of Invalid Claim

Q. In a match between A and B, A putts out of turn. B incorrectly claims that A loses the hole for putting out of turn. A protests but concedes the hole. Later, A, having consulted the Rule book, lodges an official protest with the Committee. How should the Committee rule?

A. Although B's claim was invalid — see Rule 10-1c — A lost the hole when he conceded it — Rule 2-4.

Handicap Stroke Claimed After Hole Conceded — See 6-2a/4.

2-4/13 Implied Concession of Hole Withdrawn

Q. A, unable to find his ball after a two-minute search, suggests to B, his opponent, that they move on to the next hole. A's ball is then found. A withdraws his suggestion to move on to the next hole and play is resumed. Before A plays his ball, B plays a stroke with a wrong ball. What is the ruling?

A. A's suggestion amounted to a concession of the hole and B won the hole. Concession of a hole may not be withdrawn — Rule 2-4. B's actions after A's concession could not deprive him of a hole already won.

2-4/14 Player Concedes Match Due to Misconception as to Opponent's Score at Last Hole

Q. In a match, A and B were all square playing the last hole. A had a short putt for a 4. B holed a putt for a 4. A, mistakenly believing that B had holed out in three strokes, shook hands with B, conceded the match and lifted his ball. At that point B told A that he (B) had scored a 4. What is the ruling?

A. A conceded the match. Even if A had not conceded the match, he lost it when he lifted his ball without marking its position and thereby incurred a penalty stroke under Rule 20-1.

2-4/15 Player Concedes Match After Winning It When Opponent Lodges Invalid Claim Regarding Strokes Taken

Q. In a match, A and B were all square playing the last hole. A incurred a penalty without knowing it, and accordingly did not advise B of the penalty. B was aware of what had happened but did not realize it was a breach of the Rules either.

A won the hole and the match, and the result was posted.

Subsequently, a spectator informed B that A had incurred a penalty at the 18th hole. B then claimed the hole and the match, and A conceded the match to B.

Who was the rightful winner?

A. A won the match because a match can only be conceded prior to its conclusion (Rule 2-4).

A gave wrong information when he did not advise B that he had incurred a penalty and would have lost the hole had a timely claim been made — Rule 9-2. However, a belated claim by B was not valid for two reasons:

(1) it was not based on facts previously unknown to B, and

(2) the claim was made after the result of the match was announced — see Rule 2-5.

Agreement That Side Losing After 18 Holes of 36-Hole Match Will Concede Match — See 1-3/7.

Conceding Match to Avoid Disqualification — See 2-3/4 and 33-1/6.

2-4/16 Valid Timely Claim Made After Concession of Match

Q. In a match, A and B are playing the last hole. B is 1 up. A holes out for a 4. B putts from a wrong place and holes the putt for a 4. A congratulates B and concedes the match. Before leaving the putting green, A asks B if he (B) had putted from a wrong place. B acknowledges that he did so. A claims that B loses the hole under Rule 20-7a. Is the claim valid?

A. Yes. Concession of a match is not binding if subsequently a valid claim is timely made. A's valid claim was made within the time limit in Rule 2-5.

Player Omits Penalty Stroke When Advising Opponent as to Score for Hole; Error Discovered After Match Conceded by Opponent — See 9-2/10.

2-4/17 Player in Erroneous Belief Match Is Over Shakes Opponent's Hand and Picks Up Opponent's Ball

Q. In match play, A holes a putt and, thinking he has won the match, shakes hands with B and picks up B's ball. The referee advises B that he had a putt to win the hole and keep the match alive. Has B conceded the match by his acquiescence in A's action of shaking hands and picking up B's ball?

A. No. B was entitled to replace his ball and hole out. Since A incurred a one-stroke penalty under Rule 18-3b, B now had two putts to win the hole.

Player's Conscious Failure to Correct Opponent's Misunderstanding of State of Match Results in Opponent Conceding Match When in Fact Player Is Dormie — See 9-2/12.

2-4/18 Defaulting Player Plays Informal Match with Opponent and Wins

Q. B concedes a match to A. A and B then play an informal match and B wins it, 5 and 4. Should the Committee post A as the winner by default or B as the winner by 5 and 4?

A. A should be posted as the winner by default.

2-4/19 Winner of Match Wishes to Default to Beaten Opponent

Q. In match play, A defeats B and then concedes the match to B because he (A) cannot continue in the competition. Is this permissible?

A. No. A won the match. A beaten player may not be reinstated in such circumstances. A should be posted as the winner and, since A cannot continue, A's opponent in the next round would win by default.

Under Rule 2-4, a side may concede a match at any time prior to conclusion of the match, but not thereafter.

2-4/20 Player Unable to Meet Match Play Schedule Defaults; Schedule Then Changed and Player Requests Reinstatement

Q. The final matches in a competition were to be played on a Saturday. A was to play B in one match. On Thursday, A defaulted to B, saying that he would be out of town on Saturday.

On Saturday, the course was unplayable and the matches were postponed until the following Saturday. On Monday, A requested that he be reinstated. Should the Committee reinstate A?

A. No. A conceded the match as provided for in Rule 2-4. In the circumstances concession is irrevocable.

2-5/1 Player's Obligation re Lodging Claim

In match play, a player may disregard a breach of the Rules by his opponent, provided there is no agreement between the players. There is a difference between overlooking an opponent's breach and agreement with the opponent to waive a penalty. Rule 1-3 prohibits the latter.

2-5/2 Procedure for a Valid Claim

For a claim to be valid, the claimant must indicate the facts he believes give rise to the claim and must also indicate that he wants the Rules of Golf applied. He must do both within the time required by Rule 2-5. For example, Rule 16-1e prohibits putting from a stance astride an extension of the line of putt behind the ball. In a match between A and B, if A putts from a stance astride an extension of the line and B states "that is not allowed, you are penalized" or "I'm making a claim because of that stroke," the Committee should uphold the claim.

Statements by B such as "I'm not sure that's allowed" or "I don't think you can do that" do not by themselves constitute a valid claim because each statement does not contain both a reference to the facts giving rise to the claim and a desire to have the Rules of Golf applied.

2-5/3 Player Lifts Ball Before Holing Out; Opponent Then Picks Up His Ball Claiming Player Loses Hole

Q. In match play, A's ball was resting against the flagstick but it was not holed. A, believing he had holed out, lifted his ball without first marking its position. In doing so, A incurred a penalty stroke under Rule 20-1. Since A was not aware that he had incurred a penalty, he did not inform B. B, who had not witnessed A's actions, played his next sΩtroke. A's actions were then brought to the attention of B and he picked up his ball, claiming that A's lifting of his ball entailed a penalty of loss of hole. A and B agreed to continue the match and refer B's claim to the Committee later. How should the Committee have ruled?

A. The Committee should have ruled that B won the hole. B's claim was valid since he indicated the facts that gave rise to the claim (A's lifting of the ball) and that he wanted the Rules of Golf applied (A and B agreed to refer B's claim to the Committee). Although the penalty for A's lifting of the ball without first marking its position is one stroke, he lost the hole for giving wrong information (Rule 9-2) when he failed to inform B before he (B) played his next stroke that he (A) had incurred the penalty stroke. (Revised)

2-5/4 Player Wins Hole with Own Ball After Playing Wrong Ball; Opponent Lodges Belated Claim

Q. In a match, A and B are all square playing the last hole. A plays a wrong ball in the rough and discovers the error before his next stroke. A and B go back to look for A's ball without any question being raised as to whether A had incurred a penalty. A's ball is found. A plays out the hole with his original ball and wins the hole and the match. Several days later B claims the last hole and the match by virtue of the fact that A played a wrong ball.

Is the claim valid?

A. No. A gave wrong information when he did not advise B that he (A) had incurred a penalty — Rule 9-2. However, a belated claim by B was not valid for two reasons:

(1) it was not based on facts previously unknown to B, and

(2) the claim was made after the result of the match was announced — See Rule 2-5.

Player Wins Hole with Wrong Ball; Error Discovered at Next Hole; Opponent Claims Previous Hole — See 9-2/8.

Player Wins Hole with Wrong Ball and Partner Picks Up; Error Discovered at Next Hole; Opponents Claim Hole — See 30-3d/2.

2-5/5 Invalid Claim Not Disputed

Q. In a match, A played a wrong ball to a green and then found his own ball in the hole. His own ball had been holed in three strokes, which was fewer strokes than B had taken. However, B claimed the hole on the ground that A had played a wrong ball. A did not dispute the claim. A lost the match.

Later, A learned that, because he had completed the hole when his own ball was holed and before play of a wrong ball, the play of the wrong ball was irrelevant and he was the rightful winner of the hole in question. A then lodged a claim with the Committee. Was the claim valid?

A. No. Since A did not dispute B's invalid claim before B played from the next teeing ground, B's claim stands and B won the hole in question — Rule 2-5.

Player Concedes Hole on Basis of Invalid Claim — See 2-4/12.

Player Concedes Match After Winning It When Opponent Lodges Invalid Claim Regarding Strokes Taken — See 2-4/15.

2

2-5/5.5 Breach of 14-Club Rule Discovered After Match Concluded But Before Result Officially Announced

Q. On completion of the 14th hole in a match between A and B, A wins by 5 and 4. The players continue the round. After the 16th hole, it is discovered by the players that A has 15 clubs in his bag.

Before the result of the match has been officially announced, B reports the facts to the Committee and asks for a ruling. Is the claim valid?

A. Yes. Although the players had left the putting green of the last hole of the match, B's claim is based on facts previously unknown to him and he is deemed to have been given wrong information by A (Rule 9-2). The players must return to the 15th hole and resume the match. A is penalized under Rule 4-4a and is three up with four holes to play.

2-5/6 Players Mistakenly Believe Match Is All Square After 18 Holes and Play Extra Hole Without Claim Being Made

Q. In a match between A and B, A is 1 up after the prescribed 18 holes. However, both A and B believe the match is all square. So they play extra holes and B wins at the 20th hole. The error is then discovered. What is the ruling?

A. Since A did not make a claim before either player played from the tee at the 19th hole, the match must be considered all square at that point. Thus, B was the winner.

Players Under Impression Match Is Over Later Realize It Was All Square — See 2-3/1.

2-5/7 Rightful Winner of Match Makes No Claim and Agrees to Play Extra Holes

Q. In a match, A and B are all square going to the 18th hole. On completion of the 18th hole, B states that he has scored 7; A states that he (A) has scored 6. A and B go into the clubhouse under the impression that A has won the match. At that point B tells A that, on reflection, he (B) believes A scored 7 at the 18th hole. On recounting, A acknowledges that he had a 7.

By agreement, A and B resume the match; A wins it at the 20th hole and the result is posted.

That night, B discovers that, because A gave wrong information after completion of the 18th hole, under Rule 9-2 he (B) was rightfully the winner of the 18th hole and the match. B reports the matter to the Committee and claims the match. What is the ruling?

A. The match stands as played, with A the winner.

B's claim was not made within the time limit in Rule 2-5. B's claim would have been valid if he had refused to play extra holes or had played the extra holes under protest.

2-5/8 Status of Valid Claim If Players Accept Wrong Ruling from Someone Not on Committee and Continue Match

Q. In an 18-hole match between A and B, A's ball strikes the flagstick which was attended by B. A and B believe that a loss-of-hole penalty is incurred but they are in doubt as to which one of them incurs the penalty. Accordingly, before teeing off at the next hole, they agree to refer the matter to the Committee later.

At the conclusion of 18 holes, A and B agree that if B incurred a loss-of-hole penalty at the hole in question, the match is all square; if A incurred it, B has won the match by two holes. A and B seek a ruling from X, who is not on the Committee. X incorrectly advises A and B that B incurred the penalty and that the match is therefore all square.

A and B accept X's ruling, play extra holes and A wins.

Subsequently, the incident was brought to the attention of the Committee. What should the Committee do?

A. When A and B accepted X's incorrect ruling, they, in effect, settled the doubt themselves and, after A and B began playing extra holes, the Committee was no longer entitled to consider a claim. The match stands as played, with A the winner.

Valid Timely Claim Made After Concession of Match — See 2-4/16.

2-5/9 Player Agreeing with Opponent That Hole Was Halved Later Realizes He Has Won Hole; Player Then Makes Claim

Q. In a match between A and B, at the 16th hole A scored 6 and B scored 5. When leaving the putting green, B commented to A: "A half?" and A replied: "Yes."

A won the match at the 20th hole and the result was posted. Later, B realized that he had won the 16th hole and, if the mistake had not been made, he would have won the match 1 up.

A admitted that he had made a mistake. B reported the matter to the Committee and claimed the match. Is the claim valid?

A. No. The match stands as played, with A the winner. After the result of the match was posted, the claim by B could have been considered only if A had knowingly given wrong information as to the number of strokes he (A) had taken at the 16th hole — see Rule 2-5.

2-5/10 Player Accepting Erroneous Claim Disputes It After Result Announced

Q. In a match, A was in breach of a Rule. Although the penalty for a breach of the Rule in question was only one stroke, B, his opponent, claimed that A lost the hole. A did not dispute the claim. B won the match and the result was posted. Three days later, A protested to the Committee that B had misinformed him with respect to the Rules. What is the ruling?

A. The match stands as played. Under Rule 2-5, no claim may be considered after the result of a match has been announced unless the opponent knowingly gave wrong information. Incorrect information on the Rules is not wrong information. It is up to each player to know the Rules.

2-5/11 Wrong Information Given After Play of Last Hole; Claim Made After Result Announced

Q. In a match, A and B came to the last hole all square. After completion of the hole, A stated that he had scored 9 and B stated that he (B) had scored 8, making B the winner, 1 up. The result was recorded by the Committee.

A few minutes later, a spectator told A that B had scored 9 at the last hole. B reviewed the hole and acknowledged that he had made a mistake and that his actual score was 9. What is the ruling?

A. The match stands as played, with B the winner. Under Rule 2-5 no claim may be considered after the result of a match is announced unless wrong information has been given knowingly.

2-5/12 Imposition of Penalty by Referee After Any Player in Match Has Played from Next Tee

Q. In match play, may a referee penalize a player for a breach of a Rule at a hole if he does not become aware of the breach until someone in the match has played from the next teeing ground?

A. Yes, unless the facts giving rise to the penalty were known to the opponent.

2-5/13 Extra Stroke Taken by Mistake in Handicap Match; Status of Late Claim

Q. Prior to the start of a handicap match, the two players correctly advised one another as to the handicaps to which they were entitled. However, during the match, A, by mistake, took a stroke to which he was not entitled at a certain hole. The error was discovered several holes later. Could B, the opponent, then claim the hole in question?

A. No. A late claim would not be valid unless it was based on facts previously unknown to B and B had been given wrong information by A. In this case A did not give B wrong information as to the number of strokes to which he was entitled during the round, and it was B's responsibility to know the holes at which handicap strokes were to be given (see Note under Rule 6-2). The hole in question stands as played.

2

2-5/14 Opponent Disputes Player's Claim That Ball Is Unfit for Play

Q. In a match, A considers his ball unfit for play. A's opponent, B, disagrees. There is no referee or Committee member available for a ruling. In spite of B's disagreement, may A substitute another ball?

A. Yes. However, if B then makes a claim (Rule 2-5) and the Committee, after examination of the original ball, upholds B's claim, A would lose the hole. Otherwise, the result of the hole would stand as played.

A must ensure that the condition of the ball he considered unfit for play is preserved until the Committee examines it. Otherwise, the Committee should uphold B's claim.

Other Decisions relating to Rule 2-5:

Player with Lost Ball Concedes Hole; Ball Then Found in Hole and Player Claims Hole — See 2-4/11.

Second Ball Played in Match Play; No Claim Made — See 3-3/9.

Wrong Handicap Used in Match by Mistake; Error Discovered After Result Officially Announced; Status of Claim by Opponent — See 6-2a/5.

Match Discontinued by Agreement Due to Rain; One Player Subsequently Wishes to Resume; Opponent Refuses on Ground Course Unplayable and Makes Claim — See 6-8a/6.

Player Omits Penalty Stroke When Advising Opponent as to Score for Hole; Error Discovered After Match Conceded by Opponent; Opponent Lodges Claim — See 9-2/10.

Doubt Whether Ball Moved by Outside Agency; Opponent Lodges Claim — See 18-1/4.

In Foursome Side Drives for Three Holes in Wrong Order and Then Claim Is Made — See 29-2/2.

Rule 3. Stroke Play

3-1. Winner

The *competitor* who plays the *stipulated round* or rounds in the fewest strokes is the winner.

3-2. Failure to Hole Out

If a *competitor* fails to *hole* out at any hole and does not correct his mistake before he plays a *stroke* from the next *teeing ground* or, in the case of the last hole of the round, before he leaves the *putting green*, he shall be disqualified.

3-3. Doubt as to Procedure

a. Procedure

In stroke play only, when during play of a hole a *competitor* is doubtful of his rights or procedure, he may, without penalty, play a second ball. After the situation which caused the doubt has arisen, the *competitor* should, before taking further action, announce to his *marker* or a *fellow-competitor* his decision to invoke this Rule and the ball with which he will score if the *Rules* permit.

The *competitor* shall report the facts to the *Committee* before returning his score card unless he scores the same with both balls; if he fails to do so, he shall be disqualified.

b. Determination of Score for Hole

If the *Rules* allow the procedure selected in advance by the *competitor*, the score with the ball selected shall be his score for the hole.

If the *competitor* fails to announce in advance his decision to invoke this Rule or his selection, the score with the original ball or, if the original ball is not one of the balls being played, the first ball put into play shall count if the *Rules* allow the procedure adopted for such ball.

Note 1: If a *competitor* plays a second ball, *penalty strokes* incurred solely by playing the ball ruled not to count and *strokes* subsequently taken with that ball shall be disregarded.

Note 2: A second ball played under Rule 3-3 is not a *provisional ball* under Rule 27-2.

3-4. Refusal to Comply with a Rule

If a *competitor* refuses to comply with a *Rule* affecting the rights of another *competitor,* he shall be disqualified.

3-5. General Penalty

The penalty for a breach of a *Rule* in stroke play is two strokes except when otherwise provided.

3/1 Disqualification in Play-Off

Q. A competitor in a stroke play play-off incurs a penalty of disqualification. Does the disqualification apply to the play-off only or to the entire competition?

A. The disqualification applies only to the play-off.

3/2 Competitors Play Two Holes Not Included in Stipulated Round

Q. In stroke play, the stipulated round was 16 holes, *i.e.*, the 13th and 14th holes were omitted. After play of the 12th hole, one group elected to play the 13th and 14th holes without counting their scores for those holes. They then completed the round. What is the ruling?

A. The stipulated round consists of playing the holes of the course in the sequence prescribed by the Committee — see Definition of "Stipulated Round." These competitors were in breach of the conditions of the competition and the Committee should in this case impose a penalty of disqualification under Rule 33-7.

3-2/1 Fellow-Competitor's Ball Knocked from Lip of Hole by Competitor Not Replaced

Q. In stroke play, a competitor concedes his fellow-competitor a short putt and knocks the ball away. The fellow-competitor lifts his ball, does not replace it as required by Rule 18-4 and plays from the next tee. What is the ruling?

A. The fellow-competitor is disqualified — Rule 3-2.

Ball Played from Putting Green Deflected by Moving Outside Agency; Stroke Not Replayed — See 19-1/3.

3-2/2 Ball Blown into Hole by Competitor Not Replaced and Holed Out

Q. In stroke play, a competitor's ball stopped on the lip of the hole and on impulse he blew the ball into the hole. He did not replace the ball, as required by Rule 18-2a, and hole out. He played from the next tee. Is the competitor disqualified under Rule 3-2 for failing to hole out?

A. Yes.

Player Who Putts with One Hand and Catches Ball in Hole with Other Hand Does Not Place Ball on Lip of Hole and Hole Out — See 1-2/5.

3-2/3 Competitor in Error Does Not Hole Out; Error Corrected Before Playing from Next Tee

Q. In four-ball stroke play, A holed out in 4. B, A's partner, who was lying 3 and had marked and lifted his ball, forgot he had a handicap stroke. He did not replace his ball and hole out or pick up his ball-marker. On the way to the next teeing ground, B remembered his stroke, returned to the green, replaced his ball where it previously lay and holed out for a net 3. Was this in order?

A. Yes, since B had not played from the next teeing ground (Rule 3-2).

Competitor Picks Up Second Ball — See 3-3/8.

Modifying Penalty for Not Holing Out — See 33-7/2.

3-3/0.5 Guidelines for Determining Which Ball Counts When Player Proceeds Under Rule 3-3

The purpose of Rule 3-3 is to allow a competitor to avoid a penalty when he is in doubt as to the proper procedure. The following are guidelines for determining the ball with which the competitor scores in various situations:

(1) If both balls are played in accordance with the Rules, the ball selected shall count if the competitor announces in advance his decision to invoke this Rule and announces in advance the ball with which he wishes to score. If the competitor does not announce or select in advance, the score with the original ball counts if played in accordance with the Rules. Otherwise the score with the second ball counts if played in accordance with the Rules.

(2) If the procedure with the ball selected in advance is not in accordance with the Rules, the other ball must count (see Decision 3-3/5).

(3) If neither ball is played in accordance with the Rules, the following applies:

(a) In a case where the competitor plays both balls from a wrong place but is not guilty of a serious breach with either ball, the score with the original ball counts, with an additional penalty under the applicable Rule (see Rule 20-7b).

(b) In a case where the competitor is guilty of a serious breach with one ball and not guilty of a serious breach with the other ball, the score with the other ball counts, with an additional penalty under the applicable Rule (see Rule 20-7b and Decision 3-3/5.5).

(c) In a case where the competitor is guilty of a serious breach with both balls, the competitor shall be disqualified.

(4) If the original ball is played and then Rule 3-3 is invoked, the score with the original ball must count, even if the Rules do not allow the procedure adopted for that ball, *i.e.*, Rule 3-3 is not applicable in such circumstances.

3-3/1 Provisional Ball Used as Second Ball When Not Determinable Whether Original Ball Is Out of Bounds

Q. In stroke play, a player is in doubt as to whether his drive may be out of bounds. He plays a provisional ball under Rule 27-2. He finds the original ball and cannot determine whether it is out of bounds or not. The player wishes to consider the provisional ball as his second ball under Rule 3-3 and complete the play of the hole with both balls. Is this permissible?

A. Yes. In invoking Rule 3-3 after playing a provisional ball, the player must treat the provisional ball as a second ball. Although the Note to Rule 3-3 provides:"A second ball played under Rule 3-3 is not a provisional ball under Rule 27-2," the reverse is not true in the present case.

3-3/2 Second Ball Played Despite Adverse Ruling

Q. In stroke play, a competitor believes he is entitled to relief under a Rule, but a member of the Committee disagrees. In spite of the ruling by the Committee member, the competitor invokes Rule 3-3 and opts to score with the second ball. He plays his original ball as it lies and the second ball under the Rule he believes is applicable.

May a competitor invoke Rule 3-3 in such circumstances?

A. The answer depends upon whether or not the Committee has given authority to make final decisions to its individual members.

If the Committee member concerned has not been given authority to make final decisions, the competitor is entitled to invoke Rule 3-3.

If, on the other hand, the Committee member has been given authority to make final decisions, he may, despite his own view that the competitor is not entitled to relief, permit the competitor to invoke Rule 3-3. However, if the Committee member exercises his authority and gives the competitor a final decision that he is not entitled to the relief he claims, there is then no justification for the competitor invoking Rule 3-3, and he will incur a penalty of two strokes for undue delay (Rule 6-7) if he, nevertheless, goes ahead and invokes Rule 3-3. The score with his original ball, including this two-stroke penalty, must count.

3-3/3 Ball Dropped in Wrong Place and Played; Rule 3-3 Then Invoked and Second Ball Dropped in Right Place; Both Balls Played Out

Q. In stroke play, a competitor's ball comes to rest through the green on a paved path. He lifts the ball, drops it off the path at a point almost two club-lengths from the nearest point of relief (*i.e.*, he drops in a wrong place) and plays it. The competitor's marker advises the competitor that he (the marker) believes the ball must be dropped within one club-length of the nearest point of relief. The competitor, in doubt, invokes Rule 3-3, drops a second ball within one club-length of the nearest point of relief and otherwise in accordance with Rule 24-2b(i) and opts to score with the second ball. The competitor holes out with both balls. What is the ruling?

A. Rule 20-7b states in part: "If a competitor plays a stroke with his ball in play which has been dropped or placed in a wrong place, he shall incur the penalty prescribed by the applicable Rule and play out the hole with the ball." Thus, the competitor's score with the original ball, with a penalty of two strokes added, must count.

Rule 20-7b does not permit the second ball to count. However, the competitor incurs no penalty for having played the second ball.

3-3/4 Ball Dropped in Wrong Place But Not Played; Rule 3-3 Then Invoked and Second Ball Dropped in Right Place; Both Balls Played Out

Q. With reference to Decision 3-3/3, what would have been the ruling if the marker had advised the competitor of his possible error before the ball dropped in a wrong place was played and the competitor had invoked Rule 3-3 at that point?

A. Rule 20-7b would not have applied because Rule 3-3 was invoked before the ball dropped in a wrong place was played.

The score with the second ball would have counted and no penalty would have been incurred.

The competitor, had he not been in doubt, could have lifted the ball dropped in the wrong place, without penalty — Rule 20-6.

3-3/5 Whether Score with Second Ball Counts If Ball Dropped in Wrong Place and Played

Q. In stroke play, a competitor's ball came to rest on an artificially-surfaced road which had not been declared an integral part of the course. The competitor, not sure whether the road was an obstruction or an integral part of the course, invoked Rule 3-3 and announced that he wished his score with the second ball to count. He played his original ball as it lay and dropped and played a second ball under Rule 24-2b(i). He met all the requirements of that Rule, except that he dropped the second ball almost two club-lengths from the nearest point of relief, instead of within one club-length. Does the score with the second ball count?

A. No. Rule 3-3b states in part: "If the Rules allow the procedure selected in advance by the competitor, the score with the ball selected shall be his score for the hole." In this case, the procedure selected in advance (*i.e.*, dropping the second ball almost two club-lengths from the nearest point of relief) is not allowed under the Rules. Accordingly, the score with the original ball counts.

3-3/5.5 Procedure If Both Original and Second Balls Dropped in Wrong Place and Played

Q. A competitor's ball crosses a water hazard in front of a putting green and then rolls back into the hazard. The competitor incorrectly believes that he is entitled to drop the ball on the green side of the hazard within two club-lengths of the point where the ball crossed the hazard margin when it rolled back into the hazard. A fellow-competitor incorrectly advises the competitor that he must drop the ball on the line of flight of his previous shot.

The competitor invokes Rule 3-3. He drops the original ball on the green side of the hazard and elects to score with that ball. He then drops a second ball on the line of flight of his previous shot. He holes out with both balls and then plays from the next tee.

Under Rule 3-3b and Decision 3-3/5, it would appear that the score with neither ball can count since both balls were dropped at a wrong place and played, and thus the Rules do not allow the procedure adopted for either ball. How should the Committee rule when the competitor reports the facts?

A. Rule 3-3 does not contemplate such a case. Therefore, the ruling must be made in accordance with equity (Rule 1-4).

In dropping the original ball on the green side of the hazard, the competitor was guilty of a serious breach of Rule 26-1. If the competitor was not guilty of a serious breach with respect to the second ball, the score with that ball counts, with an additional two-stroke penalty added for breach of Rule 26-1. See also Rule 20-7b.

In a case where the competitor has played both balls from a wrong place but is not guilty of a serious breach with either ball, the score with the original ball counts, with a two-stroke penalty added.

In a case where the competitor is guilty of a serious breach with both balls, the competitor is disqualified.

Meaning of Serious Breach — See 20-7b/0.5.

3-3/6 Competitor Plays Original Ball After Doubtful Situation Has Arisen and Then Invokes Rule 3-3

Q. In stroke play, a competitor's ball lies in a water hazard. A movable stake defining the margin of the hazard interferes with the area of his intended swing. He plays his next stroke, avoiding the stake. It then occurs to him that he may have been entitled to remove the stake. The competitor informs his marker that he is invoking Rule 3-3 and elects to score with a second ball. He removes the stake and drops a second ball at the spot from which his original ball was played. He holes out with both balls. What is the ruling?

A. The situation which caused the doubt arose when the competitor's ball lay in the water hazard and the stake interfered with his swing. Since the competitor took further action, *i.e.*, played the original ball, after the situation which caused the doubt had arisen, the score with the original ball must count — see last paragraph of Rule 3-3b.

However, the competitor incurs no penalty for having played the second ball.

3-3/6.5 Competitor Plays Second Ball Without Announcing Intention to Invoke Rule 3-3 and Fails to Report Facts to Committee

Q. In stroke play, a competitor's ball came to rest on an artificially-surfaced road which had not been declared an integral part of the course. Without announcing his decision to invoke Rule 3-3 or the ball with which he would score if the Rules permitted, the competitor dropped and played a second ball in accordance with Rule 24-2b. The competitor then played the original ball as it lay and completed play of the hole with both balls, scoring 4 with the original ball and 5 with the dropped ball.

The competitor returned his score card to the Committee with a score of 4 on the hole in question and failed to report the facts to the Committee.

What is the ruling?

A. Although the competitor did not announce his decision to invoke Rule 3-3, it is clear from the facts that he intended to invoke such Rule. As the competitor did not score the same with both balls and failed to report the facts to the Committee before returning his score card, he is disqualified under Rule 3-3a.

3-3/7 Original Ball Strikes Second Ball or Vice Versa

Q. A competitor invokes Rule 3-3 and plays a second ball. Subsequently, the competitor makes a stroke at one ball and it strikes and moves the other ball. What is the ruling?

A. If both balls lay on the putting green prior to the stroke, the competitor incurs a penalty of two strokes if the score with the striking ball ultimately becomes the competitor's score for the hole — Rule 19-5. Otherwise, there is no penalty.

The striking ball must be played as it lies — Rule 19-5.

The moved ball must be replaced — Rule 18-5.

3-3/7.5 Competitor Announces Intention to Play Two Balls; Plays Original Ball Before Dropping Second Ball; Elects Not to Play Second Ball

Q. A competitor's ball comes to rest in a rut made by a maintenance vehicle. Believing the Committee might declare the rut to be ground under repair, he announces that he will invoke Rule 3-3 and play a second ball in accordance with Rule 25-1b and that he wishes his score with the second ball to count if the Rules permit. He hits his original ball from the rut to one foot from the hole and then states he will not play a second ball. He completes the hole with his original ball. On completion of the round, the facts are reported to the Committee. What is the ruling?

A. The answer depends on whether the Committee declares the rut to be ground under repair. If the Committee declares the rut to be ground under repair, the competitor is disqualified for failing to hole out (Rule 3-2) since the score with the second ball would have counted — see Rule 3-3 and Decision 3-3/8. Otherwise, the score with the original ball counts.

If a player declares his intention to invoke Rule 3-3, he may change his mind at any time before he takes further action, such as making another stroke at his original ball or putting a second ball into play. Once he invokes the Rule and takes further action, he is bound by the procedures in Rule 3-3. (New)

3-3/8 Competitor Picks Up Second Ball

Q. In stroke play, a competitor, uncertain whether the road his ball lies on is an obstruction or not, invokes Rule 3-3. He plays his original ball as it lies on the road and a second ball under Rule 24-2b(i), telling his marker he wishes his score with the second ball to count if the Rules permit. Having hit his original ball onto the green and the second ball into a bunker, the competitor picks up the second ball, holes out with the original ball and plays from the next tee. At this point the matter is referred to the Committee, which establishes that the road on which the competitor's ball lay was an obstruction. What is the ruling?

A. Since the road on which the competitor's ball lay was an obstruction and therefore Rule 24-2b(i) allowed the procedure selected by the competitor, the score with the second (or selected) ball would have counted if it had been holed out. However, since the competitor did not hole out with that ball, he is disqualified — Rule 3-2.

If, on the other hand, the road had not been an obstruction, there would have been no penalty. In that case, since the Rules would not have allowed the selected procedure, a score with the second ball would not have counted, and the competitor's score with his original ball would have been his score for the hole. There is no penalty for picking up a ball played under Rule 3-3 if that ball cannot count.

3-3/9 Second Ball Played in Match Play

Q. In a match between A and B, A was unsure of his rights at a hole. Neither A nor B was aware that Rule 3-3 applies only in stroke play, so A played a second ball and holed out with both balls. At the end of the round, the matter was referred to the Committee. What is the ruling?

3

A. A second ball played in match play is a wrong ball — See Definition of "Wrong Ball." Accordingly, A would have lost the hole had B claimed it under Rule 2-5 before either player had played from the next tee. However, B made no claim. Therefore, the score with A's original ball counts.

Local Rule Allowing Play of Second Ball in Match Play — See 33-8/3.

3-3/10 Competitor Plays Three Balls When Doubtful of Rights

Q. Are there any circumstances under which a competitor in stroke play, who is doubtful of his rights or procedure, may play a third ball under Rule 3-3?

A. No. If a competitor so proceeds, the score with the original ball or, if the original ball is not one of the balls being played, the first ball put into play shall count. If the Rules do not allow the procedure adopted for the original ball or the first ball put into play, the competitor incurs the penalty prescribed for the improper procedure.

3-3/11 Competitor Drops One Ball in Accordance with Two Different Rules Instead of Playing Second Ball

Q. In stroke play, a competitor's ball comes to rest through the green in a deep rut which has not been defined as ground under repair by the Committee. The ball is not playable due to the rut. The competitor believes that the Committee might declare the rutted area to be ground under repair. He announces to his marker or a fellow-competitor that he will drop the ball at a spot which conforms to the procedures prescribed in both Rule 25-1b(i) (Ground Under Repair) and Rule 28b (Ball Unplayable), seek a ruling from the Committee before returning his score card, and accept the penalty stroke in Rule 28 if the Committee does not declare the rutted area to be ground under repair. Is such a procedure permissible?

A. Yes. Although it would have been advisable for the competitor to proceed under Rule 3-3 in this situation, the Rules do not prohibit such a procedure — see also Decision 3-3/12.

3-3/12 Competitor Drops One Ball in Accordance with Two Different Rules Instead of Playing Second Ball; Dropped Ball Rolls Back into the Condition from Which Relief Taken

Q. In the circumstances described in Decision 3-3/11, what is the ruling if the competitor drops the ball and it rolls and comes to rest where there is still interference from the same rutted area?

A. If this occurred it would be advisable for the competitor to obtain a ruling from the Committee before proceeding further or invoke Rule 3-3.

If the Committee determines that the area is ground under repair, the ball must be re-dropped (Rule 20-2c(v)). Otherwise, the dropped ball is in play and the competitor must either play the ball as it lies or, for a second time, proceed under the unplayable ball Rule (Rule 28) incurring an additional penalty stroke.

Other Decisions relating to Rule 3-3:

Wrong Ball Played in Belief It Is Second Ball — See 15/7.

Ball Dropped from Ground Under Repair Area Rolls to Position Where Area Interferes with Stance; Whether Re-Drop Required — See 20-2c/0.5.

Ball Dropped and Played Under Water Hazard Rule; Original Ball Then Found in Hazard and Holed Out as Second Ball — See 26-1/5.

3-4/1 Competitor Not Given Opportunity to Lift Ball Assisting Fellow-Competitor

Q. In stroke play, A's ball lies near the hole in a position to assist B, whose ball lies off the green. A states his intention to lift his ball under Rule 22. However, B says that he does not want A's ball lifted. B plays before A has an opportunity to lift, and B's ball strikes A's ball. Should B be penalized?

A. B is disqualified under Rule 3-4.

CLUBS AND THE BALL

The United States Golf Association reserves the right to change the *Rules* and make and change the interpretations relating to clubs, balls and other implements at any time.

Rule 4. Clubs

A player in doubt as to the conformity of a club should consult the United States Golf Association.

A manufacturer should submit to the United States Golf Association a sample of a club which is to be manufactured for a ruling as to whether the club conforms with the *Rules*. If a manufacturer fails to submit a sample before manufacturing and/or marketing the club, the manufacturer assumes the risk of a ruling that the club does not conform with the *Rules*. Any sample submitted to the United States Golf Association will become its property for reference purposes.

4-1. Form and Make of Clubs

a. General

The player's clubs shall conform with this Rule and the provisions, specifications and interpretations set forth in Appendix II.

b. Wear and Alteration

A club which conforms with the *Rules* when new is deemed to conform after wear through normal use. Any part of a club which has been purposely altered is regarded as new and must, in its altered state, conform with the *Rules*.

4

4-2. Playing Characteristics Changed and Foreign Material

a. Playing Characteristics Changed

During a *stipulated round,* the playing characteristics of a club shall not be purposely changed by adjustment or by any other means.

b. Foreign Material

Foreign material must not be applied to the club face for the purpose of influencing the movement of the ball.

PENALTY FOR BREACH OF RULE 4-1 or -2:
Disqualification.

4-3. Damaged Clubs: Repair and Replacement

a. Damage in Normal Course of Play

If, during a *stipulated round,* a player's club is damaged in the normal course of play, he may:

(i) use the club in its damaged state for the remainder of the *stipulated round;* or

(ii) without unduly delaying play, repair it or have it repaired; or

(iii) *as an additional option available only if the club is unfit for play,* replace the damaged club with any club. The replacement of a club must not unduly delay play and must not be made by borrowing any club selected for play by any other person playing on the *course.*

PENALTY FOR BREACH OF RULE 4-3a:
See Penalty Statement for Rule 4-4a or b.

Note: A club is unfit for play if it is substantially damaged, e.g., the shaft breaks into pieces or the clubhead becomes loose, detached or significantly deformed. A club is not unfit for play solely because the shaft is bent, the club's lie or loft has been altered or the clubhead is scratched.

b. Damage Other Than in Normal Course of Play

If, during a *stipulated round,* a player's club is damaged other than in the normal course of play rendering it non-conforming or changing its playing characteristics, the club shall not subsequently be used or replaced during the round.

c. Damage Prior to Round

A player may use a club damaged prior to a round provided the club, in its damaged state, conforms with the *Rules*.

Damage to a club which occurred prior to a round may be repaired during the round, provided the playing characteristics are not changed and play is not unduly delayed.

PENALTY FOR BREACH OF RULE 4-3b or c: Disqualification.

(Undue delay — see Rule 6-7.)

4-4. Maximum of Fourteen Clubs

a. Selection and Addition of Clubs

The player shall start a *stipulated round* with not more than fourteen clubs. He is limited to the clubs thus selected for that round except that, if he started with fewer than fourteen clubs, he may add any number provided his total number does not exceed fourteen.

The addition of a club or clubs must not unduly delay play (Rule 6-7) and must not be made by borrowing any club selected for play by any other person playing on the *course*.

b. Partners May Share Clubs

Partners may share clubs, provided that the total number of clubs carried by the *partners* so sharing does not exceed fourteen.

PENALTY FOR BREACH OF RULE 4-4a or b, REGARDLESS OF NUMBER OF EXCESS CLUBS CARRIED:

Match play — At the conclusion of the hole at which the breach is discovered, the state of the match shall be adjusted by deducting one hole for each hole at which a breach occurred. Maximum deduction per round: Two holes.

Stroke play — Two strokes for each hole at which any breach occurred; maximum penalty per round: Four strokes.

4

Bogey and par competitions — Penalties as in match play.

Stableford competitions — see Note to Rule 32-1b.

c. Excess Club Declared Out of Play

Any club carried or used in breach of this Rule shall be declared out of play by the player immediately upon discovery that a breach has occurred and thereafter shall not be used by the player during the round.

PENALTY FOR BREACH OF RULE 4-4c: Disqualification.

4-1/1 Non-Conforming Club Carried But Not Used

Q. If a player unwittingly carries a non-conforming club but does not use it, would the Committee be justified, under Rule 33-7, in waiving or modifying the disqualification penalty?

A. No.

4-1/2 Material in Head of Metal Wood Club Broken Away from Shell

Q. A piece of material in the head of a metal wood club, which conformed with the Rules when manufactured, has broken away from the shell due to use, and it rattles around in the head. Appendix II, 1a states in part: "All parts of the club shall be fixed so that the club is one unit." Is this metal wood club now non-conforming because of the loose piece of material?

A. No, because Rule 4-1b states in part: "A club which conforms with the Rules when new is deemed to conform after wear through normal use." The piece of material in the metal wood club in question broke loose from the shell due to wear through normal use. (Revised)

Attachment to Grip or Shaft of Club of Player with Artificial Arm — See 14-3/15.

4-1/3 Status of a Chipper

Q. What Rules apply to "chippers"?

A. A "chipper" is an iron club designed primarily for use off the putting green, generally with a loft greater than ten degrees. As most players adopt a "putting stroke" when using a chipper, there can be a tendency to design the club as if it was a putter. To eliminate confusion, the Rules which apply to "chippers" include:

(1) The club must not be designed to be adjustable except for weight (Appendix II, 1b);

(2) The shaft must be attached to the clubhead at the heel (Appendix II, 2c);

(3) The grip must be circular in cross-section (Appendix II, 3(i)) and only one grip is permitted (Appendix II, 3(v));

(4) The clubhead must be generally plain in shape (Appendix II, 4a) and have only one striking face (Appendix II, 4c); and

(5) The face of the club must conform to specifications with regard to hardness, surface roughness, material and markings in the impact area (Appendix II, 5). (New)

4-1/4 Lead Tape Applied to Clubhead or Shaft Before Start of Round

Q. Before the start of a round, may a player attach lead tape to a clubhead or shaft for the purpose of adjusting weight?

A. Yes. The use of lead tape is an exception to Appendix II, 1b(ii). (New)

4-2/0.5 Lead Tape Applied to Clubhead or Shaft During Round

Q. With regard to Decision 4-1/4, may a player remove, add or alter lead tape during a round?

A. No. However, lead tape that becomes detached from the club in the normal course of play may be replaced (i.e., placed back on to the club in the same location). If the tape is altered or damaged other than in the normal course of play, the club may not be used for the remainder of the round, under penalty of disqualification (see Rules 4-2a and 4-3). (New)

4-2/1 Material Applied to Top of Clubhead to Reduce Glare

Q. During a round, may a player put a bandaid or a strip of tape on the top of a clubhead to reduce glare?

A. Yes. This would not change the playing characteristics of the club.

Caddie Shields Player from Sun During Stroke — See 14-2/3.

Competitor Changes Weight of Club During Round; Breach Discovered After Competition Closed — See 34-1b/4.

4-2/2 Playing Characteristics of Club Changed While Play Suspended; Error Discovered Before Play Resumed

Q. While play is suspended, a player changes the lie of four of his clubs. Before play is resumed, he becomes aware that Rule 4-2a prohibits changing the playing characteristics of a club purposely during a round. If the original lie of the four clubs is restored, or if the player discards them before play is resumed, can he avoid the disqualification penalty prescribed by Rule 4-2?

A. Rule 4-2a is intended to ensure that, apart from damage sustained in the normal course of play, the playing characteristics of the clubs with which the player starts the stipulated round shall not be altered until he has finished it. Accordingly, although the stipulated round has been suspended and the player did not technically change the playing characteristics during the round, in equity (Rule 1-4):

(1) the player incurs no penalty if he discards the clubs in question before play is resumed and, assuming he started the round with 14 clubs, finishes the round with the remaining ten clubs, or

(2) if the player resumes play carrying the four clubs, whether or not he has attempted to restore the origi-

nal playing characteristics, he should be disqualified, in view of the purpose of Rule 4-2a. If the lie of a club has been changed, it would be impossible exactly to restore the original lie. (Revised)

4-2/3 Applying Chalk to Club Face

Q. During a round, may a player apply chalk to the face of an iron club in order to obtain more backspin?

A. No. (Formerly 4-3/1)

4-2/4 Applying Saliva to Face of Club

Q. A player spat on the face of his club and did not wipe the saliva off before playing his next stroke. Is this permissible?

A. If the purpose of doing this was to influence the movement of the ball, the player was in breach of Rule 4-2b as saliva is "foreign material." (Revised — formerly 4-3/2)

4-3/1 Meaning of Damage Sustained in "Normal Course of Play"

Q. What is meant by the term "normal course of play" in Rule 4-3a?

A. A club is considered damaged in the "normal course of play" when an action related to making a stroke, a practice swing or a practice stroke results in the club being damaged. If a club is damaged by the player having subjected it to a strain which is not related to making a stroke, it is not considered damaged in the normal course of play. Examples of actions which are not covered by the term "normal course of play" include removing or replacing a club in the bag, using a club to search for or retrieve a ball, leaning on a club while waiting to play, in teeing a ball or removing a ball from the hole. (New)

Leaning on Club in Hazard While Waiting to Play — See 13-4/2.

4-3/2 Meaning of "Repair"

Q. During a round, a player may repair a club damaged in the normal course of play, or he may have it repaired by someone else. What does the term "repair" mean within the context of Rule 4-3a(ii)?

A. The term "repair" in Rule 4-3a(ii) means to restore the club, as nearly as possible, to its condition prior to the incident which caused the damage. (New)

4-3/3 Club Damaged in Normal Course of Play Breaks into Pieces When Repaired

Q. The shaft of a player's club is bent in the normal course of play. The player, in attempting to repair the damaged club as permitted by Rule 4-3a(ii), breaks the shaft into pieces. What is the ruling?

A. Since the player was entitled to repair the damaged club, the further damage to the club, which has rendered it unfit for play, is also considered to have occurred in the normal course of play. Thus, Rule 4-3a permits the player to use the club in its damaged state, repair it or have it repaired, or replace it with any club. (New)

4-3/4 Modifying Penalty for Holing Short Putt with Club Whose Playing Characteristics Changed Other Than in Normal Course of Play

Q. A player leaves a putt about an inch short of the hole. In disgust, he hits his shoe with the head of his putter. The impact bends the neck of the putter, changing its playing characteristics. The player then holes the one-inch putt with the putter.

Rule 4-3b states in part: "If, during a stipulated round, a player's club is damaged other than in the normal course of play . . . changing its playing characteristics, the club shall not subsequently be used or replaced during the round." The penalty for breach of Rule 4-3b is disqualification. Would the Committee be justified in waiving or modifying the disqualification penalty in these circumstances, provided the player does not subsequently use the altered putter during the round?

A. No. (Revised — formerly 4-2/1.5)

4-3/5 Changing Clubs Because of Wet Grips

Q. May a player change clubs during a round if the grips become wet?

A. No. A club is "unfit for play" if it is substantially damaged, but not if the grip becomes slippery — see Note to Rule 4-3a. (Revised — formerly 4-4a/1)

4-3/6 Replacing Club When Grip Becomes Loose During Round

Q. The grip of a player's club becomes loose during a round. Is the club considered "unfit for play," in which case the player would be entitled to replace it under Rule 4-3a?

A. Yes, the club is considered to be substantially damaged — see Note to Rule 4-3a. (Revised — formerly 4-4a/2).

4-3/7 Club Broken While Used as Cane

Q. A player uses one of his clubs as a cane while climbing a hill and the shaft breaks. May he replace the club during the round?

A. No. A club broken in such circumstances is not considered to have become "damaged in the normal course of play" as its use as a cane is not an action related to making a stroke. (Revised — formerly 4-4a/3).

4-3/8 Player Starting with 13 Clubs Breaks Putter in Anger and Replaces It

Q. A player who started a round with 13 clubs broke his putter in anger, i.e., other than in the normal course of play, during the first nine holes. He bought another putter in the pro shop after the first nine holes and used it for the remainder of the round. Rule 4-3a(iii) permits replacing a club only if it becomes unfit for play in the normal course of play. Was the player subject to penalty?

A. No. Since he started with 13 clubs, he was entitled to add another club under Rule 4-4a. (Revised — formerly 4-4a/4).

4-3/9 Club Broken Due to Habit of Hitting Head of Club on Ground

Q. Rule 4-3a states that a club may be replaced if it becomes "damaged in the normal course of play." A player has a habit of hitting the head of his putter on the ground as he walks to the next tee, especially after missing a putt. On one occasion, after missing a short putt, the player hit the head of his putter on the ground so hard that the putter broke. The player said that he often taps the putter on the ground, and that it was not done in anger or with the intention of breaking the club. Should he be allowed to replace the club?

A. No. A club broken by hitting it hard on the ground or tapping it on the ground is not considered to have become "damaged in the normal course of play" as such actions are not related to making a stroke. (Revised — formerly 4-4a/5).

4-3/10 Replacement of Club Lost During Round

Q. A player who started a round with 14 clubs lost his putter. May he replace it during the round?

A. No. A lost club is not one which has become unfit for play in the normal course of play — see Rule 4-3. (Revised — formerly 4-4a/6).

4-3/11 Replacement of Club Broken on Practice Ground While Play Suspended

Q. Play has been suspended by the Committee. Prior to resuming play, a player is practicing on the practice ground. While hitting a ball, the shaft of his sand wedge breaks. In such circumstances, is the club considered to have become unfit for play in the normal course of play, in which case the player would be entitled to replace the broken club under Rule 4-3a(iii)?

A. Yes. (Revised — formerly 4-4a/6.5).

4-3/12 Replacing Club for Stroke Play Play-Off

Q. In stroke play, a competitor broke a club in anger, finished the round with 13 clubs and then learned that he would be involved in a sudden-death play-off. May the competitor replace his broken club for the play-off?

A. The play-off constituted a new round — see Definition of "Stipulated Round." The competitor was therefore entitled to replace his broken club. (Formerly 4-4a/9)

4-4a/1 When Club Is Considered Added

Q. A player finds on the first green that he has no putter and is carrying only 13 clubs. He continues play but sends his caddie back to the clubhouse. The caddie fetches one of two putters which he finds and gives it to the player. May the player then tell the caddie to take it back and fetch the other one instead?

A. Yes, provided he did not play a stroke with any club when the first putter was in his possession. (Formerly 4-4a/7)

4-4a/2 Changing Clubs Between Rounds in 36-Hole Match

Q. In a 36-hole match, may a player who started with 14 clubs change putters after play of the first 18 holes and before the start of the second 18 holes?

A. Yes. Rule 4-4a prohibits such procedure only during a stipulated round. A 36-hole match comprises two stipulated rounds of 18 holes each — Definition of "Stipulated Round." (Formerly 4-4a/8)

4-4a/3 Competitor Withdraws During Round and Puts His Clubs in Fellow-Competitor's Bag

Q. In stroke play, B withdrew during a round, put his clubs in A's bag, making the total number of clubs in the bag exceed 14, and carried A's bag for the remainder of the round. Should A be penalized under Rule 4-4a?

A. No, provided he did not use any of B's clubs. (Formerly 4-4a/10)

4-4a/4 Partners' Clubs Carried in One Bag

Q. In a foursome competition, is it permissible for partners to put both sets of clubs in one golf bag, provided each player uses only his own clubs?

A. Yes, provided each player's clubs are clearly identifiable. (Formerly 4-4a/11)

4-4a/5 Fellow-Competitor's Club Put in Competitor's Bag by Mistake During Round Used Unintentionally by Competitor

Q. In stroke play, A and B both started with 14 clubs. They were using iron clubs of the same model. At one hole, B's caddie inadvertently put one of B's clubs into A's bag. At a subsequent hole, A played a stroke with B's club by mistake. What is the ruling?

A. Rule 4-4a states: "The player shall start a stipulated round with not more than 14 clubs. He is limited to the clubs thus selected..." A complied with the first sentence and therefore incurred no penalty for carrying B's club. However, when A played a stroke with B's club, he did not comply with the second sentence and was subject to penalty under Rule 4-4a. (Formerly 4-4a/12)

4-4a/6 Excess Club Put in Player's Golf Bag After Player Has Counted His Clubs at 1st Tee; Error Discovered After Player Has Started Round

Q. A arrives at the 1st tee, counts his clubs and confirms that he is carrying fourteen. He then removes his driver from his golf bag, leaves the bag beside the tee and checks in with the starter. At this point, X, a player in another match or group, by mistake puts his putter in A's golf bag, which was identical to X's bag. A then drives from the 1st tee. During play of the 1st hole, A discovers that X's club has been put in his (A's) golf bag. Does A incur a penalty for starting the round with more than 14 clubs?

A. Yes. (Formerly 4-4a/13)

4-4a/7 Carrying Weighted Training Club

Q. May a player carry a weighted training club in addition to the 14 clubs selected for the round?

A. No, but a weighted training club may be selected as one of 14 clubs carried by a player, provided it conforms with Rule 4-1. Rule 4 does not regulate the weight of the golf club. (Formerly 4-4a/14)

4-4a/8 Retrieving Another Player's Lost Club

Q. A player carrying 14 clubs found another player's club on the course. He picked up the lost club, put it in his bag but did not use it, and handed it in at the pro shop when the round was completed. Was the player in breach of Rule 4-4a for carrying 15 clubs?

A. No. (Formerly 4-4a/15)

4-4a/9 Clarification of Match Play Penalty

Q. Please confirm that the following is a correct interpretation of Rule 4-4a in a match between A and B:

1. After the 1st hole, it is discovered that B has more than 14 clubs:
   a. If B won the hole — the match is all square.
   b. If the hole was halved — A is 1 up.
   c. If A won the hole — A is 2 up.

2. After the 2nd hole, it is discovered that B has more than 14 clubs:
   a. If B won both holes — the match is all square.
   b. If B was 1 up — A is 1 up.
   c. If the match was all square — A is 2 up.
   d. If A was 1 up — A is 3 up.
   e. If A was 2 up — A is 4 up.

3. Later in the match, but before the players leave the last green, it is discovered that B has more than 14 clubs:
   a. If B was more than 2 up — 2 "ups" are deducted.
   b. If B was 2 up — the match is all square.
   c. If B was 1 up — A is 1 up.
   d. If the match was all square — A is 2 up.
   e. If A was 1 up — A is 3 up.

f. If A was 2 up — A is 4 up.
g. If A was more than 2 up — 2 "ups" are added to his "ups."

A. As the loss of hole penalty for a breach of Rule 4-4a is not applied to a specific hole, but to the state of the match at the conclusion of the hole at which the breach is discovered, your interpretation is correct. (Formerly 4-4a/16)

Breach of 14-Club Rule Discovered After Match Concluded But Before Result Announced — See 2-5/5.5.

4-4a/10 Breach of 14-Club Rule in Stroke Play Discovered at 8th Hole; Where Penalty Strokes Applied

Q. In stroke play, A discovers during play of the 8th hole that he has 15 clubs in his bag and thus has incurred a penalty of four strokes under Rule 4-4a. How should the four-stroke penalty be applied?

A. A must add penalties of two strokes to his scores for the 1st and 2nd holes.

In four-ball stroke play, both A and his partner would add penalties of two strokes to their scores for the 1st and 2nd holes — see Rule 31-3. (Formerly 4-4a/17)

4-4a/11 Excess Club Discovered Before Player Plays from 2nd Tee But After Opponent or Fellow-Competitor Has Played

Q. A player starts a round with 15 clubs. He discovers his error at the 2nd tee after his opponent or a fellow-competitor has played but before he has played. Does the player incur the maximum penalty of (a) deduction of two holes in match play or (b) four strokes in stroke play?

A. No. Since the player has not started play of the 2nd hole, he incurs a penalty of (a) deduction of one hole in match play or (b) two strokes in stroke play. (Formerly 4-4a/18)

4-4a/12 Competitor Who Misplaces Putter Borrows Fellow-Competitor's Putter

Q. In stroke play, A, who had mistakenly left his putter at the previous green, borrows a putter from B, a fellow-competitor, and uses it. At the next tee, the Committee is advised of the situation. What is the ruling?

A. A was not entitled to borrow a club selected for play by any other person on the course— Rule 4-4a. A incurs a penalty of two strokes for a breach of Rule 4-4a and must immediately declare B's putter out of play as prescribed in Rule 4-4c. If A recovers his own putter, he may use it.

B may have his putter returned to him and use it for the remainder of the round. (Formerly 4-4a/19)

[4-4a/13 Reserved]

[4-4a/14 Reserved]

[4-4a/15 Reserved]

4-4b/1 Borrowing Partner's Putter

Q. Neither A nor B, who were partners in a four-ball match, had 14 clubs, but between them they had more than 14 clubs. Several times during the round A borrowed B's putter. Is this permissible?

A. No. A and B should have had two holes deducted. The penalty would be applied to the state of the match at the conclusion of the hole at which it became known that a breach had occurred.

Whether Player May Borrow Balls from Another Player — See 5-1/5.

Borrowing Club for Measuring Purposes — See 20/2.

[4-4b/2 Reserved]

4-4c/1 Excess Club Declared Out of Play Before Round and Placed on Floor of Golf Cart

Q. Before the start of a round, a player discovers that there are 15 clubs in his golf bag. He declares one of the clubs out of play, removes it from his bag, places it on the floor of his golf cart and begins the round. Is the player subject to penalty?

A. Yes, for starting the round with more than 14 clubs. Rule 4-4c has to do with declaring an excess club out of play on discovery of a breach after a round has started. There is nothing in the Rules to permit carrying, during a round, an excess club declared out of play before the round.

Rule 5. The Ball

5-1. General

The ball the player uses shall conform to requirements specified in Appendix III.

Note: The *Committee* may require, in the conditions of a competition (Rule 33-1), that the ball the player uses must be named on the current List of Conforming Golf Balls issued by the United States Golf Association.

5-2. Foreign Material

Foreign material must not be applied to a ball for the purpose of changing its playing characteristics.

PENALTY FOR BREACH OF RULE 5-1 or -2:
Disqualification.

5-3. Ball Unfit for Play

A ball is unfit for play if it is visibly cut, cracked or out of shape. A ball is not unfit for play solely because mud or other materials adhere to it, its surface is scratched or scraped or its paint is damaged or discolored.

If a player has reason to believe his ball has become unfit for play during the play of the hole being played, he may during the play of such hole lift his ball without penalty to determine whether it is unfit.

Before lifting the ball, the player must announce his intention to his opponent in match play or

5

his *marker* or a *fellow-competitor* in stroke play and mark the position of the ball. He may then lift and examine the ball without cleaning it and must give his opponent, *marker* or *fellow-competitor* an opportunity to examine the ball.

If he fails to comply with this procedure, he shall incur a penalty of one stroke.

If it is determined that the ball has become unfit for play during play of the hole being played, the player may substitute another ball, placing it on the spot where the original ball lay. Otherwise, the original ball shall be replaced.

If a ball breaks into pieces as a result of a *stroke*, the *stroke* shall be cancelled and the player shall play a ball without penalty as nearly as possible at the spot from which the original ball was played (see Rule 20-5).

*PENALTY FOR BREACH OF RULE 5-3:
Match play — Loss of hole;
Stroke play — Two strokes.

*If a player incurs the general penalty for breach of Rule 5-3, no additional penalty under the Rule shall be applied.

Note: If the opponent, *marker* or *fellow-competitor* wishes to dispute a claim of unfitness, he must do so before the player plays another ball.

(Cleaning ball lifted from *putting green* or under any other Rule — see Rule 21.)

5-1/1 Use of Ball Not Conforming with Prescribed Specifications

Q. If a player unwittingly plays one stroke with a ball which does not meet the prescribed specifications, would the Committee be justified, under Rule 33-7, in waiving or modifying the disqualification penalty?

A. No — but see Decision 5-1/3 with regard to a provisional ball.

5-1/2 Condition Requiring Use of Ball on List of Conforming Golf Balls; Penalty for Breach

Q. If it is a condition of a competition that players must use a brand of ball on the current List of Conforming Golf Balls, may the Committee provide that the penalty for breach of the condition is loss of hole in match play or two strokes in stroke play for each hole at which a breach occurs rather than disqualification?

A. Yes, unless the ball obviously does not meet the prescribed specifications — see Decision 5-1/1.

5-1/3 Condition Requiring Use of Ball on List of Conforming Golf Balls; Ball Not on List Played as Provisional Ball

Q. It is a condition of the competition that players must use a brand of ball on the current List of Conforming Golf Balls. A player, believing his ball may be lost or out of bounds, plays a provisional ball. He subsequently finds his original ball and then discovers that the ball he played as his provisional ball was not on the List. What is the ruling?

A. The player incurs no penalty as the provisional ball was never the ball in play.

5-1/4 Status of an 'X-out' Ball

Q. 'X-out' is the common name used for a golf ball which a manufacturer considers to be imperfect and has, therefore, crossed out the brand name on the golf ball. What is the status of an 'X-out' ball?

A. The vast majority of 'X-out' balls are rejected for aesthetic reasons only, i.e., paint or printing errors. In the absence of strong evidence to suggest that an 'X-out' ball does not conform to the Rules, it is permissible for such a ball to be used. However, in a competition where the Committee has adopted the condition that the ball the player uses must be named on the List of Conforming Golf Balls (see Note to Rule 5-1), an 'X-out' ball may not be used, even if the ball in question (without the X's) does appear on the List. (New)

Another Decision Relating to Rule 5-1:

Golf Ball Artificially Warmed — See 14-3/13.5.

5-1/5 Whether Player May Borrow Balls from Another Player

Q. During a stipulated round, a player runs out of balls. May he borrow one or more balls from another player?

A. Yes. Rule 4-4a prohibits a player from borrowing a club from another player playing on the course but the Rules do not prevent a player from borrowing other items of equipment (balls, towels, gloves, tees, etc.) from another player or an outside agency.

If the "One Ball" Condition in Appendix I is in effect, the player would need to obtain the same brand and type of ball as required by that condition. (New)

Borrowing Partner's Putter — See 4-4b/1.

5-3/1 Ball Internally Damaged

Q. A player hit his tee shot and expressed the view that the ball behaved erratically in flight. Before his next shot he examined the ball but he could find no external damage and the ball was not out of shape. He commented that the ball must have been damaged internally by his last stroke and claimed the right to substitute another ball under Rule 5-3. Was the player entitled to invoke Rule 5-3?

A. No.

5-3/2 Ball Declared Unfit for Play Played at Later Hole

Q. A player damaged his ball at a certain hole, declared it unfit for play and substituted another ball. At a subsequent hole he played the damaged ball. What is the ruling?

A. There is no penalty. However, the player may not again declare the ball (in the same condition) unfit for play.

5-3/3 Ball Not Unfit for Play Deemed Unfit

Q. In stroke play, a competitor, after announcing his intention of doing so, lifted his ball to check for damage, showed it to his marker and claimed that it was unfit for play. The marker disputed this claim, but the competitor insisted on substituting and playing another ball. Before completion of the hole, however, a Committee member was consulted and ruled that the ball taken out of play by the competitor was not, after all, unfit for play. What is the ruling?

A. The competitor should be penalized two strokes for a breach of Rule 5-3 or 15-1 and must hole out with the substituted ball.

In similar circumstances in match play, the player would lose the hole for a breach of Rule 5-3 or 15-1.

5-3/3.5 Player Lifts Ball on Putting Green, Throws Ball into Lake and Then Announces That Ball Is Unfit for Play

Q. A player mis-hits his approach shot but the ball comes to rest on the putting green. The player marks the position of his ball, inspects it and throws it into an adjacent lake from which it cannot be retrieved.

The player then announces to his opponent, marker or fellow-competitor that the ball was unfit for play and that he is substituting another ball. The player did not, as required by Rule 5-3, announce his intention in advance to his opponent in match play or his marker or a fellow-competitor in stroke play and give his opponent, marker or fellow-competitor an opportunity to examine the ball.

What is the ruling?

A. The player was entitled under Rule 16-1b to lift his ball without announcing his intentions. However, when he threw the ball into the lake, he deprived his opponent, marker or fellow-competitor of the opportunity to examine the ball and dispute the claim of unfitness, and he made it impossible to replace the original ball should such a dispute be resolved against him. Accordingly, he incurs a penalty of loss of hole in match play or two strokes in stroke play for a breach of Rule 5-3 or 15-1, but he may substitute another ball to complete the hole.

5-3/4 Ball Breaks into Pieces as a Result of Striking Paved Cart Path

Q. A player plays a stroke and the ball strikes a paved cart path. As a result of the impact with the cart path, the ball breaks into pieces. Should the ball be considered to have broken into pieces "as a result of a stroke," in which case the player must replay the stroke without penalty under the last paragraph of Rule 5-3?

A. Yes.

5-3/5 Ball Embedded in Hazard Lifted to Determine Whether Unfit for Play

Q. Under Rule 5-3, a ball in a hazard may be lifted to determine whether it is unfit for play. If a ball embedded in a bunker is lifted to determine whether it is unfit for play and the lie is altered in the lifting process, Rule 20-3b seems to make it clear that the original lie must be recreated and the ball must be placed in that lie. However, if the ball is embedded in a water hazard and the lie is altered in the lifting process, it would appear that, under Rule 20-3b, the ball must be placed in the nearest lie most similar to that which it originally occupied, not more than one club-length from the original lie. Is this correct?

A. No. Rule 5-3 states: "If it is determined that the ball has become unfit for play during play of the hole being played, the player may substitute another ball, placing it on the spot where the original ball lay. Otherwise, the original ball shall be replaced." Therefore, if a ball is embedded in a bunker or in a water hazard and Rule 5-3 is invoked, the original ball or a substituted ball must be embedded in the original lie to the extent that the original ball was embedded before Rule 5-3 was invoked. Rule 20-3b does not apply in such cases.

5-3/6 Ball Thought to Be Unfit for Play Lifted Under Another Rule and Cleaned; Ball Then Determined to Be Unfit for Play

Q. A player believes that his ball may have become unfit for play as a result of his previous stroke, but he is unable to determine whether the ball is unfit due to a large piece of mud adhering to it. He lifts his ball to take relief from an area of ground under repair. He then cleans the ball as permitted under Rule 25-1b and determines that the ball is unfit for play. Is the player subject to penalty under Rule 5-3 which prohibits cleaning the ball?

A. No. The player is entitled to clean the ball as provided in Rule 25-1b.

5-3/7 Ball Thought to Be Unfit for Play; Committee Involvement When Opponent, Marker or Fellow-Competitor Not Readily Available

Q. A player wishes to lift his ball to determine if it is unfit for play, but his opponent, marker or fellow-competitor is not readily available. May a referee or a member of the Committee fulfill the responsibilities of the opponent, marker or fellow-competitor in the relief procedure under Rule 5-3?

A. Yes. However, every effort should be made to have the opponent, marker or fellow-competitor fulfill his responsibilities under Rule 5-3. A referee or a member of the Committee should only become involved if the opponent, marker or fellow-competitor is not readily available.

The same ruling would apply if a player wishes to lift his ball for identification (Rule 12-2) or to determine if it is in a hole made by a burrowing animal (Rule 25-1) or if it is embedded (Rule 25-2).

Another Decision relating to Rule 5-3:

Opponent Disputes Player's Claim That Ball Unfit for Play — See 2-5/14.

PLAYER'S RESPONSIBILITIES

Rule 6. The Player

Definition

A *"marker"* is one who is appointed by the *Committee* to record a *competitor*'s score in stroke play. He may be a *fellow-competitor.* He is not a *referee.*

6-1. Conditions of Competition

The player is responsible for knowing the *Rules* and the conditions under which the competition is to be played (Rule 33-1).

6-2. Handicap

a. Match Play

Before starting a match in a handicap competition, the players should determine from one another their respective handicaps. If a player begins the match having declared a higher handicap which would affect the number of strokes given or received, he shall be disqualified; otherwise, the player shall play off the declared handicap.

b. Stroke Play

In any round of a handicap competition, the *competitor* shall ensure that his handicap is recorded on his score card before it is returned to the *Committee.* If no handicap is recorded on his score card before it is returned, or if the recorded handicap is higher than that to which he is entitled and this affects the number of strokes received, he shall be disqualified from the handicap competition; otherwise, the score shall stand.

Note: It is the player's responsibility to know the holes at which handicap strokes are to be given or received.

6-3. Time of Starting and Groups

a. Time of Starting

The player shall start at the time laid down by the *Committee.*

b. Groups

In stroke play, the *competitor* shall remain throughout the round in the group arranged by the *Committee* unless the *Committee* authorizes or ratifies a change.

PENALTY FOR BREACH OF RULE 6-3:
Disqualification.

(Best-ball and four-ball play — see Rules 30-3a and 31-2.)

Note: The *Committee* may provide in the conditions of a competition (Rule 33-1) that, if the player arrives at his starting point, ready to play, within five minutes after his starting time, in the absence of circumstances which warrant waiving the penalty of disqualification as provided in Rule 33-7, the penalty for failure to start on time is loss of the first hole in match play or two strokes at the first hole in stroke play instead of disqualification.

6-4. Caddie

The player may have only one *caddie* at any one time, under penalty of disqualification.

For any breach of a *Rule* by his *caddie,* the player incurs the applicable penalty.

6-5. Ball

The responsibility for playing the proper ball rests with the player. Each player should put an identification mark on his ball.

6-6. Scoring in Stroke Play

a. Recording Scores

After each hole the *marker* should check the score with the *competitor* and record it. On completion of the round the *marker* shall sign the card and hand it to the *competitor.* If more than one *marker* records the scores, each shall sign for the part for which he is responsible.

b. Signing and Returning Card

After completion of the round, the *competitor* should check his score for each hole and settle any doubtful points with the *Committee.* He shall ensure that the *marker* has signed the card, countersign the card himself and return it to the *Committee* as soon as possible.

PENALTY FOR BREACH OF RULE 6-6b:
Disqualification.

c. Alteration of Card

No alteration may be made on a card after the *competitor* has returned it to the *Committee.*

d. Wrong Score for Hole

The *competitor* is responsible for the correctness of the score recorded for each hole on his card. If he returns a score for any hole lower than actually taken, he shall be disqualified. If he returns a score for any hole higher than actually taken, the score as returned shall stand.

Note 1: The *Committee* is responsible for the addition of scores and application of the handicap recorded on the card — see Rule 33-5.

Note 2: In four-ball stroke play, see also Rule 31-4 and -7a.

6-7. Undue Delay; Slow Play

The player shall play without undue delay and in accordance with any pace of play guidelines which may be laid down by the *Committee.* Between completion of a hole and playing from the next *teeing ground,* the player shall not unduly delay play.

6

PENALTY FOR BREACH OF RULE 6-7:
Match play — Loss of hole;
Stroke play — Two strokes.

Bogey and par competitions — See Note 2 to Rule 32-1a.

Stableford competitions — See Note 2 to Rule 32-1b.

For subsequent offense — Disqualification.

Note 1: If the player unduly delays play between holes, he is delaying the play of the next hole and the penalty applies to that hole.

Note 2: For the purpose of preventing slow play, the *Committee* may, in the conditions of a competition (Rule 33-1), lay down pace of play guidelines including maximum periods of time allowed to complete a *stipulated round*, a hole or a *stroke*.

In stroke play only, the *Committee* may, in such a condition, modify the penalty for a breach of this Rule as follows:

First offense — One stroke;
Second offense — Two strokes.
For subsequent offense — Disqualification.

6-8. Discontinuance of Play; Resumption of Play

a. When Permitted

The player shall not discontinue play unless:

(i) the *Committee* has suspended play;

(ii) he believes there is danger from lightning;

(iii) he is seeking a decision from the *Committee* on a doubtful or disputed point (see Rules 2-5 and 34-3); or

(iv) there is some other good reason such as sudden illness.

Bad weather is not of itself a good reason for discontinuing play.

If the player discontinues play without specific permission from the *Committee*, he shall report to the *Committee* as soon as practicable. If he does so and the *Committee* considers his reason satisfactory, the player incurs no penalty. Otherwise, the player shall be disqualified.

Exception in match play: Players discontinuing match play by agreement are not subject to disqualification unless by so doing the competition is delayed.

Note: Leaving the *course* does not of itself constitute discontinuance of play.

b. Procedure When Play Suspended By Committee

When play is suspended by the *Committee,* if the players in a match or group are between the play of two holes, they shall not resume play until the *Committee* has ordered a resumption of play. If they are in the process of playing a hole, they may continue provided they do so without delay. If they choose to continue, they shall discontinue either before or immediately after completing the hole.

The players shall resume play when the *Committee* has ordered a resumption of play.

PENALTY FOR BREACH OF RULE 6-8b:
Disqualification.

Note: The *Committee* may provide in the conditions of a competition (Rule 33-1) that, in potentially dangerous situations, play shall be discontinued immediately following a suspension of play by the *Committee.* If a player fails to discontinue play immediately, he shall be disqualified unless circumstances warrant waiving such penalty as provided in Rule 33-7.

c. Lifting Ball When Play Discontinued

When a player discontinues play of a hole under Rule 6-8a, he may lift his ball without penalty only if the *Committee* has suspended play or there is a good reason to lift it. Before lifting the ball the player must mark its position. If the player discontinues play and lifts his ball without specific permission from the *Committee,* when reporting to the *Committee* (Rule 6-8a), he shall, at that time, report the lifting of the ball.

6

If the player lifts the ball without a good reason to do so, fails to mark the position of the ball before lifting it or fails to report the lifting of the ball, he shall incur a penalty of one stroke.

d. Procedure When Play Resumed

Play shall be resumed from where it was discontinued, even if resumption occurs on a subsequent day. The player shall, either before or when play is resumed, proceed as follows:

(i) if the player has lifted the ball, he shall, provided he was entitled to lift it under Rule 6-8c, place a ball on the spot from which the original ball was lifted. Otherwise, the original ball must be replaced;

(ii) if the player entitled to lift his ball under Rule 6-8c has not done so, he may lift, clean and replace the ball, or substitute a ball on the spot from which the original ball was lifted. Before lifting the ball he must mark its position; or

(iii) if the player's ball or ball-marker is moved (including by wind or water) while play is discontinued, a ball or ball-marker shall be placed on the spot from which the original ball or ball-marker was moved.

(Spot not determinable — Rule 20-3c.)

*PENALTY FOR BREACH OF RULE 6-8d:
Match play — Loss of hole;
Stroke play — Two strokes.

*If a player incurs the general penalty for a breach of Rule 6-8c or d, no additional penalty under Rule 6-8c shall be applied.

6-1/1 Wrong Form of Play Used in Match Play Event

Q. In a foursome match play competition, four players begin their match on a four-ball match play basis. The error is discovered after play of the 9th hole. What is the ruling?

A. It would be improper to decide any match by a form of play other than the prescribed form.

If the wrong form of play is used as a result of a Committee error, the match should be replayed. If the wrong form of play is used unintentionally by players, the match should be replayed; if, however, this would delay the competition, both sides should be disqualified unless one side concedes the match to the other — see Rules 2-4 and 6-1. If the wrong form of play is used intentionally by players, they should be disqualified — Rule 1-3.

Wrong Handicap Allowance Used in Match — See 6-2a/6.

Other Decisions relating to Rule 6-1:

Agreement to Waive Condition — See 1-3/7.

Responsibility for Knowing Stipulated Round — See 11-5/2.

6-2a/1 Failure to Determine Handicaps Prior to Start of Match

There is no penalty if players fail to determine one another's handicaps before starting a match. If this results in one of them not receiving a handicap stroke at a hole at which he is entitled to receive one, the hole stands as played.

6-2a/2 Handicap Stroke Given at Incorrect Hole in Error

Q. In a match between A and B, under the Handicap Stroke Table A was to receive a handicap stroke at the 9th hole. However, both A and B mistakenly believed that A should receive a handicap stroke at the 7th hole, and the match was played on this basis. Subsequently, the Committee became aware of the error. What should the Committee do?

A. The Committee should take no action. Since the players did not agree to deviate from the Handicap Stroke Table and did so by mistake, there was no breach of Rule 1-3. The match should stand as played. See Note under Rule 6-2.

6-2a/3 Handicap Stroke Wrongly Claimed at Hole; Error Discovered Before Hole Completed

Q. In match play, on the tee of a hole A states in error that he is to receive a handicap stroke at that hole. When A is preparing to putt, his opponent, B, recalls that A does not receive a handicap stroke. B so advises A and claims the hole on the ground that A gave wrong information. What is the ruling?

6

A. The hole should have been completed without a stroke being given to A, and with no penalty to either side. A did not give wrong information. It is up to each player to know the holes at which handicap strokes are to be given or received — see Note under Rule 6-2.

Extra Stroke Taken by Mistake in Handicap Match; Error Discovered Several Holes Later — See 2-5/13.

6-2a/4 Handicap Stroke Claimed After Hole Conceded

Q. In a handicap match, A holed out in 3. B, having a putt for a gross 4 and forgetting that he was entitled to a handicap stroke at the hole, conceded the hole to A. Before A or B played from the next teeing ground, B remembered that he had a handicap stroke at the last hole. What is the ruling?

A. A won the hole when B conceded it — Rule 2-4. It was B's responsibility to know the holes at which he received handicap strokes — see Note under Rule 6-2. Since B forgot about his handicap stroke, he must suffer the consequences.

6-2a/5 Wrong Handicap Used in Match by Mistake; Error Discovered After Result Officially Announced

Q. In a handicap match between A and B, A stated by mistake before the match began that his handicap was ten strokes, whereas in fact his handicap was nine strokes. The match was played on the basis that A's handicap was ten strokes. A won the match. The error was discovered after the result had been officially announced. What is the ruling?

A. The match stands as played. No claim by B could be considered unless A had known he was giving wrong information about his handicap — See Rules 2-5, 6-2a and 34-1a.

Wrong Handicap Used Due to Committee Misinformation — See 33-1/12.

6-2a/6 Wrong Handicap Allowance Used in Match

Q. In a handicap match play competition, the conditions provided that, where handicaps were different, an allowance of 3/4 of the difference would be used. In one match, however, the players, unaware of this condition, used the full difference, and the higher handicapped player won. How should the Committee rule?

A. The Committee should rule that the match stands as played. The players failed to take note of the conditions of the competition (Rule 6-1) and have only themselves to blame.

Determination of Handicap Allowances in Four-Ball Match If One Player Unable To Compete — See 30-3a/3.

6-2b/1 Wrong Handicap Used in Stroke Play by Mistake; Error Discovered After Competition Closed

Q. In a stroke play competition, A believed that his handicap was ten strokes, which he recorded on his score card. In fact his handicap was nine strokes. He won the event because of the error. The result of the competition was announced and the error was then discovered.

What is the ruling?

A. The competition should stand as played. Under Rule 34-1b, a penalty under Rule 6-2b may not be imposed after a handicap stroke play competition has closed unless the competitor has knowingly played off a handicap higher than that to which he was entitled.

6-2b/2 Wrong Handicap Knowingly Used in Stroke Play; Error Discovered After Competition Closed

Q. In late June, A submitted an entry form for a handicap stroke play competition to be held on July 10 and stated therein that his handicap was seven strokes, which was his correct handicap. On July 1, A's handicap was reduced to six strokes and he was aware of the reduction.

On July 10, he played in the stroke play competition and returned his score card with a handicap of seven strokes recorded thereon. Under the conditions for the event he should have recorded his up-to-date handicap of six strokes. After the competition was closed, it was discovered that A had played off seven, instead of six.

The Committee questioned A, and A stated that he had assumed he should play off the handicap recorded on his entry form. What should the Committee do?

A. A should not have assumed he should play off seven. Under 34-1b, he should be disqualified for knowingly playing off a handicap higher than that to which he was entitled.

6-2b/2.5 Competitor Records Incorrect Handicap for Partner in Foursome Stroke Play Competition; Error Discovered After Competition Closed

Q. A and B were partners in a foursome stroke play competition. At the conclusion of the round, A recorded on the score card that his handicap was eight strokes but, mistakenly and without B's knowledge, recorded B's handicap as ten strokes, whereas B knew that his handicap was nine. The mistake affected the number of strokes received by the side, but was not discovered until after the competition had closed. What is the ruling?

A. The side should be disqualified for returning a score card on which B's recorded handicap was higher than that to which he was entitled and this affected the number of strokes received (Rule 6-2b). Since B knew that his handicap was nine, the fact that the competition had closed makes no difference — see Rule 34-1b(ii).

6-2b/3 Competitor Wins Competition with Handicap Which Was Incorrect Due to Committee Error; Error Discovered Several Days Later

Q. The Committee incorrectly calculated a competitor's handicap and posted it on the notice board as 17 when it should have been 16. The competitor won an 18-hole stroke play event as a result of the error. May the Committee correct the error several days later and retract the prize?

A. Yes. There is no time limit on correcting such an error. Rule 34-1b is not applicable since it deals with penalties, not with Committee errors.

The competitor should not be disqualified but his net score should be increased by one stroke.

6-2b/3.5 Wrong Handicap Recorded on Score Card by Committee; Error Discovered Before Competition Closed

Q. In a stroke play competition, the Committee issues the score cards containing the competitor's handicap in addition to his name and the date.

The Committee mistakenly records a competitor's handicap as seven instead of six and this affects the number of strokes received. The error remains unnoticed until after the card is returned, but before the competition has closed. What is the ruling?

A. The competitor should be disqualified under Rule 6-2b. It is the responsibility of the competitor to ensure that his correct handicap is recorded on his score card before it is returned to the Committee.

6-2b/4 Competitors in Foursome Competition Fail to Record Individual Handicaps on Score Card

Q. In a foursome stroke play competition, partners A and B correctly calculated their combined handicap allowance and recorded it on their score card, rather than their individual handicaps.

A and B were disqualified. Was the ruling correct?

A. Yes. In any round of a handicap stroke play competition, it is the responsibility of the competitor to ensure that his handicap is recorded on his score card before it is returned to the Committee (Rule 6-2b).

The word "competitor" includes his partner in a stroke play foursome competition — see Definition of "Competitor." Therefore, the individual handicaps of A and B should have been recorded on the score card. As only the combined handicap allowance was recorded, A and B were correctly disqualified.

6-2b/5 Competition in Which Best Two of Four Scores Used to Determine Winner; Competitor Returns Score Card with Higher Handicap

Q. A handicap competition is based on the best two of four scores. In the first round, a competitor returns his score card with a handicap higher than that to which he is entitled and it affects the number of strokes received. What is the ruling?

A. The competitor is disqualified only from the first round of the competition and now has three rounds in which to determine his best two net scores. (New)

6-3a/1 Postponement of Final Match Due to Injury of Player

If a player who reaches the final of a match play event suffers an injury and is unable to play at the time arranged, the Committee may, with the concurrence of the opponent, postpone the match for a reasonable period. This applies in all forms of match play.

6-3a/2 Time of Starting; All Competitors Must Be Present

Q. In a stroke play competition, A, B and C were drawn by the Committee to play together starting at 9:00 a.m. A and B were present at the appointed time. C arrived at 9:02 a.m. after A and B had played from the teeing ground, but just in time to play in the correct order.

What is the ruling?

A. C is disqualified for failure to start at the time laid down by the Committee (Rule 6-3a) unless circumstances warrant waiving the penalty under Rule 33-7.

All competitors in a group must be present and ready to play at the time laid down by the Committee, in this case 9:00 a.m. The order of play is not relevant.

If the Committee had adopted the Note to Rule 6-3 as a condition of the competition, the five-minute period would have started at the time laid down by the Committee. Therefore, in this case the time started at 9:00 a.m. and C would incur a penalty of two strokes, rather than be subject to disqualification.

6-3a/3 Circumstances Which Warrant Waiving of Disqualification Penalty Under Rule 6-3a

Q. A Committee may in exceptional circumstances waive the penalty of disqualification under Rule 6-3a for failure to start on time (Rule 33-7). With reference to the following examples, what circumstances are considered exceptional such that the Committee would be justified in waiving the penalty if the player failed to start at the time laid down:

(1) The player gets lost on the way to the course.

(2) Heavy traffic results in the journey to the course taking longer than expected.

(3) A major accident results in the journey to the course taking longer than expected.

(4) The player's car breaks down on the way to the course.

(5) The player was present at the scene of an accident and provided medical assistance or was required to give a statement as a witness and otherwise would not have failed to start on time.

A. There is no hard-and-fast Rule. The proper action depends on the circumstances in each case and must be left to the judgement of the Committee.

Generally, only example (5) constitutes exceptional circumstances which might justify waiving the disqualification penalty under Rule 6-3a.

It is the player's responsibility to ensure that he allows enough time to reach the course and he must make allowances for possible delays. (New)

Other Decisions relating to Rule 6-3a:

6

Competitor Refuses to Start Because of Weather Conditions; Round Subsequently Canceled — See 33-2d/3.

Status of Starting Time Fixed by Players — See 33-3/1.

Player Not Present at Time of Starting; Course Closed at the Time — See 33-3/2.

6-4/1 Meaning of "Specific Directions" in Definition of "Caddie"

Q. A and B are sharing a caddie. A asks the caddie to bring him a club. The caddie removes A's club from his bag, places both bags behind the green and walks towards A to give him his club. At that point B plays and his ball strikes one of the bags. What is the ruling?

A. B incurred a penalty under Rule 19-2 (Ball in Motion Deflected or Stopped by Player's Equipment).

The Definition of "Caddie" (second paragraph) provides that, when a caddie is shared by two players, the equipment he carries is deemed to belong to the player whose ball is involved in any incident (in this case, B).

The only exception to the above provision occurs when the shared caddie is acting upon the specific directions of another player. In this case, although A asked the caddie to bring him a club, he did not instruct the caddie, when complying with his request, to place the two bags in a particular position. In placing the bags where he did, therefore, the caddie was not acting on "specific directions" of A within the meaning of that term in the Definition of "Caddie." Before playing, B could have asked the caddie to move the bags if he thought his ball might strike them.

6-4/2 Who May Serve as Caddie

There is no restriction in the Rules of Golf as to whom

a player may employ as his caddie. Restrictions may be imposed by a Committee, however, in the conditions of a competition.

6-4/2.5 Status of Individual Who Transports Player's Clubs on Motorized Golf Cart or Trolley

Q. During a round, a player's clubs are transported on a motorized golf cart or trolley by a friend who performs no other functions of a caddie. Is the friend considered to be the player's caddie?

A. Yes. By driving the cart or pulling the trolley, the friend is deemed to be carrying the player's clubs — see Definition of "Caddie."

Breach of Transportation Condition by Caddie — See 33-1/9.5.

Condition Banning Use of Caddies — See 33-1/10.

Condition Restricting Player in Choice of Caddie — See 33-1/11.

6-4/3 Player Whose Clubs Are Transported on Motorized Golf Cart Hires Individual to Perform All Other Functions of a Caddie

Q. A player whose clubs are transported on a motorized golf cart hires an individual to perform all the other duties of a caddie. Is this permissible, and is the individual considered to be a caddie?

A. The individual is considered to be a caddie.

This arrangement is permissible provided the player has not engaged someone else to drive the cart. In such a case, the cart driver, since he is transporting the player's clubs, is also a caddie. Rule 6-4 prohibits a player from having two caddies at any one time.

Thus, the arrangement is permissible (a) if the player and an opponent or a fellow-competitor are sharing the cart, even if the player walks and the opponent or fellow-competitor drives the cart, or (b) if the cart is not being shared with an opponent or a fellow-competitor and the player drives the cart.

6-4/4 Caddie Hires Boy to Carry All of Player's Clubs Except Putter

Q. A player's caddie hires a young boy to carry all of the player's clubs except his putter, which the caddie carries. The caddie assists the player in other ways, *i.e.*, attends the flagstick and gives advice. The young boy does not so assist. Is this permissible?

A. No. The player would be considered to have two caddies in contravention of Rule 6-4.

6-4/4.5 Another Caddie or Friend Carries Clubs While Player's Caddie Returns to Tee with Player's Glove

Q. A player walks from the putting green of the previous hole to the next tee with his driver while his caddie walks ahead with the clubs in order to save time. The caddie realizes he has his player's glove and gives the clubs to another player's caddie or friend to be carried while he takes the player his glove.

Did the player have two caddies in breach of Rule 6-4?

A. No. The casual act of someone assisting the player or his caddie in these circumstances does not constitute a breach of Rule 6-4.

6-4/5 Umbrella Carrier Employed in Addition to Caddie

Q. May a player employ both a caddie and a second person to carry his umbrella and hold it over his head (except when a stroke is being made) to protect him from the sun or rain?

A. Yes. The second person would be an outside agency. However, the Committee may prohibit the employment of an umbrella carrier in the conditions of the competition.

6-4/6 Status of Carts Pulled by Double Caddie

Q. A and B are sharing a caddie who is pulling A's bag on one cart and B's on another. A plays a stroke and his ball strikes B's cart. With reference to the Definition of "Caddie," since B's cart was not being carried by the caddie, would it be considered B's equipment?

A. No. The cart is considered A's equipment in these circumstances. The word "carried" in the Definition should not be taken so literally as to exclude the pulling of a cart by a caddie.

6-4/7 Changing Caddies During Round

Q. May a player have more than one caddie during a round? If so, may each caddie give the player advice?

A. A player may have more than one caddie during a round, provided he has only one at a time. He is entitled to receive advice from whoever is his caddie at the time — see Definition of "Caddie."

6-4/8 Player in Competition Caddies for Another Player in Same Event

Q. Two players playing in the same competition at different times on the same day caddie for each other. Is this permissible?

A. Yes.

6-4/9 Competitor Withdraws During Round and Carries Fellow-Competitor's Clubs for Remainder of Round

Q. In stroke play, A, B's fellow-competitor and marker, withdrew during a round and ceased to play. He continued to mark B's card, and also carried B's clubs for the rest of the round. Is this permissible?

A. Yes. A became B's caddie as well as his marker when he started carrying B's clubs.

6-4/10 Acts Which Caddie May Perform

While the Rules do not expressly so state, the following are examples of acts which the caddie may perform for the player without the player's authority:

1. Search for the player's ball as provided in Rule 12-1.
2. Place the player's clubs in a hazard — Exception 1 under Rule 13-4.
3. Repair old hole plugs and ball marks — Rule 16-1a(vi) and -1c.
4. Remove loose impediments on the line of putt or elsewhere — Rules 16-1a and 23-1.
5. Mark the position of a ball, without lifting it — Rule 20-1.
6. Clean the player's ball — Rule 21.
7. Remove movable obstructions — Rule 24-1.

Competitor's Caddie Practices on or Tests Putting Green Surfaces of the Course Before Stroke Play Round — See 7-1b/5.

Ball Thrown into Bounds by Outside Agency and Played; Caddie Aware of Action of Outside Agency — See 15/9.

Caddie Roughens Surface of Putting Green But Player Does Not Benefit — See 16-1d/6.

Caddie on Own Initiative Lifts Ball Considering It Unplayable — See 18-2a/15.

Caddie Lifts Ball in Water Hazard Without Player's Authority — See 26-1/9.

6-6a/1 Lone Competitor Appoints Own Marker

Q. In a stroke play competition, a lone competitor had no marker. No member of the Committee was present to appoint one. So the competitor played with two players playing a friendly game, and one of them served as his marker. Should the Committee accept the card?

A. Yes. Since the Committee failed to provide a marker, the Committee should give retrospective authority to the player who acted as the competitor's marker.

Retrospective Appointment of Marker by Committee — See 33-1/5.

6-6a/2 Competitor Plays Several Holes Without Marker

Q. A plays three holes by himself while his marker, B, rests. B then resumes play and marks A's scores for the holes he (A) played alone as well as his scores for the remainder of the holes. Should A's card be accepted?

A. No. A should have insisted on B accompanying him or have discontinued play and reported to the Committee. Since A was not accompanied by a marker for three holes, he did not have an acceptable score.

6-6a/3 Hole Scores Entered in Wrong Boxes; Marker Corrects Error by Altering Hole Numbers on Card

Q. In stroke play, a marker recorded some of the competitor's hole scores in the wrong boxes. He altered the hole numbers on the card to correct the error. Should the card be accepted?

A. Yes.

Hole Scores for First Nine Holes Recorded in Boxes for Second Nine and Vice Versa — See 6-6d/3.

6-6a/4 Marker Refuses to Sign Competitor's Card After Dispute Resolved in Favor of Competitor

Q. In stroke play, B, who was A's fellow-competitor and marker, refused to sign A's score card on the ground that A had played outside the teeing ground at the 15th hole. A claimed that he played from within the teeing ground.

The Committee decided in favor of A. Despite the Committee's decision, B continued to refuse to sign A's card. Should B be penalized?

A. No. A marker is not obliged to sign a card he believes to be incorrect, notwithstanding the determination of the Committee. However, the marker must report the facts and authenticate those scores which he considers correct.

The Committee should accept certification of A's score at the 15th hole by anyone who witnessed the play of the hole. If no witness is available, the Committee should accept A's score without certification.

6

6-6a/5 Marker Attests Wrong Score Knowingly But Competitor Unaware Score Wrong

Q. In stroke play, a competitor returned a wrong score because his score card did not include a penalty he had incurred. The competitor was unaware that he had incurred the penalty. The competitor's marker (a fellow-competitor) was aware of the penalty but nevertheless signed the card. The facts were discovered before the result of the competition was officially announced.

The competitor is, of course, disqualified — Rule 6-6d. Is the marker also subject to disqualification?

A. Yes. The Committee should disqualify the marker under Rule 33-7.

Marker Attests Wrong Score Knowingly and Competitor Aware Score Wrong — See 1-3/6.

6-6a/6 Requirement That Alteration on Score Card Be Initialed

Q. May a Committee require that alterations made on score cards be initialed?

A. No. Nothing is laid down in the Rules of Golf as to how alterations should be made on a score card.

6-6a/7 Duplicate Card Returned When Original Lost

Q. At the end of a round in stroke play, A discovered that he had lost B's card. A duplicate card was prepared, signed by both A and B and returned promptly. Should it be accepted?

A. Yes.

6-6b/1 Competitor and Marker Sign Score Card in Wrong Places

There is no penalty if a marker signs the competitor's score card in the space provided for the competitor's signature, and the competitor then signs in the space provided for the marker's signature.

6-6b/2 Competitor Records Initials in Space Reserved for Signature

Q. Instead of recording his usual signature on his score card, a competitor records his initials. Has the competitor met the requirements of Rule 6-6b?

A. Yes

6-6b/3 Competitor Fails to Sign First-Round Card; Error Discovered on Completion of Last Round

Q. In a 36-hole stroke play event, it was discovered just before the results were announced that a competitor had omitted to sign his score card at the end of the first round. In all other respects the cards for both rounds were correct. Should he be disqualified?

A. Yes, because he was in breach of Rule 6-6b.

Signing of Score Card in Foursome Stroke Play — See 29/6.

Competitor's Failure to Countersign Card Blamed on Lack of Time Provided by Committee — See 33-7/3.

Competitor's Failure to Countersign Card Discovered After Competition Closed — See 34-1b/2.

6-6b/4 Score Cards Not Returned Promptly Due to Committee Failure to Advise Competitors Where to Return Cards

It is a duty of the Committee to inform competitors where and to whom to return their score cards. If the Committee fails to do so, and as a result some competitors delay in returning cards, a penalty of disqualification under Rule 6-6b or any other Rule would not be justified.

6-6b/5 Marker Not Appointed by Committee Signs Cards

Q. In stroke play, A and B were appointed by the Committee as markers for one another. During the round, C joined them as a spectator; from that point, C marked the cards of both A and B, signed them at the end of the round and returned them to A and B. A and B checked their respective cards, signed them and returned them to the Committee. Before the competition closed, the Committee became aware that A had not signed B's card and vice versa. What is the ruling?

A. Since C had not been appointed as a marker by the Committee and there were no exceptional circumstances, A and B should be disqualified under Rule 6-6b.

6-6b/6 Marker Disappears with Competitor's Score Card

Q. In a stroke play event, competitors were instructed to return their score cards at the scoreboard. Unbeknownst to a competitor, his marker leaves the course hastily at the end of the round and does not report to the scoreboard. He takes the competitor's score card with him. What should the Committee do?

A. The Committee should make every effort to reach the marker. If unsuccessful, the Committee should accept certification of the score by someone else who witnessed the round, perhaps the marker's caddie or the competitor's caddie. If no one other than the marker witnessed the round, the score should be accepted without attestation by a marker.

6-6b/7 Score Corrected by Competitor After Marker Leaves Area in Which Card Returned

Q. A marker signed a competitor's score card, gave it to the competitor and left the area. The competitor discovered an error in his score for the 14th hole; the marker had recorded a 5 when, in fact, the competitor had scored 4. Without consulting the Committee, the competitor corrected the card, signed it and handed it in to the Committee. Later, the Committee heard what had happened, interviewed the competitor and his marker and established that the competitor did, in fact, score 4 at the 14th hole. Was the competitor in breach of Rule 6-6b and thus disqualified?

A. Yes. When the competitor altered the score card, he invalidated the attestation of his score by the marker.

Therefore, he effectively returned a score card which was not signed by the marker.

If the competitor had informed the Committee, before returning his card, that he was correcting the error, he would not have been subject to penalty.

6-6b/8 Requirement That Score be Entered Into Computer

Q. May a Committee, as a condition of competition, provide that a competitor must enter his score into a computer?

A. No. Such a condition would modify Rule 6-6b. (New)

Making Competitors Responsible for Adding Scores — See 33-1/7.

6-6d/1 No Score Entered for One Hole But Total Correct

Q. In stroke play, A returned his score card. The Committee discovered that no score had been entered for the 17th hole; however, A's total score for the round as recorded on the card by A or his marker was correct. What is the ruling?

A. A should be disqualified for a breach of Rule 6-6d.

Gross Score of Partner with Better Net Score Omitted from Card — See 31-4/1.

6-6d/2 Total Score Recorded by Competitor Incorrect

Q. In stroke play, a competitor returns his score card to the Committee. The hole by hole scores are correct, but the competitor records a total score which is one stroke lower than his actual total score. Is the competitor subject to penalty?

A. No. The competitor is responsible only for the correctness of the score recorded for each hole — Rule 6-6d. The Committee is responsible for the addition of scores — Rule 33-5. If the competitor records a wrong total score, the Committee must correct the error, without penalty to the competitor.

6

6-6d/3 Hole Scores for First Nine Holes Recorded in Boxes for Second Nine and Vice Versa

Q. A competitor who started at the 10th hole returns a card with scores for the first nine holes recorded in the boxes for the second nine holes, and vice versa. Should he be disqualified since the scores for some holes were lower than actually taken?

A. Yes.

Hole Scores Entered in Wrong Boxes; Marker Corrects Error by Altering Hole Numbers on Card — See 6-6a/3.

6-6d/4 Competitor's Scores Recorded on Fellow-Competitor's Card and Vice Versa

Q. A and B are playing together in stroke play. A is B's marker and B is A's marker. The starter, by mistake, gives A his own card instead of B's, and vice versa. Or A and B are given each other's cards by the starter, and, by mistake, they exchange them. This results in A recording B's scores on his (A's) card and B recording A's scores on his (B's) card.

The error is discovered after the cards are returned. What is the ruling?

A. Assuming that at least one of the scores on A's card is lower than the score actually taken by A and at least one of the scores on B's card is lower than the score actually taken by B, both A and B are disqualified under Rule 6-6d.

If the error had been discovered before the cards were returned, no penalty would be incurred if A struck B's name from B's card and inserted his own, and vice versa.

6-6d/5 Spectators Allege Competitor's Score Incorrect

Q. All strokes played by A at the 18th hole were observed by spectators, but when the card was returned the recorded score for that hole was lower than that which the spectators alleged had been taken. What should the Committee do?

A. If any doubt arises as to the correctness of a card, the Committee should consult with the competitor and marker and also take into account the testimony of other witnesses.

If the evidence indicates that the recorded score for the 18th hole was lower than actually taken, the Committee should disqualify A — Rule 6-6d. Otherwise, no penalty should be applied.

Other Decisions relating to Rule 6-6d:

Competitor in Four-Ball Stroke Play Records Score for Hole Not Completed — See 31-7a/1.

Competitor in Four-Ball Stroke Play Attributes Lower Gross Score to Wrong Partner — See 31-7a/2.

Handicap Stableford Competition; Recording of Lower Gross Score Affects Result of Hole — See 32-2a/3.

Handicap Stableford Competition; Recording of Lower Gross Score Does Not Affect Result of Hole — See 32-2a/4.

Handicap Bogey or Par Competition; Recording of Lower Gross Score Does Not Affect Result of Hole— See 32-2a/5.

Modifying Penalty for Returning Wrong Score — See 33-7/4.

Competitor Unaware of Penalty Returns Wrong Score; Whether Waiving or Modifying Disqualification Penalty Justified — See 33-7/4.5.

Omission of Penalty Stroke When Score Returned — See 34-1b/1.

Omission of Penalty Strokes When Score Returned Is Due to Incorrect Ruling — See 34-3/1.

6-7/1 Player Returns to Tee to Retrieve Forgotten Club

Q. A player arrives at a green and discovers that he has left his putter at the tee. He returns to the tee to retrieve the putter. If this delays play, is the player subject to penalty?

A. Yes. Rule 6-7 (Undue Delay) and not Rule 6-8a (Discontinuance of Play) applies in this case.

6-7/2 Searching Ten Minutes for Lost Ball

Q. If a player searches for a lost ball for ten minutes, is he subject to penalty under Rule 6-7 for undue delay?

A. Yes.

Other Decisions relating to Rule 6-7:

Second Ball Played Despite Adverse Ruling — See 3-3/2.

Entering Clubhouse or Half-Way House for Refreshment During Round — See 6-8a/2.7.

Ascertaining Whereabouts of Opponent's Ball Before Playing — See 9-2/16.

Player Requests Another Player to Lift His Ball in Absence of Reasonable Possibility That Ball Might Interfere or Assist — See 22/3.

Removal of Large Loose Impediment Delays Play — See 23-1/2.

Player Searches for Lost Ball After Putting Another Ball into Play — See 27/9.

6-8a/1 Watching Television for 45 Minutes After Nine Holes

Q. In stroke play, a group went into the clubhouse after nine holes and watched the final round of a golf tournament on television for 45 minutes. Then the group resumed play. Should the members of the group be penalized under Rule 6-7 (Undue Delay) or Rule 6-8 (Discontinuance of Play)?

A. The competitors should be disqualified under Rule 6-8a.

6-8a/2 Taking Shelter While Waiting to Play

Q. In stroke play, a group preparing to start a hole is waiting for the group ahead to get out of range. May the group take shelter from the rain in a rain shelter close to the tee?

A. Yes, but the group must leave the shelter and resume play as soon as the group in front is out of range.

6-8a/2.5 Discontinuing Play for Refreshment

The Committee may not permit players to discontinue play for refreshment for an extended period during a stipulated round. Such a condition would modify Rule 6-8a.

The Committee may, however, in the conditions of a competition, permit players to discontinue play for a short period of time (*e.g.*, up to five minutes), if it considers there to be good reason (*e.g.*, a danger of dehydration or heat exhaustion in hot climates or a need to warm up in cold climates).

However, since the Rules make specific provision for players to play without undue delay (Rule 6-7) and continuously (Rule 6-8a), such a condition is not recommended.

6-8a/2.7 Entering Clubhouse or Half-Way House for Refreshment During Round

Q. May a player, between the play of two holes, enter the clubhouse or a "half-way house" to obtain a refreshment if he then proceeds immediately to the next tee and consumes the food and/or drink while continuing his round?

A. Yes. A player may enter the clubhouse or a half-way house without penalty (see Note to Rule 6-8a).

However, the player must not unduly delay either his own play or that of his opponent or any other competitor (Rule 6-7).

6-8a/3 Discontinuing Play Due to Physical Problem

Q. During a round, a player is incapacitated by heat exhaustion, a bee sting or because he has been struck by a golf ball. The player reports his problem to the Committee and requests the Committee to allow him some time to recuperate. Should the Committee comply with the request?

A. The matter is up to the Committee. Rule 6-8a(iv) permits a player to discontinue play because of sudden illness and the player incurs no penalty if he reports to the Committee as soon as practicable and the Committee considers his reason satisfactory. It would seem reasonable for a Committee to allow a player ten or 15 minutes to recuperate from such a physical problem but ordinarily allowing more time than that would be inadvisable.

6-8a/4 Discontinuing Play Due to Inoperable Motorized Cart

Q. In stroke play, two competitors are sharing a motorized golf cart. During the round the cart becomes inoperable. The competitors discontinue play and return to the clubhouse to obtain another cart. Should the competitors be penalized for discontinuing play?

A. If the competitors reported to the Committee as soon as practicable after discontinuing play (as required by Rule 6-8a), it is recommended that, since it may not always be reasonable to expect players to carry their own bags, the Committee may consider the reason for discontinuance satisfactory, in which case there would be no penalty provided the competitors resume play when directed to do so by the Committee.

6-8a/5 Match Discontinued by Agreement Due to Rain; One Player Subsequently Wishes to Resume; Opponent Refuses Although Course Playable

6

Q. In accordance with the Exception under Rule 6-8a, A and B discontinue a match due to rain. Subsequently, although the rain continues to fall, A wishes to resume play. B refuses because he does not want to play in the rain, not because he considers the course unplayable. What is the ruling?

A. B is disqualified — Rule 6-8a. The Exception to Rule 6-8a permits discontinuance of a match by mutual agreement. However, when A decided that he wanted to resume play, there was no longer an agreement and B was obliged to resume play.

6-8a/6 Match Discontinued by Agreement Due to Rain; One Player Subsequently Wishes to Resume; Opponent Refuses on Ground Course Unplayable

Q. In accordance with the Exception under Rule 6-8a, A and B discontinue a match due to rain. Subsequently, A wishes to resume play. B refuses on the ground that the course is unplayable. What is the ruling?

A. B is entitled to refer the dispute to a representative of the Committee if one is available within a reasonable time. If a Committee member is not available within a reasonable time, B is obliged to continue the match without delay — Rule 2-5. If B does not do so, he is disqualified under Rule 6-8a, which allows a player to discontinue play for a decision on a disputed point, but only within the limits prescribed in Rule 2-5.

However, before continuing the match B is entitled to make a claim that the course is unplayable — Rule 2-5. If B does so, (a) the match should be resumed at the spot at which it was discontinued if the Committee subsequently upholds B's claim, or (b) the match should stand as played if the Committee subsequently rejects B's claim.

Replaying Match When Play Discontinued Instead of Resuming from Where Play Stopped — See 2-3/5.

Player Returns to Tee to Retrieve Forgotten Club — See 6-7/1.

Discontinuing Play Because Hole-Liner Not Sunk Deep Enough — See 16/4.

Discontinuing Play Due to Raised or Sunken Hole Plug on Line of Putt — See 16-1c/3.

Competitor Discontinues Play Because of Weather Conditions; Round Subsequently Canceled — See 33-2d/3.

6-8b/1 Competitors Playing Hole When Play Suspended Discontinue Play Immediately But Then Complete Hole Before Committee Orders Resumption of Play

Q. In stroke play, a group was playing a hole when it was announced that play was suspended. The group discontinued play for 10 to 15 minutes and then decided to complete the hole, even though the Committee had not yet announced resumption of play. Is this permissible?

A. No. Competitors playing a hole when play is suspended may only continue play of that hole if they do so without delay — Rule 6-8b. The group in question was in breach of Rule 6-8b. The penalty is disqualification.

6-8b/2 Options If Play Suspended After One Competitor in Group Has Played from Tee

Q. In stroke play, A plays a stroke from the teeing ground and the competition is at that point suspended. May B, A's fellow-competitor, also play from the teeing ground, even though play has been suspended?

A. Yes. When A played from the teeing ground, play had commenced for that hole and thus A and B may continue play of the hole provided they do so without delay and then discontinue play either before or immediately after completing it.

6-8b/3 Completion of Hole by One Competitor in Group After Play Suspended During Play of Hole

Q. In stroke play, A plays a stroke from the teeing ground and play is at that point suspended. B, A's marker and fellow-competitor, decides not to play the hole until play is officially resumed. May A play alone and complete the hole?

A. Yes, provided B accompanies A until the hole is completed. Otherwise, A would have no marker for the hole and thus would not have an acceptable score for the round.

6-8b/4 Player Unable to Resume Suspended Match at Scheduled Time

Q. During a match play competition, the course becomes unplayable and play is suspended. The Committee announces that the suspended matches will be completed the next day. One player states that he is unable to play the next day. What is the ruling?

A. The player is disqualified under Rule 6-8b.

6-8b/5 Player Claiming Danger from Lightning Refuses to Resume Play When Resumption Ordered by Committee

Q. In a stroke play competition, the Committee, after having suspended play because of lightning, orders play to be resumed. Must a player resume play if he considers that there is still danger from lightning?

A. Rule 6-8a authorizes a player to discontinue play if he considers that there is danger from lightning. This is one of the rare occasions on which the player is virtually the final judge. The safety of players is paramount, especially as there is a common natural fear of lightning. Committees should not risk exposing players to danger.

However, if the Committee has used all reasonable means to ascertain the weather prospects and has concluded that no danger from lightning exists, it has the power to order resumption of play and to disqualify under Rule 6-8b any player who refuses to comply.

6-8b/6 Play Suspended by Committee; Competitor Does Not Resume Play at Time Ordered by Committee

Q. In stroke play, the Committee suspends play. Subsequently, the Committee advises all competitors that a siren will signify resumption of play at a specific time.

A competitor in one group resumed play about two minutes before the siren sounded, because he saw a group of competitors walking down an adjacent fairway. Should the competitor be disqualified under Rule 6-8b?

A. No. Due to the exceptional nature of resumption of play, such minor errors are inevitable, and a penalty of disqualification is too severe. Accordingly, if the Committee has ordered a resumption of play and a competitor is no more than five minutes late (or five minutes early) in resuming play, the Committee would be justified in modifying the disqualification penalty to two strokes or, if circumstances warrant, waiving it entirely under Rule 33-7.

In this case, modifying the penalty to two strokes would be appropriate.

6-8b/7 Condition Requiring Immediate Discontinuance of Play; Guidelines for Waiving or Modifying Disqualification Penalty for Failure to Discontinue Play Immediately

Q. It is a condition of the competition (Note under Rule 6-8b) that players must discontinue play immediately following a suspension of play by the Committee in a potentially dangerous situation. In what circumstances should the Committee consider waiving or modifying the disqualification penalty under Rule 33-7?

A. The intent of the condition is to enable the course to be cleared as quickly as possible when a potentially dangerous situation, such as lightning, exists. A player who breaches this condition may place others at serious risk by creating the impression that no danger exists. Therefore, it is generally recommended that the penalty of disqualification should not be waived or modified and that any doubt on this matter should be resolved against the player.

However, if a player plays a stroke after play has been suspended by the sounding of a siren, the Committee must consider all of the relevant facts in determining if the player should be disqualified or if the penalty should be waived or modified.

The following are examples of Committee decisions that are justified in light of the circumstances:

After the siren has sounded:

(a) a player finished assessing his shot, selects a club and plays his stroke, taking approximately 30 seconds to do so — disqualification.

(b) a player approaches the ball and taps in a short putt, all within a few seconds — disqualification.

(c) a player, having addressed the ball, steps away momentarily, addresses the ball again and then completes his stroke within a few seconds — disqualification.

(d) a player, having addressed the ball, completes his stroke without hesitation — no penalty.

Another Decision relating to Rule 6-8b:

Time Permitted for Search for Lost Ball if Play Suspended During Search — See 27/1.5.

6-8c /1 Explanation of "Good Reason to Lift"

When play has been suspended by the Committee under Rule 6-8a(i) and a player discontinues play of a hole, he is entitled to lift his ball without penalty. If a player discontinues play of a hole under Rule 6-8a(ii), (iii) or (iv) he is not entitled to lift his ball unless there is a "good reason" to lift it (Rule 6-8c). It is a matter for the Committee to decide in each case whether a "good reason" exists.

Generally, the ball should not be lifted unless the player is required to leave the area where his ball is located and it is likely that the ball may be moved or taken by an outside agency in his absence.

If the player lifts his ball without a "good reason" to do so, the player is penalized one stroke under Rule 6-8c, unless he was proceeding under another Rule which entitled him to lift the ball, such as Rule 16-1b. (New)

[6-8c/2 Reserved]

6-8d/1 Resuming Play from Where It was Discontinued; Lie Altered by Natural Causes

Q. Rule 6-8d states that following a discontinuance of play under Rule 6-8a, play shall be resumed "from where it was discontinued" and a ball shall be placed on the spot where it was prior to the discontinuance. Does this mean the player is always entitled to the lie he had prior to discontinuance?

A. No. Natural causes such as wind, rain and water may change the conditions at the spot where the ball is to be replaced and the player must accept those conditions, whether they worsen or improve the lie of the ball. (New)

Ball Visible from Tee Disappears or is Moved While Play Suspended — See 18-1/2.

Ball Moved by Wind or Casual Water While Play Suspended — See 18-1/11.

Ball-Marker Moved Off Green by Wind or Casual Water While Play Suspended — See 20-1/10.

Rule 7. Practice

Definition
The *"course"* is the whole area within which play is permitted (see Rule 33-2).

7-1. Before or Between Rounds

a. Match Play

On any day of a match play competition, a player may practice on the competition *course* before a round.

b. Stroke Play

On any day of a stroke competition or play-off, a *competitor* shall not practice on the competition *course* or test the surface of any *putting green* on the *course* before a round or play-off. When two or more rounds of a stroke competition are to be played over consecutive days, a competitor shall not practice between those rounds on any competition *course* remaining to be played, or test the surface of any *putting green* on such course.

Exception: Practice putting or chipping on or near the first *teeing ground* before starting a round or play-off is permitted.

PENALTY FOR BREACH OF RULE 7-1b:
Disqualification.

Note: The *Committee* may in the conditions of a competition (Rule 33-1) prohibit practice on the competition *course* on any day of a match play competition or permit practice on the competition *course* or part of the *course* (Rule 33-2c) on any day of or between rounds of a stroke competition.

7-2. During Round

A player shall not play a practice *stroke* either during the play of a hole or between the play of two holes except that, between the play of two holes, the player may practice putting or chipping on or near the *putting green* of the hole last played, any practice *putting green* or the *teeing ground* of the next hole to be played in the round, provided such practice *stroke* is not played from a *hazard* and does not unduly delay play (Rule 6-7).

Strokes played in continuing the play of a hole, the result of which has been decided, are not practice *strokes.*

Exception: When play has been suspended by the *Committee,* a player may, prior to resumption of play, practice (a) as provided in this Rule, (b) anywhere other than on the competition *course* and (c) as otherwise permitted by the *Committee.*

PENALTY FOR BREACH OF RULE 7-2:
Match play — Loss of hole;
Stroke play — Two strokes.

In the event of a breach between the play of two holes, the penalty applies to the next hole.

Note 1: A practice swing is not a practice *stroke* and may be taken at any place, provided the player does not breach the *Rules.*

Note 2: The *Committee* may prohibit practice on or near the *putting green* of the hole last played.

7-1b/1 One Practice Stroke Played on Course Before Stroke Play Round

Q. On the day of a stroke play competition, a competitor, before starting his round, played one practice stroke from a forward tee at the first hole into an out-of-bounds area. What is the ruling?

A. The competitor infringed Rule 7-1b and was subject to disqualification. However, the Committee would be justified, in the circumstances, in modifying the penalty to two strokes under Rule 33-7. If the competitor played more than one such stroke, modification of the disqualification penalty would not be appropriate.

7-1b/2 Waiving Penalty for Practice on Course

Q. A 36-hole stroke play competition was scheduled over consecutive days. After completing his first round, a competitor who was a member of the club at which the event was being held played several more holes and thus was subject to disqualification under Rule 7-1b.

Would the Committee be justified in waiving or modifying the penalty?

A. No.

7-1b/3 Competitor Who Practices on Competition Course After Qualifying Round Subsequently Is in Play-Off on Same Day

Q. After early completion of a stroke play qualifying round for a match play event, a competitor practiced on the competition course after the last group in the competition had teed off. After the conclusion of play, the competitor was tied for the last place in the match play event. Such a tie was to be decided by a sudden-death play-off which was scheduled to be played immediately. Was the competitor subject to disqualification from the play-off under Rule 7-1b? If so, would the Committee have been justified in waiving the penalty under Rule 33-7?

A. The competitor was subject to disqualification. Waiving the penalty is not recommended in such circumstances.

7-1b/4 Stroke Play Over 36 Holes on Two Courses; Player Completes First Round, Practices on Same Course and Is Later in Play-Off on That Course

Q. Stroke play to determine the qualifiers for match play was scheduled over 36 holes on consecutive days.

Eighteen holes were to be played on the East Course and 18 on the North Course. Any play-off was to be held on the East Course.

Several competitors who played their first qualifying round on the East Course wanted to play more golf. They knew that they would be in breach of Rule 7-1b if they played the North Course, so they played the East Course again.

7 After the second qualifying round, one of the competitors was tied for the last qualifier's place. Should he be disqualified from the play-off on the East Course under Rule 7-1b?

A. Yes.

7-1b/5 Competitor's Caddie Practices on or Tests Putting Green Surfaces of the Course Before Stroke Play Round

Q. In stroke play, a competitor's caddie practices on or tests the putting green surfaces of the course before the competitor tees off. In view of the second paragraph of Rule 6-4, is the competitor disqualified under Rule 7-1b?

A. No. A competitor is responsible for the actions of his caddie only during a round.

[7-1b/5.5 Reserved]

7-1b/6 Stroke Play Over 54 Holes on Consecutive Days ; Second Round Canceled and Competitor Practices on Course Following Cancellation

Q. A 54-hole stroke play competition was scheduled to be played on consecutive days. The second round was canceled when the course became unplayable, and the competition was reduced to 36 holes. A competitor practiced on the course on the day of the second round after that round was canceled. Was the competitor subject to disqualification for a breach of Rule 7-1b?

A. Yes, because the competition was scheduled to be played over consecutive days. It is irrelevant that at the time the competitor practiced the competition was no longer to be played over consecutive days.

However, the Committee may in such circumstances permit practice on the course between rounds — see Note under Rule 7-1b.

7-1b/7 Competitor Practices Putting on 3rd Green After Finishing Hole During First Round of 36-Hole Stroke Play Competition

Q. A 36-hole stroke play competition was scheduled to be played on one day. During the first round a competitor, having holed out at the 3rd hole, plays a practice putt on the 3rd green. Is the competitor disqualified under Rule 7-1b for practicing on the course before his second round?

A. No. A competitor is entitled to do anything which the Rules permit him to do during a stipulated round. Rule 7-2 permits a player between the play of two holes to practice putting or chipping on or near the putting green of the hole last played, any practice putting green or the teeing ground of the next hole to be played in the round, provided such practice stroke is not played from a hazard and does not unduly delay play (Rule 6-7).

Competitor Practices Putting on 18th Green Immediately After Finishing First Round of Stroke Play Competition Played Over Consecutive Days — See 7-2/8.

Competitor Practices Putting on 3rd Green of 9-Hole Course During 18-Hole Stroke Play Round — See 7-2/9.

7-2/1 When Practice Between Holes Permitted

Q. When is play of a hole completed by a player so that he may practice as permitted in Rule 7-2?

A. *Match play: Singles* — When he has holed out, his next stroke has been conceded, or the hole has been conceded by either player.

Four-ball — When both he and his partner have holed out, their next strokes have been conceded, or either side has conceded the hole.

Stroke play: Individual — When he has holed out.

Four-ball — When both he and his partner have holed out or picked up.

Bogey, Par and Stableford — When he has holed out or picked up.

7-2/1.5 Continuing Play of Hole in Match Play After Result of Hole Decided

Q. In a match between A and B, A holes out for a 4. B has played four strokes and his ball lies in a bunker. Thus, the hole has been decided. If B plays from the bunker, would the stroke be considered a practice stroke?

A. No. Strokes played in continuing play of a hole, the result of which has been decided, are not practice strokes — see Rule 7-2.

7-2/1.7 Explanation of "Strokes Played in Continuing the Play of a Hole"

Q. Rule 7-2 states that strokes played in continuing the play of a hole, the result of which has been decided, are not practice strokes. What is meant by "continuing the play of a hole?"

A. This phrase covers situations in which a player plays the remainder of the hole with one ball in play. Its interpretation is not restricted to continuing the play of the hole in accordance with the Rules and includes, for example, situations where a player plays a ball from a spot close to where his original ball went out of bounds or in the area where it was lost.

7-2/2 Putting on Fairway While Waiting to Play to Green

Q. While waiting to play to the putting green, a player dropped a ball on the fairway and struck it several times with his putter. When questioned, he stated that he was not practicing but was "killing time." What is the ruling?

A. The player was in breach of Rule 7-2.

In Anger Player Hits Ball Played by Player in Following Group — See 1-4/4.

7-2/3 Player Practices Putting Off Green While Waiting to Putt

Q. A player lifted his ball on the putting green and, while waiting for his opponent or a fellow-competitor to play, dropped his ball off the green and played a few practice putts. What is the penalty?

A. Under Rule 7-2 the player lost the hole in match play or incurred a penalty of two strokes in stroke play.

7-2/4 Hitting Plastic Ball Before Playing Ball in Play

Q. During play of a hole, a player plays a stroke with a plastic ball before playing his ball in play. Is he in breach of Rule 7-2?

A. Yes.

7-2/5 Hitting Practice Range Ball Back to Range

Q. During play of a hole, a player saw some balls from the adjoining practice range lying on the course and flicked one back to the range with his club. Is there a penalty under Rule 7-2?

A. In some circumstances the hitting of a practice range ball back towards the range during the play of a hole would be a breach of Rule 7-2, but the casual flicking of a range ball, apparently only for the purpose of tidying up the course, is not a breach.

7-2/5.5 Player Finds Ball and Hits It to Player Who Lost It

Q. As A was playing the 13th hole, X, who was playing the adjoining 14th, was searching for his ball on the 13th fairway. X could not find his ball and walked off down the 14th. A then found X's ball plugged in the 13th fairway and called to him. X requested that the ball be returned to him. As X was out of throwing range, A hit the ball to him with a short iron.

In doing so, should A be considered to have played a practice stroke in contravention of Rule 7-2?

A. No. Since A was acting out of courtesy, there is no penalty.

[7-2/6 Reserved]

7

7-2/7 Practice Swing Dislodges Concealed Ball

Q. A player makes a practice swing in the rough and dislodges a concealed ball. Is there any penalty?

A. No. Since the player had no intention of striking the concealed ball, his swing remained a practice swing and was not a stroke. Consequently, there is no question of his having played either a practice stroke (Rule 7-2) or a stroke with a wrong ball (Rule 15).

Ball Moved Accidentally by Practice Swing — See 18-2a/19 and 18-2a/20.

7-2/8 Competitor Practices Putting on 18th Green Immediately After Finishing First Round of Stroke Play Competition Played Over Consecutive Days

Q. In a 72-hole stroke play competition held over four consecutive days, a competitor, immediately after holing out at the 18th hole of the first round, plays a practice putt on the 18th green. Is the competitor disqualified under Rule 7-1b for practicing on the course between rounds?

A. No. Rule 7-2 permits practice putting or chipping on or near the putting green of the hole last played between the play of two holes. It follows that the same privilege applies immediately after completion of the last hole of the round, even though technically such practice would be between rounds, not during a round.

Rule 7-1b would apply if a competitor, after holing out at the 18th hole, left the course and later returned and played a practice putt on the 18th green.

7-2/9 Competitor Practices Putting on 3rd Green of 9-Hole Course During 18-Hole Stroke Play Competition

Q. An 18-hole stroke play competition is played on a 9-hole course. A competitor, having holed out at the 3rd hole, plays a practice putt on the 3rd green. Since the stipulated round requires that the competitor play the 3rd hole as the 12th hole later in the round, is the competitor penalized for practicing?

A. No. Rule 7-2 permits a player between the play of two holes to practice putting or chipping on or near the putting green of the hole last played.

Penalty Strokes Incurred by Playing Ball Ruled Not to Count — See 20-7b/6.

7-2/10 Match Discontinued by Agreement Cannot be Resumed Until Three Days Later; One Player Wishes to Play on Competition Course Prior to Resumption

Q. In accordance with the Exception under Rule 6-8a, a match is discontinued due to fading light. The players establish that the only mutually convenient time for play to be resumed, which will not delay the competition, is three days later.

They agree to resume play at that time, but one of them wishes to take part in another competition on the course the following day. What is the ruling?

A. Rule 7-2 does not contemplate such a case and as it is unreasonable to prohibit a player from playing on the competition course in such circumstances, in equity (Rule 1-4), either player may play on the course at any time prior to the resumption of play. (New)

7-2/11 Match Discontinued by Agreement on 13th Tee Cannot be Resumed Until Following Day; May Players Play First Twelve Holes Prior to Resuming Match

Q. In accordance with the Exception under Rule 6-8a, a match is discontinued at the 13th tee due to fading light. The players agree to resume the match the following afternoon. However, the next day, it is not possible for the players to resume play on the competition course at the 13th tee, due to heavy play on the course.

The players wish to play the first twelve holes and resume the match at the 13th tee. What is the ruling?

A. Rule 7-2 does not contemplate such a case. In equity (Rule 1-4), the players may play the first twelve holes and resume the match at the 13th tee. (New)

Other Decisions relating to Rule 7-2:

Competitor Practices Putting on 3rd Green After Finishing Hole During First Round of 36-Hole Stroke Play Competition — See 7-1b/7.

Player in Foursome Match Practices Putts on Previous Green After Partner Has Driven from Next Tee — See 29/3.

Player After Picking Up Drops Ball Where Partner's Ball Lies and Plays Practice Stroke — See 30-3f/7.

In Four-Ball Player Disqualified for Next Hole Plays That Hole; Whether Strokes Played on That Hole Were Practice Strokes — See 30-3f/8.

Rule 8. Advice; Indicating Line of Play

Definitions

"Advice" is any counsel or suggestion which could influence a player in determining his play, the choice of a club or the method of making a *stroke.*

Information on the *Rules* or on matters of public information, such as the position of hazards or the *flagstick* on the *putting green,* is not *advice.*

The *"line of play"* is the direction which the player wishes his ball to take after a *stroke,* plus a reasonable distance on either side of the intended direction. The *line of play* extends vertically upwards from the ground, but does not extend beyond the *hole.*

8-1. Advice

During a *stipulated round,* a player shall not give *advice* to anyone in the competition except his *partner* and may ask for *advice* only from his *partner* or either of their *caddies.*

8-2. Indicating Line of Play

a. Other Than On Putting Green

Except on the *putting green,* a player may have the *line of play* indicated to him by anyone, but no one shall be positioned by the player on or close to the line or an extension of the line beyond the *hole* while the *stroke* is being played. Any mark placed during the play of a hole by the player or with his knowledge to indicate the line shall be removed before the *stroke* is played.

Exception: Flagstick attended or held up — see Rule 17-1.

b. On the Putting Green

8

When the player's ball is on the *putting green*, the player, his *partner* or either of their *caddies* may, before but not during the stroke, point out a line for putting, but in so doing the *putting green* shall not be touched. No mark shall be placed anywhere to indicate a line for putting.

PENALTY FOR BREACH OF RULE:
Match play — Loss of hole;
Stroke play — Two strokes.

Note: The *Committee* may, in the conditions of a team competition (Rule 33-1), permit each team to appoint one person who may give *advice* (including pointing out a line for putting) to members of that team. The *Committee* may lay down conditions relating to the appointment and permitted conduct of such person, who must be identified to the *Committee* before giving *advice.*

8/1 Conditions of Team Competition Stipulate Who Is Authorized to Give Advice

Q. A condition of a team competition stipulates that only the Team Captain may give advice or that the person to be appointed by each team to give advice must be an amateur. Is this permitted?

A. Yes — see Note to Rule 8.

8/2 Team Captain Gives Advice While Playing

Q. If the Committee has adopted the Note to Rule 8 as a condition of the competition, may a Team Captain, while playing in the competition, give advice to a team mate other than his partner?

A. No.

Advice Given by Team Mate in Another Group in Stroke Play — See 8-1/21.

8-1/1 Seeking Information About Length of Hole

Q. A player asks his opponent or fellow-competitor the length of the hole about to be played. This information was not displayed on the teeing ground. Was the player in breach of Rule 8-1 which prohibits asking for advice?

A. No. Information as to the length of a hole is not advice within the meaning of the term in the Rules. This is factual information normally available to all players through score cards, tee signs, etc.

8-1/2 Inquiring as to Distance from Certain Object to Green

A player may ask anyone to inform him as to the distance from a permanent object to another permanent object (*e.g.*, from a tee board to a fairway bunker, from a tree to a water hazard, from a sprinkler head to a putting green, etc.). Such information is public information.

A player may ask only his partner or either of their caddies to inform him as to the distance from a non-permanent object, *e.g.*, his ball, to the putting green.

8-1/2.5 Players Exchange Distance Information to Determine Order of Play

Q. During the play of a hole, players exchange information concerning the distance of their respective balls from the hole for the purpose of determining the order of play (Rules 10-1 or 10-2). Is this permissible?

A. Yes. However, it is recommended that the players determine the order of play in another manner to eliminate any question as to whether a breach of the advice Rule (Rule 8-1) has occurred. Any doubt on this point must be resolved against the players.

8-1/3 Asking If Distance Marker Accurate

Q. A player inquires of another player as to the accuracy of a 150-yard marker. Was the player in breach of Rule 8-1?

A. No.

[8-1/4 Reserved]

8-1/5 Seeking Information on Whereabouts of Another Player's Ball

Q. A player preparing to play to a putting green asks a spectator to advise him how far his opponent's or fellow-competitor's ball, which is on the green, lies from the flagstick. Was the player in breach of Rule 8-1?

A. No.

8-1/6 Asking Opponent or Fellow-Competitor What Club He Used at Previous Hole

Q. During play of the 6th hole, A asked B what club he had used for a shot at the 4th hole. Was A in breach of Rule 8-1?

A. No.

8-1/7 After Player Has Played to Green He Asks Opponent or Fellow-Competitor What Club He Used in Playing to Green

Q. A plays his second shot which lands on the green. B does likewise. A then asks B what club he used for his second shot. Was A in breach of Rule 8-1?

A. No.

8-1/8 Comment About Club Selection After Stroke

Q. After playing a stroke, a player says: "I should have used a 5-iron." Was the player in breach of Rule 8-1?

A. If the statement was made casually, there was no breach. If the statement was made to another player who had a shot to play from about the same position, there was a breach.

8-1/9 Misleading Statement About Club Selection

Q. A made a statement regarding his club selection which was purposely misleading and was obviously intended to be overheard by B, who had a similar shot. What is the ruling?

A. A was in breach of Rule 8-1 and lost the hole in match play or incurred a two-stroke penalty in stroke play.

8-1/10 Looking into Another Player's Bag to Determine Club Used

Q. A looks into B's bag to determine which club B used for his last stroke. Is this the equivalent of asking for advice?

A. No. Information obtained by observation is not advice. But see also Decision 8-1/11.

8-1/11 Removing Towel Covering Another Player's Clubs to Determine Club Used

Q. Decision 8-1/10 states that it is not a breach of Rule 8-1 for A to look into B's golf bag to determine which club B used for his last stroke. Suppose a towel was covering B's clubs and A removed the towel in order to determine which club B had used, would that be a breach of Rule 8-1?

A. Yes. A player is prohibited from obtaining such information through a physical act.

8-1/12 Double Caddie Informs One Employer About Club Used by Other

Q. When one caddie is employed by two players, A and B, who are not partners, is it permissible for A, who is about to play, to ask the caddie which club B used for a stroke from a nearby position?

A. Yes. A is entitled to seek from the caddie any information the caddie might possess.

8-1/13 Player Giving Opponent or Fellow-Competitor Instruction During Round

Q. During a round a player tells an opponent or a fellow-competitor that he is overswinging. Is this giving advice in breach of Rule 8-1?

A. Yes.

8-1/14 Competitor, After Finishing Hole, Demonstrates to Fellow-Competitor How to Play Shot

Q. In individual stroke play, A, who had holed out, demonstrated to B, whose ball was just off the green, how he should play his chip shot. What is the ruling?

A. B incurred no penalty as he did not seek advice. A incurred a penalty of two strokes for giving advice to B. As both competitors had not completed the hole, the penalty would be applied to the hole being played.

8-1/15 Caddie Swings Club to Show Player How to Play Shot

Q. A player's caddie takes one of his clubs and swings it to show him how to play a certain shot. Is this permissible?

A. Yes, provided there is no undue delay. A player may always seek and accept advice from his caddie — Rule 8-1.

8-1/16 Suggesting to Competitor That He Declare His Ball Unplayable

Q. B's ball was lying badly. B was deliberating what action to take when A, his fellow-competitor, said: "You have no shot at all. If I were you, I would declare the ball unplayable." Was A giving advice, contrary to Rule 8-1?

A. Yes. A's suggestion could have influenced B "in determining his play." Thus, it constituted advice — see Definition of "Advice." It did not constitute "information on the Rules," which is not advice.

8-1/17 Request for Advice Made in Error to Opponent's Caddie Withdrawn Before Advice Given

Q. While surveying his putt, A sought advice from B's caddie, whom he mistook for his own caddie. A immediately realized his mistake and told B's caddie not to answer. The caddie said nothing. What is the ruling?

A. There should be no penalty.

8-1/18 Player Who Has Not Yet Played Seeks Advice from Player Who Has Finished Round

Q. May a player about to start his round seek advice as to clubs used at various holes from a player who has just finished?

A. Yes. Rule 8-1 applies only during the play of a round.

8-1/19 Advice Between Rounds in 36-Hole Match

Q. May a player seek advice, other than from his partner or caddie, after 18 holes in a 36-hole match?

A. Yes. Rule 8-1 applies only during a stipulated round. A 36-hole match consists of two 18-hole stipulated rounds — see Definition of "Stipulated Round."

8-1/20 Asking Advice When Play Suspended

Q. A is about to play the 6th hole, a par-3, when play is suspended by the Committee. Prior to the resumption of play, A asks X, who had already played the 6th, what club he used for his tee shot. Is A penalized under Rule 8-1?

A. No. The prohibition against giving or asking for advice applies only during a stipulated round. In this case, the stipulated round had been suspended.

8-1/21 Advice Given by Team Mate in Another Group in Stroke Play

Q. Individual and team competitions are being played concurrently in stroke play. A competitor is given advice by a team mate who is playing in another group. What is the ruling?

A. The team mate would be penalized two strokes.

8-1/22 Team Mates Playing as Fellow-Competitors Exchange Advice

Q. The format for a competition between two teams is as follows: Individual stroke play, with the winner being the team with the lowest aggregate score. Play is in groups of four, with two players from each team in each group.

In such an event, may two team members playing in the same group give each other advice?

A. No. The team mates are fellow-competitors and not partners in this type of event, which is not the same as four-ball stroke play (Rule 31, Preamble), and they would be penalized for each breach of Rule 8-1.

8-1/23 Player's Team Mate in Gallery Hits Ball to Green to Show Player Whether Green Will Hold

Q. In a team competition, A, a member of one team, is playing against B, a member of the opposing team. X, a team mate of A, is in the gallery. X drops a ball close to A's ball and hits it to the green to show A whether or not the green will hold. What is the ruling?

A. In equity (Rule 1-4), if A did nothing to stop X's irregular action, he should lose the hole in view of the purpose of Rule 8-1.

8-1/24 Advice Given by Team Coach or Captain

Q. A team competition is being played, and in the conditions the Committee has not authorized captains or coaches to give advice under the Note to Rule 8. A non-playing coach or captain gives advice during a round to one of the members of his team. What is the ruling?

A. There is no penalty. However, the player should take action to stop this irregular procedure. If he does not do so, he should, in equity (Rule 1-4), incur a penalty of loss of hole in match play or two strokes in stroke play in view of the purpose of Rule 8-1.

Conditions of Team Competition Stipulate Who is Authorized to Give Advice — See 8/1.

Team Captain Authorized to Give Advice; Whether Advice May be Given While Playing — See 8/2.

Status of Team Captain or Coach — See 33-1/11.5.

8-1/25 Advice Given on Request; Penalties in Various Forms of Play

In singles match play, if A asks for advice from B, it is irrelevant whether B gives advice because A lost the hole as soon as he asked.

In a four-ball match, A and B versus C and D, if A asks for advice from C and C gives advice, A and C are disqualified for the hole. The penalties do not apply to their partners — Rule 30-3f.

In stroke play, if A asks for advice from B, a fellow-competitor, A incurs a penalty of two strokes. If B gives advice, he also incurs a penalty of two strokes.

Penalty Strokes Incurred by Playing the Ball Ruled Not to Count — See 20-7b/6.

Absent Partner Gives Advice Before Joining Four-Ball Match — See 30-3a/2.

8-2a/1 Club Placed on Ground to Align Feet

Q. A player places a club on the ground parallel to the line of play to assist him in aligning his feet properly. Is this permissible?

A. Yes, provided the player removes the club before playing his stroke. Otherwise, a breach of Rule 8-2a would occur.

8-2a/2 Object Placed Beside or Behind Ball to Indicate Line of Play

Q. May a player place his pipe or a club beside his ball, or an object behind his ball, to indicate the line of play and leave the object there while playing a stroke?

A. No. Such action would be a breach of Rule 8-2a.

8-2a/3 Player Places Mark to Indicate Distance for Pitch Shot

Q. A player who has a pitch shot places a club on the ground off his line of play to indicate the distance he would like his ball to carry and leaves the club there during the stroke. What is the ruling?

A. In view of the purpose of Rule 8-2a, in equity (Rule 1-4), the player incurs the general penalty of loss of hole in match play or two strokes in stroke play. (New)

8-2b/1 Caddie Casts Shadow to Indicate Line of Putt

Q. A caddie cast his shadow on the putting green for the purpose of indicating to the player a line for putting. Is this permissible?

A. No. Such action is a breach of Rule 8-2b if the shadow remains in position while the stroke is being played.

[8-2b/2 Reserved]

8-2b/3 Caddie Touches Putting Green to Indicate Line of Play Before Player Chips from Off Green

Q. The caddie of a player who is preparing to play a chip shot from off the putting green touches the green with a club to indicate the line of play. What is the ruling?

A. There is no penalty. The prohibition against touching the putting green to indicate the line of play applies only if the player's ball lies on the putting green.

8-2b/4 Whether Team Captain Who Is Authorized to Give Advice May Be Required to Keep Off Putting Greens

Q. In a team competition, the Committee wishes to introduce a condition of competition permitting a team captain to give advice to members of his team, including pointing out a line for putting. However, it wishes to stipulate that he must keep off the putting greens. Is such a condition permitted?

A. Yes — see Note to Rule 8.

Other Decisions relating to Rule 8-2b:

Ball-Marker in Position to Assist Another Player — See 20-1/11.

Trademark Aimed Along Line of Putt When Ball Replaced — See 20-3a/2.

Player Touches Putting Green in Pointing Out Line for Putting for Partner and Incidentally Touches Own Line of Putt — See 30/2.5.

Rule 9. Information as to Strokes Taken

9-1. General

The number of *strokes* a player has taken shall include any *penalty strokes* incurred.

9-2. Match Play

A player who has incurred a penalty shall inform his opponent as soon as practicable, unless he is obviously proceeding under a *Rule* involving a penalty and this has been observed by his opponent. If he fails so to inform his opponent, he shall be deemed to have given wrong information, even if he was not aware that he had incurred a penalty.

An opponent is entitled to ascertain from the player, during the play of a hole, the number of *strokes* he has taken and, after play of a hole, the number of *strokes* taken on the hole just completed.

If during the play of a hole the player gives or is deemed to give wrong information as to the number of *strokes* taken, he shall incur no penalty if he corrects the mistake before his opponent has played his next *stroke*. If the player fails so to correct the wrong information, he shall lose the hole.

If after play of a hole the player gives or is deemed to give wrong information as to the number of *strokes* taken on the hole just completed and this affects the opponent's understanding of the result of the hole, he shall incur no penalty if he corrects his mistake before any player plays from the next *teeing ground* or, in the case of the last hole of the match, before all players leave the *putting green*. If the player fails so to correct the wrong information, he shall lose the hole.

9-3. Stroke Play

A *competitor* who has incurred a penalty should inform his *marker* as soon as practicable.

9

9/1 Incorrect Information on Rules

A player incurs no penalty for giving incorrect information on the Rules (see Definition of "Rules"); this is not wrong information as that term is used in Rule 9. It is up to each player to know the Rules and conditions of competition (Rule 6-1). However, if it is established that a player has knowingly given incorrect information on the Rules, the Committee would be justified in imposing a penalty of disqualification under Rule 33-7. (Revised)

9-2/1 Meaning of "As Soon as Practicable" in Rule 9-2

Rule 9-2 requires a player who has incurred a penalty to inform his opponent "as soon as practicable." This phrase is purposely broad so as to allow for consideration of the circumstances in each situation, especially the proximity of the player to his opponent. Thus, informing the opponent "as soon as practicable" of a penalty incurred does not, in all circumstances, mean that the player must do so before the opponent plays his next stroke. (New)

9-2/2 Wrong Information Given by Caddie or Partner

Q. If wrong information as to the number of strokes a player has taken is given to an opponent, not by the player himself, but by the player's partner or caddie, is the player liable to a penalty under Rule 9-2?

A. Yes.

9-2/3 Wrong Information on Strokes Taken Given Voluntarily

Q. In a match between A and B, A voluntarily told B during play of a hole that he had played three strokes, whereas in fact he had played four strokes. A did not correct the error before B played his next stroke. Was A subject to penalty under Rule 9-2?

A. Yes. When a player gives wrong information, it is irrelevant whether the error is contained in a response to a question from the player's opponent or in a voluntary statement by the player. It must be corrected before the opponent's next stroke is played.

9-2/4 Withholding Information on Strokes Taken Until Opponent's Turn to Play

Q. In a match between A and B, A asks B during play of a hole how many strokes he (B) has taken. B, whose turn it is to play, withholds the information until he has played his next stroke. Is B subject to penalty under Rule 9-2?

A. No, provided B gave the information before A played his next stroke.

9-2/5 Wrong Information Causes Opponent to Lift His Ball-Marker

Q. Rule 9-2 provides that, if during play of a hole a player gives wrong information to the opponent and does not correct the error before the opponent plays his next stroke, the player loses the hole. During play of a hole, a player gives wrong information to his opponent and the wrong information results in the opponent lifting the coin marking the position of his ball. Is the lifting of the coin by the opponent the equivalent of the opponent playing his next stroke?

A. Yes; the player loses the hole.

9-2/6 Player Reporting Wrong Score Causes Opponent with Chance for Half to Pick Up Ball

Q. In match play, A holed out and stated to B, his opponent, that he had scored a 4. B, having played four strokes, picked up assuming he had lost the hole. A then realized that he had scored a 5. He immediately told B. What is the ruling?

A. A gave wrong information as to the number of strokes taken and, under the principle of Rule 9-2, A would normally lose the hole. However, since A had holed out for no worse than a half, the hole was halved — see Rule 2-2.

Player Lifts Ball Before Holing Out; Opponent Then Picks Up His Ball and Claims Player Loses Hole — See 2-5/3.

In Four-Ball Match Player with Putt for Half Picks Up at Suggestion of Opponent Due to Misunderstanding — See 30/5.

Player's Ball Resting Against Flagstick Lifted Before Being Holed; Others in Four-Ball Match Pick Up Mistakenly Believing Player Won Hole — See 30-3f/3.

Wrong Information Given by Player Out of Contention in Four-Ball Match — See 30-3f/4.

9-2/7 Wrong Information Given by Player Corrected Before Opponent Plays Next Stroke But After Opponent Has Conceded Player's Putt

Q. In a match, A's ball was a few inches from the hole. B asked A, "How many will that be in the hole?" A answered, "6," whereupon B conceded A's next stroke, holed a putt for a 6 and assumed that he had halved the hole. B was then informed by A that he (A) had actually scored 5. The Committee ruled that A won the hole. Was this correct?

A. No. A gave wrong information as to his score during play of the hole and did not correct his mistake before B played his next stroke. Therefore, under Rule 9-2, A lost the hole.

However, the penalty would still have applied even if A had corrected his mistake after B had conceded A's next stroke and before B putted. The principle of Rule 9-2 applies if, after receiving wrong information, a player takes some action (*e.g.*, picks up or concedes the opponent's next stroke) which he might not have taken if wrong information had not been given.

In such a case, the answer does not turn on how close A's ball was to the hole or on the fact that B sank his putt and could not have done any better.

9-2/8 Player Wins Hole with Wrong Ball; Error Discovered at Next Hole; Opponent Claims Previous Hole

Q. In a match, A holed out in 3 at the 5th hole. His opponent, B, holed out in 4. After driving from the next tee, it was discovered that A had played a wrong ball at the 5th hole. B claimed the 5th hole. What is the ruling?

A. Since A failed to inform B as soon as practicable that he had incurred a penalty for playing a wrong ball, he is deemed to have given wrong information even though he was not aware he had incurred a penalty (Rule 9-2). Thus, B's belated claim was valid (Rule 2-5) and the Committee should have ruled that B won the 5th hole. (Revised)

Player Wins Hole with Own Ball After Playing Wrong Ball; Opponent Lodges Belated Claim — See 2-5/4.

Player Wins Hole with Wrong Ball and Partner Picks Up; Error Discovered at Next Hole — See 30-3d/2.

Players on Opposite Sides Exchange Balls During Play of Hole and Their Partners Pick Up; Error Discovered at Next Hole — See 30-3d/3.

Player Plays Partner's Ball; Error Discovered After Opponents Have Played Next Strokes — See 30-3d/3.5.

9-2/9 Player Reports Wrong Score for Hole; Error Discovered Several Holes Later

Q. In match play, after completion of a hole, A inadvertently reports to B, his opponent, that he scored a 5, whereas in fact he scored a 6. This results in the hole being halved or won by A. A realizes his mistake several holes later. What is the ruling?

A. In either case, A loses the hole and the state of the match must be adjusted accordingly (Rule 9-2).

9-2/10 Player Omits Penalty Stroke When Advising Opponent as to Score for Hole; Error Discovered After Match Conceded by Opponent

Q. In a match, A and B were all square after 18 holes and were playing the 19th hole. A incurred a penalty stroke but was unaware of that fact. A holed out and told B that he had scored a 6. B played his sixth shot, missed the hole and conceded the match to A.

When returning to the clubhouse, A learned that he had incurred a penalty stroke and that his score had been 7, not 6. B claimed the match on the ground that A gave wrong information. What is the ruling?

A. B's claim was valid since the result had not been announced — see Rule 2-5. A lost the hole for giving wrong information, even though he may not have been aware that he had incurred a penalty — Rule 9-2.

Player Concedes Match After Winning It When Opponent Lodges Invalid Claim Regarding Strokes Taken — See 2-4/15.

Player Wins Match; Breach of 14-Club Rule Discovered Before Result Announced — See 2-5/5.

Winner of Match Due to Wrong Information by Opponent Makes No Claim and Loses in Extra Holes — See 2-5/7.

9-2/11 Player Concluding He Played Wrong Ball When Opponent Misread Number on Player's Ball Concedes Hole

Q. In a match, A and B are playing the same brand of ball (Brand X). The identification number on A's ball is "3" and A's name is imprinted on his ball. The identification number on B's ball is "5."

On completion of the 2nd hole, which A won, B picks up both balls and says, "Both 5's — which is yours?" A states that he was playing a "3" and therefore he must have played a wrong ball. A concedes the hole to B.

B wins the match and then discovers he has in his possession a Brand X ball with the identification number "3" and A's name imprinted on it. A and B conclude that B misread the number at the 2nd hole. Did B give A wrong information?

A. No. Wrong information as the term is used in Rule 9 refers to the number of strokes taken.

A's concession of the 2nd hole must stand and the match must stand as played. It would have been advisable for A to inspect the two balls at the 2nd hole before conceding the hole.

9-2/12 Conscious Failure to Correct Opponent's Misunderstanding of State of Match; What Constitutes Wrong Information

Q. In a match, B is 1 up on A playing the 14th hole. A and B take 6's at the 14th hole, but B assuming A scored a 5, says: "We are now all square." A says nothing although he knows that both have scored 6 and he is still 1 down.

At the end of the 17th hole, B believing he is 2 down, concedes the match, although in fact he is only 1 down. Is A subject to penalty under Rule 9-2 for giving wrong information?

A. No. Rule 9-2 deals with giving wrong information as to the number of strokes taken at a hole and would include acquiescence by the player (whether oral or tacit) in a misstatement by his opponent of the number of strokes taken by the player. Wrong information does not include acquiescence by the player in a misstatement by his opponent of the result of a hole or the state of the match.

However, A's conscious failure to correct B's misunderstanding of the state of the match is so contrary to the spirit of the game that the Committee should disqualify A under Rule 33-7 and reinstate B.

9-2/13 Player Who Told Opponent He Would Proceed Under Water Hazard Rule Changes Mind After Opponent Plays

Q. In a match, B hit his tee shot short of a water hazard and A hit his into the hazard. Before B played his second shot he asked A what he was going to do. A said he was going to drop out and take a one-stroke penalty. B then played his second shot, after which A changed his mind and played his ball out of the hazard. Did A give wrong information, contrary to Rule 9-2?

A. No. A could have refused to answer B's question or replied that he would await B's play before deciding his own tactics. The fact that A did tell B what he planned to do does not preclude A from changing his mind.

9-2/14 Wrong Information Causes Opponent Mistakenly to Think He Has Putt for Half; Opponent Holes Putt and Then Error Discovered

Q. In a match between A and B, A's ball was a few inches from the hole. B conceded A's next stroke and then asked, "How many strokes did you take?" A answered, "6". B, lying 5, then holed a putt for a 6 and assumed that he had halved the hole. At that point, A told B that he (A) had actually scored 5. The Committee ruled that A won the hole. Was this correct?

A. Yes. The hole was over when A's putt was conceded and he had won the hole with a 5. Since A corrected the error before either player played from the next tee, no penalty was incurred — see Rule 9-2.

9-2/15 Wrong Information After Play of Hole; When Penalty Applicable

Q. Decision 9-2/14 implies that, if A had not corrected the error before playing from the next tee, he would have lost the hole under Rule 9-2. Is this correct? It would seem that A would not incur a penalty because he won the hole, and therefore the wrong information did not affect the result of the hole.

A. There is a penalty for giving wrong information after play of a hole which is not corrected before play from the next teeing ground unless the wrong information does not affect the opponent's understanding of the result of the hole just completed. Wrong information would not affect the opponent's understanding of the result of the hole in the following circumstances: A and B are playing a match. After play of a hole, A states that he scored 5 and B states that he (B) scored 7. After teeing off at the next hole, A states that he was incorrect in saying that he scored 5 and that, in fact, he scored 6.

In Decision 9-2/14, the wrong information caused B to believe that the hole in question had been halved, when in fact B lost the hole. Accordingly, if A had not corrected the error before playing from the next tee, under Rule 9-2 the hole should have been awarded to B.

9-2/16 Ascertaining Whereabouts of Opponent's Ball Before Playing

Q. In a match, B's tee shot may be lost, out of bounds or in a water hazard. In view of the second paragraph of Rule 9-2, under which an opponent is entitled to ascertain from the player the number of strokes he has taken, may A go forward to determine the status of B's ball before he (A) plays from the tee?

A. No. A would be in breach of Rule 6-7 (Undue Delay) if he did so. A player may make such a determination only if it can be done without unduly delaying play.

Another Decision relating to Rule 9-2:

In Foursome Side Drives for Three Holes in Wrong Order and Then Claim Is Made — See 29-2/2.

9-3/1 Competitor in Sudden-Death Play-Off Gives Wrong Information

Q. In a stroke play sudden-death play-off, B has completed the hole in 5 strokes. A, who has a putt for a 5, inquires as to B's score for the hole, and B wrongly states that he (B) has holed out in 4 strokes. A picks up his ball without marking its position. B then corrects his mistake. What is the ruling?

A. B incurs no penalty. Rule 9 imposes no penalty for giving wrong information as to the number of strokes taken in stroke play.

A incurs a penalty of one stroke under Rule 20-1 for lifting his ball at rest without marking its position. Since this leaves A with a putt for a 6, he loses the play-off.

ORDER OF PLAY

Rule 10. Order of Play

Definition

The player who is to play first from the *teeing ground* is said to have the *"honor."*

10-1. Match Play

a. Teeing Ground

The *side* which shall have the *honor* at the first *teeing ground* shall be determined by the order of the draw. In the absence of a draw, the *honor* should be decided by lot.

The *side* which wins a hole shall take the *honor* at the next *teeing ground.* If a hole has been halved, the *side* which had the *honor* at the previous *teeing ground* shall retain it.

b. Other Than on Teeing Ground

When the *balls are in play,* the ball farther from the *hole* shall be played first. If the balls are equidistant from the *hole,* the ball to be played first should be decided by lot.

Exception: Rule 30-3c (best-ball and four-ball match play).

c. Playing Out of Turn

If a player plays when his opponent should have played, the opponent may immediately require the player to cancel the *stroke* so played and, in correct order, play a ball without penalty as nearly as possible at the spot from which the original ball was last played (see Rule 20-5).

10

10-2. Stroke Play

a. Teeing Ground

The *competitor* who shall have the *honor* at the first *teeing ground* shall be determined by the order of the draw. In the absence of a draw, the *honor* should be decided by lot.

The *competitor* with the lowest score at a *hole* shall take the *honor* at the next *teeing ground*. The *competitor* with the second lowest score shall play next and so on. If two or more *competitors* have the same score at a hole, they shall play from the next *teeing ground* in the same order as at the previous *teeing ground*.

b. Other Than on Teeing Ground

When the *balls are in play,* the ball farthest from the *hole* shall be played first. If two or more balls are equidistant from the *hole,* the ball to be played first should be decided by lot.

Exceptions: Rules 22 (ball interfering with or assisting play) and 31-5 (four-ball stroke play).

c. Playing Out of Turn

If a *competitor* plays out of turn, no penalty is incurred and the ball shall be played as it lies. If, however, the *Committee* determines that *competitors* have agreed to play in an order other than that set forth in Clauses 2a, 2b and 3 of this Rule to give one of them an advantage, they shall be disqualified.

(Incorrect order of play in threesomes and foursomes stroke play — see Rule 29-3.)

(Playing stroke while another ball in motion after stroke from putting green — see Rule 16-1f.)

10-3. Provisional Ball or Second Ball from Teeing Ground

If a player plays a *provisional ball* or a second ball from a *teeing ground,* he shall do so after his opponent or *fellow-competitor* has played his first *stroke.* If a player plays a *provisional ball* or a second ball out of turn, Clauses 1c and 2c of this Rule shall apply.

10-4. Ball Moved in Measuring

If a ball is *moved* in measuring to determine which ball is farther from the *hole*, no penalty is incurred and the ball shall be replaced.

10/1 Order of Play When Two Balls Lie in Ground Under Repair and Both Players Take Relief

Q. A and B hit their balls into ground under repair. The balls are approximately 18 inches apart. A's ball is farther from the hole. Both players decide to take relief. Is the order of play for the next shot determined by the relative positions of the balls before relief is taken, or after?

A. The order of play is determined by the relative positions of the balls before relief is taken. A should play before B — see Rules 10-1b and -2b.

10/2 Order of Play When Two Balls Lie in Lateral Water Hazard and Both Players Take Relief

Q. A and B hit their balls into a lateral water hazard. The balls are approximately 18 inches apart. A's ball is farther from the hole but B's ball last crossed the hazard margin farther from the hole than A's ball. Both players decide to take relief from the hazard. What is the proper procedure?

A. Since A's ball lies farther from the hole, under Rule 10-1b or -2b A should play before B.

10/3 Order of Play When Two Balls Are Lost in Lateral Water Hazard

Q. A and B hit their balls into the same general area of a lateral water hazard. Both balls are lost in the hazard and therefore it is not known which ball is farther from the hole. However, B's ball last crossed the hazard margin farther from the hole than A's ball. What is the proper procedure?

A. The ball to be played first should be decided by lot, just as would be the case if the balls were equidistant from the hole — see Rules 10-1b and -2b.

Players Exchange Distance Information to Determine Order of Play — See 8-1/2.5.

10-1a/1 Determination of Honor in Handicap Match

Q. A and B are playing a match on a handicap basis. B has the honor at the 1st hole.

Both players score 5's at the 1st hole but A receives a handicap stroke and therefore has a net 4. Does A take the honor at the 2nd hole?

A. Yes. See Rules 2-1 and 10-1a.

10-1a/2 Determination of Honor at Hole Following Disputed Hole

Q. A dispute arises in a match between A and B, and A lodges a claim. A and B agree to continue the match and get a ruling later. Which player has the honor at the next hole?

A. In equity (Rule 1-4), the honor should be decided by lot, except that, if A's claim was to gain a half, B would retain the honor if he had it at the previous hole.

Other Decisions relating to Rule 10-1a:

Players Agree Not to Tee Off in Prescribed Order to Save Time — See 1-3/1.

Determination of Honor in Four-Ball Match in Which Points Awarded for Both Better-Ball and Aggregate Scores — See 30/3.

10-1b/1 Procedure for Referee in Determining Ball Farther from Hole

Q. In a match, A's ball is on one side of the fairway and B's ball is on the other side. Both balls are about 100 yards from the hole. A plays and B questions whether A played out of turn. Is the referee obliged to pace off the distances to the hole to resolve the question?

A. No. In view of the distances involved, the referee would be justified in resolving the question by eye. If he could not do so, he would be justified in deciding by lot which player should have played first. If it was decided by lot that B should have played first, B would have the option of recalling A's stroke under Rule 10-1c.

Other Decisions relating to Rule 10-1b:

Player Who Walks Off Green Under Mistaken Impression Partner Halved Hole Returns and Putts for Half — See 30/5.

Waiving Turn to Putt in Four-Ball Match — See 30-3c/2.

10-1c/1 Request for Player to Replay Stroke Withdrawn After Opponent Plays

Q. In a match between A and B, A played his tee shot out of turn. B requested A to abandon the ball and play in the correct order. However, after B played, he told A not to bother playing another ball. What is the ruling?

A. A was not obliged to comply with B's instruction to continue with the original ball. B incurred no penalty for giving the instruction.

Whether A continued with his original ball or played another ball in correct order as was his right, the result of the hole should stand as played.

10-1c/2 Player Requested to Lift Ball Due to Interference Plays Out of Turn Instead

Q. In match play, A's ball is on B's line of putt. B requests A to lift his ball under Rule 22. Instead of complying with the request, A putts out of turn. Does A lose the hole for a breach of Rule 22 or does Rule 10-1c apply, in which case there would be no penalty but B would have the right to require A to replay the stroke in correct order?

A. Rule 10-1c governs.

Other Decisions relating to Rule 10-1c:

Player Smooths Irregularities in Bunker After Playing Out of Turn; Opponent Then Recalls Stroke and Player Must Drop Ball in Smoothed Area — See 13-4/39.

Player Wishing to Render Original Ball Lost Plays Provisional Ball Out of Turn — See 27-2b/1.

In Four-Ball Match Side Plays Out of Turn from Tee; Opponents Require One Member of Side to Replay But Not Other — See 30-1/1.

Player Plays Out of Turn from Tee in Three-Ball Match; One Opponent Requests Replay and Other Does Not — See 30-2/1.

10-2a/1 Determination of Honor in Handicap Stroke Play

Q. In a stroke play competition on a handicap basis, the handicap is deducted at the end of the round and not at individual holes. In such a competition, how is the honor determined?

A. According to gross scores.

Determination of Honor in Handicap Stableford Competition — See 32-1/3.

10-2b/1 Competitor Objects to Fellow-Competitor Putting Out of Turn

Q. In stroke play, A's ball is 40 feet from the hole and B's is 30 feet away. A putts and his ball comes to rest four feet from the hole. A prepares to hole out before B putts. B objects and claims that under the Rules (Rule 10-2b) he is entitled to putt before A.

Although putting out of turn in stroke play is generally condoned, should the Committee allow A to putt out of turn in these circumstances?

A. If A had lifted his ball when the objection was lodged, the Committee should rule that A is not entitled to putt out of turn, in view of Rule 10-2b.

If A had not lifted his ball at the time the objection was lodged, the answer depends on whether B would require A to lift his ball under Rule 22 (Ball Interfering with or Assisting Play) before he (B) putts. If so, the

Committee should rule that A is entitled to play out of turn, provided he does so without first lifting his ball, *i.e.*, Rule 22 permits a competitor in stroke play who is required to lift his ball because of interference to "play first rather than lift."

If B would not require A to lift his ball before he (B) putts, the Committee should rule that A is not entitled to putt out of turn.

Although condoning putting out of turn in stroke play may be questionable in view of the explicit language of Rule 10-2b, there is no penalty for doing so (Rule 10-2c), it is not in conflict with the intent of Rule 10-2b, and it may tend to speed play.

Accordingly, it is considered that the practice should not be discouraged.

Other Decisions relating to Rule 10-2b:

Waiving Turn to Play in Four-Ball Stroke Play — See 31-5/1.

Extent to Which Side May Play in Order It Considers Best — See 31-5/2.

10-2c/1 Ball Played Out of Turn from Tee Abandoned and Another Ball Played in Proper Order

Q. In stroke play, a competitor played out of turn from the teeing ground and, although he should have continued play with the ball played out of turn without penalty, he abandoned the ball and played another ball in proper order. What is the ruling?

A. When the competitor played another ball from the tee, the original ball was lost and the other ball was in play under penalty of stroke and distance — see Decision 27/17.

10-2c/2 Competitors in Stroke Play Agree to Play Out of Turn But Not for Purpose of Giving One of Them an Advantage

Q. In stroke play, A and B agree to play out of turn at the 10th hole to save time. There is no penalty under Rule 10-2c because they did not do so in order to give one of them an advantage. However, are they liable to disqualification under Rule 1-3 for agreeing to exclude the operation of Rule 10-2a or 10-2b as the case may be?

A. No. Rule 10-2c specifically governs and permits the procedure in stroke play. Accordingly, Rule 1-3 does not apply. As to match play, see Decision 1-3/1.

TEEING GROUND

Rule 11. Teeing Ground

11

Definition

The *"teeing ground"* is the starting place for the hole to be played. It is a rectangular area two club-lengths in depth, the front and the sides of which are defined by the outside limits of two tee-markers. A ball is outside the *teeing ground* when all of it lies outside the *teeing ground.*

11-1. Teeing

In teeing, the ball may be placed on the ground, on an irregularity of surface created by the player on the ground or on a tee, sand or other substance in order to raise it off the ground.

A player may stand outside the *teeing ground* to play a ball within it.

11-2. Tee-Markers

Before a player plays his first *stroke* with any ball from the *teeing ground* of the hole being played, the tee-markers are deemed to be fixed. In such circumstances, if the player moves or allows to be moved a tee-marker for the purpose of avoiding interference with his *stance,* the area of his intended swing or his *line of play,* he shall incur the penalty for a breach of Rule 13-2.

11-3. Ball Falling Off Tee

If a ball, when not in play, falls off a tee or is knocked off a tee by the player in *addressing* it, it may be re-teed without penalty, but if a *stroke* is made at the ball in these circumstances, whether the ball is moving or not, the *stroke* counts but no penalty is incurred.

11-4. Playing from Outside Teeing Ground

a. Match Play

If a player, when starting a hole, plays a ball from outside the *teeing ground,* the opponent may immediately require the player to cancel the *stroke* so played and play a ball from within the *teeing ground,* without penalty.

b. Stroke Play

If a *competitor,* when starting a hole, plays a ball from outside the *teeing ground,* he shall incur a penalty of two strokes and shall then play a ball from within the *teeing ground.*

If the *competitor* plays a *stroke* from the next *teeing ground* without first correcting his mistake or, in the case of the last hole of the round, leaves the *putting green* without first declaring his intention to correct his mistake, he shall be disqualified.

The *stroke* from outside the *teeing ground* and any subsequent strokes by the *competitor* on the hole prior to his correction of the mistake do not count in his score.

11-5. Playing from Wrong Teeing Ground

The provisions of Rule 11-4 apply.

Decisions relating to Rule 11-1:

Breaking Off Grass Behind Ball on Teeing Ground — See 13-2/3.

Breaking Branch Interfering with Backswing on Teeing Ground — See 13-2/14.

Player Who Misses Tee Shot Presses Down Irregularities Before Next Stroke — See 13-2/2.

Standing on Mat on Teeing Ground — See 13-3/1.

Player Who Misses Tee Shot Tees Ball Lower Before Playing Next Stroke — See 18-2a/1.

Teed Ball Missed Then Hit Out of Bounds — See 20-5/1.

Interference by Immovable Obstruction Within Teeing Ground — See 24-2a/3.

Casual Water Covering Teeing Ground — See 25-1b/4.

Mixed Foursome in Which Different Tees Used by Men and Women; Tee Shot Out of Bounds — See 29/2.

11-2/1 Status of Tee-Markers After First Stroke

Q. Under Rule 11-2, tee-markers are deemed to be fixed when playing the first stroke with any ball from the teeing ground. Are tee-markers obstructions thereafter?

A. Yes. (Revised)

11-2/2 Tee-Marker Moved by Player

Rule 11-2 states that before a player plays his first stroke with any ball from the teeing ground, the tee-markers are deemed to be fixed. Thereafter, Decision 11-2/1 clarifies that they are obstructions and if movable, may be moved (see Definition of "Obstruction").

In view of the fact that tee-markers are initially fixed, and when moved can have a significant effect on the competition, the following are examples of the appropriate ruling in various circumstances. In all cases a moved tee-marker should be replaced. In some cases, the replacement of the tee-marker may affect the penalty to the player.

(a) A player moves a tee-marker before playing his first stroke with any ball from the teeing ground because the tee-marker interferes with the lie of the ball, his stance or his area of intended swing — loss of hole in match play or two strokes in stroke play for breach of Rule 13-2.

(b) A player moves a tee-marker before or after playing a stroke from the teeing ground because, in his view, the tee-markers are too close together, too far back, aimed in the wrong direction, or some similar reason — disqualification under Rule 33-7, unless the tee-marker is replaced before the player or any other player plays from the teeing ground, in which case the penalty is modified to loss of hole in match play or two strokes in stroke play.

(c) A player moves a tee-marker before or after playing a stroke from the teeing ground as a result of falling over the marker — no penalty and the tee-marker should be replaced.

(d) A player moves a tee-marker before or after playing a stroke from the teeing ground as a result of intentionally kicking it or striking it with a club — no penalty and the tee-marker should be replaced.

(e) A player lifts a tee-marker before or after playing a stroke from the teeing ground for no apparent reason and without authority under the Rules — no penalty and the tee-marker should be replaced. (Revised)

11-3/1 Stroke Misses Ball; Ball Then Accidentally Knocked Off Tee

Q. A player teed his ball within the teeing ground. He made a stroke at the ball but missed it. He addressed the ball again and accidentally knocked it off the tee. What is the ruling?

A. When the player made a stroke at the ball, it was in play and Rule 11-3 no longer applied. When the ball in play moved after it was addressed, the player incurred a penalty stroke and was obliged to replace the ball-Rule 18-2b.

Ball Falling Off Tee When Stroke Just Touches It Is Picked Up and Re-Teed — See 18-2a/2.

11-3/2 Lifting Ball in Play But Still Within Teeing Ground

Q. A player played his first stroke from a teeing ground and barely moved the ball, which remained within the teeing ground. The player re-teed the ball claiming that, since the ball was still within the teeing ground, he was entitled to do so. Was the player correct?

A. No. When the player made a stroke, the ball was in play — see Definition of "Ball in Play." If a player moves his ball in play without authority, he incurs a penalty stroke under Rule 18-2a and he must replace his ball before playing his next stroke. Otherwise, he loses the hole in match play or he incurs a total penalty of two strokes in stroke play — see penalty statement under Rule 18.

11-3/3 Original Ball Out of Bounds; Ball Played Under Stroke-and-Distance Procedure Falls Off Tee at Address

Q. A player played his original ball out of bounds from the teeing ground. Under Rule 27-1, he teed up another ball. When addressing the ball, he touched it and it fell off the tee. What is the ruling?

A. There is no penalty, because a teed ball is not in play until a stroke has been made at it (see Definition of "Ball in Play"). The ball may be re-teed (Rule 11-3).

Decisions relating to Rule 11-4a:

Ball Played Out of Bounds from Wrong Teeing Ground not Recalled — See 11-5/3.

Ball Played from Outside Teeing Ground in Foursome Match — See 29-1/1.

11

[11-4a/1 Reserved]

[11-4b/1 Reserved]

11-4b/2 Competitors Estimate Area of Teeing Ground When One Tee-Marker Missing

Q. In stroke play, competitors in a group, finding one tee-marker missing from a teeing ground, determine for themselves the area of the teeing ground based on the position of the remaining tee-marker and the shape of the tee. What is the ruling?

A. The correct procedure is to discontinue play until the Committee resolves the problem.

However, if the Committee is satisfied that the competitors did not gain an advantage by playing from the place they judged to be the teeing ground, it would be appropriate for the Committee, in equity (Rule 1-4), to accept their scores, without penalty. Otherwise, they incur the penalty prescribed in Rule 11-4b.

11-4b/3 Competitors Determine Spot from Which to Play from Tee When Both Tee-Markers Are Missing

Q. In stroke play, the competitors in a group, finding no tee-markers on a particular hole, determine for themselves the spot from which to begin play on the hole, and tee off. What is the ruling?

A. It would be appropriate for the Committee to accept without penalty the scores of the competitors in question if there was evidence as to where the tee-markers were intended to be and the competitors determined the teeing ground from such evidence and played from within such teeing ground. Sufficient evidence might include spots of paint established to show where the tee-markers were to be installed or, if the tee-markers were removed during a round, depressions or other marks on the ground indicating where the tee-markers had been located.

In the absence of such evidence, the competitors should be disqualified under Rule 11-4b unless, before playing from the next tee, they discontinue play, get the Committee to establish tee-markers and replay the hole from within the established teeing ground. Any competitor so replaying would incur a penalty of two strokes — Rule 11-4b.

[11-4b/4 Reserved]

[11-4b/4.5 Reserved]

[11-4b/5 Reserved]

11-4b/6 Ball Played from Outside Teeing Ground Goes Out of Bounds

Q. In stroke play, A played from outside the teeing ground and his ball came to rest out of bounds. He played another ball from within the teeing ground. Is he penalized stroke and distance under Rule 27-1, as well as two strokes under Rule 11-4b?

A. No. A is penalized only two strokes under Rule 11-4b. The ball played from outside the teeing ground was not in play. Therefore, the fact that it came to rest out of bounds was irrelevant and the stroke itself did not count.

Competitor Plays from Outside Teeing Ground in Foursome Stroke Play; Partner Replays Stroke — See 29-1/2.

11-5/1 Explanation of "Next Teeing Ground" When Competitors Have Played From Wrong Teeing Ground

Q. In stroke play, two competitors, have completed the 11th hole, played from the 15th tee, completed the hole and played from the 16th tee. Before playing their second shots they realized their mistake, returned to the 12th tee and completed the round. On reporting the incident the competitors were each penalized two strokes, as the Committee interpreted the "next teeing ground" referred to in Rule 11-4b to be that of the 12th hole. Was this correct?

A. No. When the competitors played from the 16th tee, they had played from the "next teeing ground" and could not correct their error. Therefore, they should have been disqualified.

11-5/2 Use of Wrong Teeing Ground Attributable to Committee Failure to Indicate Hole Numbers on Teeing Ground

Q. In a stroke play competition, the Committee failed to place a sign at each teeing ground indicating the hole number. As a result, a group which had just finished the 4th hole played from the teeing ground of the 12th hole, rather than the 5th hole. Should the members of the group be penalized under Rule 11-4b in the circumstance?

A. Yes

The Committee was remiss in not placing a sign at each teeing ground. However, each player is responsible for knowing the stipulated round, this being one of the conditions of the competition.

11-5/3 Ball Played Out of Bounds from Wrong Teeing Ground Not Recalled

Q. A played B in a match. A drove out of bounds from the wrong teeing ground. B did not recall the stroke. What is the ruling?

A. As A played from the wrong teeing ground and B did not require him to cancel the stroke and play a ball from within the correct teeing ground, A's ball is deemed to have been put into play.

11 Therefore, under Rule 27-1 A must drop a ball, under penalty of one stroke, as nearly as possible at the spot from which the original ball was played, *i.e.*, on the wrong teeing ground. He could not tee the ball because the original ball was not played from the teeing ground of the hole being played (Rule 20-5).

Ball Played from Outside Teeing Ground in Foursome Match — See 29-1/1.

11-5/4 Ball Played From Wrong Teeing Ground in Stroke Play; Error Corrected

Q. In stroke play, after finishing the 10th hole, A and B played from the teeing ground of the 15th hole instead of the 11th hole. They realized their error before completing the 15th hole, returned to the 11th tee and completed the round. What is the ruling?

A. A and B each incurred a penalty of two strokes under Rule 11-4b. They were correct in discontinuing play at the 15th hole and returning to the 11th hole. Strokes played at the 15th hole, when it was played out of order, did not count.

11-5/5 Ball Played from Teeing Ground of Hole to Be Played Later in Round Lifted; Ball Replaced at Spot from Which Lifted and Played Out When That Hole Subsequently Reached

Q. In stroke play, after playing the 8th hole, A, by mistake, played from the teeing ground of the 18th hole, instead of the 9th hole. A marked the position of the ball, lifted it and played from the teeing ground of the 9th hole. He added a two-stroke penalty to his score for the 9th hole under Rule 11-4b for playing from the wrong teeing ground, *i.e.*, playing from the 18th tee. A played the holes from the 10th to the 17th. He then replaced his ball at the spot on the 18th hole from which he had lifted it, played out the hole and returned his score card. Did A proceed correctly?

A. No. A should have disregarded the original stroke played from the 18th tee and replayed from that tee after completion of the 17th hole. In failing to do so, A did not play the stipulated round — see Definition of "Stipulated Round" — and thus did not have an acceptable score.

PLAYING THE BALL

Rule 12. Searching for and Identifying Ball

Definitions

A *"hazard"* is any *bunker* or *water hazard.*

A *"bunker"* is a *hazard* consisting of a prepared area of ground, often a hollow, from which turf or soil has been removed and replaced with sand or the like. Grass-covered ground bordering or within a *bunker* is not part of the *bunker.* The margin of a *bunker* extends vertically downwards, but not upwards. A ball is in a *bunker* when it lies in or any part of it touches the *bunker.*

A *"water hazard"* is any sea, lake, pond, river, ditch, surface drainage ditch or other open water course (whether or not containing water) and anything of a similar nature.

All ground or water within the margin of a *water hazard* is part of the *water hazard.* The margin of a *water hazard* extends vertically upwards and downwards. Stakes and lines defining the margins of *water hazards* are in the *hazards.* Such stakes are obstructions. A ball is in a *water hazard* when it lies in or any part of it touches the *water hazard.*

Note 1: *Water hazards* (other than *lateral water hazards*) should be defined by yellow stakes or lines.

Note 2: The *Committee* may make a Local Rule prohibiting play from an environmentally-sensitive area which has been defined as a *water hazard*.

12-1. Searching for Ball; Seeing Ball

In searching for his ball anywhere on the *course*, the player may touch or bend long grass, rushes, bushes, whins, heather or the like, but only to the extent necessary to find and identify it, provided that this does not improve the lie of the ball, the area of his intended swing or his *line of play*.

A player is not necessarily entitled to see his ball when playing a *stroke*.

12 In a *hazard*, if a ball is believed to be covered by *loose impediments* or sand, the player may remove by probing, raking or other means as much thereof as will enable him to see a part of the ball. If an excess is removed, no penalty is incurred and the ball shall be re-covered so that only a part of the ball is visible. If the ball is *moved* in such removal, no penalty is incurred; the ball shall be replaced and, if necessary, re-covered. As to removal of *loose impediments* outside a *hazard*, see Rule 23.

If a ball lying in an *abnormal ground condition* is accidentally *moved* during search, no penalty is incurred; the ball shall be replaced, unless the player elects to proceed under Rule 25-1b if applicable.

If a ball is believed to be lying in water in a *water hazard*, the player may probe for it with a club or otherwise. If the ball is *moved* in so doing, no penalty is incurred; the ball shall be replaced, unless the player elects to proceed under Rule 26-1.

PENALTY FOR BREACH OF RULE 12-1:
Match play — Loss of hole;
Stroke play — Two strokes.

12-2. Identifying Ball

The responsibility for playing the proper ball rests with the player. Each player should put an identification mark on his ball.

Except in a *hazard,* the player may, without penalty, lift a ball he believes to be his own for the purpose of identification and clean it to the extent necessary for identification. If the ball is the player's ball, he shall replace it. Before lifting the ball, the player must announce his intention to his opponent in match play or his *marker* or a *fellow-competitor* in stroke play and mark the position of the ball. He must then give his opponent, *marker* or *fellow-competitor* an opportunity to observe the lifting and replacement. If he lifts his ball without announcing his intention in advance, marking the position of the ball or giving his opponent, *marker* or *fellow-competitor* an opportunity to observe, or if he lifts his ball for identification in a *hazard,* or cleans it more than necessary for identification, he shall incur a penalty of one stroke and the ball shall be replaced.

If a player who is required to replace a ball fails to do so, he shall incur the penalty for a breach of Rule 20-3a, but no additional penalty under Rule 12-2 shall be applied.

12-1/1 Searching with Clubhead for Ball Covered by Sand in Bunker

Q. If a ball is covered by sand in a bunker, may a clubhead be used in searching?

A. Yes.

12-1/2 Ball Covered by Sand in Bunker Removed from Buried Lie During Search

Q. A ball buried in sand in a bunker is removed from the buried lie during search. The player replaces and re-covers it as required by Rule 12-1, third paragraph. May the player then remove as much sand as will enable him to see a part of the ball?

A. Yes.

12-1/3 Top of Ball in Hazard Covered by Leaves But Part of Ball Visible from Another Angle

Q. The top of a ball in a hazard is covered by leaves so that it is not visible when the player addresses it. However, a portion of the ball is visible from another angle. Is it permissible for the player to remove enough leaves to see the ball when addressing it?

A. No. A player is entitled to remove loose impediments covering a ball in a hazard only if the ball is not visible from any angle.

[12-1/4 Reserved]

12-1/5 Player Kicks Ball While Probing for It In Water In Water Hazard

Q. A player is probing for his ball in the water in a water hazard and accidentally kicks the ball which is in fact lying in long grass on the bank within the hazard. What is the ruling?

A. As the movement of the ball was not related to the probing for the ball, the player incurs a penalty stroke under Rule 18-2a for moving his ball in play. The player may replace the ball and play it or, under an additional penalty of one stroke, proceed under Rule 26-1. If the player proceeds under Rule 26-1 he is not required to replace the ball. (New)

Ball Accidentally Kicked by Player Asked to Lift It Due to Interference — See 20-1/13.

12-2/1 Identifying Ball by Brand and Number Only

Q. In the area in which his ball presumably came to rest, a player finds a ball of the same brand and identification number as the ball he is playing. The player assumes it is his ball, even though it does not carry an identification mark as suggested in Rule 12-2, and plays it. Should the player be considered to have played a wrong ball?

A. No, unless (1) there is reasonable evidence that, because of the ball's condition, it is not the player's ball or (2) subsequently it is established that another ball of the same brand and identification number was lying in the area at the time the player played and either ball, from a condition standpoint, could be the player's ball.

Player Unable to Distinguish His Ball from Another Ball — See 27/10.

Provisional Ball Not Distinguishable from Original Ball — See 27/11.

Identification of Ball Through Testimony of Spectator — See 27/12.

Refusal to Identify Ball — See 27/13.

12-2/2 Touching and Rotating Half-Buried Ball in Rough for Identification Purposes

Q. A ball is half buried in the rough. Having announced his intention in advance to his opponent, marker or fellow-competitor, the player, for the purpose of identifying the ball, touches the ball and rotates it. By so doing he identifies the ball as his ball. Is there a penalty?

A. Yes, for touching the ball other than as provided for in the Rules — Rule 18-2a. Under Rules 12-2 and 20-1, a ball may be lifted (or touched and rotated) for identification purposes after its position has been marked. If the player had marked the position of the ball before rotating it, there would have been no penalty, assuming the rotating did not result in the ball being cleaned beyond the extent necessary to identify it.

12-2/3 Touching and Rotating Half-Buried Ball in Hazard for Identification Purposes

Q. A ball is half buried in a water hazard and is not identifiable. Having announced his intention in advance to his opponent, marker or fellow-competitor, the player touches the ball and rotates it. By so doing he is able to identify the ball as his ball. Is such procedure permissible?

A. No. Neither Rule 12-2 nor any other Rule permits a player to touch his ball in a hazard for identification purposes. Accordingly, the player was in breach of Rule 18-2a for touching his ball purposely and incurred a penalty of one stroke.

Two Balls Lie Together in Hazard and Neither Is Identifiable — See 1-4/6.

Caddie on Own Initiative Lifts Ball for Identification — See 18-2a/14.

Ball Dislodged from Tree for Identification Purposes by Shaking Tree or Throwing Club — See 18-2a/27.

Position of Ball Lifted for Identification Not Marked, Intention to Lift Not Announced and Ball Cleaned Beyond Extent Necessary to Identify It — See 21/4.

Ball in Tree Identified But Not Retrieved — See 27/14.

Ball in Tree Visible But Not Identifiable — See 27/15.

Rule 13. Ball Played as It Lies

Definitions

A *"hazard"* is any *bunker* or *water hazard.*

A *"bunker"* is a *hazard* consisting of a prepared area of ground, often a hollow, from which turf or soil has been removed and replaced with sand or the like. Grass-covered ground bordering or within a *bunker* is not part of the *bunker.* The margin of a *bunker* extends vertically downwards, but not upwards. A ball is in a *bunker* when it lies in or any part of it touches the *bunker.*

A *"water hazard"* is any sea, lake, pond, river, ditch, surface drainage ditch or other open water course (whether or not containing water) and anything of a similar nature.

All ground or water within the margin of a *water hazard* is part of the *water hazard.* The margin of a *water hazard* extends vertically upwards and downwards. Stakes and lines defining the margins of *water hazards* are in the *hazards.* Such stakes are *obstructions.* A ball is in a *water hazard* when it lies in or any part of it touches the *water hazard.*

The *"line of play"* is the direction which the player wishes his ball to take after a *stroke,* plus a reasonable distance on either side of the intended direction. The *line of play* extends vertically upwards from the ground, but does not extend beyond the *hole.*

Taking the "*stance*" consists in a player placing his feet in position for and preparatory to making a *stroke.*

13-1. General

The ball shall be played as it lies, except as otherwise provided in the *Rules.*

(Ball at rest *moved* — see Rule 18.)

13-2. Improving Lie, Area of Intended Stance or Swing, or Line of Play

Except as provided in the *Rules,* a player shall not improve or allow to be improved:

- the position or lie of his ball,
- the area of his intended *stance* or swing,
- his *line of play* or a reasonable extension of that line beyond the *hole,* or
- the area in which he is to drop or place a ball

by any of the following actions:

- moving, bending or breaking anything growing or fixed (including immovable *obstructions* and objects defining *out of bounds*),
- creating or eliminating irregularities of surface,
- removing or pressing down sand, loose soil, replaced divots or other cut turf placed in position, or
- removing dew, frost or water

except as follows:

- as may occur in fairly taking his *stance,*
- in making a *stroke* or the backward movement of his club for a *stroke,*
- on the *teeing ground* in creating or eliminating irregularities of surface, or
- on the *putting green* in removing sand and loose soil as provided in Rule 16-1a or in repairing damage as provided in Rule 16-1c.

The club may be grounded only lightly and shall not be pressed on the ground.

Exception: Ball in *hazard* — see Rule 13-4.

13-3. Building Stance

A player is entitled to place his feet firmly in taking his *stance,* but he shall not build a *stance.*

13-4. Ball in Hazard

Except as provided in the *Rules,* before making a *stroke* at a ball which is in a *hazard* (whether a *bunker* or a *water hazard*) or which, having been lifted from a *hazard,* may be dropped or placed in the *hazard,* the player shall not:

a. Test the condition of the *hazard* or any similar *hazard,*

b. Touch the ground in the hazard or water in the water hazard with a club or otherwise, or

c. Touch or move a loose impediment lying in or touching the hazard.

Exceptions:

(1) Provided nothing is done which constitutes testing the condition of the *hazard* or improves the lie of the ball, there is no penalty if the player (a) touches the ground in any *hazard* or water in a *water hazard* as a result of or to prevent falling, in removing an *obstruction,* in measuring or in retrieving, lifting, placing or replacing a ball under any *Rule* or (b) places his clubs in a *hazard.*

(2) The player after playing the *stroke,* or his *caddie* at any time without the authority of the player, may smooth sand or soil in the *hazard,* provided that, if the ball is still in the *hazard,* nothing is done which improves the lie of the ball or assists the player in his subsequent play of the hole.

Note: At any time, including at *address* or in the backward movement for the *stroke,* the player may touch with a club or otherwise any *obstruction,* any construction declared by the *Committee* to be an integral part of the *course* or any grass, bush, tree or other growing thing.

PENALTY FOR BREACH OF RULE:
Match play — Loss of hole;
Stroke play — Two strokes.

(Searching for ball — see Rule 12-1.)

13/1 Sand Spilling Over Margin of Bunker

Q. If sand spills over the margin of a bunker, is the sand part of the bunker?

A. No.

13/2 Status of Tree in Bunker

Q. Is a tree in a bunker part of the bunker?

A. No. Grass-covered ground within a bunker is not part of the bunker. The same principle applies to a tree. The margin of a bunker does not extend upwards.

13/3 Ball on Edge of Bunker Overhanging Sand

Q. Is a ball in a bunker if it lies on the edge of the bunker overhanging, but not touching, the sand?

A. No. The margin of a bunker, unlike that of a water hazard, does not extend vertically upwards.

13/4 Ball Completely Embedded in Lip of Bunker

Q. A player's ball is completely embedded in the vertical lip of a bunker. The lip is not grass-covered, so it is part of the bunker. Is the ball considered to be lying through the green? If so, the player would be entitled to drop the ball behind the bunker if he declares it unplayable.

A. No. An embedded ball is considered to be lying in the part of the course where it entered the ground.

Ball Embedded in Grass Bank or Face of Bunker — See 25-2/5.

13/5 Ball Lying on Obstruction in Bunker

Q. If a ball is lying on either a movable or an immovable obstruction in a bunker, is the ball considered to be in the bunker?

A. Yes. Although the margin of a bunker does not extend upwards, a ball lying on an obstruction in a bunker is in the bunker.

13-2/1 Explanation of "Fairly Taking His Stance"

Q. Rule 13-2 states that a player shall not improve the position or lie of his ball, the area of his intended stance or swing or his line of play or a reasonable extension of that line beyond the hole by moving, bending or breaking anything growing or fixed. An exception permits a player to do so in "fairly taking his stance." What is the significance of "fairly?"

A. Without "fairly," the exception would permit improvement of position or lie, area of intended stance or swing or line of play by anything which could be said to be taking a stance. The use of "fairly" is intended to limit the player to what is reasonably necessary to take a stance without unduly improving his lie, area of intended stance or swing or line of play. The player is not entitled to a normal stance or swing. He must accommodate the situation in which the ball is found and take a stance as normal as the circumstances permit. What is fair must be determined in the light of all the circumstances.

Examples of actions which do constitute fairly taking a stance are:

— backing into a branch or young sapling if that is the only way to take a stance (see Definition of "Stance"), even if this causes the branch to move out of the way or the sapling to bend or break.

— bending a branch of a tree with the hands in order to get under the tree to play a ball.

Examples of actions which do not constitute fairly taking a stance are:

— deliberately moving, bending or breaking branches with the hands to get them out of the way of the backswing or stroke.

— standing on a branch to prevent it interfering with the backswing or stroke.

— hooking one branch on another or braiding two weeds for the same purpose.

— bending with a hand a branch obscuring the ball after the stance has been taken.

— bending an interfering branch with a leg in taking a stance when the stance could have been taken without bending the branch. (Revised)

13-2/2 Player Who Misses Tee Shot Presses Down Irregularities Before Next Stroke

Q. In playing a tee shot A misses the ball. Before playing his next stroke, A presses down turf behind the ball. Is this permissible, since the ball is in play?

A. Yes. Rule 13-2 permits eliminating irregularities of surface on the teeing ground, whether or not the ball is in play.

13-2/3 Breaking Off Grass Behind Ball on Teeing Ground

Q. Under Rule 13-2, it is permissible to eliminate irregularities of surface on the teeing ground. Is it also permissible to break off or pull out grass growing behind a ball on the teeing ground?

A. Yes.

13-2/4 Greenkeeping Staff Member Rakes Bunker When Player's Ball Lies Therein

Q. If a member of the greenkeeping staff rakes a bunker when the player's ball lies therein and the raking improves the lie of the ball or the line of play, is the player penalized under Rule 13-2?

A. If the staff member raked the bunker on the instructions, or with the sanction, of the player, the player would incur a penalty. Otherwise, there would be no penalty.

13-2/4.5 Divots Replaced and Pressed Down in Area in Which Ball Is to Be Dropped

Q. A player plays a stroke. He replaces and presses down his divot and other divots nearby. He then discovers that his ball is lost or out of bounds. The player must now drop a ball as nearly as possible at the spot from which his previous stroke was played — Rule 27-1. In these circumstances, is the player in breach of Rule 13-2, which prohibits improving the area in which a ball is to be dropped by eliminating irregularities of surface and pressing down a replaced divot?

A. No. When the player replaced and pressed down the divots, he was unaware that he would be required to drop a ball in the area. Therefore, in equity (Rule 1-4) he is not penalized. (Revised)

13-2/5 Replacing or Removing Undetached Divot

Q. A player's ball comes to rest in front of a divot which is folded over but not completely detached. The divot interferes with his backswing. May the player replace or remove the divot before playing?

A. No. A divot which is not completely detached is not a loose impediment. It is something fixed and therefore its removal or replacement would be a breach of Rule 13-2 as the lie and area of intended swing would be improved.

13-2/6 Replacing Divot in Divot Hole on Line of Play

Q. A player's ball comes to rest close to the putting green and he wishes to use his putter for his next stroke. However, there is a divot hole just in front of his ball on his line of play. May the player replace the divot before playing his next stroke?

A. No. Rule 13-2 prohibits a player from improving his line of play by eliminating an irregularity of surface. (Revised)

13-2/7 When Divot Replaced

Q. Under Rule 13-2 a player may not remove or press down a replaced divot. When is a divot considered replaced?

A. When substantially all of it, with the roots downwards, lies in a divot hole. The hole need not be the one from which the divot was extracted.

13-2/8 Player's Lie or Line of Play Affected by Pitch-Mark Made by Partner's, Opponent's or Fellow-Competitor's Ball

Q. A player's lie or line of play through the green is affected by a pitch-mark made by his partner's, his opponent's or a fellow-competitor's ball. Is the player entitled to relief?

13

A. If the pitch-mark was there before the player's ball came to rest, he is not entitled to relief without penalty.

If the pitch-mark was created after the player's ball came to rest, in equity (Rule 1-4) he may repair the pitch-mark. A player is entitled to the lie which his stroke gave him.

13-2/8.5 Player's Lie Affected by Sand from Partner's, Opponent's or Fellow-Competitor's Stroke from Bunker

Q. A's ball is on the apron between the green and a bunker. A's partner, opponent or fellow-competitor (B) plays from the bunker and deposits sand on and around A's ball. Is A entitled to any relief?

A. Yes. A is entitled to the lie and line of play he had when his ball came to rest. Accordingly, in equity (Rule 1-4) he is entitled to remove the sand deposited by B's stroke and lift his ball and clean it, without penalty.

13-2/9 Lie Through the Green Improved When Sand Behind Ball Removed by Backswing

Q. A player's ball lies in a sandy area through the green and there is a mound of sand a few inches behind his ball. The player makes his stroke and in the process he removes the mound of sand with the clubhead on his backswing, improving his lie. Is the player subject to penalty?

A. No, provided that he did not ground his club other than lightly and that he took a normal backswing.

13-2/10 Pitch-Mark in Dropping Area Repaired Before Ball Dropped

Q. Through the green, a player's ball was embedded in its own pitch-mark in a closely mown area. He lifted the ball under Rule 25-2 but, before dropping it, repaired the pitch-mark. Is such repair permissible?

A. No. The player was in breach of Rule 13-2 when he improved the area in which his ball was to be dropped by eliminating an irregularity of surface. (Revised)

13-2/11 Removing Sand or Loose Soil from Dropping Area

Q. Through the green, may a player remove or brush away sand or loose soil from the area in which he is preparing to drop a ball?

A. No. Rule 13-2 prohibits improving the area in which a ball is to be dropped by removing sand or loose soil. Sand and loose soil are loose impediments only on the putting green.

Ball Played from Bunker Is Out of Bounds or Lost; Player Tests Condition of Bunker or Smooths Footprints Before Dropping Another Ball in Bunker — See 13-4/37.

[13-2/12 Reserved]

13-2/13 Bending Grass in Removal of Loose Impediments

Q. A player whose ball was in long grass rolled a stone away from the ball, pressing down some of the long grass in the process. Was he in breach of Rule 13-2?

A. Yes, if the pressing down of the grass improved the position or lie of his ball, the area of his intended swing or his line of play.

13-2/14 Breaking Branch Interfering with Backswing on Teeing Ground

Q. On the teeing ground, a player broke off a branch of a tree which was interfering with his swing. The player maintained that such action was not a breach of Rule 13-2 because his ball was not yet in play. Was the player correct?

A. No. The player was in breach of Rule 13-2 for improving the area of his intended swing. Although Rule 13-2 allows a player to eliminate irregularities of surface on the teeing ground, it does not allow him to break a branch interfering with his swing. The penalty would apply even if the player, before playing his next stroke, re-teed elsewhere on the teeing ground — see Decision 13-2/24.

13-2/14.5 Branch Broken on Backswing and Swing Discontinued

Q. A player's ball lies under a tree. The player fairly takes his stance and starts his backswing with the intention of making a stroke. Near the top of his backswing his club strikes a branch and breaks it. At that point he discontinues his swing.

Rule 13-2 states in part: "... a player shall not improve ... the area of his intended stance or swing ... except ... in making a stroke or the backward movement of his club for a stroke." Is the player exempt from penalty under this exception?

A. No, because the swing was discontinued the backward movement of the club was not in fact the backward movement for a stroke. (Revised)

13-2/15 Area of Intended Swing Improved by Removing Immovable Obstruction

Q. A player's swing is interfered with by an immovable obstruction. The player and his caddie, with great effort, remove the obstruction. Is the player subject to penalty?

A. Yes, for a breach of Rule 13-2. An immovable obstruction is something fixed. Rule 13-2 prohibits a player from improving the area of his intended swing by moving anything fixed.

13-2/15.5 Position of Ball Worsened When Obstruction Removed; Player Replaces Obstruction

Q. A player's ball comes to rest near a tree. A branch of the tree is being held back by a rope installed for gallery control. The player removes the rope (movable obstruction). This releases the branch and worsens the position of the ball. The player then re-installs the rope which results in the branch being held back as before. Was the player in breach of Rule 13-2 when he reinstalled the rope?

A. Yes.

If an outside agency had removed the rope without the player's authority or sanction, the player would be entitled to re-install the rope without penalty.

Grounding Club, Removing Leaves and Improving Area of Intended Swing in Water Hazard — See 13-4/28.

Lie Altered by Act of Marking Position of Ball — See 20-1/15.5.

13-2/16 Stake Supporting Tree Broken in Attempt to Remove It

Q. A stake supporting a young tree interferes with a player's stroke. He tries to remove it, but it cannot readily be removed and it breaks. What is the ruling?

A. The player was in breach of Rule 13-2 for breaking the stake. However, as the stake was not readily removable, it was an immovable obstruction and relief could have been taken, without penalty, under Rule 24-2b.

13-2/17 Removal of Boundary Stake Interfering with Swing

Q. A player removes a stake defining out of bounds

which interferes with his swing. Is this permissible?

A. No. Objects defining out of bounds are fixed. Improving the position of a ball by moving anything fixed is a breach of Rule 13-2.

Boundary Post on Line of Play Removed But Replaced Before Stroke — See 13-2/25.

13-2/18 Improving Position of Ball by Bending Boundary Fence

Q. Part of a boundary fence is bowed towards the course so that it is inside the out of bounds line formed by the fence posts. A player's ball comes to rest against this part of the fence. Decision 24/4 states that the player is not entitled to drop the ball away from the fence under Rule 24-2b. May the player push back the bowed section of the fence to obtain a measure of relief?

A. No. Such action would be a breach of Rule 13-2, which prohibits improving the position or lie of his ball or the area of his intended stance or swing by moving or bending anything fixed (including objects defining out of bounds). (Revised)

Part of Boundary Fence Within Boundary Line — See 24/4.

Gate in Boundary Fence — See 27/18.

13-2/19 Improving Area of Intended Swing by Moving Growing or Fixed Object Situated Out of Bounds

Q. A young tree or a fixed artificial object situated out of bounds interferes with a player's swing. May the player move, bend or break the tree or fixed artificial object without penalty?

A. No. Such action would be a breach of Rule 13-2.

13-2/20 Part of Fence Off Course Leans Across Boundary and Interferes with Swing

Q. Part of a fence which is beyond white stakes defining out of bounds, and therefore not a boundary fence, leans onto the course and interferes with a player's swing.

May the player push the fence back into an upright position or treat it as an obstruction?

A. Rule 13-2 prohibits improving the position of the ball by moving anything fixed, even if such thing is off the course. Therefore, the player may not push the fence back. However, that part of the fence leaning onto the course is an immovable obstruction and the player is entitled to relief under Rule 24-2b.

13-2/21 Area of Intended Swing Improved by Repairing Pitch-Mark Made by Ball on Previous Stroke

Q. A pitch-mark made by the ball as a result of the previous stroke interferes with a player's backswing. Before playing his next stroke, the player steps on the pitch-mark, improving the area of his intended swing. Is this permissible?

A. No. The player was in breach of Rule 13-2 which prohibits improving the area of the intended swing by eliminating irregularities of surface. (Revised)

13-2/22 Knocking Down Leaves with Practice Swing

Q. A player's ball lies near a tree or bush. The player knocks down leaves with a practice swing. Is this a breach of Rule 13-2?

A. It depends on the circumstances. In some cases, the knocking down of a number of leaves would not improve the area of the intended swing, in which case there would be no breach of the Rules. In other cases, the knocking down of one large leaf might improve the area of the intended swing, in which case there would be a breach of Rule 13-2.

13-2/23 Shaking Water from Tree Branch Interfering with Backswing

Q. After heavy rain, a player plays a stroke that comes to rest under a tree. A branch of the tree interferes with the player's backswing. Before playing his next stroke, the player shakes the water off this branch in order to eliminate the possibility of dislodged water distracting him. Is this a breach of Rule 13-2?

A. Yes. In moving the branch, the player removed water which could have caused a distraction and thereby improved the area of his intended swing in breach of Rule 13-2. (Revised)

13-2/24 Area of Originally Intended Swing Improved by Breaking Branch; Area of Swing Finally Used Not Affected by Branch

Q. A player, intending to play in a certain direction, took a practice backswing for a stroke in that direction and broke a branch impeding his backswing. The player then decided to play in a different direction. The area of his intended swing for a stroke in this new direction was not improved by the breaking of the branch. In such circumstances, would the player incur a penalty under Rule 13-2?

A. Yes. The player was in breach of Rule 13-2 as soon as he improved the area of the originally intended swing. The penalty is not avoided if he subsequently plays in another direction, even if the breaking of the branch had no effect on the area of the swing for a stroke in the new direction.

13-2/25 Player Removes Boundary Post on Line of Play But Replaces It Before Playing

Q. A player removes a post defining out of bounds on his line of play. He realizes he has made a mistake and replaces it before playing his next stroke. What is the ruling?

A. The player was in breach of Rule 13-2 the moment he moved the post and there was nothing he could do to avoid the penalty. The replacement of the post before the next stroke was irrelevant.

13-2/26 Natural Object Interfering with Swing Moved to Determine Whether It Is Loose

Q. A player cannot determine whether a long blade of grass, a twig, a tumbleweed or some similar natural object interfering with his swing through the green is loose or is attached to its roots. The player moves the object to the extent necessary to make a determination and discovers that the object is attached. If the movement of the natural object results in the area of the player's intended swing being improved, is the player subject to penalty under Rule 13-2?

A. No, provided he returns the natural object to its original position before playing his next stroke. A player is entitled to determine whether such a natural object which interferes with the area of his intended swing is loose provided that, if the object is found not to be loose, (1) it has not become detached and (2) it is returned to its original position before the next stroke.

13-2/27 Probing Near Ball for Tree Roots or Rocks

Q. A player's ball comes to rest through the green in such a position that he believes tree roots or rocks may be just below the surface of the ground. May he, without penalty, probe the area around his ball with a tee to see if his club would strike a root or rock in the course of making a stroke?

A. Yes, provided there is a reasonable possibility that there are roots or rocks in the area and the lie of the ball, the area of intended stance or swing or the line of play is not improved (Rule 13-2) and the ball is not moved (Rule 18-2). The same principles would apply if the player wished to probe to determine the presence of an immovable obstruction. (Revised)

13-2/28 Smoothing Irregularities in Bunker Situated Between Ball and Hole

Q. There is a bunker between A's ball and the hole. Before playing, A smooths footprints and other irregularities in the bunker on his line of play. Was A in breach of Rule 13-2?

A. Yes, such action would improve the line of play, contrary to Rule 13-2.

13-2/29 Creating and Then Smoothing Footprints in Bunker on Line of Play

Q. There is a bunker between a player's ball and the hole. The player walks through the bunker to remove a rake on his line of play, to measure the distance to the hole or for any other reason. On his way back to his ball, he smooths the footprints he made, restoring the line to its original condition. Is such smoothing permissible?

A. No. If a player worsens his line of play, he is not entitled to restore the line to its original condition. If he does so, he has improved the line in breach of Rule 13-2 and incurs a penalty of loss of hole in match play or two strokes in stroke play.

13-2/29.5 Extension of Line of Play Affected When Opponent or Fellow-Competitor Creates Footprints in Bunker

Q. A's ball lies behind the green. The ball of his opponent or fellow-competitor (B) lies in a bunker in front of the green, which is on an extension of A's line of play.

It is A's turn to play but before he does so, B walks into the bunker to assess his next stroke, thereby creating footprints. A believes that his ball might come to rest in the bunker. Is A entitled to have the bunker restored to the condition which existed when A's ball came to rest?

A. Yes. In equity (Rule 1-4), A may have the bunker restored to its former condition because the footprints were created by B after A's ball came to rest. The bunker may be restored by anyone.

13-2/30 Testing Condition of Bunker Before Deciding Whether to Play Through It

Q. A player's ball lies behind a bunker. May he test the condition of the bunker to determine whether it is feasible to putt through it?

A. The Rules do not prohibit a player from testing the condition of a hazard except when his ball lies in or touches the hazard — see Rule 13-4. However, if such testing improved the line of play, the player would be in breach of Rule 13-2.

13-2/31 Ball Outside Bunker; Stone in Bunker on Line of Play Pressed Down or Removed

Q. A player's ball is lying behind a bunker and he decides to putt through the bunker. There is a small stone (loose impediment) in the bunker on his line of play. May he push the stone down into the sand or remove it?

A. Sand may not be pressed down if the act would improve the line of play — Rule 13-2. However, Rule 23-1 permits the removal of a loose impediment in a hazard when the ball is not lying in the hazard.

13-2/32 Improving Line of Play by Removing Stone from Wall

Q. A stone wall on the course (immovable obstruction) is on A's line of play. A removes a stone from the top of the wall. Is this permissible?

A. No. An immovable obstruction is fixed. In removing part of an immovable obstruction, A was in breach of Rule 13-2. The same ruling would apply if the wall had been declared an integral part of the course.

13-2/32.5 Improving Line of Play by Removing Part of Fence

Q. A fence which is not a boundary fence does not interfere with a player's swing but it is on his line of play. May the player remove a part of the fence, which is readily movable, in order to improve his line of play?

A. No. A fence is an immovable obstruction and thus is something fixed. If a player removes a part of something fixed and in so doing improves his line of play, he is in breach of Rule 13-2.

13-2/33 Outside Agency Removes Immovable Obstruction on Player's Line of Play

Q. A stake supporting a young tree has been deemed an immovable obstruction by the Committee. A player's ball comes to rest in such a position that the stake intervenes on his line of play but does not interfere with his swing or stance. At that point, an outside agency removes the stake. What is the ruling?

A. If the player allowed the outside agency to remove the stake, the player loses the hole in match play or incurs a penalty of two strokes in stroke play for a breach of Rule 13-2.

If the player did not know the stake had been removed, or if he knew it but was not in a position to prevent it, there is no penalty and the player may replace the stake, but he is not required to do so.

Relief from Obstruction Incidentally Gives Relief from Intervention on Line of Play — See 24-2b/7.

Window of Clubhouse Opened and Ball Played Through Window — See 24-2b/14.

Opening Barn Doors to Play Shot Through Barn — See 24-2b/15.

Improving Line of Play When Taking Relief from Abnormal Ground Condition — See 25-1b/3.

13

13-2/34 Mopping Up Casual Water on Line of Play

Q. A pool of casual water was on the putting green between the player's ball, which was lying short of the green, and the hole. The player's caddie mopped up the water. Was this permissible?

A. No. When the player's caddie improved the line of play by removing the water, the player was in breach of Rule 13-2 and incurred a penalty of loss of hole in match play or two strokes in stroke play. (Revised)

Brushing Aside or Mopping Up Casual Water on Line of Putt — See 16-1a/1.

Ball Mark Partially On and Partially Off Putting Green Is on Line of Play — See 16-1c/1.5.

13-2/35 Removal of Dew or Frost

The removal of dew or frost from the area immediately behind or to the side of a player's ball is not permitted. Such action is deemed to improve the position or lie of the ball or the area of the player's intended swing and is a breach of Rule 13-2, unless it occurs incidentally to some other action permitted under the Rules, such as in addressing the ball or removing loose impediments.

Additionally, the removal of dew or frost from the

player's line of play or line of putt is not permitted. Such action is deemed to improve the line and is a breach of Rule 13-2 or, on the putting green, Rule 16-1a, unless it occurs incidentally to some other action permitted under the Rules, such as in removing loose impediments, repairing ball marks on the putting green or addressing the ball. (Revised)

Removing Dew or Frost from Line of Putt — See 16-1a/3.

13-2/36 Competitor Sanctions Repair of Spike Damage on His Line of Putt by Fellow-Competitor

Q. If a fellow-competitor purposely improves the competitor's line of putt by repairing spike damage, the fellow-competitor is penalized under Rule 1-2. If the fellow-competitor's action is sanctioned, tacitly or otherwise, by the competitor, is the competitor also subject to penalty? 13

A. Yes, under Rule 13-2, for allowing his line of play to be improved.

Repair of Spike Mark Damage Around Hole — See 16-1c/4.

13-2/37 Status of Moss or Creepers in Tree

Q. May moss, or a creeper, in a tree be removed if its removal would improve the line of play?

A. No. Trees are the natural habitat of some mosses and creepers. Accordingly, such plants growing in a tree may not be moved — see Rule 13-2.

Moss or a creeper which has fallen to the ground, and is not growing there, is a loose impediment and may be removed, without penalty — see Rule 23-1.

13-3/1 Standing on Mat on Teeing Ground

Q. Is it permissible for a player to carry a mat and stand on it when playing from the teeing ground?

A. No. The player would be building a stance in breach of Rule 13-3.

13-3/2 Playing Stroke While Kneeling on Towel

Q. A player's ball was under a tree in such a position that he found it expedient to play his next stroke while on his knees. Because the ground was wet, the player placed a towel on the ground at the spot where his knees would be situated so that the knees of his trousers would not get wet. He then knelt on the towel and played his stroke. Was the player subject to penalty under Rule 13-3 for building a stance?

A. Yes.

13-3/3 Knocking Down Side of Bunker to Get Level Stance

Q. A player knocks down the side of a bunker with his foot in an effort to get his feet on the same level. Is this permissible?

A. No. Such action constitutes building a stance in breach of Rule 13-3.

[13-3/4 Reserved]

13-3/5 Player Builds Stance But Corrects Error Before Playing Stroke

Q. A player's ball is lodged in the branch of a tree just beyond his reach with a club. The player positions his motorized golf cart under the tree, stands on the cart and prepares to make a stroke at his ball. At that point, the player is advised that he is building a stance, contrary to Rule 13-3. If the player removes the cart and does not play a stroke while standing on it, does he nevertheless incur a penalty for a breach of Rule 13-3?

A. No. If a player builds a stance through use of an object such as a golf cart, stone or brick, he incurs no penalty if he removes the object before playing his next stroke.

However, if a player builds a stance through alteration of the ground on which he is taking his stance, it is impossible for him to restore the ground to its original state. Accordingly, a player who builds a stance in such manner incurs the penalty prescribed in Rule 13-3, whether or not he attempts to restore the ground to its original state before playing his next stroke.

13-4/1 Touching Sand in Bunker When Ball Lies Outside Bunker

Q. A ball lies just outside a bunker. The player takes his stance in the bunker. May the player ground his club on the sand in the bunker or touch the sand during his backswing?

A. Yes. Since the ball was not in or touching the bunker, Rule 13-4 does not apply. However, the player may ground his club only lightly — see Rule 13-2.

13-4/2 Leaning on Club in Hazard While Waiting to Play

Q. A, whose ball lies in a hazard, casually leans on his club in the hazard while waiting for B to play. What is the ruling?

A. A was in breach of Rule 13-4b for touching the ground in the hazard with his club before making a stroke. The Exceptions to Rule 13-4 do not apply.

13-4/3 Touching Ground in Hazard with Several Practice Swings

Q. In stroke play, a competitor in ignorance of the Rules took several practice swings in a hazard, touching the ground each time. What is the penalty?

A. Two strokes for a breach of Rule 13-4.

13-4/3.5 Player Uses Cane or Club to Enter or Leave Hazard When Ball Lies in Hazard

Q. A player, to prevent falling, uses a cane or club to enter or leave a hazard when his ball lies in the hazard.

Is the player in breach of Rule 13-4b which prohibits touching ground in the hazard?

A. No, provided nothing is done which constitutes testing the condition of the hazard or improves the lie of the ball — see Exception 1 to Rule 13-4. (Revised)

13-4/4 Touching Grass with Club During Practice Swing in Hazard

Q. A player takes a practice swing in a water hazard without grounding his club, but his club touches some long grass. Is there a penalty?

A. No, provided the player did not improve his lie or test the condition of the hazard — see Note to Rule 13-4.

When Club Grounded in Grass — See 18-2b/5.

13-4/5 Touching Mound Made by Burrowing Animal with Backswing in Bunker

Q. A player's ball and a mound made by a burrowing animal are in a bunker. The mound interferes with the player's backswing, but the player elects not to take relief under Rule 25-1b(ii). During his backswing, the player's club touches the mound. Is the player in breach of Rule 13-4?

A. Yes. Rule 13-4 prohibits touching the ground in a hazard before making a stroke, which is the forward movement of the club. In a hazard, a mound made by a burrowing animal is ground in the hazard.

13-4/6 Touching Solidly Embedded Stone in Hazard with Club During Backswing

Q. A player's ball lies in a hazard. In making his backswing for the stroke, the player's club touches a solidly embedded stone in the hazard. Is the stone considered "ground in the hazard"?

A. Yes.

[13-4/7 Reserved]

[13-4/8 Reserved]

[13-4/8.5 Reserved]

[13-4/9 Reserved]

[13-4/10 Reserved]

13-4/11 Smoothing Footprints Made in Search for Ball in Bunker Before Playing Stroke from Bunker

Q. A player searches for his ball in a bunker and in the process makes numerous footprints. He subsequently finds his ball. Before playing his stroke, may the player smooth the footprints?

A. No, such action would be a breach of Rule 13-4. However, there would be no breach if the player's caddie smoothed the footprints on his own initiative, provided that the smoothing did not improve the lie of the ball or assist the player in his subsequent play of the hole — see Exception 2 to Rule 13-4.

13-4/12 Ball Touched Accidentally with Club in Hazard But Not Moved

Q. A player, when addressing his ball which was lying in a bunker or was partially submerged in water in a water hazard, accidentally touches the ball with his club, but without moving it. Does this constitute touching the ground in a hazard or water in a water hazard in breach of Rule 13-4?

A. No.

13-4/13 Accidentally Moving Loose Impediment in Hazard

Q. A player accidentally moves a loose impediment in a hazard. Does the player incur a penalty?

A. No, provided the loose impediment was not moved in making the backswing and the lie of the ball or area of the intended swing was not improved.

13-4/14 Player Accidentally Kicks Pine Cone into Bunker and Picks It Up

Q. A player's ball went into a bunker. The player accidentally kicked a pine cone, and it rolled into the bunker. He picked up the pine cone which was not interfering with his stance or the area of his intended swing. Did he incur a penalty?

A. Yes. A pine cone is a loose impediment — see Definition of "Loose Impediments" — and may not be removed when both the impediment and the ball lie in a hazard (Rule 13-4c). By removing the pine cone from the bunker, the player incurred a penalty of loss of hole in match play or two strokes in stroke play for a breach of Rule 13-4c.

13-4/15 Ball in Hazard Moves When Loose Impediment Removed

Q. In stroke play, a competitor's ball in a hazard moves due to his removal of a loose impediment in the hazard. What is the ruling?

A. The competitor incurs a penalty of three strokes — two for moving a loose impediment in a hazard (Rule 13-4c) and one because the ball moved (Rule 18-2a). The ball must be replaced (Rule 18-2a).

Ball in Hazard Moves After Loose Impediment Outside Hazard Moved — See 18-2c/4.

13-4/16 Removal of Loose Impediment in Water Hazard Covering Wrong Ball

Q. A player plays his ball into a water hazard. He finds a ball in the hazard and removes a loose impediment partially covering it. He discovers that the ball is not his ball. He searches for his ball but does not find it. He proceeds under Rule 26-1. Is the player subject to penalty under Rule 13-4 for removing the loose impediment?

A. Yes.

Removal of Obstruction in Hazard Would Move Loose Impediment — See 1-4/5.

13-4/16.5 Flying Insect in Water Hazard

Q. A player's ball is in a water hazard. The player is being distracted by an insect (a loose impediment) flying in the hazard. May the player swat away the insect?

A. Although the margin of a water hazard extends vertically upwards such that the insect is in the hazard, the Rules do not contemplate such a case. Thus, in equity (Rule 1-4), the player may swat away the insect whether it be flying or on the player. (New)

Removal of Insect on Ball — See 23-1/5.

Status of Insect on Ball in Bunker — See 23-1/5.5.

13-4/17 Loose Impediment Removed from Water Hazard; Player Then Decides Not to Play from Hazard

Q. A player whose ball was in a water hazard removed a loose impediment from the hazard. He then decided not to play from the hazard. He proceeded under Rule 26-1. Was the player absolved from the penalty incurred under Rule 13-4 for removing the loose impediment in view of the fact that he subsequently invoked Rule 26-1 and did not play his ball from the hazard?

A. No.

Player Removes Loose Impediment Affecting Opponent's Lie in Hazard — See 1-2/6.

Player Lifts Loose Impediment in Bunker When His Ball and Partner's Ball in Bunker — See 30-3f/1.

Competitor Lifts Loose Impediment in Bunker When His Ball and Partner's Ball in Bunker — See 31-8/1.

13-4/18 Partner's, Opponent's or Fellow-Competitor's Divot Comes to Rest Near Player's Ball in Bunker

Q. A player's partner, opponent or fellow-competitor plays a stroke from near a bunker and the divot comes to rest near the player's ball lying in the bunker. May the divot be removed?

A. A player is entitled to the lie which his stroke gave him. Accordingly, in equity (Rule 1-4) the divot may be removed without penalty.

The same would apply if the player's ball was lying in a water hazard.

13-4/18.5 Pine Cone Falls from Tree and Comes to Rest Behind Ball Lying in Bunker

Q. A pine cone falls from a tree and comes to rest behind a ball which is lying in a bunker. Under the principle in Decision 13-4/18, may the player remove the pine cone without penalty?

A. No. The principle in Decision 13-4/18 is applied only in cases in which the lie of a ball has been altered as a result of an act by another player or caddie, or by a spectator or other animate outside agency. In this case, the lie was altered through natural causes.

13-4/19 Player Preparing to Play from Bunker Requests Another Player Who Has Just Played from Bunker to Smooth His Footprints

Q. In a match between A and B, both balls lie in a bunker and B's ball is farther from the hole. B plays out of the bunker. A then asks B to rake the bunker in case A's ball rolls backwards into B's footprints if A fails to get out of the bunker. What is the ruling?

A. B was entitled to rake the bunker under Exception 2 to Rule 13-4. A incurs no penalty for having asked B to rake the bunker.

13-4/20 Umbrella or Rake Placed in Hazard Before Stroke

Q. May a player place an umbrella or a rake in a bunker before playing a stroke from the bunker?

A. Placing an umbrella or rake in a hazard is equivalent to placing clubs in the hazard — see Exception 1 to Rule 13-4. There is no penalty, providing nothing is done which may constitute testing the soil or improving the lie of the ball. But see Decision 13-4/22.

13-4/21 Rake Thrown into Bunker Before Stroke

Q. A player's ball lies in a bunker. He casually throws a rake into the bunker for use after his stroke. The rake does not move his ball or improve the lie of the ball. Does the player incur a penalty?

A. No. Placing a rake in a bunker is permissible. In this case, throwing the rake into the bunker was the equivalent of placing it.

If the rake had moved the ball, the player would incur a penalty of one stroke for causing his ball to move; and the ball would have to be replaced — Rule 18-2a.

13-4/22 Rake Handle Stuck in Bunker Before Stroke

Q. A takes a rake into a bunker so that he can smooth his footprints after playing from the bunker. He sticks the handle of the rake into the sand prior to playing his stroke. Is this permissible?

A. No. A was in breach of Rule 13-4 which prohibits testing the condition of a hazard when the ball lies in the hazard.

13-4/23 When Stance Taken in Bunker

Q. In a bunker, when is a player deemed to have taken his stance and thus to have addressed the ball?

A. Whether a stance has been taken is a question of fact to be determined in the light of the circumstances in each case. In a bunker, some "digging in" with the feet would normally precede the completion of the stance.

13-4/24 Stance in Bunker Taken Without Club

Q. A player whose ball was in a bunker entered it without a club, dug in with his feet and simulated a stroke. He then left the bunker, got a club, dug in again with his feet at the same place and made a stroke.

The Committee asked the player why he had gone through this exercise. He replied that he had wanted to get the "feel" of the shot he was about to make and that the purpose of the simulated stroke was to determine which club to use and what kind of stroke to make. He stated that he was not testing the condition of the haz-

ard or building a stance when he dug his feet in for the simulated stroke.

How should the Committee have ruled?

A. The Committee should have ruled that no penalty was incurred.

Rule 13-3 states: "A player is entitled to place his feet firmly in taking his stance."

The Definition of "Stance" states: "Taking the 'stance' consists in a player placing his feet in position for and preparatory to making a stroke."

On the first occasion, the player was "placing his feet in position for and preparatory to making a stroke," even though he had no club in his hands. If it were ruled otherwise, a player would be in breach of Rule 13-4 if he selected a club for a bunker shot, took his stance with the club in hand and then decided to play the stroke with another club.

Ball Moves After Stance Taken in Hazard Without Club — See 18-2b/2.

13-4/25 Taking Firm Stance in Bunker Some Distance from Where Ball Lies in Bunker to Simulate Next Stroke

Q. While waiting to play a bunker shot, A went to another part of the bunker, took a firm stance and simulated his bunker shot without using a club. Was A in breach of Rule 13-4?

A. Yes. A tested the condition of the bunker in breach of Rule 13-4a.

13-4/26 Taking Stance in Bunker and Then Changing Clubs

Q. A player takes his stance in a bunker and firmly places his feet in the sand. He then leaves his position to change clubs and thereafter takes his stance a second time. Is the player considered to have tested the condition of the hazard, contrary to Rule 13-4? 13

A. No. Rule 13-3 allows a player to place his feet firmly in taking his stance in a bunker or elsewhere. There is nothing in the Rules to prohibit changing clubs or taking a stance twice in a bunker.

Ball Moves While Player in Process of Taking Stance in Bunker — See 18-2b/3.

13-4/27 Player in Bunker Takes Firm Stance and Then Smooths Footprints When He Decides to Play Different Type Shot

Q. A player places his feet firmly in the sand in a bunker, intending to play an explosion shot. He then changes his mind and decides to play a chip shot. He takes a different club and, before playing, smooths out his original footprints because he does not want his feet so firmly implanted for a chip shot. Is this permissible?

A. No. The player incurs a penalty under Rule 13-4a for testing the condition of the hazard. Rule 13-3 allows him to place his feet firmly in taking his stance. However, there is nothing in the Rules to permit the player to place his feet firmly and then smooth the footprints before the stroke, even if the smoothing is due to the player having changed his mind as to the type of stroke. If it were otherwise, the way would be open for a player to test the condition of a bunker with his feet beyond any testing incidental to taking his stance.

13-4/28 Grounding Club, Removing Leaves and Improving Area of Intended Swing in Water Hazard

Q. In stroke play, a player whose ball lies in a water hazard takes several practice swings, touching the ground each time and removing leaves. He also bends a shrub, improving the area of his intended swing. What is the penalty?

A. Four strokes — two strokes for grounding his club and removing leaves (Rule 13-4) and two strokes for improving the area of his intended swing by bending a shrub (Rule 13-2).

13-4/29 Grounding Club Outside Water Hazard When Playing Stroke at Ball in Hazard

Q. A player's ball touches a line defining the margin of a water hazard. So the ball is in the hazard. In addressing the ball for his next stroke, may the player's club be grounded outside the hazard?

A. Yes.

13-4/30 Grounding Club on Bridge in Water Hazard

Q. A player's ball lies on a bridge over a water hazard within the margins of the hazard when extended upwards. May the player ground his club?

A. Yes. A bridge is an obstruction. In a hazard, the club may touch an obstruction at address or in the backward movement for the stroke — see Note under Rule 13-4. Touching the bridge prior to address is also permissible, since an obstruction in a water hazard is not "ground in the hazard."

This applies even if the bridge has been declared an integral part of the course.

13-4/31 Touching Sand in Bunker During Backswing

Q. A player playing a shot in a bunker accidentally touched the sand when making his backswing. What is the ruling?

A. The player was in breach of Rule 13-4b when he touched the ground in the bunker with his club before making the stroke — see Definition of "Stroke."

13-4/32 Club Touches Partially Embedded Pine Needle on Backswing in Bunker

Q. A player whose ball lies in a bunker touches a partially embedded pine needle with his club on his backswing. What is the ruling?

A. The player is in breach of Rule 13-4c. A partially embedded pine needle is not solidly embedded and is not considered to be fixed; therefore, it is a loose impediment (see Definition of "Loose Impediments").

13-4/33 Bunker Covered by Leaves; Player Touches Leaves During Backswing

Q. A player hits a ball into a bunker which is covered by leaves (loose impediments). The player removes as many leaves as will enable him to see a part of the ball in accordance with Rule 12-1. If the player then touches some of the leaves on his backswing, is he in breach of the Rules?

A. Yes. If the player touches leaves on his backswing, he is in breach of Rule 13-4c which prohibits a player from touching a loose impediment in a hazard before making a stroke in the hazard. A stroke does not begin until after the completion of the player's backswing — see Definition of "Stroke."

If fallen leaves in bunkers seasonally create an abnormal problem, the Committee may make a Local Rule declaring accumulations of leaves in bunkers to be ground under repair. Rule 25-1b(ii) would then apply.

13-4/34 Touching Bare Earth Wall of Bunker on Backswing

Q. In playing from a bunker, a player touches a bare earth wall of the bunker with his club on his backswing. What is the ruling?

A. The player touched the ground in the hazard in breach of Rule 13-4b. The Note to Rule 13-4 permits a player's club to touch an obstruction (such as an artificial wall) on his backswing. However, an earth wall of a bunker is not an artificial wall.

Local Rule for Bunker Faces Consisting of Stacked Turf — See 33-8/39.

13-4/35 Hitting Sand in Bunker with Club After Failing to Extricate Ball

13

Q. A played a stroke in a bunker and failed to get the ball out. He then swung his club into the sand, but his action did not affect his new lie in the bunker. However, since A had to play another stroke in the bunker, was he in breach of Rule 13-4?

A. Yes. Neither of the Exceptions under Rule 13-4 applies to A's action.

Hitting Sand in Bunker with Club After Failing to Extricate Ball; Foursome Match — See 29/5.

Hitting Sand in Bunker with Club After Failing to Extricate Ball; Partner's Ball in Same Bunker — See 30-3f/2.

13-4/35.5 Ball Played from Bunker onto Grass Bank; Player Hits Sand with Club; Ball Then Rolls Back into Bunker

Q. A player plays from a bunker and the ball lands on the grass bank of the bunker. Before the ball comes to rest, the player swings his club into the sand, after which the ball rolls back into the bunker.

Rule 13-4b prohibits touching the ground in a hazard when the ball lies in the hazard. Does the player incur a penalty under this Rule even though the ball was outside the bunker when the club was swung into the sand?

A. No. However, if the club was still touching the sand when the ball rolled back into the bunker, a breach of Rule 13-4 occurred, and any doubt on this point should be resolved against the player.

13-4/35.7 Player Declares Ball Unplayable in Bunker; Lifts Ball and Then Removes Loose Impediment from Bunker

Q. A player lifts his ball in a bunker after declaring it unplayable. Before selecting an option under Rule 28, he removes a loose impediment from the bunker. Since this action took place while his ball was lifted, *i.e.*, it was not lying in the hazard, was the player in breach of Rule 13-4?

A. Yes. The prohibitions of Rule 13-4 apply when a ball is in a hazard or when a ball, having been lifted from a hazard, may be dropped or placed in the hazard. Under the unplayable ball Rule, two of the player's options require him to drop a ball in the bunker. The player would incur the penalty even if he subsequently elected to drop a ball outside the bunker under Rule 28a.

Loose Impediments Affecting Lie Removed While Ball Lifted — See 23-1/8.

13-4/36 Smoothing Irregularities in Bunker After Stroke But Before Ball Extricated

Q. A plays a stroke in a bunker but he hits too far behind the ball and fails to extricate it from the bunker. He smooths irregularities in the area where the stroke was played. Exception 2 to Rule 13-4 permits smoothing provided that the lie of the ball is not improved and the player is not assisted in his subsequent play of the hole. The smoothing does not improve the new lie of the ball. However, B claims that the smoothing assisted A in his subsequent play of the hole because it constituted testing the consistency of the sand. Is B right?

A. No. A was able to test the consistency of the sand during his first stroke in the bunker, and he would gain no additional information by smoothing the sand at the place where that stroke was played.

No claim by B that A's smoothing of the sand assisted him in his subsequent play of the hole would be valid unless, as a result of a subsequent stroke in the bunker, A's ball rolled back into the smoothed area.

13-4/37 Ball Played from Bunker Is Out of Bounds or Lost; Player Tests Condition of Bunker or Smooths Footprints Before Dropping Another Ball in Bunker

Q. A player plays from a bunker and his ball comes to rest out of bounds or is lost. He smooths his footprints in the bunker at the place where he must drop a ball under Rule 27-1 or, before dropping a ball under Rule 27-1, he takes a few practice swings touching the sand in the bunker. Is the player in breach of Rule 13-4?

A. No. The prohibitions in Rule 13-4 apply only when the player's ball is in the hazard or when it has been lifted from a hazard and may be dropped or placed in the hazard. In this case, the player's ball has been played from the hazard rather than lifted.

Furthermore, Exception 2 under Rule 13-4 allows a player, after playing his ball out of a hazard, to smooth sand or soil in the hazard, without restriction. This right supersedes any conflicting provisions in other Rules, including Rule 13-2.

13-4/38 Sand Smoothed After Ball Played Out of Bunker; Ball Later Returns to Smoothed Area

Q. After playing his ball out of a greenside bunker, the player smooths his footprints. He then discovers that his ball is in another bunker on the other side of the green. He plays out of the second bunker and the ball comes to rest in the smoothed area of the first bunker. What is the ruling?

A. No penalty was incurred. The player did not smooth his footprints in the first bunker while his ball still lay in that bunker — see Exception 2 to Rule 13-4.

If, however, the player had failed to extricate his ball from the first bunker with his first stroke and had smoothed his footprints while his ball still lay in that bunker, he would have incurred a penalty if, as a result of a subsequent stroke in the bunker, his ball had rolled back into the smoothed area.

Other Decisions relating to Rule 13-4:

Greenkeeping Staff Member Rakes Bunker When Player's Ball Lies Therein — See 13-2/4.

Smoothing Irregularities in Bunker Situated Between Ball and Hole — See 13-2/28.

Extension of Line of Play Affected When Opponent or Fellow-Competitor Creates Footprints in Bunker — See 13-2/29.5.

Testing Condition of Bunker Before Deciding Whether to Play Through It — See 13-2/30.

Ball Outside Bunker; Stone in Bunker on Line of Play Pressed Down or Removed — See 13-2/31.

13-4/39 Player Smooths Irregularities in Bunker After Playing Out of Turn in Match Play; Opponent Then Recalls Stroke and Player Must Drop Ball in Smoothed Area

Q. In a match between A and B, A's ball lay in a bunker near the green and B's ball was on the green. B's ball was farther from the hole but A played first. B recalled the stroke under Rule 10-1c. In the meantime A had raked his footprints. Did A incur a penalty?

A. If A's ball played out of turn came to rest outside the bunker, there was no breach of Rule 13-4b because A's ball was not lying in the bunker when he raked the footprints, *i.e.*, the prohibitions in Rule 13-4 apply only when the player's ball lies in or touches the hazard.

If A's ball still lay in the bunker, he was in breach of Rule 13-4 because it must be assumed that the smoothing assisted him in his subsequent play of the hole. Exception 2 to Rule 13-4 exempts the player from penalty for assisting himself in the subsequent play of a hole by smoothing footprints if the ball lies outside the hazard when the smoothing takes place, but not if the ball still lies in the hazard.

13-4/40 Player Cleans Clubhead in Water Hazard When Ball Lies in Hazard

Q. A player plays a stroke from within a water hazard but does not extricate the ball from the hazard. The player sees the ball land in deep water and it is clearly unreasonable for him to play a stroke at the ball from its new position. Before leaving the hazard, the player cleans mud off his clubhead by rinsing it in the water. Is the player in breach of Rule 13-4?

A. No, provided that there is no doubt or it is reasonable to assume from the player's actions or statements that he will play his next stroke from outside the hazard.

Other Decisions relating to Rule 13-4:

Ball Lying on Grass-Covered Ground in Bunker Declared Unplayable — See 28/9.

Ball Unplayable in Bunker Dropped Outside Bunker Under Option Requiring Drop in Bunker — See 28/10.

Rule 14. Striking the Ball

Definition

A "*stroke*" is the forward movement of the club made with the intention of fairly striking at and moving the ball, but if a player checks his downswing voluntarily before the clubhead reaches the ball he is deemed not to have made a *stroke.*

14-1. Ball to Be Fairly Struck At

The ball shall be fairly struck at with the head of the club and must not be pushed, scraped or spooned.

14-2. Assistance

In making a *stroke*, a player shall not:

a. Accept physical assistance or protection from the elements,

or

b. Allow his *caddie*, his *partner* or his *partner's caddie* to position himself on or close to an extension of the *line of play* or the *line of putt* behind the ball.

PENALTY FOR BREACH OF RULE 14-1or -2:
Match play — Loss of hole;
Stroke play — Two strokes.

14-3. Artificial Devices and Unusual Equipment

A player in doubt as to whether use of an item would constitute a breach of Rule 14-3 should consult the United States Golf Association.

A manufacturer may submit to the United States Golf Association a sample of an item which is to be manufactured for a ruling as to whether its use during a *stipulated round* would cause a player to be in breach of Rule 14-3. Such sample will become the property of the United States Golf Association for reference purposes. If a manufacturer fails to submit a sample before manufacturing and/or marketing the item, he assumes the risk of a ruling that use of the item would be contrary to the Rules of Golf.

Except as provided in the *Rules,* during a *stipulated round* the player shall not use any artificial device or unusual *equipment:*

a. Which might assist him in making a *stroke* or in his play; or
b. For the purpose of gauging or measuring distance or conditions which might affect his play; or

c. Which might assist him in gripping the club, except that:
   (i) plain gloves may be worn;
   (ii) resin, powder and drying or moisturizing agents may be used; and
   (iii) a towel or handkerchief may be wrapped around the grip.

PENALTY FOR BREACH OF RULE 14-3:
Disqualification.

14-4. Striking the Ball More than Once

If a player's club strikes the ball more than once in the course of a *stroke,* the player shall count the *stroke* and add a *penalty stroke,* making two strokes in all.

14-5. Playing Moving Ball

A player shall not play while his ball is moving.

Exceptions:

Ball falling off tee — Rule 11-3.
Striking the ball more than once — Rule 14-4.
Ball moving in water — Rule 14-6.

When the ball begins to *move* only after the player has begun the *stroke* or the backward movement of his club for the *stroke,* he shall incur no penalty under this Rule for playing a moving ball, but he is not exempt from any penalty incurred under the following Rules:

Ball at rest *moved* by player — Rule 18-2a.

Ball at rest moving after *address* — Rule 18-2b.

Ball at rest moving after *loose impediment* touched — Rule 18-2c.

(Ball purposely deflected or stopped by player, *partner* or *caddie* — see Rule 1-2.)

14-6. Ball Moving in Water

When a ball is moving in water in a *water hazard,* the player may, without penalty, make a *stroke,* but he must not delay making his *stroke* in order to allow the wind or current to improve the position of the ball. A ball moving in water in a *water hazard* may be lifted if the player elects to invoke Rule 26.

PENALTY FOR BREACH OF RULE 14-5 or -6:
Match play — Loss of hole;
Stroke play — Two strokes.

14/1 Club Stopped on Downswing by Agency Other Than Player

Q. If a player starts his downswing and his clubhead is deflected or stopped by an agency other than himself, *e.g.,* the branch of a tree, is he deemed to have made a stroke?

A. Yes.

14/1.5 Intent to Strike Ball Ceases During Downswing; Club Not Stopped But Path of Clubhead Altered to Avoid Striking Ball

Q. A player begins his downswing with the intention of striking the ball but decides during the downswing not to strike the ball. The player is unable to stop the club before it reaches the ball, but he is able to swing intentionally over the top of the ball. Is the player deemed to have made a stroke?

A. No. The player has checked his downswing voluntarily by altering the path of his downswing and missing the ball even though the swing carried the clubhead beyond the ball.

However, any doubt in such a case must be resolved against the player. If, for example, the clubhead struck the ball there would be insufficient evidence to support a claim that the player had not made a stroke.

14/2 Club Breaks During Backswing; Swing Completed

Q. The head of a player's club separated from the shaft during his backswing. The player completed the swing but missed the ball. Is the player deemed to have made a stroke?

14

A. No. A stroke is "the forward movement of the club… " A shaft by itself is not a club — see Rule 4-1a.

14/3 Clubhead Separates from Shaft on Downswing

Q. A player starts his downswing and the clubhead separates from the shaft. The player continues his swing but no contact is made with the ball. Did the player make a stroke?

A. Yes.

14/4 Club Breaks During Downswing; Swing Stopped Short of Ball; Clubhead Falls and Moves Ball

Q. The shaft of a player's club broke during his downswing. The player stopped his swing short of the ball, but the clubhead fell and moved the ball. What is the ruling?

A. The player did not make a stroke — see Definition of "Stroke."

If the ball was not in play, *i.e.*, the incident involved a tee shot, no penalty was incurred, and a ball must be played from the teeing ground.

If the ball was in play, the player would incur a one-stroke penalty under Rule 18-2a or -2b and the ball must be replaced.

14/5 Club Breaks During Downswing; Swing Completed But Misses Ball; Clubhead Falls and Moves Ball

Q. The shaft of a player's club broke during his downswing. The player continued his swing and missed the ball. However, the clubhead fell and moved the ball. What is the ruling?

A. The stroke counts but the player incurs no penalty. The ball must be played as it lies.

14/6 Ball Popped Up Swung at in Disgust

Q. A player's ball is lying against a root. He makes a stroke and the ball pops up into the air. In disgust, he swings at it on the way down, but misses. Was the swing in disgust a stroke?

A. No. Such an instinctive swing in anger is not a stroke. Nor should the player be considered to have taken action to influence the movement of the ball in breach of Rule 1-2. However, if the player had struck the ball accidentally while it was in motion, he would have incurred a penalty of loss of hole in match play or two strokes in stroke play — Rules 19-2a and -2b.

Ball Knocked from Lip of Hole in Disgust — See 18-2a/23.

14/7 Striking at Tree Branch to Move Ball Lodged Higher in Branch

Q. A player's ball is lodged in a tree branch beyond the reach of a club. The player swings at a lower part of the branch with a club for the purpose of dislodging the ball, and the ball falls to the ground. Has the player made a stroke?

A. No, because the player did not strike at the ball — see Definition of "Stroke." The player incurred a one-stroke penalty under Rule 18-2a (Ball at Rest Moved by Player) and must replace the ball.

Since the spot where the ball lay is unreachable and the ball therefore cannot be replaced, the player must proceed under the unplayable ball Rule, incurring an additional penalty stroke — see Decisions 18-1/9 and 18-2a/29.

Meaning of Damage Sustained in "Normal Course of Play" — See 4-3/1.

Other Decisions relating to Rule 14:

Stroke at Own Ball Dislodges Concealed Ball — See 15/2.

Ball Moved Accidentally by Practice Swing Prior to Tee Shot — See 18-2a/19.

Ball Moved Accidentally by Practice Swing Through the Green — See 18-2a/20.

Ball Moved Accidentally by Backward Movement of Club After Stroke Misses — See 18-2a/22.

Player Misses Ball Purposely in Foursome So Partner Would Play Ball Over Water — See 29-1/7.

14-1/1 Playing Stroke with Back of Clubhead

Q. May a player play a left-handed stroke with the back of the head of a right-handed club?

A. Yes. A player may play a stroke with any part of the clubhead, provided the ball is fairly struck at (Rule 14-1) and the club conforms with Rule 4-1.

14-1/2 Striking Ball with Billiard-Type Motion

Q. A player holed a short putt by squatting behind the ball (but not on an extension of the line of putt behind the ball) and striking the ball with the bottom of the clubhead, using a motion similar to that used in playing a shot in billiards or shuffleboard. Was the player in breach of Rule 14-1?

A. Yes. Such a manner of moving the ball constitutes a push in golf.

14-1/3 Putting with Wrong End of Putter

Q. A player misses a short putt and hastily holes the ball with the wrong (handle) end of his putter. What is the ruling?

A. The player incurs a penalty of loss of hole in match play or two strokes in stroke play for a breach of Rule 14-1, which requires that the ball be struck at with the head of the club. In stroke play, the stroke with the wrong end of the putter counts, and, since the ball was holed, the player had completed play of the hole.

14-1/4 Striking Ball with Half an Inch Backswing

Q. A player's ball lies close to an out of bounds fence, but there is room behind the ball to insert an iron club or a putter and leave a space of half an inch between the ball and the face of the club. If the player plays a stroke with such a limited backswing, is he in breach of Rule 14-1?

A. It is possible to strike a ball fairly with a half inch backswing. However, in most such cases the player would be pushing the ball, contrary to Rule 14-1. In the absence of strong evidence to the contrary, it should be ruled that the player has pushed the ball.

In order to strike the ball fairly, it must be swung at with the clubhead. If the ball is moved by any other method, it has been pushed, scraped or spooned.

If a ball is fairly struck at, there is only momentary contact between the clubhead and the ball or whatever intervenes between the clubhead and the ball.

14-1/5 Moving Ball Lying Against Fence by Striking Other Side of Fence

Q. A player's ball lies against a board at the base of an out of bounds fence. He swings a club from the out of bounds side of the fence against the board, *i.e.*, swings at the ball with the board intervening between the club and the ball. The stroke moves the board which causes the ball to move away from the fence. Is such a stroke permissible?

A. Yes. The player fairly struck at the ball even though other material intervened between the club and the ball. The Definition of "Out of Bounds" allows a player to "stand out of bounds to play a ball lying within bounds."

14-1/6 Player Holds Club with Left Hand and Moves Ball by Striking Shaft with Other Hand

Q. A player addresses his ball lying in high grass on a steep bank. His ball does not move, but the player believes it will move if he takes a backswing. Accordingly, the player holds the club with his left hand and strikes the shaft of the club with his right hand, thereby moving the ball. Is this permissible?

A. No. The player pushed the ball, contrary to Rule 14-1.

14-1/7 Using More Than One Club to Make Stroke

Q. A player, whose ball was lodged in a bush, swung at the ball with three clubs to minimize the chance of missing it. Is this permissible?

A. No. Rule 14-1 requires that the ball be struck at with the "head of the club;" the word "club" is in the singular. The player was in breach of this Rule when he swung at the ball with three clubs.

14-2/1 Player Aligns Partner's Club Before Stroke

Q. A player aligns his partner's putter and then moves away before his partner plays. Is this permissible?

A. Yes. Rule 14-2 (Assistance) does not apply prior to making a stroke.

14-2/2 Player Holds Umbrella Over Own Head When Playing Stroke

Q. A player playing in the rain holds an umbrella over his head with one hand while holing a very short putt, gripping the putter with the other hand. Is this permissible?

A. Yes. Rule 14-2 prohibits a player, while making a stroke, from accepting protection from the elements from someone other than himself. However, it does not prohibit him from protecting himself.

14-2/3 Caddie Shields Player from Sun During Stroke

Q. May a player's caddie purposely stand between the player and the setting sun so that the sun's glare is not in the player's face while he is playing a stroke?

A. No. Such procedure is a breach of Rule 14-2.

Material Applied to Top of Clubhead to Reduce Glare — See 4-2/1.

14-2/4 Caddie Inadvertently Positioned on Extension of Line of Putt Behind Ball

Q. A player's caddie inadvertently stood on an extension of the player's line of putt behind the ball when the player made a stroke on the putting green. The caddie was on the edge of the green watching another player drive from the next tee. Neither the player nor the caddie was aware that the caddie was so positioned. Was the player subject to penalty under Rule 14-2?

A. No. The main purpose of Rule 14-2 is to prohibit a caddie from positioning himself behind the player while the player makes a stroke in order to advise the player on alignment or otherwise assist him. In this case, the caddie was not so positioned. (Revised — formerly 16-1f/2)

14-3/1 Distance Meter Attached to Golf Cart

Q. May a player attach a meter to his golf cart for the purpose of measuring the distances of shots?

A. No. Use of such a meter during a round would be a breach of Rule 14-3.

14-3/2 Pencil or Score Card Used to Assist in Gauging Distance

Q. It is possible to gauge distance to a putting green by holding a score card or pencil at arm's length and comparing it with the height of the flagstick. Is such a practice permissible?

A. Yes, provided the score card or pencil has not been specially marked. Use of anything specially marked to gauge distance is a breach of Rule 14-3.

14-3/3 Standard Spectacles and Field Glasses

Neither standard spectacles nor field glasses which have no range-finder attachments are artificial devices within the meaning of the term in Rule 14-3.

14-3/4 Use of Compass During Round

Q. A player uses a compass during a round to assist him in determining wind direction or the direction of the grain in the greens or for some other similar reason. Is the player in breach of Rule 14-3?

A. Yes.

14-3/5 Booklet Providing Distances to Hole from Various Points

Q. A booklet contains illustrations of the holes on a course, including isolated trees, bunkers, etc. Superimposed on each illustration is a yardage scale in increments of ten yards. Thus, a player using such a booklet can determine how far his ball lies from a putting green or a tee. Is use of such a booklet during a round contrary to Rule 14-3?

A. No.

14-3/6 Holding Ball in Hand Against Grip When Putting

Q. A player putts with a golf ball held in his left hand against the grip. He claims the pressure transmitted to the grip through the ball assists him in putting. Is such use of a ball permissible?

A. No. A ball is an artificial device when used in such a manner.

14-3/7 Player with Injured Right Wrist Inserts Left Thumb Under Elastic Bandage on Right Wrist and Hand

Q. A player, who wore an elastic bandage around his right wrist and hand because of an injury, inserted his left thumb under the bandage where it crosses his right palm, and played a number of strokes with his left thumb so located. Is this permissible?

A. No. Because of the injury, the player was entitled to wear the elastic bandage. However, when he inserted his left thumb under the bandage, he was in breach of Rule 14-3.

14-3/8 Adhesive Tape

Q. May a player bind certain fingers together with adhesive tape or apply such tape to a golf glove?

A. The use of adhesive tape for any medical reason, *e.g.*, to reduce blisters or to eliminate the possibility of skin splits between the fingers, is not contrary to the Rules. However, if a player binds fingers together with tape solely to aid himself in gripping the club, he is in breach of Rule 14-3.

Applying tape to a golf glove to prevent the glove from slipping or to reduce wear is not a breach of Rule 14-3.

14-3/9 Player Putts with One Hand and Steadies Himself with Club Held in Other Hand

Q. A player, while putting with one hand, uses another club to lean on and steady himself. In the circumstances, is the club the player leans on an artificial device, contrary to Rule 14-3?

A. Yes.

Player Uses Cane or Club to Enter or Leave Hazard When Ball Lies in Hazard — See 13-4/3.5.

14-3/10 Use of Training or Swing Aid During Round

Q. During a round, may a player make a stroke or a practice swing using a club with a weighted headcover or "doughnut" on it, or use any other device designed as a training or swing aid?

A. No — but see Decision 4-4a/7.

14-3/11 Plumb-Line

Q. Is a plumb-line, *i.e.*, a weight suspended on a string, an artificial device within the meaning of the term in Rule 14-3?

A. Yes.

14-3/12 Club Used as Plumb-Line

Q. May a player use his putter as a plumb-line to assist him in determining the slope on a putting green?

A. Yes. Such a practice is not a breach of Rule 14-3.

14-3/13 Hand Warmer

Q. A player uses a device to warm his hands during a round. Is the player in breach of Rule 14-3?

A. No.

14-3/13.5 Golf Ball Artificially Warmed

Q. Is the use of a golf ball which is purposely warmed during a round with a golf ball warmer, hand warmer or any such device a breach of Rule 14-3?

A. Yes.

14-3/14 Electronic Instrument Used to Find Ball

Q. Transmitters have been embedded in a brand of golf ball. When used with a special radio receiver, a player may find such a ball readily because the transmitter emits a signal which grows louder as the receiver moves closer to the ball. Is the use of such a ball permissible?

A. Use of such a ball is not, of itself, contrary to the Rules. However, use of such a ball in conjunction with the receiver is a breach of Rule 14-3.

14-3/15 Artificial Limbs

An artificial leg or arm is not an artificial device within the meaning of the term in Rule 14-3, even if an artificial leg has been modified to aid a player in playing the game or an artificial arm has a fitting specially designed for gripping a golf club. However, if the Committee believes that an artificial limb so modified would give the player an undue advantage over other players, the Committee has authority to deem it to be an artificial device contrary to Rule 14-3.

Clubs used by a player with an artificial arm must conform with Rule 4-1 except that an attachment may be fitted to the grip or shaft to assist the player to hold the club. However, if the Committee believes that the use of a club modified in this way would give the player an undue advantage over other players, it should deem the attachment an artificial device contrary to Rule 14-3.

14-3/16 Use of Instructional Material

During a round it is a breach of Rule 14-3 to listen to audio tapes or view video tapes containing instructional or other information which might assist a player in his play, or use any electronic device containing such information.

14-4/1 Ball Falls on Club Face After Stroke and Sticks to Mud Thereon

Q. A player, playing a stroke at his ball on the bank of a bunker, hit the ball straight up. The ball came down and adhered to mud on the face of the club. Was the player in breach of Rule 14-4?

A. No. However, the player stopped his ball and was in breach of Rule 19-2.

In match play, the player loses the hole — Rule 19-2a.

In stroke play, the player incurs a penalty of two strokes and must drop the ball as near as possible to the spot where the ball adhered to the club — Rule 19-2b.

But see Decision 1-4/2.

14-4/2 Ball Strikes Pipeline and on Rebound Is Deflected by Face of Club

Q. A player's ball strikes a pipeline and on the rebound hits the face of his club. Is the player considered to have struck the ball more than once in breach of Rule 14-4?

A. No. The player did not strike the ball more than once. He struck it once and it rebounded and hit the face of his club. Rule 19-2 applies.

14-5/1 Ball Moving During Backswing Struck While Moving

Q. A player's ball starts moving during his backswing and he strikes the ball while it is still moving. What is the ruling?

A. There is no penalty under Rule 14-5 because the ball began to move after the player had begun his backswing. However, if the player caused the ball to move, had addressed it or had removed a loose impediment within a club-length of it, he incurred a penalty stroke — Rule 18-2a, b or c.

14-6/1 Ball Moving in Water Hazard After Address Played While Moving

Q. A ball was at rest in shallow, rapidly-running water in a water hazard. After the player addressed it, the ball moved, presumably due to the current, and while it was moving the player played it. What is the ruling?

A. There is no penalty. Rule 14-6 supersedes Rule 18-2b (Ball Moving After Address) in such a case.

Rule 15. Wrong Ball; Substituted Ball

Definition

A *"wrong ball"* is any ball other than the player's:

a. *Ball in play,*
b. *Provisional ball* or
c. Second ball played under Rule 3-3 or Rule 20-7b in stroke play.

Note: *Ball in play* includes a ball substituted for the *ball in play,* whether or not such substitution is permitted.

15-1. General

A player must hole out with the ball played from the *teeing ground* unless a *Rule* permits him to substitute another ball. If a player substitutes another ball when not so permitted, that ball is not a *wrong ball;* it becomes the *ball in play* and, if the error is not corrected as provided in Rule 20-6, the player shall incur a penalty of loss of hole in match play or two strokes in stroke play.

(Playing from wrong place — see Rule 20-7.)

15-2. Match Play

If a player plays a *stroke* with a *wrong ball* except in a *hazard,* he shall lose the hole.

If a player plays any *strokes* in a *hazard* with a *wrong ball,* there is no penalty. *Strokes* played in a *hazard* with a *wrong ball* do not count in the player's score. If the *wrong ball* belongs to another player, its owner shall place a ball on the spot from which the *wrong ball* was first played.

If the player and opponent exchange balls during the play of a hole, the first to play the *wrong ball* other than from a *hazard* shall lose the hole; when this cannot be determined, the hole shall be played out with the balls exchanged.

15-3. Stroke Play

If a *competitor* plays a *stroke* or *strokes* with a *wrong ball*, he shall incur a penalty of two strokes, unless the only *stroke* or *strokes* played with such ball were played when it was in a *hazard*, in which case no penalty is incurred.

The *competitor* must correct his mistake by playing the correct ball. If he fails to correct his mistake before he plays a *stroke* from the next *teeing ground* or, in the case of the last hole of the round, fails to declare his intention to correct his mistake before leaving the *putting green*, he shall be disqualified.

Strokes played by a *competitor* with a *wrong ball* do not count in his score.

If the *wrong ball* belongs to another *competitor*, its owner shall place a ball on the spot from which the *wrong ball* was first played.

(Lie of ball to be placed or replaced altered — see Rule 20-3b.)

15/1 Stroke Misses Wrong Ball

Q. A player swings at and misses a wrong ball. What is the ruling?

A. Since the player made a stroke with a wrong ball, he lost the hole in match play (Rule 15-2) or incurred a two-stroke penalty in stroke play (Rule 15-3).

15/2 Player's Stroke at Own Ball Dislodges Concealed Ball

Q. A player plays a stroke with his own ball in the rough and also hits an old abandoned ball which was hidden beneath his ball. Since he struck the hidden ball, did he play a wrong ball?

A. No. The player played a stroke with his own ball, not with the hidden ball. Since he did not play a stroke with the hidden ball, Rule 15 is not applicable. The player must play his ball as it lies.

Practice Swing Dislodges Concealed Ball — See 7-2/7.

Ball Moved Accidentally by Player in Playing Wrong Ball — See 18-2a/21.

15/3 Player Plays Stroke at Part of Abandoned Ball Which Had Broken into Pieces

Q. A ball had broken into pieces and had been abandoned. Part of it was lying in heavy grass. A player mistook the part for his ball in play and played a stroke with it. The player asserts that part of a ball is not a ball and, therefore, that he has not played a wrong ball. Is the player correct?

A. No. Since the player made a stroke with a wrong ball, he lost the hole in match play (Rule 15-2) or incurred a two-stroke penalty in stroke play (Rule 15-3).

15/4 Player Lifts Ball, Sets It Aside and Plays It from Where Set Aside

Q. A player marks the position of his ball on the putting green, lifts the ball and sets it aside. By mistake, he putts the ball from the spot at which he set it aside. What is the ruling?

A. When a ball is lifted under Rule 20-1, it is out of play — see Definition of "Ball in Play." When the player played a stroke with his ball while it was out of play, he played a wrong ball (Rule 15).

In match play, the player lost the hole — Rule 15-2.

In stroke play, he incurred a penalty of two strokes and was required to correct the error before playing from the next tee; otherwise, he would be disqualified — Rule 15-3.

Ball Lifted by Player from Putting Green Replaced by Caddie Behind Ball-Marker — See 20-4/2.

15/5 Original Ball Found and Played After Another Ball Put into Play

Q. A player unable to find his ball after a brief search plays another ball (Ball B) under Rule 27-1. His original ball is then found within five minutes after search for it began. The player lifted Ball B and continued to play with the original ball. Was this correct?

A. No. The original ball was lost when Ball B was put into play — see Definition of "Lost Ball." When the player lifted Ball B, he incurred a penalty stroke under Rule 18-2a. When he played a stroke with the original ball after it was out of play, he played a wrong ball — see Definitions of "Ball in Play" and "Wrong Ball" — and incurred a penalty of loss of hole in match play or an additional two strokes in stroke play — Rule 15. In stroke play, the player would be disqualified if, before playing from the next teeing ground, he did not replace Ball B and play out the hole with it — Rule 15-3.

Original Ball Played After Provisional Ball Played from Point Nearer Hole Than Original Ball Likely to Be — See 27-2b/5.

Ball Found After Search Exceeding Five Minutes Is Then Played — See 27/8.

Provisional Ball Played from Point Nearer Hole Than Original Ball Because Player Erroneously Thought Original Ball, Which Was Visible, Was Out of Bounds — See 27-2c/3.

15/6 Stroke Played with Ball Lying Out of Bounds

Q. A player plays a stroke at his ball which is lying out of bounds. What is the ruling?

A. A ball lying out of bounds is no longer in play and thus is a wrong ball — see Definitions of "Ball in Play" and "Wrong Ball." Accordingly, in match play, the player loses the hole. In stroke play, he incurs a two-stroke penalty and must proceed under Rule 27-1, incurring the additional one-stroke penalty prescribed in that Rule.

Stroke Played from Environmentally-Sensitive Area Defined as Out of Bounds — See 33-8/43.

15/6.5 Ball Changed During Play of Hole to Aid Identification

Q. A and B realized after playing their tee shots on a par-5 hole that they were playing balls with identical markings. Based on the location of both tee shots, A knew which ball was his. To avoid subsequent confusion, A lifted his ball before playing his second shot, substituted a ball with different markings and played out the hole. Is this permissible?

A. No. A was not entitled to substitute a ball.

In match play, A loses the hole — Rule 15-1.

In stroke play, A incurs a total penalty of three strokes — two strokes under Rule 15-1 and one stroke under Rule 18-2a for lifting his ball in play without authority.

Second Ball Played in Match Play — See 3-3/9.

15/7 Wrong Ball Played in Belief It Is Provisional or Second Ball

Q. A player, thinking his original ball may be lost or out of bounds, plays a provisional ball under Rule 27-2a. Before reaching the place where his original ball is likely to be, he plays a wrong ball, believing it is his provisional ball. He then finds his original ball in bounds and, correctly, abandons the provisional ball. Does the player incur a penalty under Rule 15 for playing a wrong ball, even though that wrong ball was played in mistake for a provisional ball which never became the ball in play?

A. Yes. Although a penalty incurred in play of a provisional ball is normally cancelled if the provisional ball has to be abandoned under Rule 27-2c (e.g., a one-stroke penalty under Rule 18-2b if the provisional ball moves after being addressed), this does not apply when the penalty is for playing a wrong ball.

The same ruling would apply if a competitor played a wrong ball in the belief that it was a second ball played under Rule 3-3 (Doubt as to Procedure in Stroke Play) or Rule 20-7b (Serious Breach of Playing from a Wrong Place in Stroke Play). However, in similar circumstances, there would have been no penalty under Rule

15-3 if the competitor had first holed out with his ball in play and then played a stroke with a wrong ball when proceeding under Rule 3-3 or 20-7b. (Revised)

Penalty Strokes Incurred by Playing the Ball Ruled Not to Count — See 20-7b/6.

15/8 Ball Played Under Rule for Ball Lost in Ground Under Repair After Another Ball Played Under Stroke-and-Distance Procedure

Q. A player's ball was lost in ground under repair. He played another ball under the lost ball Rule (Rule 27-1). The player then realized that Rule 25-1c provides for relief without penalty for a ball lost in ground under repair. He decided to proceed under that Rule, lifted the ball played under Rule 27-1, dropped another ball in accordance with Rule 25-1c and played out the hole. What is the ruling?

15

A. The ball played under Rule 27-1 was the player's ball in play and he should have continued with that ball. The player, having put another ball into play under Rule 27-1, was no longer entitled to proceed under Rule 25-1c. Therefore, when he lifted his ball in play, dropped another ball elsewhere under Rule 25-1c and played it, he was in breach of Rule 18 (for lifting his ball in play and failing to replace it) and Rule 15-1 (for wrongly substituting a ball).

In match play, he loses the hole — Rule 15-1, or Rule 18.

In stroke play, in addition to the stroke-and-distance penalty incurred when he proceeded under the lost ball Rule (Rule 27-1), he incurs a penalty of two strokes under Rule 18 and an additional two-stroke penalty for a breach of Rule 15-1.

Ball Dropped and Played Under Ground Under Repair Rule in Absence of Reasonable Evidence Original Ball Lost in Ground Under Repair — See 25-1c/2.

Ball Played Under Water Hazard Rule; Original Ball Then Found Outside Hazard — See 26-1/3.

Ball Played Under Water Hazard Rule Without Reasonable Evidence Original Ball in Hazard; Original Ball Then Found in Hazard — See 26-1/4.

Lost Ball Treated as Moved by Outside Agency in Absence of Reasonable Evidence to That Effect — See 27-1/2.5.

15/9 Ball Thrown into Bounds by Outside Agency and Played; Caddie Aware of Action of Outside Agency

Q. A's ball was found lying in bounds and A played a shot towards the green. Then a man appeared and said that A's ball had come to rest out of bounds in his garden. He said he had thrown it onto the course and had told A's caddie what he had done. The caddie had not reported this to A. What is the ruling?

A. Under Rule 6-4, A must assume responsibility for his caddie's failure to tell him what the man said.

A's ball was no longer the ball in play when it came to rest out of bounds. Therefore, it was a wrong ball — see Definitions of "Ball in Play" and "Wrong Ball." When A played a stroke with the wrong ball, he incurred the penalty prescribed in Rule 15 and, in stroke play, was obliged to proceed under Rule 27-1.

15/10 Ball Thrown into Bounds by Outside Agency and Played; Neither Player Nor His Caddie Aware of Action of Outside Agency

Q. Decision 15/9 states that, if an outside agency throws a player's ball back onto the course from out of bounds and advises the player's caddie to this effect, the player is penalized for playing a wrong ball if he plays the ball from its position in bounds. What would be the ruling if neither the player nor his caddie knew the player's ball had been thrown back onto the course?

A. In equity (Rule 1-4), there would be no penalty for playing a wrong ball (Rule 15). If the player discovers before playing from the next teeing ground that his original ball was out of bounds, he must go back and proceed under Rule 27-1. If the discovery is not made until later than this, the score with the wrong ball stands.

15/11 Wrong Ball Hit Out of Bounds; Another Ball Played Under Rule 27-1; Original Ball Then Found Nearby

Q. A player plays what he believes to be his ball and hits it out of bounds. He plays another ball under Rule 27-1 and then discovers that the ball he hit out of bounds was a wrong ball and that his original ball is lying in bounds. What is the ruling?

A. In match play, the player loses the hole for playing a wrong ball (Rule 15-2).

In stroke play, the ball the player hit out of bounds was a wrong ball, and the ball played under Rule 27-1 was a continuation of the play of that wrong ball.

The player incurred a penalty of two strokes under Rule 15-3 and he was obliged to hole out with his original ball.

15/12 Wrong Ball Found Out of Bounds Played Under Stroke-and-Distance Procedure; Original Ball Then Found in Bounds

Q. A player finds a ball out of bounds, thinks it is his original ball, plays it at the spot from which the original ball was played and then finds his original ball in bounds. What is the ruling?

A. The original ball is lost and the ball found out of bounds is in play under penalty of stroke and distance. See Decision 27/17.

15/13 Wrong Ball Dropped Under Unplayable Ball Rule But Not Played

Q. A player finds a ball he believes is his ball, declares it unplayable and drops it under Rule 28b or c. He then discovers that the ball is not his, *i.e.*, it is a wrong ball. What is the ruling?

A. There is no penalty for lifting and dropping a wrong ball. A penalty is applicable only if a stroke is played with a wrong ball (Rule 15). The player would be entitled to resume search for his own ball.

Wrong Ball Declared Unplayable Played Under Stroke-and-Distance Procedure; Original Ball Then Found — See 28/14.

Wrong Ball Declared Unplayable, Dropped Within Two Club-Lengths and Played Before Error Discovered — See 28/15.

15/14 Ball in Bunker Deemed Unplayable, Dropped in Bunker and Played; Ball Then Discovered to Be Wrong Ball

Q. A player, believing that a ball lying very badly in a bunker is his ball, declares it unplayable, drops it in the bunker under Rule 28, plays it out and then discovers that he has played a wrong ball. Is he liable to penalty for playing a wrong ball since he had ample opportunity to examine the ball when he lifted it under Rule 28?

A. No. Rule 15 exempts a player from penalty for playing a wrong ball in a hazard, even in the circumstances described.

Other Decisions relating to Rule 15:

Player Discovers Own Ball in Hole After Playing Wrong Ball — See 1-1/4.

In Anger Player Hits Ball Played by Player in Following Group — See 1-4/4.

Player Wins Hole with Wrong Ball; Error Discovered at Next Hole — See 9-2/8.

Competitor's Ball Played by Fellow-Competitor in Bunker Not Replaced — See 18-4/1.

Ball Moved by Wrong Ball Played by Opponent — See 18-5/1.

Competitor's Ball Played by Fellow-Competitor; Competitor Substitutes Another Ball at Wrong Place, Plays It and Then Abandons It and Plays Out Original Ball from Right Place — See 20-7b/5.

Casual Water Mistaken for Water Hazard; Substituted Ball Played Under Water Hazard Rule — See 25-1b/13.

Time Permitted for Search for Lost Ball After Wrong Ball Played — See 27/2.

Order of Play in Foursome Stroke Play When Wrong Ball Played — See 29-1/8.

Player Plays Partner's Ball — See 30-3d/1.

Player Wins Hole with Wrong Ball and Partner Picks Up; Error Discovered at Next Hole — See 30-3d/2.

Players on Opposite Sides Exchange Balls During Play of Hole and Their Partners Pick Up; Error Discovered at Next Hole — See 30-3d/3.

Player Plays Partner's Ball; Error Discovered After Opponents Have Played Next Strokes — See 30-3d/3.5.

15-1/1 Balls Inadvertently Exchanged by Players Between Holes

Q. After completion of a hole, the balls of A and B were inadvertently exchanged and A played B's ball from the next teeing ground. Did A play a wrong ball?

A. No. A ball played from the teeing ground into the hole is not a wrong ball, even if it does not belong to the player — see Definitions of "Ball in Play" and "Wrong Ball."

15-1/2 Balls Inadvertently Exchanged by Competitors at Unknown Place

Q. In stroke play, it was discovered after play of a hole that A had holed out with B's ball and vice versa. Both A and B were certain that they had holed out at this hole with the balls they played from the teeing ground. Thus, it was concluded that they had exchanged balls during play of a previous hole or between two holes. What is the ruling?

A. If it cannot be established that the balls were exchanged during play of a hole, A and B should be given the benefit of the doubt and it should be assumed that the balls were inadvertently exchanged between play of two holes, in which case no penalty would be imposed.

15-1/2.5 Balls Inadvertently Exchanged by Players After One Ball Struck and Moved the Other

Q. A plays to the green and his ball strikes and moves B's ball which was lying on the green. Both balls come to rest on the green. B, acting under Rules 18-5 and 20-3c, lifts A's ball by mistake and places it as near as possible to where his (B's) ball lay before it was moved. B then holes out with A's ball after which A, by mistake, holes out with B's. What is the ruling?

A. In both forms of play, A has played a "wrong ball," whereas B has, in effect, substituted another ball when not so permitted.

In match play, B lost the hole when he played A's ball (Rule 15-1). A's subsequent play of a wrong ball is irrelevant.

In stroke play, A incurs a penalty of two strokes, must retrieve his ball from B, replace it on the spot from which B had lifted it and hole out with it before playing from the next tee; otherwise A is disqualified (Rule 15-3).

B incurs a penalty of two strokes under Rule 15-1, which must be added to his score for the hole.

15-1/3 Hole at Which Wrong Ball Played Unknown

Q. A player discovers after the 6th hole that he is not playing the ball with which he started the round. He does not know when he first played the different ball. What is the ruling in:

(a) stroke play?
(b) match play when:
  (i) he has won every hole?
  (ii) he has lost every hole?
  (iii) he has won 4 holes, lost 1 hole and halved 1 hole?
  (iv) he has lost 4 holes, won 1 hole and halved 1 hole?

A. The Committee must determine whether the different ball is a wrong ball or not and give the player the benefit of any doubt — see Decision 15-1/2. Thus, if the different ball might have been put into play under a Rule or if the player might have put the different ball into play at the start of a hole, the Committee should rule in favor of the player and the player incurs no penalty in either match play or stroke play.

If, however, the conclusion is that a wrong ball has been played:

(a) in stroke play, the player is disqualified, unless the conclusion is that the wrong ball was played at the 6th hole and the player rectifies his mistake as prescribed in Rule 15-3.
(b) in match play, the Committee must determine on a balance of probabilities the hole at which the wrong ball was played and the player loses that

hole, the state of the match being adjusted accordingly, if necessary. If it is impossible to determine the hole at which the wrong ball was played, in equity (Rule 1-4):

(i) the player loses one of the holes which he had won and becomes 4 up instead of 6 up.
(ii) the player remains 6 down.
(iii) the player becomes one hole worse off, *i.e.*, he becomes 2 up instead of 3 up.
(iv) as in (iii), *i.e.*, he becomes 4 down instead of 3 down.

15-1/4 Players Inadvertently Exchange Balls Recovered from Water Hazard

Q. A and B played into a water hazard at approximately the same spot. One caddie was authorized to retrieve both balls and he handed A's ball to B and B's ball to A. Each player dropped the ball handed to him behind the hazard under Rule 26-1b and played to the green. On reaching the green, they discovered the exchange of balls. Should they be penalized under Rule 15-1?

A. No. Rule 26-1b authorizes the player to drop "a ball." Accordingly, the substitution of another ball is permissible.

[15-1/5 Reserved]

15-1/6 Player Substitutes Another Ball on Putting Green Because Original Ball Thrown to Caddie for Cleaning Came to Rest in Lake

Q. A player, whose ball was on the putting green, marked the ball's position, lifted it and threw it to his caddie for cleaning. The caddie failed to catch the ball and it went into a lake and could not be retrieved. The player holed out with another ball. Should he be penalized under Rule 15-1?

A. Yes. Rule 16-1b, under which the ball was lifted, does not permit substitution of another ball. Accordingly, the player incurred a penalty of loss of hole in match play or two strokes in stroke play.

Ball Lifted and Thrown Into Pond in Anger — See 18-2a/13.5.

15-1/7 Player Mistakenly Substitutes Another Ball on Putting Green; Error Discovered Before Stroke Played

Q. A player marks the position of his ball on the putting green and lifts the ball. By mistake he places another ball on the spot from which his original ball was lifted. He discovers his error before playing his next stroke, places his original ball on the spot from which it was lifted and holes out with it. What is the ruling?

A. There is no penalty. The player corrected the error and did not play a stroke with the other ball. Therefore, a penalty under Rule 15-1 was not applicable. Further, the other ball effectively marked the position of his original ball. So a penalty under Rule 20-1 was not applicable.

Ball Not Unfit for Play Deemed Unfit — See 5-3/3.

Ball Mistakenly Substituted When Dropped; Correction of Error — See 20-6/3.

15-1/8 Competitor Mistakenly Substitutes Another Ball on Putting Green; Error Discovered After Stroke Played from Next Teeing Ground

Q. A competitor in stroke play lifted his ball on the putting green and by mistake replaced it with another ball. He holed out and drove off the next tee. What is the ruling?

A. The competitor incurs a penalty of two strokes — Rule 15-1.

15-1/9 Competitor Who Lifts His Ball and Fellow-Competitor's Ball Inadvertently Exchanges Balls When Replacing Them

Q. In stroke play, A's ball and B's ball are in the same area on the putting green. A marks the position of, and lifts, both balls with B's consent. When A replaces them, they are inadvertently exchanged and A putts out, from the right place, with B's ball and vice versa. What is the ruling?

A. Each player is penalized two strokes under Rule 15-1.

Because he authorized A to lift his ball, B cannot be exempted from penalty (Rule 20-1).

Competitor's Ball Lifted Without Authority by Fellow-Competitor's Caddie Who Subsequently Substitutes Another Ball Which Competitor Plays — See 20-1/5.

Decisions relating to Rule 15-2:

Player Concedes Hole After Which It Is Discovered That Opponent Had Played Wrong Ball — See 2-4/9.

Player Concedes Hole After Which Opponent Plays Wrong Ball — See 2-4/10.

Player Wins Hole with Own Ball After Playing Wrong Ball; Opponent Lodges Belated Claim — See 2-5/4.

Player Wins Hole with Wrong Ball; Error Discovered at Next Hole — See 9-2/8.

Ball Moved by Wrong Ball Played by Opponent — See 18-5/1.

15-3/1 Competitor Plays Wrong Ball and Loses It; Wrong Ball May Have Been Fellow-Competitor's Ball

Q. In stroke play, A and B drive into the same area in the rough. B finds a ball and hits it into the middle of a deep water hazard. A finds a ball which turns out to be B's ball. No other ball is found in the area, so presumably B played A's ball. B incurs a penalty of two strokes under Rule 15-3 and he must play his own ball. What is the proper procedure for A?

A. Since there was reasonable evidence that B played A's ball, A should place another ball at the spot from which B played the wrong ball, without penalty — Rule 15-3.

15-3/2 Play of Two Different Wrong Balls Between Strokes with Ball in Play

Q. In stroke play, a competitor plays a wrong ball to a putting green. He discovers his error and returns to the spot from which the wrong ball was played. He finds another ball and plays it to the green. He then discovers that he has played another wrong ball. Is the penalty two strokes or four strokes?

A. Two strokes for a breach of Rule 15-3. A penalty of four strokes for playing two wrong balls in succession before a stroke with the correct ball would not be justified.

15-3/3 Fellow-Competitor Lifts Competitor's Ball and Sets It Aside; Competitor Plays Ball from Where Set Aside

Q. In stroke play, B marked the position of A's ball on the putting green, lifted it and placed it nearby on the green. A failed to replace the ball. He putted it from where it lay and holed out. The error was then discovered. What is the ruling?

A. When a ball is lifted, it is out of play — see Definition of "Ball in Play." When A played a stroke with his ball which was out of play, he played a wrong ball.

If A knew that B had lifted his ball, he incurred a penalty of two strokes under Rule 15-3 and was required to replace his ball on the correct spot and play out the hole.

If A did not know that B had lifted his ball, A could not be penalized for playing a wrong ball. If he became aware of the mistake before playing from the next tee, he was required to replace his ball on the correct spot, without penalty, and complete the hole. If he learned of the mistake after playing from the next tee, the score with the wrong ball would stand and there would be no penalty.

Other Decisions relating to Rule 15-3:

Play of Wrong Ball Not Rectified on Advice of Committee Member — See 33-7/5.

Play of Wrong Ball Not Rectified; Error Discovered After Competition Closed — See 34-1b/3.

THE PUTTING GREEN

Rule 16. The Putting Green

Definitions

The *"putting green"* is all ground of the hole being played which is specially prepared for putting or otherwise defined as such by the *Committee.* A ball is on the *putting green* when any part of it touches the *putting green.*

The *"line of putt"* is the line which the player wishes his ball to take after a *stroke* on the *putting green.* Except with respect to Rule 16-1e, the *line of putt* includes a reasonable distance on either side of the intended line. The *line of putt* does not extend beyond the *hole.*

A ball is *"holed"* when it is at rest within the circumference of the *hole* and all of it is below the level of the lip of the *hole.*

16-1. General

a. Touching Line of Putt

The *line of putt* must not be touched except:

(i) the player may move sand and loose soil on the *putting green* and other *loose impediments* by picking them up or by brushing them aside with his hand or a club without pressing anything down;

(ii) in *addressing the ball,* the player may place the club in front of the ball without pressing anything down;

(iii) in measuring — Rule 10-4;

(iv) in lifting the ball — Rule 16-1b;

(v) in pressing down a ball-marker;
(vi) in repairing old *hole* plugs or ball marks on the *putting green* — Rule 16-1c; and
(vii) in removing movable *obstructions* — Rule 24-1.

(Indicating line for putting on putting green — see Rule 8-2b.)

b. Lifting Ball

A ball on the *putting green* may be lifted and, if desired, cleaned. A ball so lifted shall be replaced on the spot from which it was lifted.

c. Repair of Hole Plugs, Ball Marks and Other Damage

The player may repair an old *hole* plug or damage to the *putting green* caused by the impact of a ball, whether or not the player's ball lies on the *putting green*. If a ball or ball-marker is accidentally *moved* in the process of such repair, the ball or ball-marker shall be replaced, without penalty. Any other damage to the *putting green* shall not be repaired if it might assist the player in his subsequent play of the hole.

d. Testing Surface

During the play of a hole, a player shall not test the surface of the *putting green* by rolling a ball or roughening or scraping the surface.

e. Standing Astride or on Line of Putt

The player shall not make a *stroke* on the *putting green* from a *stance* astride, or with either foot touching, the *line of putt* or an extension of that line behind the ball.

f. Playing Stroke While Another Ball in Motion

The player shall not play a *stroke* while another ball is in motion after a *stroke* from the *putting green*, except that, if a player does so, he incurs no penalty if it was his turn to play.

(Lifting ball interfering with or assisting play while another ball in motion — see Rule 22.)

PENALTY FOR BREACH OF RULE 16-1:
Match play — Loss of hole;
Stroke play — Two strokes.

(Position of *caddie* or *partner* — see Rule 14-2.)

(*Wrong putting green* — see Rule 25-3)

16-2. Ball Overhanging Hole

When any part of the ball overhangs the lip of the *hole*, the player is allowed enough time to reach the *hole* without unreasonable delay and an additional ten seconds to determine whether the ball is at rest. If by then the ball has not fallen into the *hole*, it is deemed to be at rest. If the ball subsequently falls into the *hole*, the player is deemed to have *holed* out with his last *stroke*, and he shall add a *penalty stroke* to his score for the hole; otherwise there is no penalty under this Rule.

(Undue delay — see Rule 6-7.)

16/1 Mud on Ball Touches Putting Green But Ball Itself Does Not Touch Green

Q. A player's ball lies off the putting green, overhanging but not touching the green. A clump of mud adhering to the ball touches the green. Is the ball considered to be on the green?

A. No. However, if a ball lies on the green but does not actually touch the green because it is perched on mud, the ball is considered to be on the green.

Status of Half of Double Green Serving Hole Not Being Played — See 25-3/1.

16/2 Ball Embedded in Side of Hole; All of Ball Below Lip of Hole

Q. A player's ball embeds in the side of a hole. All of the ball is below the level of the lip of the hole. What is the ruling?

A. The ball should be considered holed even though all of the ball is not within the circumference of the hole as required by the Definition of "Holed."

16/3 Ball Embedded in Side of Hole; All of Ball Not Below Lip of Hole

Q. A player's ball embeds in the side of a hole. Part of the ball is above the level of the lip of the hole. What is the ruling?

A. The ball is not holed — see Definition of "Holed." The player may play the ball as it lies or lift the ball under Rule 16-1b, repair the damage under Rule 16-1c and place the ball on the lip of the hole.

16/4 Hole-Liner Not Sunk Deep Enough

Q. Players discover that a hole-liner is not sunk at least one inch below the putting green surface as prescribed in the Definition of "Hole." What should they do?

A. The players should call the matter to the attention of a Committee member if one is present. If feasible, the Committee member should attempt to have the fault corrected.

However, the players must not discontinue play in the meantime, because correction might not be possible and, if possible, might take considerable time.

16/5 Ball Strikes Edge of Hole-Liner and Bounces Out of Hole

Q. A player's ball struck the rim of a hole-liner, which had not been sunk deep enough, and bounced out of the hole. Should the ball be considered holed in such circumstances?

A. No. Under the Definition of "Holed," the ball must be at rest within the circumference of the hole.

16/5.5 Player Holes Short Putt and Allegedly Removes Ball from Hole Before It Is at Rest

Q. A player strikes a short putt into the hole and removes the ball from the hole. His opponent or a fellow-competitor claims he heard the ball bouncing in the bottom of the hole-liner at the time the player was removing the ball from the hole, and therefore the ball cannot be considered holed in view of the Definition of "Holed" which states: "A ball is holed when it is at rest within the circumference of the hole ... " What is the ruling?

A. The ball is holed. The words "at rest" are in the Definition of "Holed" to make it clear that if a ball falls below the lip and thereafter bounces out, it is not holed.

16/6 Cutting Hole on Slope

Q. If a new hole is to be located in a part of a putting green having a gentle slope, should the hole be cut vertically or should it be cut at a slight angle to take the slope into consideration? If the hole is cut vertically, all points on the rim of the hole-liner will not be equidistant from the surface of the green.

A. The hole should be cut vertically, regardless of slope. It is not required that all points on the rim of the hole-liner be equidistant from the surface of the green, but they should be at least one inch below the surface — see Definition of "Hole."

16/7 Two Holes on Each Green of Nine-Hole Course

Q. 1. Is it permissible for a Committee to make two holes on each green of a nine-hole course, one (A) for use in play of the first nine holes and the other (B) for use in play of the second nine?

Q. 2. If so, what is the status of hole B on each green when hole A is in use, and vice versa?

A. 1. Yes.

A. 2. The hole not in use on each green is a hole made by a greenkeeper — see Definition of "Ground Under Repair" — and Rule 25-1 is applicable.

Other Decisions relating to Rule 16:

Player Putts with One Hand and Catches Ball in Hole with Other Hand — See 1-2/5.

Marking Position of Ball on Putting Green — See Decisions under Rule 20-1.

16-1a/1 Brushing Aside or Mopping Up Casual Water on Line of Putt

Q. May a player whose ball lies on a putting green brush aside casual water on his line of putt, or mop it up with a towel?

A. No. Such action would be a breach of Rule 16-1a (Touching Line of Putt).

Mopping Up Casual Water on Line of Play — See 13-2/34.

[16-1a/2 Reserved]

16-1a/3 Removing Dew or Frost from Line of Putt

Q. May a player brush dew or frost from his line of putt?

A. No. Rule 16-1a prohibits touching the line of putt except in removal of loose impediments, repair of ball marks, etc. Dew or frost is not a loose impediment — see Definition of "Loose Impediments." Accordingly, such action would be a breach of Rule 16-1a.

16

Removal of Dew or Frost Other Than from Line of Putt — See 13-2/35.

16-1a/4 Scooping Casual Water from Hole

Q. A player scoops casual water from the hole with a paper cup. Is this permissible?

A. Yes, provided the line of putt, which includes the rim of the hole, is not touched.

16-1a/5 Touching Inside Edge of Hole

Q. Prior to putting, a player touched the inside of the hole. Should he be considered to have touched his line of putt in breach of Rule 16-1a?

A. Yes, unless the hole was materially damaged and the player was entitled to repair it. In this connection, see Decision 16-1a/6.

Player Repairs Hole After Holing Out But Before Opponent, Fellow-Competitor or Partner Holes Out — See 1-2/3.5.

16-1a/6 Damaged Hole; Procedure for Player

Q. Prior to putting, a player discovers that the hole has been damaged. What is the proper procedure?

A. If the damage is not clearly identifiable as a ball mark, then:

(a) If the damage is such that the proper dimensions of the hole have not been changed materially, the player should continue play without repairing the hole. If he touches the hole in such circumstances, a breach of Rule 16-1a occurs.

(b) If the proper dimensions of the hole have been changed materially, the player should request the Committee to have the hole repaired. If a Committee Member is not readily available, the player may repair the damage, without penalty.

If a player repairs a materially damaged hole when a Committee Member is readily available, he incurs a penalty for a breach of Rule 16-1a.

16-1a/7 Player Repairs Depression on Line of Putt Created When Partially Embedded Acorn Removed

Q. A player removed with his hand an embedded acorn on his line of putt. The acorn was not solidly embedded, so it was a loose impediment. The player then repaired the depression in which the acorn lay. Was the repair of the depression a breach of Rule 16-1a?

A. Yes.

16-1a/8 Loose Impediments Removed from Line of Putt with Cap or Towel

Q. A player touches his line of putt in brushing aside loose impediments with his cap or with a towel. Is this permissible?

A. No. Such action is a breach of Rule 16-1a, which permits the player to touch his line of putt in removing loose impediments only with his hand or a club.

Worm Partially Underground on Line of Putt — See 23/8.

16-1a/9 Brushing Loose Impediments Off Line of Putt with Palm of Hand

Q. A player, with about one dozen strokes with the whole palm of his hand, attempted to remove small leaves, which are difficult to remove by any method, from his line of putt. Is this permissible under Rule 16-1a?

A. The action described exceeded that authorized by Rule 16-1a and was a breach of the Rule.

16-1a/10 Loose Impediments Brushed Along Line of Putt Rather Than to Side

16

Q. In removing loose impediments from his line of putt by brushing with a putter, a player brushed along the line for about one foot before brushing the impediments to the side. Did the player infringe Rule 16-1?

A. Under Rule 16-1a a player is allowed to brush aside loose impediments on his line of putt. The casual movement of the putter along the line of putt would not be a breach of the Rules unless in the process the player did something to the putting green which might influence the movement of his ball when played (Rule 1-2).

16-1a/11 Raised Tuft of Grass on Line of Putt Brushed to Determine Whether It Is Loose

Q. A player cannot determine whether a raised tuft of grass on his line of putt is loose or is attached to its roots. The player brushes the raised tuft lightly with his hand and discovers that it is attached. The position of the raised tuft is altered slightly by the brushing, but it has not become detached. Is the player in breach of Rule 16-1a?

A. No, provided he restores the raised tuft to its original position before the next stroke.

A player is entitled to determine whether such a natural object on his line of putt is loose provided that, if the object is found not to be loose, (1) it has not become detached and (2) it is restored to its original position before the next stroke if its position is altered.

16-1a/12 Player Walks on Line of Putt

Q. A player walked on his line of putt. Did he incur a penalty for a breach of Rule 16-1a?

A. Yes, if he did so intentionally. No, if he did so accidentally and the act did not improve the line.

16-1a/13 Line of Putt Stepped on Accidentally by Opponent or Fellow-Competitor

Q. An opponent or a fellow-competitor accidentally steps on the player's line of putt. What is the ruling?

A. There is no penalty. Rule 1-2 is not applicable.

If the line of putt has been damaged (e.g., a spike mark has been created), in equity (Rule 1-4) it may be restored to its previous condition. The player is entitled to the lie and line of putt he had when his ball came to rest. The line of putt may be restored by anyone. (Revised)

Line of Putt Altered Purposely by Opponent or Fellow-Competitor by Stepping on It — See 1-2/1.

16-1a/14 Line of Putt Damaged Accidentally by Fellow-Competitor's Caddie

Q. In a stroke play competition, a fellow-competitor holes a long putt for an eagle. His caddie jumps in the air in excitement and makes a deep footprint on the competitor's line of putt. Is the competitor entitled to any relief?

A. Yes. The competitor would be justified in requesting the Committee to grant relief. The Committee should repair the damage or, if it is not possible to do so promptly, declare the damaged area to be ground under repair, in which case the competitor may take relief under Rule 25-1b(iii).

If a Committee member is not readily available, the competitor may repair the damage, without penalty.

If the competitor repairs the damage when a Committee member is readily available, he incurs a penalty of two strokes for a breach of Rule 16-1a.

16-1a/15 Mushroom Growing on Line of Putt

Q. A mushroom is growing on a player's line of putt. Is the player entitled to relief?

A. The player would be justified in discontinuing play and requesting the Committee to remove the mushroom. The Committee should comply.

If such an abnormal condition is a recurring problem on a course, the Committee should make a Local Rule to the effect that mushrooms on the putting green are to be treated as ground under repair.

16-1a/16 Spike Mark on Line of Putt Repaired During Repair of Ball Mark

Q. A player stepped on a ball mark in the act of repairing it and incidentally pressed down a spike mark on his line of putt. Did the player incur a penalty under Rule 16-1a?

A. Yes.

16-1a/16.5 Spike Mark on Line of Putt Pressed Down When Player Repairs Old Hole Plug

Q. An old hole plug is raised on the player's line of putt. The player steps on the hole plug to make it level with the surface of the putting green. In so doing he presses down a spike mark within the hole plug. Was the player in breach of Rule 16-1a when he pressed down the spike mark?

A. No. Rule 16-1a permits touching the line of putt "in repairing old hole plugs."

If the spike mark had been near but not within the old hole plug, the ruling would be different. In these circumstances, the player would have been able to step on the hole plug without affecting the spike mark.

16-1a/17 Ball Lifted on Putting Green Placed Ahead of Ball-Marker and Then Moved Back to Original Position

Q. When replacing his ball on the putting green, a player has a habit of placing the ball ahead of his ball-marker and then rolling or sliding the ball to its original position. Is such a procedure permissible?

A. Such a procedure is not recommended but is not a breach of Rule 16-1a which permits touching the line of putt in lifting (or replacing) the ball. However, if in the process the player does something to the putting green which might influence the movement of the ball when played, *e.g.*, presses down a raised tuft of grass, he is in breach of Rule 1-2.

Other Decisions relating to Rule 16-1a:

Shielding Line of Putt from Wind — See 1-2/2.

Player and Opponent or Fellow-Competitor Agree to Repair Spike Marks on One Another's Line of Putt — See 1-3/3.

Caddie Touches Putting Green to Indicate Line of Play Before Player Chips from Off Green — See 8-2b/3.

Competitor Sanctions Repair of Spike Damage on His Line of Putt by Fellow-Competitor — See 13-2/36.

Placing Ball-Marker on Line of Putt — See 20-1/19.

Player Touches Putting Green in Pointing Out Line for Putting for Partner and Incidentally Touches Own Line of Putt — See 30/2.5.

Player Putting First When Partner's Ball Farther from Hole Stands on Partner's or Opponent's Line of Putt — See 30-3c/1.

16-1b/1 Ball on Putting Green Lifted Because Player Feared Ball Might Move

Q. A player lifted his ball on the putting green under Rule 16-1b, cleaned it and replaced it. As the player approached the ball to play his next stroke, he feared the ball might move. So he lifted the ball again, replaced it and played. What is the ruling?

A. There is no penalty, provided the player marked the position of his ball both times. Rule 16-1b permits the lifting of a ball on the putting green for any reason.

Rotating Ball on Putting Green Without Marking Position — See 18-2a/33.

Ball Replaced on Putting Green But Ball-Marker Not Removed; Ball Then Moves — See 20-4/1.

Ball Lifted by Player from Putting Green Replaced by Caddie Behind Ball-Marker — See 20-4/2.

Ball Replaced at Wrong Place on Putting Green and Holed — See 20-7b/1.

16-1c/1 Repair of Ball Mark a Second Time

Q. A ball mark has been repaired by a player. The ball mark is on the line of putt of a following player. May the following player further repair the ball mark?

A. Yes, provided it is still clearly identifiable as a ball mark.

16-1c/1.5 Ball Mark Partially on and Partially Off Putting Green Is on Line of Play

Q. If a player's ball lies just off the putting green and there is a ball mark on his line of play, he is entitled to repair the ball mark if it is on the green (Rule 16-1c), but not if it is off the green (Rule 13-2). What is the ruling if a ball mark on the line of play is partially on and partially off the green?

A. Since it is impracticable to allow the repair of only that part of the ball mark which is on the putting green, the player may repair the entire ball mark.

16-1c/2 Ball Mark in Position to Assist Opponent

Q. A and B are playing a match. At a par-3 hole, both are on the green with their tee shots. A's ball comes to rest four feet from the hole. B's ball is fifteen feet from the hole. Upon reaching the green, A prepares to repair his ball mark. B tells A not to do so until he (B) has putted because A's ball mark is so situated that B's ball might be deflected into the hole by it. A objects, stating that he wishes to repair his ball mark immediately. May A do so?

A. No. If A were to repair the ball mark, he would lose the hole under Rule 1-2. A has no right to repair a ball mark affecting B's play if B requests A not to repair it, unless the ball mark also physically affects A's play and it is A's turn to play.

16-1c/3 Old Hole Plug Sunk or Raised on Line of Putt

Q. A player's ball lies on the green. An old hole plug is sunk or raised on the player's line of putt. What relief is available to the player?

A. The player may attempt to raise or lower the plug to make it level with the surface of the putting green — Rule 16-1c. If this is impossible, he may discontinue play and request the Committee to raise or lower the plug. If the Committee cannot level the plug without unduly delaying play, the Committee should declare the plug to be ground under repair, in which case the player would be entitled to relief under Rule 25-1b(iii).

Whether Sunken Hole Plug Is "Hole Made by Greenkeeper" — See 25/17.

Local Rule Permitting Repair of Turf Plugs on the Putting Green That are Not 4¼ Inches in Diameter — See 33-8/30.

16-1c/4 Repair of Spike Mark Damage Around Hole

Q. A player's ball lies on or near the putting green. Before playing his next stroke, he taps down spike marks in the vicinity of the hole. Is this permissible?

A. No. Such action would be a breach of Rule 16-1c since repair of spike marks in the vicinity of the hole might assist the player in his subsequent play of the hole.

16-1d/1 Player Concedes Opponent's Next Stroke and Rolls or Knocks Ball to Opponent

Q. A player concedes his opponent's next stroke and either picks up the opponent's ball and rolls it to the opponent or knocks it back to him with a club. The player did so only for the purpose of returning the opponent's ball to him, not to test the surface of the putting green. Was the player in breach of Rule 16-1d (Testing Surface)?

A. No. Such casual action is not a breach of Rule 16-1d.

16-1d/2 Player Concedes Opponent's Next Stroke and Knocks His Ball Away Along Own Line of Putt

Q. A player concedes his opponent's next stroke and knocks his ball away on the same line on which he (the player) must subsequently putt. Is this a breach of Rule 16-1d?

A. It is a question of fact whether or not the player's action was for the purpose of testing the surface of the putting green. The manner and apparent purpose of the action would be the determining factors in each individual case.

16-1d/3 Player Returns Ball to Spot from Which It Was Lifted by Rolling It with Putter

Q. A player marks the position of his ball on the putting green, lifts the ball and sets it aside. When it is his turn to putt, he rolls the ball with his putter back to the spot from which it was lifted. Was the player in breach of Rule 16-1d (Testing Surface)?

A. No, provided the action of rolling the ball was not for the purpose of testing the surface of the green. This method of replacing a ball is not recommended, but it is not a breach of the Rules.

16-1d/4 Testing for Wetness Surface of Putting Green Behind Ball

Q. A player placed the palm of his hand on the putting green behind his ball to determine if the green was wet. He did not roughen or scrape the surface. Was the player in breach of Rule 16-1d (Testing Surface)?

A. No. Rule 16-1d only prohibits rolling a ball or roughening or scraping the putting surface for testing purposes. Since the line of putt was not touched, Rule 16-1a also was not infringed.

16-1d/5 Rubbing Ball on Putting Green for Cleaning Purposes

Q. May a player clean his ball by rubbing it on the putting green?

A. Yes, provided the act is not for the purpose of testing the surface of the putting green. It is recommended that a ball be cleaned in other ways to eliminate any question as to the player's intentions.

16-1d/6 Caddie Roughens Surface of Putting Green But Player Does Not Benefit

Q. A caddie tests the surface of the green by roughening the grass. His employer tells him immediately that he is not allowed to do that under the Rules. The player receives no information from the caddie about the condition of the green. Is the player penalized under Rule 16-1d?

A. Yes. The reference to the player in Rule 16-1d includes his caddie. Thus, the Rule prohibits the caddie, as well as the player, from testing the surface of the putting green. Under Rule 6-4, the player incurs the applicable penalty for a breach of a Rule by his caddie.

16-1e/1 Meaning of "Line of Putt" in Context of "Standing Astride or on Line of Putt"

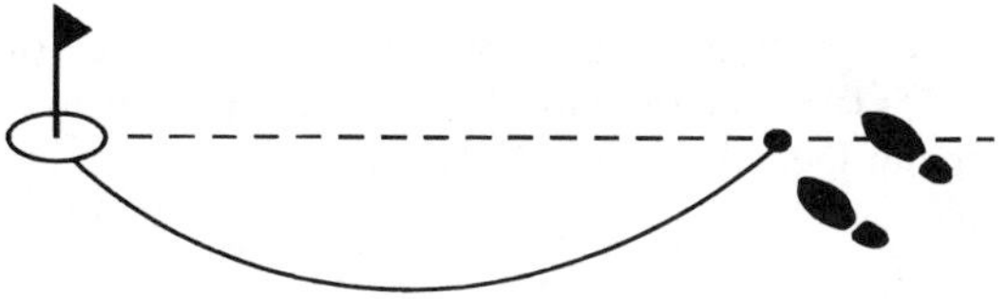

Q. With reference to the above sketch, the broken line is a direct line from the ball to the hole and the solid line is the line on which the player intends his ball to travel. Which line is "the line of putt" for purposes of application of Rule 16-1e (Standing Astride or on Line of Putt)? If the broken line is "the line of putt," the player will be in breach of Rule 16-1e. If the solid line is the "line of putt," he will not be in breach of the Rule.

A. The solid line is "the line of putt."

[16-1f/1 Reserved]

[16-1f/2 Reserved]

16-2/0.5 Ball Overhanging Hole Is Lifted, Cleaned and Replaced; Ball Then Falls into Hole.

Q. After an approach shot, a player's ball is overhanging the hole. The player walks up to the hole without unreasonable delay and notices that there is mud on the ball. The player marks the position of the ball and lifts it. He then cleans the ball and replaces it. The ball remains on the lip of the hole for about five seconds and then, as the player is preparing to tap it into the hole, the ball falls into the hole. What is the ruling?

A. Under Rule 16-2 , if a ball falls into the hole after it is deemed to be at rest, the player is deemed to have holed out with his last stroke and he shall add a penalty stroke to his score for the hole. In this case, when the player marked the position of the ball it must have been at rest. The ball must be considered to have been at rest when it was replaced; otherwise, it would have to be replaced again (Rule 20-3d).

Accordingly, the player is deemed to have holed out with his last stroke and must add a penalty stroke to his score for the hole.

16-2/1 Ball Overhanging Hole Falls into Hole After Player Waits 40 Seconds

Q. A player's ball overhangs the edge of the hole. The player walks up to the hole. He then waits about 40 seconds, after which the ball falls into the hole. Is the player subject to penalty?

A. Yes. The player incurs a penalty of one stroke—Rule 16-2.

16-2/2 Ball Overhanging Hole Knocked Away by Opponent Before Player Determines Status

Q. In a match between A and B, A putts and his ball apparently comes to rest, but is overhanging the hole. Within five seconds, B concedes A's next stroke and knocks his ball away. Was B entitled to knock A's ball away?

A. No. Under Rule 16-2, A is allowed a reasonable time to reach the hole and an additional ten seconds to determine whether his ball is at rest. Since B infringed A's rights, B was in breach of Rule 1-2 (Exerting Influence on Ball) and lost the hole, assuming that Rule 2-2 (Halved Hole) did not apply.

Player Jumps Close to Hole to Cause Ball Overhanging Hole to Drop — See 1-2/4.

Ball Falls into Hole After Concession of Next Stroke — See 2-4/2.

Ball Blown into Hole by Competitor Not Replaced and Holed Out — See 3-2/2.

Ball Overhanging Hole Falls into Hole After Being Addressed — See 18-2b/10.

16

16-2/3 Casting Shadow on Ball Overhanging Hole

Q. A player's ball came to rest overhanging the edge of the hole. The player walked up to the hole and cast his shadow on the ball, believing that this would cause the grass to wilt and his ball to fall into the hole. Was the player in breach of Rule 1-2 (Exerting Influence on Ball) when he cast his shadow on the ball?

A. No.

Rule 17. The Flagstick

Definition

The *"flagstick"* is a movable straight indicator, with or without bunting or other material attached, centered in the *hole* to show its position. It shall be circular in cross-section.

17-1. Flagstick Attended, Removed or Held Up

Before and during the *stroke,* the player may have the *flagstick* attended, removed or held up to indicate the position of the *hole.* This may be done only on the authority of the player before he plays his *stroke.*

If, prior to the *stroke,* the *flagstick* is attended, removed or held up by anyone with the player's knowledge and no objection is made, the player shall be deemed to have authorized it. If anyone attends or holds up the *flagstick* or stands near the *hole* while a *stroke* is being played, he shall be deemed to be attending the *flagstick* until the ball comes to rest.

17-2. Unauthorized Attendance

a. Match Play

In match play, an opponent or his *caddie* shall not, without the authority or prior knowledge of the player, attend, remove or hold up the *flagstick* while the player is making a *stroke* or his ball is in motion.

b. Stroke Play

In stroke play, if a *fellow-competitor* or his *caddie* attends, removes or holds up the *flagstick* without the *competitor*'s authority or prior knowledge while the *competitor* is making a *stroke* or his ball is in motion, the *fellow-competitor* shall incur the penalty for breach of this Rule. In such circumstances, if the *competitor*'s ball strikes the *flagstick*, the person attending it or anything carried by him, the *competitor* incurs no penalty and the ball shall be played as it lies, except that, if the stroke was played from the *putting green*, the *stroke* shall be cancelled, the ball replaced and the *stroke* replayed.

PENALTY FOR BREACH OF RULE 17-1 or -2:
Match play — Loss of hole;
Stroke play — Two strokes.

17-3. Ball Striking Flagstick or Attendant

The player's ball shall not strike:

a. The *flagstick* when attended, removed or held up by the player, his *partner* or either of their *caddies*, or by another person with the player's authority or prior knowledge; or

b. The player's *caddie*, his *partner* or his *partner's caddie* when attending the *flagstick*, or another person attending the *flagstick* with the player's authority or prior knowledge or anything carried by any such person; or

c. The *flagstick* in the *hole*, unattended, when the ball has been played from the *putting green*.

PENALTY FOR BREACH OF RULE 17-3:
Match play — Loss of hole; Stroke play — Two strokes and the ball shall be played as it lies.

17-4. Ball Resting Against Flagstick

If the ball rests against the *flagstick* when it is in the *hole*, the player or another person authorized by him may move or remove the *flagstick* and if the ball falls into the *hole*, the player shall be deemed to have *holed* out with his last *stroke*; otherwise, the ball, if *moved*, shall be placed on the lip of the *hole*, without penalty.

17/1 Attachment to Flagstick to Indicate Position of Hole on Green

Q. A thin disc or sleeve is attached to the flagstick to indicate the distance of the hole from the front of the green. If the disc is placed near the bottom of the flagstick it means that the hole is at the front of the green; if it is placed near the top of the flagstick it means that the hole is at the back of the green. Is this permitted?

A. Yes, provided the attachment is circular in cross-section.

17/2 Different Colored Flags Used to Indicate Position of Hole on Green

Q. May a Committee use flagsticks with flags of two different colors, one color being used when the hole is at the front of the green and the other when the hole is at the back?

A. Yes.

17/3 Flagstick Tapered or of Varying Diameters

Q. May a flagstick be tapered or have a slender metal ferrule at the base?

A. Yes. The Definition does not prohibit sections of varying diameters. The Definition requires that the flagstick be circular in cross-section. This is to prohibit non-circular features in the lower part of the flagstick.

17/4 Adjustment of Flagstick; Player's Rights

Q. A player playing from off the green and wishing to leave the flagstick in the hole may find that the flagstick is leaning towards his ball (a disadvantage) or away from his ball (an advantage). What are the player's rights in such a situation?

A. The flagstick may be left as it is or centered in the hole, as contemplated by the Definition of "Flagstick."

The flagstick may not be adjusted to a more favorable position than centered. To do so would infringe Rule 1-2 (Exerting Influence on Ball).

An opponent or fellow-competitor who centers the flagstick incurs no penalty, but the player may have it restored to its original position.

[17/5 Reserved]

17/6 Ball Lodged in Flag Attached to Flagstick

Q. A player's ball lodges in the flag attached to a flagstick. What is the procedure?

A. A flagstick is a movable obstruction and Rule 24-1 applies. The ball may be placed on the lip of the hole.

17/7 Hole-Liner Pulled Out by Flagstick Attendant and Ball Falls into Unlined Hole

Q. A flagstick attendant removes the flagstick and, in the process, pulls out the hole-liner. The player's ball rolls into the unlined hole. What is the ruling?

A. The player incurs no penalty and the ball is holed. A hole need not contain a lining — see Definition of "Hole."

17/8 Ball Strikes Hole-Liner Pulled Out with Flagstick

Q. A player played a stroke from the putting green. The ball struck the hole-liner, which had stuck to the bottom of the flagstick and had come out of the hole when the person attending the flagstick removed the flagstick. Is there any penalty?

A. No. A hole-liner is an outside agency. Accordingly, if the hole-liner was moving when the ball struck it, the stroke is cancelled and the ball must be replaced — Rule 19-1b. If the hole-liner was not moving, the ball must be played as it lies — Rule 19-1. In case of doubt, the ball must be played as it lies.

17/9 Attendant Removes Flagstick Whereupon Knob Falls from Top of Flagstick and Deflects Ball

Q. After a player putts, the flagstick attendant removes the flagstick and a knob attached to the top of the flagstick falls off. The knob strikes the player's moving ball and deflects it. What is the ruling?

A. Once detached the knob was no longer a part of the flagstick. It was an outside agency. Therefore, the stroke is cancelled and the ball must be replaced — Rule 19-1b.

Other Decisions relating to Rule 17:

Flagstick Lying on Putting Green Removed by Player to Prevent Another Player's Ball from Striking It — See 1-2/3.

Flagstick Stuck into Green Some Distance from Hole by Practical Joker — See 1-4/3.

Ball Moved by Flagstick Accidentally Dropped on Ball — See 18-2a/24.

17-1/1 Meaning of "Stands Near the Hole"

Q. Rule 17-1 states that, if anyone "stands near the hole," he is deemed to be attending the flagstick. Is such a person considered to be standing "near the hole" if he is close enough to touch the flagstick?

A. Yes.

17-1/2 Opponent or Fellow-Competitor Declines to Attend Flagstick

Q. Does a player have any redress if he requests his opponent or a fellow-competitor to attend the flagstick for him and the opponent or fellow-competitor declines?

A. No.

17-1/3 Flagstick Attended by Referee, Observer or Marker at Player's Request

Q. A player requests a referee, observer or marker to attend the flagstick and the referee, observer or marker does so. Is the player subject to penalty?

A. A referee or observer should not attend the flagstick — see Definitions of "Referee" and "Observer." However, a player incurs no penalty if he makes such a request and the referee or observer complies. A marker may attend the flagstick, even if he is not a fellow-competitor.

17-1/4 Flagstick Attendant Stands Behind Hole

Q. May a person attending the flagstick stand directly behind the hole, instead of to the side of it?

A. Yes. A flagstick attendant might have to stand behind the hole to avoid standing on the line of putt of another player.

17-1/4.5 Flagstick Attendant Removes Flagstick and Holds It Upright Behind Hole; End of Flagstick Touches Green

Q. A player preparing to putt asks his caddie to attend the flagstick. The caddie removes the flagstick from the hole and holds it upright two or three inches directly behind the hole, with the end of the flagstick touching the putting green. He attends the flagstick in this manner to eliminate the risk of the flagstick sticking in the hole. Is such a procedure a breach of the Rules?

A. No, but such a practice is not recommended because of the possibility of damage to the putting green.

17-1/5 Holding Flagstick with One Hand and Putting with Other Hand

Q. A player holds the flagstick with one hand and holes a short putt, gripping the putter with his other hand. Is this permissible?

A. Yes, provided the flagstick has been removed from the hole and the ball therefore does not strike it. If the ball were to strike the flagstick, a breach of Rule 17-3a would occur.

17-3/1 Holing Out Without Ball Touching Flagstick

Q. A player plays a stroke from the putting green without having the flagstick attended. The ball stops momentarily on the lip of the hole and then falls into the hole. The player claims that the ball fell into the hole without striking the flagstick and therefore he incurs no penalty under Rule 17-3. Is the claim valid?

A. No. A ball is not holed until it is at rest in the hole — Definition of "Holed." If the flagstick is in the hole, it is impossible for a ball to come to rest in the hole without striking the flagstick.

17-3/2 Opponent or Fellow-Competitor Attending Flagstick for Player Fails to Remove It; Player's Ball Strikes Flagstick

Q. A requests B, his opponent or a fellow-competitor, to attend the flagstick, and B complies. A putts too firmly and B fails to remove the flagstick. A's ball strikes the flagstick. What is the ruling?

A. If B failed to remove the flagstick for the purpose of causing A to incur a penalty, B is disqualified in both match play and stroke play for a serious breach of Rule 1-2. In stroke play, in equity (Rule 1-4) A must replay the stroke without penalty.

If B's failure to remove the flagstick was for the purpose of preventing A's ball from going beyond the flagstick and not for the purpose of causing A to incur a penalty, in match play B lost the hole under Rule 1-2 when he failed to remove the flagstick before A's ball reached the hole. The fact that A's ball subsequently struck the flagstick (a breach of Rule 17-3a) is irrelevant since B had already lost the hole. In stroke play, B incurs a penalty of two strokes under Rule 1-2, and A incurs the same penalty under Rule 17-3a.

If B's failure to remove the flagstick was not deliberate, *e.g.*, the flagstick stuck in the socket or B was distracted and did not see A putt, A incurs a penalty of loss of hole in match play or two strokes in stroke play under Rule 17-3. B incurs no penalty.

17-3/3 Ball Strikes Flagstick Lying on Green

Q. Consider the following situations and give a ruling in each case:

(a) A player putts too strongly and his ball strikes the flagstick which has been removed by someone in his match or group and placed on the putting green behind the hole.

(b) A player plays his second shot to the green and the ball strikes the flagstick which had been blown down by the wind and was lying on the green.

(c) A player, not believing he can reach the green which is occupied by the preceding match or group, plays his second shot at a par-5 hole and the ball rolls onto the green and strikes the flagstick which has been removed from the hole and placed on the green by someone in the preceding match or group.

A. The following are the rulings:

(a) The player incurs a penalty under Rule 17 3a.

(b) and (c) No penalty is incurred. Rule 17-3a is not applicable in either case. It applies only when the flagstick has been removed with the player's author-
 ity or prior knowledge by someone in the player's match or group.

17-3/4 Flagstick Attended by Partner Without Express Authority of Player; Ball Strikes Flagstick or Partner

Q. In four-ball play, A is preparing to play from off the putting green. B, A's partner, attends the flagstick without A's knowledge or express authority. A plays and his ball strikes B or the flagstick. What is the ruling?

A. If the flagstick is attended by the player's caddie, his partner or his partner's caddie, *i.e.*, by a member of the player's side, it is deemed to be attended with the player's knowledge and authority. Accordingly, under Rule 17-3 A incurs a penalty of loss of hole in match play or two strokes in stroke play. In stroke play, A must play the ball as it lies. B incurs no penalty.

17-3/5 Flag Struck by Ball When Flagstick Attended

Q. While the flagstick was being attended, a player's ball struck the flag attached to the flagstick. Did the player incur a penalty under Rule 17-3a?

A. Yes. The flag is part of the flagstick.

17-3/6 Marking Position of Hole with Club

Q. The flagstick has been removed. A wants the position of the hole marked but he does not want to waste time retrieving the flagstick. So A asks B to place the grip end of his putter in the hole. Is this permissible?

A. Yes, but a putter used to mark the position of the hole must be treated as a flagstick for the purposes of applying the Rules.

Ball at Rest Kicked Away from Hole by Spectator Attending Flagstick — See 18-1/10.

Player Attending Flagstick for Opponent Struck by Ball of Opponent's Partner Who Played Out of Turn — See 30-3f/5.

17-4/1 Ball Resting Against Flagstick Lifted Before Being Holed

Q. A player's ball is resting against the flagstick, but it is not holed because all of it is not below the level of the lip of the hole. However, the player, believing the ball is holed, picks it up. What is the ruling?

A. The player incurs a penalty stroke under Rule 20-1 for lifting his ball without marking its position. The player must replace the ball against the flagstick and may then apply Rule 17-4.

Player's Ball Resting Against Flagstick Lifted Before Being Holed; Others in Four-Ball Match Pick Up Mistakenly Believing Player Won Hole — See 30-3f/3.

17-4/2 Ball Resting Against Flagstick; Putt Conceded and Ball Removed Before Player Can Remove Flagstick

Q. In a match, A plays a stroke from off the green and his ball comes to rest against the flagstick. B, A's opponent, concedes A's next stroke and removes A's ball. Despite B's concession, is A entitled to have the ball replaced to enable him to exercise his rights under Rule 17-4?

A. Yes. When A's ball was resting against the flagstick, Rule 17-4 applied and A was entitled to have the flagstick moved or removed to see whether the ball would fall into the hole. B had no right to remove the ball and concede the next stroke until A had an opportunity to proceed under Rule 17-4. By removing A's ball, B was in breach of Rule 18-3b and incurred a penalty stroke; A should then have replaced his ball against the flagstick and applied Rule 17-4.

17-4/3 Ball Resting Against Flagstick Moves Away from Hole When Flagstick Removed by Opponent or Fellow-Competitor

Q. A player's ball is resting against the flagstick. Without the player's authority, his opponent or a fellow-competitor removes the flagstick and the ball moves away from the hole. What is the ruling?

A. In match play, the opponent incurs a penalty stroke and the ball must be replaced against the flagstick — Rule 18-3b.

In stroke play, the ball must be replaced against the flagstick without penalty to anyone — Rule 18-4.

In either form of play, the player may then move or remove the flagstick as prescribed in Rule 17-4.

17-4/4 Ball Resting Against Flagstick Moves Away from Hole When Flagstick Removed by Player; Ball Not Placed on Lip of Hole

Q. A player's ball is resting against the flagstick. The player removes the flagstick and the ball moves away from the hole. The player plays the ball from its new position, holing the putt. What is the ruling?

A. The player was required to place the ball on the lip of the hole (Rule 17-4).

In match play, the player loses the hole — Rules 17-4 and 2-6.

In stroke play, the player incurs a penalty of two strokes and the ball is holed — Rules 17-4 and 3-5.

BALL MOVED, DEFLECTED OR STOPPED

Rule 18. Ball at Rest Moved

Definitions

A ball is deemed to have *"moved"* if it leaves its position and comes to rest in any other place.

An *"outside agency"* is any agency not part of the match or, in stroke play, not part of the *competitor's side,* and includes a *referee,* a *marker,* an *observer* and a *forecaddie.* Neither wind nor water is an *outside agency.*

"Equipment" is anything used, worn or carried by or for the player except any ball he has played at the hole being played and any small object, such as a coin or a tee, when used to mark the position of a ball or the extent of an area in which a ball is to be dropped. *Equipment* includes a golf cart, whether or not motorized. If such a cart is shared by two or more players, the cart and everything in it are deemed to be the *equipment* of the player whose ball is involved except that, when the cart is being moved by one of the players sharing it, the cart and everything in it are deemed to be that player's *equipment.*

Note: A ball played at the hole being played is *equipment* when it has been lifted and not put back into play.

A player has *"addressed the ball"* when he has taken his *stance* and has also grounded his club, except that in a *hazard* a player has *addressed the ball* when he has taken his *stance.*

Taking the "*stance*" consists in a player placing his feet in position for and preparatory to making a *stroke.*

18-1. By Outside Agency

If a ball at rest is *moved* by an *outside agency,* the player shall incur no penalty and the ball shall be replaced before the player plays another *stroke.*

(Player's ball at rest *moved* by another ball — see Rule 18-5.)

18-2. By Player, Partner, Caddie or Equipment

a. General

When a player's *ball is in play,* if:

(i) the player, his *partner* or either of their *caddies* lifts or *moves* it, touches it purposely (except with a club in the act of *addressing* it) or causes it to *move* except as permitted by a *Rule,* or

(ii) *equipment* of the player or his *partner* causes the ball to *move,*

the player shall incur a *penalty stroke.* The ball shall be replaced unless the movement of the ball occurs after the player has begun his swing and he does not discontinue his swing.

Under the *Rules* no penalty is incurred if a player accidentally causes his ball to *move* in the following circumstances:

In measuring to determine which ball farther from *hole* — Rule 10-4

In searching for covered ball in *hazard* or for ball in *abnormal ground condition* — Rule 12-1

In the process of repairing *hole* plug or ball mark — Rule 16-1c

In the process of removing *loose impediment* on *putting green* — Rule 18-2c

In the process of lifting ball under a *Rule* — Rule 20-1

In the process of placing or replacing ball under a *Rule* — Rule 20-3a

In removal of movable *obstruction* — Rule 24-1.

b. Ball Moving After Address

If a player's *ball in play moves* after he has *addressed* it (other than as a result of a *stroke*), the player shall be deemed to have *moved* the ball and shall incur a *penalty stroke.* The player shall replace the ball unless the movement of the ball occurs after he has begun his swing and he does not discontinue his swing.

c. Ball Moving After Loose Impediment Touched

Through the green, if the ball *moves* after any *loose impediment* lying within a club-length of it has been touched by the player, his *partner* or either of their *caddies* and before the player has *addressed* it, the player shall be deemed to have *moved* the ball and shall incur a *penalty stroke.* The player shall replace the ball unless the movement of the ball occurs after he has begun his swing and he does not discontinue his swing.

On the *putting green,* if the ball or the ball-marker *moves* in the process of removing any *loose impediment,* the ball or the ball-marker shall be replaced. There is no penalty provided the movement of the ball or the ball-marker is directly attributable to the removal of the *loose impediment.* Otherwise, the player shall incur a *penalty stroke* under Rule 18-2a or 20-1.

18-3. By Opponent, Caddie or Equipment in Match Play

a. During Search

If, during search for a player's ball, the ball is *moved* by an opponent, his *caddie* or his *equipment,* no penalty is incurred and the player shall replace the ball.

b. Other Than During Search

If, other than during search for a ball, the ball is touched or *moved* by an opponent, his *caddie* or his *equipment,* except as otherwise provided in the Rules, the opponent shall incur a *penalty stroke*. The player shall replace the ball.

(Ball *moved* in measuring to determine which ball farther from the *hole* — see Rule 10-4.)

(Playing a *wrong ball* — see Rule 15-2.)

18-4. By Fellow-Competitor, Caddie or Equipment in Stroke Play

If a *competitor's* ball is *moved* by a *fellow-competitor*, his *caddie* or his *equipment*, no penalty is incurred. The *competitor* shall replace his ball.

(Playing a *wrong ball* — see Rule 15-3.)

18-5. By Another Ball

If a *ball in play* and at rest is *moved* by another ball in motion after a *stroke*, the *moved* ball shall be replaced.

*PENALTY FOR BREACH OF RULE:
Match play — Loss of hole;
Stroke play — Two strokes.

*If a player who is required to replace a ball fails to do so, he shall incur the general penalty for breach of Rule 18 but no additional penalty under Rule 18 shall be applied.

Note 1: If a ball to be replaced under this Rule is not immediately recoverable, another ball may be substituted.

Note 2: If it is impossible to determine the spot on which a ball is to be placed, see Rule 20-3c.

18/1 Ball Moves Vertically Downwards

Q. A ball lying in long grass slips vertically downwards. Or a ball is accidentally stepped on and pressed down, say a quarter of an inch, in the grass or into the ground. In each case, has the ball moved?

A. Yes, unless the ball returns to its original position. The direction of movement is immaterial.

18/2 Ball Oscillates During Address

Q. In addressing the ball, a player accidentally causes the ball to oscillate, but it returns to its original position. Has the ball "moved"?

A. No.

18/3 Ball in Fork of Tree Moves in Relation to Ground But Not in Relation to Fork

Q. A ball rests in the fork of a branch of a tree. The player climbs the tree to play his next stroke. The branch bends under his weight. Although the ball has moved relative to the ground, it has not moved relative to the fork. Is the ball deemed to have moved?

A. The ball is deemed not to have moved since it did not move in relation to the fork of the tree in which it was lodged.

18/4 When Snake Is Outside Agency

Q. Is a snake an outside agency or a loose impediment?

A. A live snake is an outside agency. A dead snake is a loose impediment.

18/5 Placing Clubhead on Ground in Front of Ball When Addressing

Q. A player takes his stance and places his clubhead on the ground in front of the ball without pressing anything down. Before the player grounds the club behind the ball, the ball moves. Has the player "addressed the ball" so that he is subject to penalty under Rule 18-2b?

A. Yes.

When Club Grounded in Grass — See 18-2b/5.

18/6 When Player Who Putts "Side-Saddle" Has Addressed Ball

Q. A player who putts "side-saddle" usually stands directly behind the ball, places the clubhead on the ground behind the ball and aligns the clubhead. The player then moves to the side so as not to infringe Rule 16-1e and makes his stroke. When is the player deemed to have addressed the ball?

A. The player has addressed the ball when he moves to the side. The player has not placed his feet in position for a stroke, and therefore has not taken his stance, until he has moved to the side, and a ball is not addressed until a player has taken his stance.

18/7 Explanation of "Any Ball He Has Played"

Q. The Definition of "Equipment" excludes "any ball he (the player) has played at the hole being played." What does this mean?

A. The phrase means any ball the player has played at the hole being played except during any period when it has been lifted and has not been put back into play. Accordingly, the ball in play, a provisional ball, a second ball played under Rule 3-3 or Rule 20-7b and a ball being used for practice are not equipment.

Player Lifts His Ball on Putting Green and Sets It Aside; Opponent's or Fellow-Competitor's Ball Played from Green Subsequently Strikes Player's Ball — See 19-5/1.

18/7.5 Player's Ball Moved by Ball Accidentally Dropped by Opponent or Fellow-Competitor

Q. A lifts his ball on the putting green. He then accidentally drops the ball and it strikes and moves B's ball, which is in play and at rest. What is the ruling?

A. A ball which has been lifted and not put back into play is equipment — see the Note under Definition of "Equipment."

In match play, A incurs a penalty stroke and B must replace his ball — Rule 18-3b.

In stroke play, there is no penalty and B must replace his ball — Rule 18-4.

Rule 19-5 (Ball in Motion Deflected or Stopped by Another Ball) does not apply because A's ball was not "in motion after a stroke."

18/8 Ball Moved by Golf Cart Shared by Two Players

Under the Definition of "Equipment," equipment includes a golf cart, whether or not motorized. If two players share a golf cart, the cart and everything in it are deemed to be the equipment of the player whose ball is involved; except that, when the cart is being moved by one of the players, the cart and everything in it are deemed to be that player's equipment.

Thus, for example, in a singles match, if A and B are sharing a cart and the cart moves A's ball which was at rest, A would be penalized one stroke if he was driving or pulling the cart (Rule 18-2a). B would be penalized one stroke if he was driving or pulling the cart (Rule 18-3b), unless the incident occurred during search (Rule 18-3a).

18/9 Whether Glove Used as Indicating Mark Is Equipment

Q. A player entitled to drop a ball marks with his glove the spot on which the ball is to be dropped or the outer limit of the area within which the ball is to be dropped. The dropped ball then strikes the glove.

If the glove is a "small object," it is not equipment of the player, and the ball would not be re-dropped. Otherwise, the glove is equipment and the ball must be re-dropped under Rule 20-2a.

What is the status of the glove?

A. A glove is not a "small object" within the meaning of that term in the Definition of "Equipment." Therefore, it is equipment and the ball must be re-dropped.

18/10 Ball Falls into Bunker When Person Walks Nearby

Q. A ball at rest on the edge of a bunker falls into the bunker when X (a spectator, the player, an opponent or a fellow-competitor) walks nearby. Should the ball be replaced in accordance with Rules 18-1 or -4 or must the ball be played as it lies in the bunker?

A. The answer depends on whether X in any way caused the ball to move. If it is determined that X did not in any way cause the ball to move, there is no penalty and the ball must be played as it lies.

If it is determined that X caused the ball to move, it must be replaced. If X is the player, the player incurs a penalty stroke under Rule 18-2a; if X is an opponent, the opponent incurs a penalty stroke under Rule 18-3b. In all other cases, there is no penalty.

Whether X caused the ball to move is a question of fact to be determined in the light of all the circumstances. Relevant circumstances might include the distance between X and the ball and the nature of the ground. In the absence of evidence that X caused the ball to move, it should be concluded that the ball's movement was a coincidence.

18/11 Meaning of "Immediately Recoverable"

Q. With reference to Note 1 under Rule 18, when is a ball to be replaced deemed not to be "immediately recoverable"?

A. When it cannot be retrieved within a few seconds.

18-1/1 Treating Ball as Moved by Outside Agency Rather Than Lost

To treat a ball which cannot be found as moved by an outside agency rather than lost (Rule 27), there must be reasonable evidence to that effect. All available testimony should be considered. In the absence of such evidence, the ball must be treated as lost.

Lost Ball Treated as Moved by Outside Agency in Absence of Reasonable Evidence to That Effect — See 27-1/2.5.

18-1/2 Ball Visible from Tee Disappears or Is Moved While Play Suspended

Q. A player's tee shot came to rest and was visible from the tee by all players in the match or group. At that point play was suspended. The player took cover and did not lift the ball. When play was resumed, the player's ball was missing or was found some distance from where it was seen to come to rest. What is the procedure?

A. It must be assumed that the ball was moved by an outside agency. Therefore, the player should place a ball at the spot from which his ball was moved, without penalty (Rule 6-8d(iii)). If this spot is not determinable, Rule 20-3c would apply. (Revised)

18-1/3 Player Unaware Ball Moved by Outside Agency Does Not Replace Ball

Q. In stroke play, a player's ball was moved by an outside agency. Neither the player nor his caddie was aware that his ball had been moved, so the player did not replace the ball. He completed the hole, teed off at the next hole and then learned that his ball had been moved at the previous hole. What is the ruling?

A. It would be inequitable to impose a penalty for failure to replace a ball moved by an outside agency as required by Rule 18-1 if neither the player nor his caddie knew the ball had been moved. Accordingly, the score made with the moved ball would stand.

18-1/4 Spectator Says Ball Was Moved by Outside Agency But Player Not Sure

Q. A spectator tells a player that his ball has been moved by an outside agency. Neither the player nor his caddie was aware the ball had been moved. Is the player obliged to take the spectator's word and replace the ball on the spot from which the spectator said it was moved?

A. No. In stroke play, if it is impractical to get a decision from the Committee, the player should, under Rule 3-3, hole out both with the original ball and a second ball played from the spot from which the original ball is alleged to have been moved, and request the Committee to decide the matter at the end of the round. In reaching a decision, the Committee should interrogate the spectator, if possible.

In match play, if there is no referee or representative of the Committee available within a reasonable time, the player and his opponent should, if possible, agree on the place from which the player should play his next stroke. If agreement cannot be reached, the player must proceed as he thinks best, and if the opponent does not agree with the action taken, he should lodge a claim under Rule 2-5 so that the Committee may make a decision under Rule 34-3.

18-1/5 Ball Stolen by Outside Agency from Unknown Spot

Q. At a par-3 hole, part of the green and the adjoining area cannot be seen from the tee. In this unseen area are a bunker, fairway and a dry water hazard.

A player plays towards this obscured area and cannot tell where the ball comes to rest. When the players are near the green, they see a boy running away with a ball in his hand. The boy throws the ball back and the player identifies it as his ball.

The player is unable to determine from where to play his next stroke under Rule 18-1. He does not know whether the ball was on the green, on the fairway or in one of the hazards.

How should he proceed?

A. As it was impossible to know where the ball should have been replaced under Rule 18-1, the player should, in equity (Rule 1-4), drop the ball in an area which was neither the most, nor the least, favorable of the various areas where it was equally possible that the ball originally lay.

18-1/6 Ball at Rest Moved by Blowing Tumbleweed

Q. A tumbleweed blowing across the course strikes a ball at rest and knocks it into the hole. What is the procedure?

A. In the circumstances, a tumbleweed is an outside agency. Rule 18-1 applies and the ball must be replaced without penalty.

18-1/7 Ball in Plastic Bag Moves When Bag Blown to New Position by Wind

Q. A player's ball comes to rest in a plastic bag that is lying on the ground. Before the player can invoke Rule 24-1b, a gust of wind blows the bag and the ball to a new position. In proceeding under Rule 24-1b, should the player drop the ball directly under the place where it originally lay in the bag or where it now lies in the bag?

A. Wind is not an outside agency. However, if an object being moved by the wind moves a ball, the object is an outside agency in the circumstances — see Decision 18-1/6.

In this case, the bag, not the wind, caused the ball to move. Accordingly, under Rules 18-1 and 24-1b, the player must drop the ball directly under the place where it originally lay in the bag.

18-1/8 Ball Moved by Stone Dislodged by Partner's or Opponent's Stroke

Q. In match play, a player played a stroke and dislodged a large stone. The stone struck his partner's or an opponent's ball which was lying about four yards ahead and moved it. What is the ruling? 18

A. The stone was an outside agency and Rule 18-1 applies. The partner or opponent must replace his ball.

In the circumstances, the player should not be held to have moved the ball. Accordingly, Rules 18-2a(i) and 18-3b are not applicable and no penalty is incurred.

18-1/9 Ball Lodged in Tree Knocked Down by Outside Agency

Q. A player's ball is lodged in a tree about eight feet off the ground. A spectator knocks the ball down from the tree. In complying with Rule 18-1, it is impossible to replace the ball in the prescribed manner in the tree because the spot where it lay in the tree is unknown or unreachable. What is the ruling?

A. Rules 20-3c and -3d cover cases in which the spot where a ball is to be placed or replaced is not determinable or a ball fails to come to rest on the spot on which it is placed. However, these Rules do not contemplate a case such as this one. Thus, in equity (Rule 1-4), if the position of the ball in the tree was such that the player could have made a stroke at it, the ball must be placed in the tree as near as possible to the spot from which it was moved, without penalty. Otherwise, the player must proceed under the unplayable ball Rule.

18-1/10 Ball at Rest Kicked Away from Hole by Spectator Attending Flagstick

Q. In stroke play, a competitor asked a spectator to attend the flagstick. The competitor putted and his ball stopped one inch short of the hole. The spectator then kicked the ball away. What is the ruling?

A. There was no infringement of Rule 17-3b because the competitor's ball had come to rest short of the hole. The spectator was not the competitor's caddie and so he was an outside agency. Under Rule 18-1 the competitor was required to replace his ball and hole out without penalty.

18-1/11 Ball Moved by Wind or Casual Water While Play Suspended

Q. While play is suspended, wind or casual water moves a ball. Since wind or water is not an outside agency, must the ball be played from its new position?

A. No. The ball must be replaced — see Rule 6-8d(iii). If the spot is not determinable, Rule 20-3c would apply. (Revised)

Ball-Marker Moved Off Green by Wind or Casual Water — See 20-1/10.

18-1/12 Ball Replaced and at Rest Is Thereafter Moved by Wind

Q. A player replaces his ball on the putting green and the ball is at rest. Before the player addresses the ball, a sudden gust of wind blows the ball farther from the hole. The player plays the ball from its new position. Is that correct?

A. Yes. Wind is not an outside agency — see Definition of "Outside Agency." Accordingly, Rule 18-1 does not apply.

18-2a/1 Player Who Misses Tee Shot Tees Ball Lower Before Playing Next Stroke

Q. A player playing from the teeing ground misses the ball completely. He pushes his tee farther into the ground and plays. Is there a penalty?

A. Yes. As the ball was in play after the player had made a stroke at it, he incurred a penalty of one stroke under Rule 18-2a when he teed the ball lower, and a penalty of loss of hole in match play or a total penalty of two strokes in stroke play because the ball was not subsequently replaced — see penalty statement under Rule 18.

Lifting Ball in Play But Still Within Teeing Ground — See 11-3/2.

18-2a/2 Ball Falling Off Tee When Stroke Just Touches It Is Picked Up and Re-Teed

Q. When starting a hole, a player, in making his first stroke, just touched the ball and it fell off the tee. He picked up the ball, re-teed it and played out the hole. What is the ruling?

A. When the player made a stroke the ball was in play. When he then lifted the ball, he was in breach of Rule 18-2a and incurred a penalty stroke. When he failed to replace the ball on the spot where it came to rest after being knocked off the tee, he incurred a penalty of loss of hole in match play or a total of two strokes in stroke play — see penalty statement under Rule 18.

Ball Putted from Wrong Place Lifted and Putted from Right Place — See 20-7b/2.

18-2a/3 Ball Lifted and Dropped Away from Boundary Stake Under Obstruction Rule

Q. A player's swing is interfered with by a stake defining out of bounds. The player mistakenly considers the stake an obstruction and he lifts his ball and drops it in the manner prescribed in Rule 24-2b. What is the ruling?

A. The player incurs a penalty of one stroke under Rule 18-2a and he must replace his ball before playing his next stroke. Otherwise, he loses the hole in match play or he incurs a total penalty of two strokes in stroke play — see penalty statement under Rule 18.

Dropped Ball Comes to Rest and Then Rolls Out of Bounds — See 20-2c/3.5.

18-2a/4 Ball Lifted and Dropped Away from Movable Obstruction

Q. A player's ball comes to rest against a movable obstruction. The player lifts the ball and drops it away from the obstruction instead of removing the obstruction as provided in Rule 24-1. What is the ruling?

A. The player incurs a penalty of one stroke under Rule 18-2a and he must replace his ball before playing his next stroke. Otherwise, he loses the hole in match play or he incurs a total penalty of two strokes in stroke play — see penalty statement under Rule 18.

Movable Obstruction Defined — See 24-1/1

[18-2a/5 Reserved]

18-2a/6 Oscillating Ball Pressed into Surface of Putting Green

Q. A ball lying on the putting green was oscillating due to wind. The player firmly pressed the ball into the surface of the green and the ball stopped oscillating. The player then holed out. Was the player in breach of the Rules?

A. Yes. The player incurred a penalty stroke under Rule 18-2a when he moved his ball by pressing on it.

Since the original lie of the ball was altered when the ball was firmly pressed down, the player was obliged to proceed under Rule 20-3b. Since he did not do so, he lost the hole in match play and incurred a total penalty of two strokes in stroke play — see penalty statement under Rule 18.

18-2a/7 Ball Moved by Wind Replaced

Q. In stroke play, a competitor's ball was moved by wind. Since wind is not an outside agency (see Definition of "Outside Agency"), he should have played it from where it came to rest, but he replaced it. What is the ruling?

A. The competitor incurred one penalty stroke under Rule 18-2a, and, before playing his next stroke, he should have replaced the ball on the spot where it came to rest after being moved by the wind. If he did not do so, he incurred a total penalty of two strokes — see penalty statement under Rule 18.

18-2a/8 Ball Played from Ground Under Repair Picked Up and Relief Taken Under Ground Under Repair Rule

Q. A player, unaware that his ball was in ground under repair, played the ball as it lay. The player then learned that his ball had been in ground under repair, picked up the ball played from the ground under repair, dropped it in accordance with Rule 25-1b and played out the hole. What is the ruling?

A. When the player played from the ground under repair, which is permissible, relief under Rule 25-1b was no longer available and the ball was in play where it lay.

When the player picked up his ball in play, he incurred a penalty stroke — Rule 18-2a. Since he did not replace the ball, he incurred a penalty of loss of hole in match play or a total penalty of two strokes in stroke play — see penalty statement under Rule 18.

Provisional Ball Lifted in Erroneous Belief Original Ball Is in Bounds — See 27-2b/8.

Provisional Ball Lifted Subsequently Becomes Ball in Play — See 27-2b/9.

Provisional Ball Lifted Subsequently Becomes Ball in Play; Competitor Then Plays from Wrong Place — See 27-2b/10.

18-2a/9 Ball Lifted Without Authority Dropped Instead of Being Replaced

Q. A player lifted his ball without being entitled to under the Rules and incurred a penalty stroke under Rule 18-2a. He then learned of his error, dropped the ball at the spot from which it was lifted instead of replacing it as required by Rule 18-2a, and played it. What is the ruling?

A. The player incurred a penalty of loss of hole in match play or a total of two strokes in stroke play — see penalty statement under Rule 18.

18-2a/10 Dropped Ball Lifted and Re-Dropped When It Should Have Been Played as It Lay; Ball Then Lifted Again and Placed

18

Q. In stroke play, a competitor whose ball was in a lateral water hazard elected to take relief under Rule 26-1c(i). When a ball was dropped, it rolled towards the hole but came to rest not more than two club-lengths from where it first struck the ground and not nearer the hole than the point where the original ball last crossed the margin of the water hazard.

Incorrectly believing that Rule 20-2c applied, the competitor lifted the ball and re-dropped it, whereupon the ball rolled towards the hole as before. The competitor again lifted the ball, placed it where it first struck the ground when re-dropped and played his next stroke. Is the competitor penalized two strokes or four strokes?

A. Two strokes. The ball when first dropped was in play — see Rule 20-4. The competitor was in breach of Rule 18-2a when he lifted it. Because the competitor failed to replace his ball at the spot at which it came to rest when first dropped, he incurred a total penalty of two strokes — see penalty statement under Rule 18. There are a number of Decisions under which a competitor who infringes the same Rule several times prior to a stroke is penalized for only one infringement, *e.g.*, Decisions 15-3/2 and 19-2/7.

18-2a/11 Ball Wrongly Thought to Be Out of Bounds Lifted; Competitor Proceeds Under Rule 27-1

Q. In stroke play, a competitor hit his tee shot into the practice area. He thought the ball was out of bounds. He lifted the ball and proceeded under Rule 27-1. After again playing from the tee, he discovered that the practice area was not out of bounds. What is the ruling?

A. The competitor was subject to a total penalty of two strokes for lifting his ball in play and failing to replace it — see Rule 18-2a and penalty statement under Rule 18.

18-2a/12 Player Entitled to Relief from Condition Lifts Ball; Player Then Replaces Ball and Plays It from Original Position

Q. A player elects to take relief from an immovable obstruction or abnormal ground condition and lifts his ball. He then realizes that the only area in which he may drop under the Rules is such that his ball, when dropped, will almost certainly be unplayable. He replaces his ball and plays it from its original position. What is the ruling?

A. The player was entitled to lift the ball to take relief under Rule 24 or 25. However, by subsequently deciding not to take relief, his right to lift the ball was negated and he incurred a penalty stroke under Rule 18-2a for having lifted his ball in play.

18

Player Unaware Ball in Water Hazard Takes Relief from Interference by Burrowing Animal Hole — See 25-1b/26.

18-2a/12.5 Player Entitled to Relief Without Penalty from Condition Lifts Ball; Chooses Not to Take Relief and Wishes to Proceed Under the Unplayable Ball Rule

Q. In the circumstances described in Decision 18-2a/12, rather than replace the ball under penalty of one stroke as required by Rule 18-2a, may the player declare the ball unplayable and proceed under Rule 28, avoiding the one-stroke penalty under Rule 18-2a?

A. In order to avoid the one-stroke penalty under Rule 18-2a, the player must indicate that he intends to proceed under the unplayable ball Rule before lifting the ball. Therefore, if the player wishes to proceed under the unplayable ball Rule in this situation, he may:

1. drop the ball in accordance with Rule 24 or 25 and then, using its new position as a reference point, proceed under Rule 28 incurring a penalty of one stroke; or

2. replace the ball in its original position under penalty of one stroke (Rule 18-2a) and then proceed under Rule 28, incurring an additional penalty of one stroke; or

3. proceed directly under Rule 28, without replacing the ball and using the spot where the ball originally lay as the reference point for the relief procedure, incurring a penalty stroke under Rule 28 and an additional penalty stroke under Rule 18-2a.

18-2a/13 Ball Lifted Without Authority and Cleaned

Q. A player's ball comes to rest on the apron of a green. Mistakenly believing that the ball is on the green, the player marks, lifts and cleans it. The player incurs a penalty stroke under Rule 18-2a for lifting the ball without authority under the Rules. Does the player incur an additional penalty stroke under Rule 21 for cleaning the ball?

A. No. Rule 21 states that a ball may be cleaned when lifted except when it has been lifted in accordance with Rule 5-3, 12-2 or 22.

Player Lifts Ball Without Authority Due to Misunderstanding Committee Member's Instructions — See 34-3/3.5.

18-2a/13.5 Ball Lifted and Thrown Into Pond in Anger

Q. A player played a poor shot and his ball came to rest through the green near a lake. In anger, the player lifted his ball and threw it into the lake from where it could not be retrieved. The player placed another ball on the spot from which the original ball was lifted and holed out. What is the ruling?

A. Although Note 1 to Rule 18 states "If a ball to be replaced under this Rule is not immediately recoverable, another ball may be substituted," as the player's ball became irrecoverable only due to the player's subsequent actions after his breach of Rule 18-2a, the Note is not applicable.

The player lost the hole in match play — Rule 15-1.

In stroke play, the player incurred a penalty of three strokes — one under Rule 18-2a for lifting his ball without authority under the Rules and two under Rule 15-1 for substituting a ball when not permitted. (New)

Player Substitutes Another Ball on Putting Green Because Original Ball Thrown to Caddie for Cleaning Came to Rest in Lake — See 15-1/6.

18-2a/14 Caddie on Own Initiative Lifts Ball for Identification

Q. During search for A's ball, A's caddie found a ball and lifted it for identification without the authority of A and without A's announcing in advance his intention to do so. The ball was identified as A's. What is the ruling?

A. Since the ball was lifted other than in accordance with the Rules, Rule 18-2a applies and A incurs a penalty of one stroke. Rule 18-2a overrides Rule 12-2 in the circumstances. Accordingly, an additional penalty of one stroke under Rule 12-2 for failing to announce the intention to lift the ball for identification purposes is not applicable.

Caddie Lifts Ball in Water Hazard Without Player's Authority — See 26-1/9.

18-2a/15 Caddie on Own Initiative Lifts Ball Considering It Unplayable

Q. A player's caddie, considering the player's ball to be in an unplayable lie, lifted the ball before the player had an opportunity to inspect the lie. What is the ruling?

A. A player's caddie may not declare the player's ball to be unplayable (Rule 28). Therefore, the player incurred a penalty of one stroke under Rule 18-2a when the caddie lifted the ball. The player may replace the ball and play it or invoke the unplayable ball Rule (Rule 28). If the player invokes Rule 28, he may choose to estimate the original location of the ball rather than replace it, but in either case, by invoking Rule 28, the player incurs an additional penalty of one stroke under that Rule. (Revised)

18-2a/16 Competitor's Ball Picked Up by Fellow-Competitor at Competitor's Request

Q. A competitor, mistakenly thinking his ball in play in the rough was a wrong ball, asked his fellow-competitor to pick up the ball. The fellow-competitor did so and then the error was discovered. Is the competitor subject to penalty under Rule 18-2a or exempt from penalty by virtue of Rule 18-4?

A. Because the lifting of the ball by the fellow-competitor was at the request of the competitor, it would not be correct to exonerate the competitor under Rule 18-4.

The competitor incurred a one-stroke penalty under Rule 18-2a and he was required to replace his ball.

18-2a/17 Towel Dropped by Player Is Blown onto and Moves Ball

Q. A player dropped a towel on the ground. The wind blew the towel onto the player's ball and moved it. What is the ruling?

A. As the player's equipment caused the ball to move, the player incurred a penalty stroke and must replace the ball — Rule 18-2a.

Ball Blown into Hole by Competitor Not Replaced and Holed Out — See 3-2/2.

18-2a/18 Opponent's Ball Knocked Away by Player After Concession Moves Player's Ball

Q. In singles match play, A concedes B's next stroke and knocks B's ball away. B's ball in motion moves A's ball. What is the ruling?

A. As A caused his own ball to move, he incurred a penalty of one stroke under Rule 18-2a, and he must replace his ball.

18-2a/19 Ball Moved Accidentally by Practice Swing Prior to Tee Shot

Q. Before playing from the teeing ground, a player took a practice swing, in the course of which he accidentally struck and moved the teed ball with his club. Did the player play a stroke or incur a penalty?

A. The player did not make a stroke — see Definition of "Stroke." Since the ball was not in play — see Definition of "Ball in Play" — he incurred no penalty under Rule 18-2a. The player must put a ball into play from the teeing ground.

18-2a/20 Ball in Play Moved Accidentally by Practice Swing

Q. A player makes a practice swing and accidentally moves his ball in play with his club. Has he made a stroke?

A. No. He had no intention of moving the ball — see Definition of "Stroke."

However, he incurs a penalty stroke under Rule 18-2a for moving his ball in play, and the ball must be replaced.

Player Instinctively Throws Putter at Ball and Moves It — See 1-2/4.5.

Player Kicks Ball While Probing for it in Water in Water Hazard — See 12-1/5.

Club Breaks During Downswing; Swing Stopped But Clubhead Falls and Moves Ball — See 14/4.

Ball Accidentally Kicked by Player Asked to Lift It Due to Interference — See 20-1/13.

Ball Moved by Putter Dropped by Player Approaching Ball to Lift It — See 20-1/14.

Ball Moved by Ball-Marker Dropped Accidentally by Player — See 20-1/15.

Ball Moved in Removing Ball-Marker After Replacing Ball — See 20-3a/1.

18-2a/21 Ball Moved Accidentally by Player in Playing Wrong Ball in Bunker

Q. In a bunker, A plays a wrong ball. In so doing, he accidentally moves a nearby ball which turns out to be his ball. While there is no penalty for playing a wrong ball in a hazard (Rules 15-2 and 15-3), does A incur a penalty for moving his ball in play (a) if the nearby ball was visible before A played the wrong ball or (b) if the nearby ball was not visible before A played the wrong ball?

A. If the nearby ball was visible before A played, he incurs a penalty of one stroke under Rule 18-2a and he must replace his ball on the spot from which it was moved. If the lie has been altered, it should be recreated as required by Rule 20-3b. As the nearby ball was likely to interfere with his stroke, the player would have been entitled to proceed in accordance with Decision 1-4/6.

If the nearby ball was not visible before A played, in equity (Rule 1-4), there would be no penalty under Rule 18-2a, but the ball must be replaced, and if necessary, the lie recreated. (Revised)

Ball Moved by Stone Dislodged by Partner's Stroke — See 18-1/8.

Caddie Shared by Members of Opposite Sides in Four-Ball Match Moves Ball — See 30/1.

Player's Ball Moved by Partner in Playing His Own Ball — See 30-3f/9.

18-2a/21.3 Ball Moved Accidentally and Original Lie Altered; Player Places Ball in Wrong Place and Plays

Q. A player accidentally steps on his ball in the rough and pushes it into the ground, incurring a penalty stroke under Rule 18-2a. Instead of placing the ball in the nearest most similar lie within one club-length of the original lie as required by Rule 20-3b, the player places the ball almost two club-lengths away from the original lie and plays his next stroke.

In match play, it is clear that the player incurs the general penalty for a breach of Rule 18 or 20-3b, and loses the hole.

In stroke play, does the player incur an additional penalty of two strokes for a breach of Rule 20-3b or a total penalty of two strokes under Rule 18?

A. In stroke play, the player incurs a total penalty of two strokes under Rule 18.

Rule 18 requires replacement of a ball moved accidentally. If some other Rule — in this case Rule 20-3b — requires a moved ball to be placed somewhere else, the player is considered to be in breach of Rule 18 if he places the ball other than as prescribed by the other Rule.

18-2a/21.5 Ball Moved Accidentally; Spot Where Ball Originally Lay Not Determinable; Player Places Ball Instead of Dropping It

Q. A player accidentally moves his ball in the rough, incurring a penalty stroke under Rule 18-2a. The spot where the ball originally lay is not determinable. Instead of dropping the ball as near as possible to the spot where it originally lay as required by Rule 20-3c, the player places the ball as near as possible to that spot and plays his next stroke.

In match play, it is clear that the player incurs the general penalty for a breach of Rule 18 or 20-3c and loses the hole.

In stroke play, does the player incur an additional penalty of two strokes for a breach of Rule 20-3c or a total penalty of two strokes under Rule 18?

A. In stroke play, the player incurs a total penalty of two strokes under Rule 18 — see Decision 18-2a/21.3.

18-2a/22 Ball Moved Accidentally by Backward Movement of Club After Stroke Misses; Ball Comes to Rest Out of Bounds

Q. A player misses a shot completely and, in swinging his club back, he accidentally knocks his ball backwards. Was the backward swing a stroke? If the ball comes to rest out of bounds, how does the player proceed? 18

A. The backward swing was not a stroke. A stroke is the forward movement of the club made with the intention of fairly striking at, and moving, the ball — see Definition of "Stroke."

In addition to counting the missed stroke, the player incurs a penalty stroke for moving his ball with the backward swing (Rule 18-2a), and the ball must be replaced. The fact that the ball lay out of bounds is irrelevant.

18-2a/23 Ball Knocked from Lip of Hole in Disgust

Q. In stroke play, a competitor's ball stops on the lip of the hole. In disgust the competitor knocks his ball off the green with the back of his putter. What is the ruling?

A. The competitor must replace the ball under penalty of one stroke — Rule 18-2a. The competitor is not considered to have made a stroke.

Player Jumps Close to Hole to Cause Ball to Drop and Ball Drops — See 1-2/4.

Ball Stopped by Player's Foot Moves When Foot Removed — See 19-2/1.

Ball Moves Prior to Address and Is Accidentally Stopped by Player's Club; Player Removes Club and Ball Rolls Away — See 19-2/1.5.

18-2a/24 Ball Moved by Flagstick Accidentally Dropped on Ball

Q. A player accidentally dropped the flagstick on his ball and moved it. The player replaced the ball. What is the ruling?

A. The player incurred a penalty of one stroke under Rule 18-2a, unless he was exempt from penalty under a specific Rule, *e.g.*, Rule 10-4 (Ball Moved in Measuring).

Rake Thrown into Bunker Before Stroke Moves Ball — See 13-4/21.

Ball Moved in Measuring to Determine If Re-Drop Required — See 20-2c/6.

[18-2a/25 Reserved]

18-2a/26 Ball Dislodged from Tree When Player Climbs Tree to Play Stroke

Q. As a player is climbing a tree to play a ball lodged in the tree, the ball falls to the ground. Does the player incur a penalty?

A. Yes, one stroke under Rule 18-2a, and the ball must be replaced.

18-2a/27 Ball Dislodged from Tree; Circumstances in Which Player Not Penalized

Q. A player whose ball is lodged high in a tree wishes to dislodge it by shaking the tree or throwing a club so that he can identify it and proceed under the unplayable ball Rule. Is this permissible?

A. Yes. The player should state his intention before taking such action to avoid any question being raised as to whether a penalty would be incurred under Rule 18-2a.

18-2a/28 Ball Dislodged from Tree; Circumstances in Which Player Penalized

Q. A player could not find his ball. Believing the ball might be lodged in a tree, he shook the tree and his ball fell to the ground. He played the ball from where it came to rest. What is the ruling?

A. The player incurred one penalty stroke under Rule 18-2a for moving his ball. He should have replaced the ball. Since he did not do so, in match play he lost the hole and in stroke play he incurred a total penalty of two strokes — see penalty statement under Rule 18.

18-2a/29 Ball Dislodged from Tree; Replacement of Ball Not Possible

Q. A player, believing his ball is lodged in a tree, shakes the tree in order to dislodge it. His ball falls to the ground. According to Decision 18-2a/28, the player incurs a penalty of one stroke under Rule 18-2a and must replace his ball. Suppose, however, that the player cannot replace his ball either:

(1) because the spot where it lay in the tree is not determinable, or
(2) because the ball fails to remain on the correct spot when replaced, or
(3) because the player cannot reach the spot where the ball lay.

How should the player proceed in each of these three circumstances?

A. Rules 20-3c and -3d would normally cover circumstances (1) and (2), but these Rules do not contemplate a situation such as the one described. Accordingly, in equity (Rule 1-4), in the first two circumstances the ball must be placed in the tree as near as possible to the spot from which it was moved, and in the third circumstance the player must proceed under the unplayable ball Rule, incurring an additional penalty stroke.

Striking at Tree Branch to Move Ball Lodged Higher in Branch — See 14/7.

18-2a/30 Ball Moves After Player Takes Several Practice Swings Near Ball and Touches Grass Behind Ball

Q. A player took several practice swings about one foot from his ball which was lying in light rough, and his club came in contact with the ground. He then took his stance, touched grass behind the ball with the clubhead but did not ground the club. At that point the ball moved.

The player claimed that no penalty was incurred because he had not touched a loose impediment within one club-length of the ball or addressed the ball. However, the Committee judged that the practice swings and the touching of the grass behind the ball caused the ball to move, and therefore the player incurred a penalty stroke under Rule 18-2a. Was the Committee correct?

A. It is a question of fact whether the player caused his ball to move and thus incurred a penalty under Rule 18-2a. Because of the practice swings and touching of the grass, the weight of evidence is against the player and therefore the Committee's decision was correct.

18-2a/31 Ball Touched Accidentally in Removing Loose Impediments

Q. In removing loose impediments from the vicinity of his ball lying through the green, the player accidentally touches the ball with his hand but does not move it. Is there any penalty?

A. No. Under Rule 18-2a there is only a penalty if the player, his partner or either of their caddies purposely touches the player's ball; it may be touched accidentally provided it does not move.

Ball Moved Accidentally by Foot During Removal of Loose Impediment on Putting Green — See 18-2c/1.

Ball in Hazard Moves After Loose Impediment Outside Hazard Moved — See 18-2c/4.

Holding Ball in Place While Removing Obstruction — See 24-1/4.

18-2a/32 Ball Touched with Fir Cone or Stick to Prevent Movement When Loose Impediments Removed

Q. A player placed a fir cone or stick against his ball to prevent the ball from moving when he moved some loose impediments. Is this permissible?

A. No. The player purposely touched his ball in play, contrary to Rule 18-2a, and incurred a penalty of one stroke.

Touching and Rotating Half-Buried Ball in Rough for Identification Purposes — See 12-2/2.

Touching and Rotating Half-Buried Ball in Hazard for Identification Purposes — See 12-2/3.

18-2a/33 Rotating Ball on Putting Green Without Marking Position

18

Q. A player rotates his ball on the putting green to line up the trademark with the hole. He did not lift the ball, mark its position or change its position. Is there a penalty?

A. Yes, one stroke for touching the ball other than as provided for in the Rules — Rule 18-2a. Under Rules 16-1b and 20-1, a ball on the putting green may be lifted (or touched and rotated) after its position has been marked. If the player had marked the position of the ball before rotating it, there would have been no penalty.

18-2b/1 Ball Moves After Stance Taken But Before Address

Q. Outside a hazard, the player took his stance but did not ground his club. The ball moved. What is the ruling?

A. As the player had not addressed the ball, he did not incur a penalty under Rule 18-2b (see Definition of "Addressing the Ball").

If, however, the player caused the ball to move, he was subject to penalty and the ball should have been replaced — Rule 18-2a.

18-2b/2 Ball Moves After Stance Taken in Hazard Without Club

Q. A player enters a hazard without a club and positions his feet for the purpose of determining how he wishes to play the shot. Has he taken his stance (and thus addressed the ball) so that, if the ball thereafter moves, he is subject to penalty under Rule 18-2b?

A. Yes. See Decision 13-4/24.

18-2b/3 Ball Moves While Player in Process of Taking Stance in Bunker

Q. In a bunker, a player's ball moved when he was in the process of, but had not completed, taking his stance. What is the ruling?

A. Since the ball moved before the player had addressed it (see Definition of "Addressing the Ball"), the player incurred no penalty under Rule 18-2b.

If, however, the player's approach to the ball or the act of taking his stance caused the ball to move, the player incurred a penalty stroke under Rule 18-2a and the ball must be replaced.

When Stance Taken in Bunker — See 13-4/23.

Ball Moving in Water Hazard After Address — See 14-6/1.

18-2b/4 Ball Moves After Player Grounds Club But Before Stance Completed

Q. A player's routine prior to playing a stroke is as follows: He first grounds the club directly behind the ball with his feet together. Then he gradually widens his feet to shoulder width. At that point, he makes the stroke.

If the ball moves after he grounds the club but before he widens his stance to shoulder width, does he incur a penalty stroke under Rule 18-2b (Ball Moving After Address)?

A. No. A player has not addressed the ball until he completes taking his stance, *i.e.*, his feet are essentially in the position in which he normally places them when making a stroke.

However, if the ball moved after the club was placed in position but before the player had completed taking his stance, he incurs a penalty stroke under Rule 18-2a for having caused the ball to move and must replace the ball, unless there is strong evidence that wind or some other agency caused the ball to move.

18-2b/5 When Club Grounded in Grass

Q. When is a club considered grounded in long grass?

A. When the grass is compressed to the point where it will support the weight of the club.

18-2b/6 Ball Perched on Heather Moves When Club Rested on Heather

Q. A's ball is perched on a tuft of heather. He takes his stance and rests his club on the heather behind the ball. The ball moves. What is the ruling?

A. Resting the club on heather or grass behind the ball constitutes grounding it. Accordingly, A had addressed the ball and Rule 18-2b applies. A incurs a penalty stroke and must replace his ball.

18-2b/7 Ball Moves After Player Addresses It and Then Steps Away

Q. A player takes his stance and grounds his club. Realizing that the ball is precariously balanced and may move, he steps away from the ball and starts again. This time he does not ground his club, but before he strikes the ball, it moves. What is the ruling?

A. The player incurs a penalty stroke under Rule 18-2b, and the ball must be replaced.

18-2b/8 Player Addresses Ball, Steps Away, Lifts Ball and Replaces It; Ball Then Moves

Q. On the putting green, a player addressed the ball. He stepped away from the ball, marked its position and lifted it. He then replaced the ball and, before he addressed it, the ball moved. Since the ball was lifted and out of play after it was addressed, was the player subject to penalty under Rule 18-2b when it moved after it was put back into play?

A. No. The ball must be played as it lies. Once the ball has been lifted the presumption inherent in the Rule that the act of addressing the ball caused the ball to move is no longer valid.

After Ball Addressed on Putting Green Ball Moved in Removal of Loose Impediment — See 18-2c/2.

 Ball Dropped in Improper Manner Moves When Addressed; Player Then Lifts Ball and Drops It in Proper Manner — See 20-2a/4.

18-2b/9 Ball Moves After Address and Comes to Rest Out of Bounds

Q. A player's ball is lying on a slope. When he addresses the ball it moves and comes to rest out of bounds. What is the ruling?

A. If a ball moves after the player addresses it, he incurs a one-stroke penalty and the ball must be replaced — Rule 18-2b.

18-2b/10 Ball Falls into Hole After Being Addressed

Q. A player's ball overhangs the lip of the hole. He addresses the ball and it falls into the hole. What is the ruling?

A. The player incurs a penalty stroke and the ball must be replaced. Although Rule 16-2 applies when a player's ball overhangs the lip of the hole, Rule 18-2b, which specifically applies when a player's ball moves after he has addressed it, overrides Rule 16-2 in this case.

18-2b/11 Ball Moved by Another Ball After Being Addressed

Q. After a player has addressed his ball, a ball played from elsewhere strikes and moves the player's ball. Does Rule 18-5 supersede Rule 18-2b?

A. Yes. The player's ball must be replaced, without penalty.

18-2b/12 Ball Moves After Address and Is Stopped by Player's Club

Q. After a player addresses his ball, the ball moves backwards. Before the player can remove his club, the ball is stopped by the clubhead. What is the ruling? 18

A. The player incurs a penalty stroke under Rule 18-2b and the ball must be replaced. Rule 19-2 does not apply in these circumstances.

Other Decisions relating to Rule 18-2b:

Stroke Misses Ball Which Is Then Accidentally Knocked Off Tee After Being Addressed — See 11-3/1.

Ball Addressed; Club Breaks on Downswing; Swing Stopped But Clubhead Falls and Moves Ball — See 14/4.

Provisional Ball Moves After Being Addressed — See 15/7.

Ball in Rough Moves Downward When Addressed; Ball Will Not Remain at Rest When Replaced — See 20-3d/3.

Order of Play in Foursome Match If Player Accidentally Moves Ball After Address — See 29-1/5.

18-2c/1 Ball Moved Accidentally by Foot During Removal of Loose Impediment on Putting Green

Q. A player in the process of removing a loose impediment on the putting green accidentally moved his ball with his foot. What is the ruling?

A. The player incurs a penalty stroke under Rule 18-2a, and the ball must be replaced.

Rule 18-2c provides that the player incurs no penalty if, on the putting green, his ball moves in the process of removing a loose impediment. However, this Rule applies only where the moving of a ball is directly attributable to removal of a loose impediment. In this case, removal of the loose impediment did not cause the ball to move.

18-2c/2 After Ball Addressed on Putting Green Ball Moved in Removal of Loose Impediment

Q. After a player addresses his ball on the putting green, an insect alights on the ball. The player bends over without moving his feet and, in attempting to brush the insect off the ball, moves the ball several inches. Is the player subject to a penalty stroke under Rule 18-2b?

18

A. No. An insect is a loose impediment — see Definition of "Loose Impediments" and Decision 23-1/5.

Under Rule 18-2c, a player incurs no penalty if a ball on the putting green moves while he is in the process of removing a loose impediment. Rule 18-2c supersedes Rule 18-2b in this case.

Loose Impediments Affecting Lie Removed While Ball Lifted — See 23-1/8.

18-2c/3 Loose Impediments Within One Club-Length Removed; Ball Lifted and Replaced; Ball Moves Before Address

Q. A player removed loose impediments within a few inches of his ball lying through the green, lifted the ball because it interfered with the opponent's play and, after the opponent played, replaced his ball. Before the player addressed the ball, it moved. Since the ball was lifted and out of play after the loose impediments were removed, is the player penalized under Rule 18-2c?

A. No. The ball must be played as it lies. Once the ball has been lifted, the presumption inherent in the Rule that the removal of the loose impediments caused the ball to move is no longer valid.

18-2c/4 Ball in Hazard Moves After Loose Impediment Outside Hazard Moved

Q. A player's ball lies in a hazard. He moves a loose impediment which lies outside the hazard but is within one club-length of the ball. Before the player addresses the ball, it moves. Is the player penalized under Rule 18-2c?

A. No. Rule 18-2c does not apply since the ball was in a hazard.

If, however, the player caused the ball to move, he incurred a penalty stroke under Rule 18-2a and the ball must be replaced.

Ball in Hazard Moves When Loose Impediment Removed — See 13-4/15.

Another Decision relating to Rule 18-2c:

Competitor Seeks Help in Removal of Loose Impediment to Avoid Penalty — See 33-7/7.

18

18-3b/1 Ball Moved Accidentally by Opponent in Playing His Own Ball

Q. In singles match play, A's ball is lying close to B's. It is B's turn to play. Although B has the right under Rule 22 to require A to mark and lift his ball, he fails to do so. In making a stroke at his ball, B causes A's ball to move. What is the procedure?

A. B incurs a penalty of one stroke under Rule 18-3b for moving A's ball and A must replace his ball. If A's lie has been altered, Rule 20-3b applies.

Ball Moved by Stone Dislodged by Opponent's Stroke — See 18-1/8.

18-3b/2 Opponent's Stroke Disturbs Bushes Causing Player's Ball to Move

Q. In playing a stroke, an opponent disturbed some bushes, causing the player's ball to move. What is the ruling?

A. The opponent incurs a penalty stroke (Rule 18-3b) and the player must replace his ball.

18-3b/3 Ball Accidentally Stepped on by Opponent's Caddie

Q. The opponent's caddie accidentally stepped on the player's ball. What is the ruling?

A. The opponent incurs a one-stroke penalty (Rule 18-3b) unless the caddie was searching for the ball, in which case there would be no penalty — Rule 18-3a.

18-3b/4 Opponent's Caddie Lifts Player's Ball After Player Claims Another Ball

Q. In a match, the player finds a ball and claims it as his. The opponent's caddie then finds another ball and lifts it. It is subsequently discovered that the ball the opponent's caddie lifted was the player's ball. Should the opponent incur a penalty under Rule 18-3b?

A. No. Rule 18-3b does not contemplate an opponent moving a player's ball in such circumstances. The player must replace his ball, without penalty to anyone.

18-3b/5 Opponent's Caddie Lifts Player's Ball Which May or May Not Have Been Out of Bounds

Q. An opponent's caddie lifted the player's ball and informed the player that the ball was out of bounds.

The player claimed that his ball might have been in bounds. What is the ruling?

A. If the Committee establishes that the ball was in bounds, the opponent incurs a penalty stroke under Rule 18-3b and the player must replace his ball.

If the ball was out of bounds, the opponent incurs no penalty.

If the position of the ball cannot be established, the benefit of the doubt should be given to the player.

Other Decisions relating to Rule 18-3b:

Player Mistakenly Believing He Has Won Match Picks Up Opponent's Ball — See 2-4/4 and 2-4/17.

Ball Resting Against Flagstick; Putt Conceded and Ball Removed Before Player Can Remove Flagstick — See 17-4/2.

Ball Resting Against Flagstick Moves Away from Hole When Opponent Removes Flagstick — See 17-4/3.

Player's Ball Lifted by Opponent Without Authority — See 20-1/2.

Player's Ball Lifted by Opponent Without Authority; Player Lifts Ball-Marker, Claims Hole and Opponent Disputes Claim — See 20-1/3.

Caddie Shared by Members of Opposite Sides in Four-Ball Match Moves Ball — See 30/1.

Caddie Shared by Opponents' Side in Four-Ball Match Moves Player's Ball — See 30/2.

Player's Ball Lifted by Opponent Without Authority in Four-Ball Match — See 30-3f/10.

18-4/1 Competitor's Ball Played by Fellow-Competitor in Bunker Not Replaced

Q. In stroke play, A's ball in a bunker was played by his fellow-competitor, B. B failed to get the ball out of the bunker and then discovered he had played a wrong ball. A played his ball from the spot to which B had played it and then learned that he should have replaced his ball. What is the ruling?

A. Rule 18-4 required A to replace his ball. A incurred a penalty of two strokes for a breach of Rule 18-4 when he played a stroke with his ball from the spot to which it had been played by B.

B incurred no penalty. There is no penalty for playing a stroke with a wrong ball in a hazard.

18-4/2 Competitor's Ball Knocked Out of Bunker by Fellow-Competitor's Stroke at Own Ball

Q. In stroke play, B, in playing a stroke at his ball in a bunker, accidentally hits A's ball which was also in the bunker. Both balls come to rest outside the bunker. A plays his ball from the spot to which it has been moved by B's stroke. What is the ruling?

A. A was required to replace his ball in the bunker — Rule 18-4. A's breach of Rule 18-4 was a serious one and he should have been disqualified under Rule 20-7b unless the serious breach was rectified as prescribed in the Rule. B incurred no penalty — Rule 18-4.

Fellow-Competitor's Ball Knocked from Lip of Hole by Competitor Not Replaced — See 3-2/1.

18-4/3 Fellow-Competitor Lifts Competitor's Ball Conceding Next Stroke in Stroke Play Play-Off

Q. In a stroke play play-off, B picks up A's ball, conceding A a 4. B then holed a putt for a 3 to win the play-off. Is B subject to penalty for conceding a putt in stroke play?

A. B incurs no penalty — Rule 18-4. If B had not holed in 3 to win the play-off, A would have been obliged to replace his ball and hole out (Rule 18-4).

18

Other Decisions relating to Rule 18-4:

Ball Resting Against Flagstick Moves Away from Hole When Flagstick Removed by Fellow-Competitor — See 17-4/3.

Competitor's Ball Picked Up by Fellow-Competitor at Competitor's Request — See 18-2a/16.

Competitor's Ball Lifted Without Authority by Fellow-Competitor — See 20-1/4.

18-5/1 Ball Moved by Wrong Ball Played by Opponent

Q. In match play, an opponent plays a wrong ball from a bunker and the wrong ball knocks the player's ball into the hole. What is the ruling?

A. No penalty is incurred and the player must replace his ball — Rule 18-5.

18-5/2 Original Ball Struck by Provisional Ball

Q. A player's provisional ball played from the tee strikes and moves his original ball. What is the ruling?

A. There is no penalty. The original ball must be replaced — Rule 18-5.

Original Ball Strikes Second Ball or Vice Versa — See 3-3/7.

Provisional Ball Struck by Original Ball — See 19-5/5.

18-5/3 Competitor and Fellow-Competitor Unaware Ball Moved by Fellow-Competitor's Ball Until After Completion of Hole

Q. In stroke play, A then B play their second strokes to the green but, due to the contours of the green, they cannot see where their balls come to rest. Both competitors complete the hole from about 12 feet with two putts each. On their way to the next tee, it was established that A's ball had come to rest about one foot from the hole, but that B's ball in motion had struck A's ball and moved it.

(a) How should A proceed?

(b) If A decided not to take any action because the hole had been completed, how should the Committee rule if the facts of the case come to its attention:

(i) before the card was returned?

(ii) after the card was returned but before the competition was closed?

18

A. (a) If A is certain that a serious breach of Rule 18-5 has not occurred, he should take no further action — see first paragraph of Rule 20-7b. The score with the original ball would be A's score for the hole. In equity (Rule 1-4), A would incur no penalty because he did not know that he had played from a wrong place until after he had completed the hole.

If A believes that he may have committed a serious breach of Rule 18-5, then he should rectify the situation as prescribed in Rule 20-7b. If the Committee determines that A is not guilty of a serious breach of the Rules, then his score with the original ball counts. If the Committee determines that A is guilty of a serious breach of the Rules, the score with the second ball counts. In equity (Rule 1-4), no penalty is incurred in either case — see first paragraph above.

(b) (i) and (ii) The answer depends on whether or not the Committee determines that A is guilty of a serious breach of playing from a wrong place. In making that determination, the Committee must consider all the facts. If the Committee rules that a serious breach of Rule 18-5 has not occurred, the score with the original ball will be A's score for the hole in both cases and, in equity (Rule 1-4), he incurs no penalty.

If, however, the Committee determines that A has committed a serious breach of Rule 18-5, he is disqualified in both cases — see Rule 20-7b.

Player Unaware Ball Moved by Outside Agency Does Not Replace Ball — See 18-1/3.

Other Decisions relating to Rule 18-5:

Opponent's Ball Knocked Away by Player After Concession Moves Player's Ball — See 18-2a/18.

Ball Moved by Another Ball After Being Addressed — See 18-2b/11.

Competitor's Ball Played from Putting Green Moves Ball on Green Belonging to Competitor Playing in Another Group — See 19-5/2.

Rule 19. Ball in Motion Deflected or Stopped

Definitions

An *"outside agency"* is any agency not part of the match or, in stroke play, not part of the *competitor's side,* and includes a *referee,* a *marker,* an *observer* and a *forecaddie.* Neither wind nor water is an *outside agency.*

"Equipment" is anything used, worn or carried by or for the player except any ball he has played at the hole being played and any small object, such as a coin or a tee, when used to mark the position of a ball or the extent of an area in which a ball is to be dropped. *Equipment* includes a golf cart, whether or not motorized. If such a cart is shared by two or more players, the cart and everything in it are deemed to be the *equipment* of the player whose ball is involved except that, when the cart is being moved by one of the players sharing it, the cart and everything in it are deemed to be that player's *equipment.*

Note: A ball played at the hole being played is *equipment* when it has been lifted and not put back into play.

19-1. By Outside Agency

If a ball in motion is accidentally deflected or stopped by any *outside agency,* it is a *rub of the green,* no penalty is incurred and the ball shall be played as it lies except:

a. If a ball in motion after a *stroke* other than on the *putting green* comes to rest in or on any moving or animate *outside agency,* the player shall, *through the green* or in a *hazard*, drop the ball, or on the *putting green* place the ball, as near as possible to the spot where the *outside agency* was when the ball came to rest in or on it, and

b. If a ball in motion after a *stroke* on the *putting green* is deflected or stopped by, or comes to rest in or on, any moving or animate *outside agency* except a worm or an insect, the *stroke* shall be cancelled, the ball replaced and the *stroke* replayed.

If the ball is not immediately recoverable, another ball may be substituted.

(Player's ball deflected or stopped by another ball — see Rule 19-5.)

Note: If the *referee* or the *Committee* determines that a player's ball has been purposely deflected or stopped by an *outside agency*, Rule 1-4 applies to the player. If the *outside agency* is a *fellow-competitor* or his *caddie*, Rule 1-2 applies to the *fellow-competitor.*

19-2. By Player, Partner, Caddie or Equipment

a. Match Play

If a player's ball is accidentally deflected or stopped by himself, his *partner* or either of their *caddies* or *equipment*, he shall lose the hole.

19

b. Stroke Play

If a *competitor*'s ball is accidentally deflected or stopped by himself, his *partner* or either of their *caddies* or *equipment*, the *competitor* shall incur a penalty of two strokes. The ball shall be played as it lies, except when it comes to rest in or on the *competitor's*, his *partner*'s or either of their *caddies'* clothes or *equipment*, in which case the *competitor* shall *through the green* or in a *hazard* drop the ball, or on the *putting green* place the ball, as near as possible to where the article was when the ball came to rest in or on it.

Exception: Dropped ball — see Rule 20-2a.

(Ball purposely deflected or stopped by player, *partner* or *caddie* — see Rule 1-2.)

19-3. By Opponent, Caddie or Equipment in Match Play

If a player's ball is accidentally deflected or stopped by an opponent, his *caddie* or his *equipment,* no penalty is incurred. The player may play the ball as it lies or, before another *stroke* is played by either *side,* cancel the *stroke* and play a ball without penalty as nearly as possible at the spot from which the original ball was last played (see Rule 20-5).

If the ball has come to rest in or on the opponent's or his *caddie's* clothes or *equipment,* the player may *through the green* or in a *hazard* drop the ball, or on the *putting green* place the ball, as near as possible to where the article was when the ball came to rest in or on it.

Exception: Ball striking person attending *flagstick* — see Rule 17-3b.

(Ball purposely deflected or stopped by opponent or *caddie* — see Rule 1-2.)

19-4. By Fellow-Competitor, Caddie or Equipment in Stroke Play

See Rule 19-1 regarding ball deflected by *outside agency.*

19-5. By Another Ball

a. At Rest

If a player's ball in motion after a *stroke* is deflected or stopped by a *ball in play* and at rest, the player shall play his ball as it lies. In match play, no penalty is incurred. In stroke play, there is no penalty unless both balls lay on the *putting green* prior to the *stroke,* in which case the player incurs a penalty of two strokes.

b. In Motion

If a player's ball in motion after a *stroke* is deflected or stopped by another ball in motion after a *stroke,* the player shall play his ball as it lies. There is no penalty unless the player was in breach of Rule 16-1f, in which case he shall incur the penalty for breach of that Rule.

Exception: If the player's ball is in motion after a *stroke* on the *putting green* and the other ball in motion is an *outside agency* — see Rule 19-1b.

PENALTY FOR BREACH OF RULE:
Match play — Loss of hole;
Stroke play — Two strokes.

19/1 Ball Deflected or Stopped by Golf Cart Shared by Two Players

Under the Definition of "Equipment," equipment includes a golf cart, whether or not motorized. If two players share a golf cart, the cart and everything in it are deemed to be the equipment of the player whose ball is involved; except that, when the cart is being moved by one of the players, the cart and everything in it are deemed to be that player's equipment.

Thus, for example, in a singles match, if A and B are sharing a cart and A's ball in motion is deflected or stopped by the cart, A loses the hole (Rule 19-2a) unless the cart is being driven or pulled by B when the incident occurs. If B is driving or pulling the cart, there is no penalty, and A would have the option of playing his ball as it lies or replaying the stroke (Rule 19-3).

19/2 Status of Person in Shared Golf Cart

Q. The Definition of "Equipment" refers to a shared cart and everything in it as being equipment of the player whose ball is involved or, if applicable, the player moving the cart. Does the phrase "and everything in it" include any person in the cart?

A. Yes. (New)

Local Rule for Events in Which Motorized Golf Carts Permitted — See 33-8/4.

19-1/1 Ball Deflected by Direction Post

Q. A ball is deflected by a direction post. What is the ruling?

A. It is a rub of the green and the ball must be played as it lies, without penalty.

19-1/2 Player's Ball Deflected by Stroke of Player in Another Group

Q. A hit his ball over onto another fairway where, before it came to rest, it was struck by X in the course of striking his own ball. X's ball went 20 yards. A's ball could not be found. What is the ruling?

A. Each player was an outside agency in relation to the other.

Under Rule 19-1, A would have been obliged to play his ball as it lay, without penalty, if it had been found. Since it was not found, A must proceed under Rule 27-1, incurring a penalty of stroke and distance.

X must play his ball as it lies, without penalty.

Ball Played from Spot Where Original Ball Deflected Out of Bounds by Maintenance Vehicle — See 20-7/1.

19-1/3 Ball Played from Putting Green Deflected by Moving Outside Agency; Stroke Not Replayed

Q. In stroke play, a competitor putts and his ball is deflected by a moving outside agency other than a worm or an insect. The competitor did not replay the stroke as required by Rule 19-1b, holed out and then played from the next tee. What is the ruling?

A. The stroke that was deflected by the outside agency does not count in the competitor's score. When the competitor failed to replay the stroke he played from a wrong place. If the breach was a serious one, he is disqualified — Rule 20-7b. Otherwise, the score with the original ball counts and he incurs a penalty of two strokes for breach of Rule 19.

19-1/4 Ball Played from Putting Green Deliberately Deflected or Stopped by Spectator

Q. A player plays a stroke from the putting green and,

while the ball is still in motion, a spectator deliberately deflects or stops it. What is the ruling?

A. The Committee must act in equity — see Note under Rule 19-1. The stroke should be cancelled, the ball replaced and the stroke replayed, without penalty.

19-1/4.1 Ball Deliberately Deflected or Stopped Through the Green by Spectator

Q. A player overshoots a green. A spectator (X) who is standing behind the green deliberately deflects or stops the ball. According to the Note under Rule 19-1, equity (Rule 1-4) applies. What is the equitable procedure in this case?

A. In a case where the ball might have come to rest where X was situated if he had not deliberately deflected or stopped it, the player should be required to drop the ball at the spot where X was situated. For example, if another spectator (Y) had been behind X, the ball might have struck Y, if X had avoided it, and come to rest where X was situated.

If there is no question that the ball would have come to rest somewhere else if X had not deflected or stopped it, the Committee must make a judgment as to where the ball would have come to rest, giving the player the benefit of any doubt. For example, if no person or object had been behind X and without any doubt the ball would have come to rest either in a lateral water hazard behind the green or in the rough just short of the hazard, the Committee should require the player to drop the ball in the rough just short of the hazard.

19-1/5 Ball Deliberately Deflected or Stopped on Putting Green by Fellow-Competitor

Q. At the last hole of a stroke play event, A has a putt to beat B by one stroke. A putts and B, seeing that A's ball might go into the hole, deliberately deflects it. What is the ruling?

A. In equity (Rule 1-4), A should replay his stroke, without penalty — see Note under Rule 19-1. B should be disqualified for a serious breach of Rule 1-2 (Exerting Influence on Ball).

19-1/6 Ball Picked Up or Deflected by Dog on Putting Green After Stroke from Off Green

Q. A ball played from off the green was about a foot from the hole and still in motion when it was moved by a dog to a spot about ten feet from the hole. The ball was either deflected by the dog or the dog picked it up, ran with it and dropped it. What is the ruling?

A. If the ball was deflected, it would be played as it lay, without penalty, from the spot to which it was moved by the dog — Rule 19-1.

If the dog picked up the ball, the player should have placed the ball, without penalty, as near as possible to the spot where the original ball was when the dog picked it up — Rule 19-1a.

19-1/7 Ball Picked Up or Deflected by Dog on Putting Green After Stroke on Green

Q. A player plays a stroke on the putting green and, while the ball is still in motion, it is picked up and carried away, or is deflected, by a dog. What is the ruling?

A. In either case, the stroke is canceled and the ball must be replaced — Rule 19-1b.

[19-1/8 Reserved]

19

[19-1/9 Reserved]

19-1/10 Ball in Motion After Stroke on Putting Green Deflected by Ball Played at Another Hole

Q. A player plays a stroke on a putting green. While the ball is in motion, a ball played at another hole strikes the player's ball and knocks it into a bunker. What is the ruling?

A. Since the player's ball was deflected by a moving outside agency, the player's stroke is cancelled and he must replace his ball — Rule 19-1b. Rule 19-5b does not apply — see Exception under that Rule.

Ball Strikes Hole-Liner Pulled Out with Flagstick — See 17/8.

Attendant Removes Flagstick Whereupon Knob Falls from Top of Flagstick and Deflects Ball — See 17/9.

19-2/1 Ball Stopped by Player's Foot Moves When Foot Removed

Q. A player making a stroke on the bank of a bunker hits the ball to the top of the bank. The ball then rolls back down the bank and comes to rest against the player's foot. The player removes his foot and the ball rolls into his footprint. What is the ruling?

A. In match play, the player loses the hole (Rule 19-2a).

In stroke play, the player incurs a penalty of two strokes (Rule 19-2b) and must replace the ball on the spot at which it came to rest against his foot. A further penalty under Rule 18-2a (Ball at Rest Moved by Player) would not be appropriate in the circumstances.

19-2/1.5 Ball Moves Prior to Address and Is Accidentally Stopped by Player's Club; Player Removes Club and Ball Rolls Away

Q. A player's ball lies on a steep slope through the green. The player takes his stance but, fearing the ball might move, does not ground his club and so has not addressed the ball. The ball rolls backwards and is stopped accidentally by the player's club. The player then removes his club and the ball rolls farther down the slope. Is the player subject to penalty under Rule 19-2?

A. Yes, and in stroke play the ball must be replaced on the spot at which it was stopped. A further penalty under Rule 18-2a (Ball at Rest Moved by Player) would not be appropriate in the circumstances.

Ball Moves After Address and Is Stopped by Player's Club — See 18-2b/12.

19-2/2 Player's Ball Strikes Own Caddie and Comes to Rest Out of Bounds

Q. A player's ball accidentally strikes his caddie, who is standing in bounds, and the ball comes to rest out of bounds. What is the ruling?

A. In match play, the player loses the hole — Rule 19-2a.

In stroke play, the player incurs a penalty of two strokes (Rule 19-2b) and, since the ball lies out of bounds, he must proceed under Rule 27-1, incurring another penalty stroke.

19-2/3 Player's Ball Strikes Own Caddie Standing Out of Bounds and Comes to Rest on Course

Q. A player's ball accidentally strikes his caddie standing out of bounds and comes to rest in bounds. What is the ruling?

A. In match play, the player loses the hole — Rule 19-2a.

In stroke play, the player incurs a penalty of two strokes and, since the ball came to rest in bounds, it is in play — Rule 19-2b.

19-2/4 Player's Ball Strikes Own Caddie Standing Out of Bounds and Comes to Rest Out of Bounds

Q. A player's ball accidentally strikes his caddie standing out of bounds and comes to rest out of bounds. What is the ruling?

A. In match play, the player loses the hole — Rule 19-2a.

In stroke play, the player incurs a penalty of two strokes (Rule 19-2b) and, since the ball lies out of bounds, he must proceed under Rule 27-1, incurring another penalty stroke.

Other Decisions relating to Rule 19-2:

Ball Falls on Club Face After Stroke and Sticks to Mud Thereon — See 14-4/1.

Ball Strikes Pipeline and on Rebound Is Deflected by Face of Club — See 14-4/2.

Caddie Stops Dropped Ball Before It Comes to Rest; When Penalty Incurred — See 20-2c/4.

19-2/5 Ball Deflected or Stopped by Clubs Belonging to Different Side But Carried in Same Bag

Q. A had his bag of clubs on a golf cart. B had only a few clubs which A carried for him in his bag. B played a stroke which was deflected by the clubs. What is the ruling?

A. Under the principle in the Definition of "Caddie," the clubs should be deemed B's equipment.

In match play, B lost the hole — Rule 19-2a.

In stroke play, B incurred a penalty of two strokes and must play his ball as it lies — Rule 19-2b.

19-2/6 Ball Deflected or Stopped by Player's Golf Cart Being Pulled by Opponent or Fellow-Competitor

Q. A player's ball strikes his own golf cart while it is being pulled by an opponent or a fellow-competitor. What is the ruling?

A. Since the player is not sharing the cart with any other player, it remains his equipment even when it is being pulled by an opponent or a fellow-competitor.

If the player was aware that his cart was being pulled by an opponent or a fellow-competitor, in match play the player loses the hole — Rule 19-2a. In stroke play, he incurs a penalty of two strokes and must play the ball as it lies — Rule 19-2b.

But if he was not aware, in equity (Rule 1-4) no penalty is incurred, and the ball must be played as it lies.

19-2/7 Ball Strikes Competitor's Golf Bag and Then His Caddie

Q. In stroke play, a competitor's ball strikes his golf bag lying on the ground and then bounces off it and hits his caddie. Is the penalty two strokes or four strokes?

A. Two strokes — Rule 19-2b.

Ball Popped Up Swung at in Disgust and Hit — See 14/6.

19-3/1 Ball Accidentally Strikes Opponent Standing Out of Bounds and Comes to Rest Out of Bounds

Q. In match play, a player's ball accidentally strikes his opponent, who is standing out of bounds. The ball comes to rest out of bounds. What is the ruling?

A. There is no penalty and the player is entitled to replay the stroke — Rule 19-3.

Tee Marking Position of Player's Ball Deflects Opponent's Ball — See 20-1/17.

19-3/2 Dropped Ball Accidentally Deflected by Opponent or His Caddie

Q. In match play, a player drops his ball under a Rule and the ball is accidentally deflected by the opponent or his caddie. What is the ruling?

A. The player has the option of playing his ball as it lies or re-dropping it — Rule 19-3.

19-3/3 Player's Ball Strikes Opponent's or Fellow-Competitor's Trolley Then Own Trolley

Q. A player's ball strikes his opponent's or fellow-competitor's trolley and then strikes his own trolley. What is the ruling?

A. In match play, because the ball first struck his opponent's equipment the player may replay the stroke, without penalty, regardless of what happens thereafter to the ball (Rule 19-3). The player may not play the ball as it lies, because after striking his opponent's equipment but before coming to rest, his ball struck his own equipment, the penalty for which is loss of hole (Rule 19-2a).

In stroke play, although the ball first struck a fellow-competitor's equipment, the competitor incurs a penalty of two strokes and must play the ball as it lies (Rules 19-4, -1, -2).

Decisions Relating to Rule 19-4:

Ball Deliberately Deflected or Stopped on Putting Green by Fellow-Competitor — See 19-1/5.

Player's Ball Strikes Opponent's or Fellow-Competitor's Trolley Then Own Trolley — See 19-3/3.

19-5/1 Player Lifts His Ball on Putting Green and Sets It Aside; Opponent's or Fellow-Competitor's Ball Played from Green Subsequently Strikes Player's Ball

Q. B lifts his ball on the putting green and sets it aside elsewhere on the green. A then putts and his ball is deflected or stopped by B's ball. What is the ruling?

A. Since A's ball was deflected by B's equipment (see Note under Definition of "Equipment"), Rules 19-3 and -4 apply.

In match play, A incurs no penalty and has the option of playing his ball as it lies or cancelling and replaying the stroke — Rule 19-3.

In stroke play, A incurs no penalty and must play his
19 ball as it lies — Rules 19-4 and -1.

In either form of play, B must replace his ball on the spot from which it was lifted — Rule 20-3a.

Rule 19-5a does not apply because B's ball was not in play.

Explanation of "Any Ball He Has Played" — See 18/7.

[19-5/1.5 Reserved]

19-5/1.7 Ball Dropped on Putting Green by Opponent or Fellow-Competitor Falls on Player's Moving Ball

Q. A plays a stroke on the putting green. B, A's opponent or a fellow-competitor, accidentally drops his ball, which he had lifted, and it falls on A's ball which is still in motion. What is the ruling?

A. In match play, since A's ball was deflected by B's equipment (see Note under Definition of "Equipment"), Rule 19-3 applies. A has the option of playing his ball as it lies or cancelling and replaying the stroke. Neither A nor B incurs a penalty.

In stroke play, A's ball was deflected by a moving outside agency. Therefore, A must cancel and replay his stroke, without penalty, under Rule 19-1b. B incurs no penalty.

In either form of play, B must replace his ball on the spot from which it was lifted — Rule 20-3a.

Rule 19-5b does not apply because B's ball was not in motion after a stroke.

Explanation of "Any Ball He Has Played" — See 18/7.

19-5/2 Competitor's Ball Played from Putting Green Strikes Ball on Green Belonging to Competitor Playing in Another Group

Q. In stroke play, C and D are playing together. A and B are playing immediately behind C and D. C's ball lies on the putting green and, since D is searching for his ball, C and D invite A and B to play through. Subsequently, A putts and his ball strikes C's ball. What is the ruling?

A. A incurs a penalty of two strokes and must play his ball as it lies — Rule 19-5. C must replace his ball without penalty — Rule 18-5.

19-5/3 Competitor's Ball Played on Putting Green Deflected by Balls of Two Fellow-Competitors

Q. In stroke play, a competitor plays a stroke on the putting green. His ball strikes a fellow-competitor's ball and is deflected. Before the competitor's ball comes to rest it strikes another fellow-competitor's ball. Under Rule 19-5, is the competitor penalized two strokes or four strokes?

A. Two strokes.

19-5/4 Competitor's Ball Played from Putting Green Touches But Does Not Move Ball of Fellow-Competitor Lying on Green

Q. In stroke play, A putts and his ball comes to rest touching B's ball. B's ball did not move nor did B's ball prevent A's ball from rolling any farther. What is the ruling?

A. Since A's ball was not deflected or stopped by B's ball, A incurs no penalty under Rule 19-5 or any other Rule. However, if there is any doubt as to whether B's ball moved or prevented A's ball from rolling any farther, it should be resolved against A.

19-5/5 Provisional Ball Struck by Original Ball

Q. A player's original ball strikes and moves his provisional ball. What is the ruling?

A. Rule 19-5 does not apply because the provisional ball was not in play. Rule 19-2 does not apply because the provisional ball is not the equipment of the player — see Decision 18/7. In equity (Rule 1-4) and by analogy to Rule 19-5a, the player shall play the ball as it lies and no penalty is incurred except that, in stroke play, if both balls lay on the putting green prior to the stroke, the player incurs a penalty of two strokes.

Other Decisions relating to Rule 19-5:

Original Ball Strikes Second Ball or Vice Versa — See 3-3/7.

Competitor Not Given Opportunity to Lift Ball Assisting Fellow-Competitor; Fellow-Competitor's Ball Strikes Competitor's Ball — See 3-4/1.

Explanation of "Any Ball He Has Played" — See 18/7.

Player's Ball Moved by Ball Accidentally Dropped by Opponent or Fellow-Competitor — See 18/7.5.

Provisional Ball Strikes Original Ball — See 18-5/2.

Competitor's Ball Moved by Fellow-Competitor's Ball — See 18-5/3.

RELIEF SITUATIONS AND PROCEDURE

Rule 20. Lifting, Dropping and Placing; Playing from Wrong Place

20-1. Lifting and Marking

A ball to be lifted under the *Rules* may be lifted by the player, his *partner* or another person authorized by the player. In any such case, the player shall be responsible for any breach of the Rules.

The position of the ball shall be marked before it is lifted under a *Rule* which requires it to be replaced. If it is not marked, the player shall incur a penalty of one stroke and the ball shall be replaced. If it is not replaced, the player shall incur the general penalty for breach of this Rule but no additional penalty under Rule 20-1 shall be applied.

If a ball or ball-marker is accidentally *moved* in the process of lifting the ball under a *Rule* or marking its position, the ball or the ball-marker shall be replaced. There is no penalty provided the movement of the ball or the ball-marker is directly attributable to the specific act of marking the position of or lifting the ball. Otherwise, the player shall incur a *penalty stroke* under this Rule or Rule 18-2a.

Exception: If a player incurs a penalty for failing to act in accordance with Rule 5-3 or 12-2, no additional penalty under Rule 20-1 shall be applied.

Note: The position of a ball to be lifted should be marked by placing a ball-marker, a small coin or other similar object immediately behind the ball. If the ball-marker interferes with the play, *stance* or *stroke* of another player, it should be placed one or more clubhead-lengths to one side.

20-2. Dropping and Re-dropping

a. By Whom and How

A ball to be dropped under the *Rules* shall be dropped by the player himself. He shall stand erect, hold the ball at shoulder height and arm's length and drop it. If a ball is dropped by any other person or in any other manner and the error is not corrected as provided in Rule 20-6, the player shall incur a *penalty stroke.*

If the ball touches the player, his *partner,* either of their *caddies* or their *equipment* before or after it strikes a part of the *course,* the ball shall be re-dropped, without penalty. There is no limit to the number of times a ball shall be re-dropped in such circumstances.

(Taking action to influence position or movement of ball — see Rule 1-2.)

b. Where to Drop

When a ball is to be dropped as near as possible to a specific spot, it shall be dropped not nearer the *hole* than the specific spot which, if it is not precisely known to the player, shall be estimated.

A ball when dropped must first strike a part of the *course* where the applicable *Rule* requires it to be dropped. If it is not so dropped, Rules 20-6 and -7 apply.

c. When to Re-Drop

A dropped ball shall be re-dropped without penalty if it:

(i) rolls into and comes to rest in a *hazard;*
(ii) rolls out of and comes to rest outside a *hazard;*

(iii) rolls onto and comes to rest on a *putting green;*
(iv) rolls and comes to rest *out of bounds;*
(v) rolls to and comes to rest in a position where there is interference by the condition from which relief was taken under Rule 24-2 (immovable *obstruction*), Rule 25-1 (*abnormal ground conditions*), Rule 25-3 (*wrong putting green*) or a Local Rule (Rule 33-8a), or rolls back into the pitch-mark from which it was lifted under Rule 25-2 (embedded ball);
(vi) rolls and comes to rest more than two club-lengths from where it first struck a part of the *course;*
(vii) rolls and comes to rest nearer the *hole* than:
  a. its original position or estimated position (see Rule 20-2b) unless otherwise permitted by the *Rules*; or
  b. the *nearest point of relief* or maximum available relief (Rule 24-2, 25-1 or 25-3); or
  c. the point where the original ball last crossed the margin of the *water hazard* or *lateral water hazard* (Rule 26-1).

If the ball when re-dropped rolls into any position listed above, it shall be placed as near as possible to the spot where it first struck a part of the *course* when re-dropped.

If a ball to be re-dropped or placed under this Rule is not immediately recoverable, another ball may be substituted.

Note: If a ball when dropped or re-dropped comes to rest and subsequently *moves,* the ball shall be played as it lies, unless the provisions of any other *Rule* apply.

20-3. Placing and Replacing

a. By Whom and Where

A ball to be placed under the *Rules* shall be placed by the player or his *partner.* If a ball is to be replaced, the player, his *partner* or the person who lifted or *moved* it shall place it on the spot from which it was lifted or *moved.* In any such case, the player shall be responsible for any breach of the *Rules*.

If a ball or ball-marker is accidentally *moved* in the process of placing or replacing the ball, the ball or the ball-marker shall be replaced. There is no penalty provided the movement of the ball or the ball-marker is directly attributable to the specific act of placing or replacing the ball or removing the ball-marker. Otherwise, the player shall incur a *penalty stroke* under Rule 18-2a or 20-1.

b. Lie of Ball to Be Placed or Replaced Altered

If the original lie of a ball to be placed or replaced has been altered:

(i) except in a *hazard*, the ball shall be placed in the nearest lie most similar to the original lie which is not more than one club-length from the original lie, not nearer the *hole* and not in a *hazard;*

(ii) in a *water hazard*, the ball shall be placed in accordance with Clause (i) above, except that the ball must be placed in the *water hazard;*

(iii) in a *bunker*, the original lie shall be recreated as nearly as possible and the ball shall be placed in that lie.

c. Spot Not Determinable

If it is impossible to determine the spot where the ball is to be placed or replaced:

20

(i) *through the green*, the ball shall be dropped as near as possible to the place where it lay but not in a *hazard* or on a *putting green;*

(ii) in a *hazard*, the ball shall be dropped in the *hazard* as near as possible to the place where it lay;

(iii) on the *putting green*, the ball shall be placed as near as possible to the place where it lay but not in a *hazard*.

d. Ball Fails to Come to Rest on Spot

If a ball when placed fails to come to rest on the spot on which it was placed, it shall be replaced without penalty.

If it still fails to come to rest on that spot:

(i) except in a *hazard*, it shall be placed at the nearest spot where it can be placed at rest which is not nearer the *hole* and not in a *hazard;*

(ii) in a *hazard*, it shall be placed in the *hazard* at the nearest spot where it can be placed at rest which is not nearer the *hole*.

If a ball when placed comes to rest on the spot on which it is placed, and it subsequently *moves*, there is no penalty and the ball shall be played as it lies, unless the provisions of any other *Rule* apply.

PENALTY FOR BREACH OF RULE 20-1, -2 or -3: Match play — Loss of hole;
Stroke play — Two strokes.

20-4. When Ball Dropped or Placed Is in Play

If the player's *ball in play* has been lifted, it is again in play when dropped or placed.

A substituted ball becomes the *ball in play* when it has been dropped or placed.

(Ball incorrectly substituted — see Rule 15-1.)

(Lifting ball incorrectly substituted, dropped or placed — see Rule 20-6.)

20-5. Playing Next Stroke from Where Previous Stroke Played

When, under the *Rules*, a player elects or is required to play his next *stroke* from where a previous *stroke* was played, he shall proceed as follows: if the *stroke* is to be played from the *teeing ground*, the ball to be played shall be played from anywhere within the *teeing ground* and may be teed; if the *stroke* is to be played from *through the green* or a *hazard*, it shall be dropped; if the stroke is to be played on the *putting green*, it shall be placed.

PENALTY FOR BREACH OF RULE 20-5:
Match play — Loss of hole;
Stroke play — Two strokes.

20-6. Lifting Ball Incorrectly Substituted, Dropped or Placed

A ball incorrectly substituted, dropped or placed in a wrong place or otherwise not in accordance with the *Rules* but not played may be lifted, without penalty, and the player shall then proceed correctly.

20-7. Playing from Wrong Place

For a ball played from outside the *teeing ground* or from a wrong *teeing ground* — see Rule 11-4 and -5.

a. Match Play

If a player plays a *stroke* with a ball which has been dropped or placed in a wrong place, he shall lose the hole.

b. Stroke Play

If a *competitor* plays a *stroke* with his *ball in play* (i) which has been dropped or placed in a wrong place or (ii) which has been *moved* and not replaced in a case where the *Rules* require replacement, he shall, provided a serious breach has not occurred, incur the penalty prescribed by the applicable *Rule* and play out the hole with the ball.

If, after playing from a wrong place, a *competitor* becomes aware of that fact and believes that a serious breach may be involved, he may, pro-
20 vided he has not played a *stroke* from the next *teeing ground* or, in the case of the last hole of the round, left the *putting green*, declare that he will play out the hole with a second ball dropped or placed in accordance with the *Rules*. The *competitor* shall report the facts to the *Committee* before returning his score card; if he fails to do so, he shall be disqualified. The *Committee* shall determine whether a serious breach of the Rule occurred. If so, the score with the second ball shall count and the *competitor* shall add two *penalty strokes* to his score with that ball.

If a serious breach has occurred and the *competitor* has failed to correct it as prescribed above, he shall be disqualified.

Note: If a *competitor* plays a second ball, *penalty strokes* incurred solely by playing the ball ruled not to count and *strokes* subsequently taken with that ball shall be disregarded.

20/1 Club to Be Used in Measuring

Q. A player, taking relief under a Rule, uses his driver to measure the one club-length or two club-lengths prescribed in the relevant Rule. He drops a ball correctly and the ball rolls less than two driver-lengths, but more than two putter-lengths, from where the ball first struck a part of the course when dropped.

Under Rule 20-2c, a dropped ball must be re-dropped if it rolls more than two club-lengths. If the ball comes to rest in a poor lie, may the player opt to use his putter to measure the distance his ball has rolled, in which case he would re-drop under Rule 20-2c and escape the poor lie?

A. No. The player must continue to use the club he originally used for measuring for all measuring in a given situation. (Revised)

Measuring Club-Lengths — See 20-2b/2.

20/2 Borrowing Club for Measuring Purposes

For the purpose of measuring, a player may use any club he has selected for that round (Rule 4-4). If a player borrows a club to measure with, drops the ball in that area and plays it, he incurs no penalty if the spot on which the ball was dropped could have been reached with one of the player's own clubs selected for the round. If he could not have reached that spot by measuring with one of his own clubs, he incurs the penalty under the applicable Rule for playing from a wrong place (see Rule 20-7). (New)

Borrowing Partner's Putter — See 4-4b/1.

20-1/0.5 Whether Player Himself Must Lift Ball

Q. Rule 20-1 states: "A ball to be lifted under the Rules may be lifted by the player, his partner or another person authorized by the player." On the other hand, other Rules, *e.g.*, Rules 24-2b (i) and 25-1b (i), state that the player shall lift the ball. Does Rule 20-1 override other Rules which imply that the player himself must lift the ball?

A. Yes.

20-1/1 Ball Lifted from Putting Green in Mistaken Belief It Is Wrong Ball

Q. A player, mistakenly believing the ball he has played onto a putting green is a wrong ball, picks the ball up without marking its position. He then discovers that the ball is his ball in play. What is the ruling?

A. The player incurs a penalty stroke and he must replace his ball (Rule 20-1).

20-1/2 Player's Ball Lifted by Opponent Without Authority

Q. In a match between A and B, B, without A's authority, marked the position of, and lifted, A's ball on the putting green. Is B subject to penalty?

A. Yes. Under Rule 20-1, a player's ball may be lifted by his opponent only with the authority of the player. Since B was not entitled to lift A's ball, B incurred a penalty stroke — Rule 18-3b.

Player's Ball Lifted Without Authority by Opponent in Four-Ball Match — See 30-3f/10.

Other Decisions relating to Rule 20-1:

Player Lifts Ball in Mistaken Belief That Next Stroke Conceded — See 2-4/3.

Player Concedes Match Due to Misconception as to Opponent's Score at Last Hole and Picks Up Ball — See 2-4/14.

Player Lifts Ball, Sets It Aside and Plays It from Where Set Aside — See 15/4.

Ball Resting Against Flagstick Lifted Before Being Holed — See 17-4/1.

Player's Ball Resting Against Flagstick Lifted Before Being Holed; Others in Four-Ball Match Pick Up Mistakenly Believing Player Won Hole — See 30-3f/3.

Ball Putted from Wrong Place Lifted and Putted from Right Place — See 20-7b/2.

Caddie Lifts Ball in Water Hazard Without Player's Authority — See 26-1/9.

20-1/3 Ball Marked and Lifted by Opponent Without Player's Authority; Player Lifts Ball-Marker, Claims Hole and Opponent Disputes Claim

Q. In a match, B marks the position of A's ball and lifts it without A's authority. B holes out. A picks up the ball-marker with which B had marked the position of his (A's) ball and claims the hole. B disputes the claim. What is the ruling?

A. B incurs a penalty stroke — Rule 18-3b — for lifting A's ball without authority. A incurs a penalty stroke for lifting the ball-marker (Rule 20-1). A must replace his ball and hole out; otherwise, A loses the hole.

20-1/4 Competitor's Ball Lifted Without Authority by Fellow-Competitor

Q. In stroke play, a fellow-competitor lifts a competitor's ball on the putting green without the authority of the competitor. Such action is contrary to Rule 20-1. What is the ruling?

A. There is no penalty, but the competitor must replace the ball — Rule 18-4.

Competitor Who Lifts His Ball and Fellow-Competitor's Ball Inadvertently Exchanges Balls When Replacing Them — See 15-1/9.

Fellow-Competitor Lifts Competitor's Ball and Sets It Aside; Competitor Plays Ball from Where Set Aside — See 15-3/3.

20-1/5 Competitor's Ball Lifted Without Authority by Fellow-Competitor's Caddie Who Subsequently Substitutes Another Ball Which Competitor Plays

Q. A competitor's ball lying on the putting green is lifted by a fellow-competitor's caddie without the authority of the competitor. Subsequently, the fellow-competitor's caddie by mistake substitutes another ball and the competitor plays it. The error is then discovered. What is the ruling?

A. When a competitor authorizes another person to lift his ball, the competitor is responsible for any breach of the Rules (Rule 20-1). The converse is generally true, *i.e.*, the competitor is not responsible for a breach of a

Rule caused by the unauthorized lifting of his ball. Thus, in this case, the competitor should not be penalized under Rule 15-1. The competitor should hole out with the substituted ball, without penalty.

Player Mistakenly Substitutes Another Ball on Putting Green; Error Discovered Before Stroke Played — See 15-1/7.

20-1/5.5 Ball-Marker Moved Accidentally by Player

Q. A player marked the position of his ball on the putting green and lifted the ball. When it was the player's turn to play, he could not find his ball-marker. Subsequently, he found the ball-marker stuck to the sole of his shoe. He concluded that he had accidentally stepped on it while assisting his partner in lining up a putt. What is the ruling?

A. The player incurs a penalty stroke under Rule 20-1 which requires that the position of a ball be marked before it is lifted, and contemplates that the ball-marker will remain in position until the ball is replaced. The player must place the ball as near as possible to its original position but not nearer the hole — Rule 20-3c.

Under the last paragraph of Rule 20-1, a player is exempt from penalty if his ball-marker is accidentally moved in the process of lifting the ball or marking its position. In this case the ball-marker was not moved during such process.

20-1/6 Ball-Marker Moved Accidentally by Player in Process of Marking Position of Ball

Q. A player marked the position of his ball with a coin, lifted the ball and pressed down the coin with the sole of his putter. He walked to the edge of the green and then noticed that the coin had stuck to the sole of the putter. What is the ruling?

A. In this case, the movement of the ball-marker was directly attributable to the specific act of marking the position of the ball.

Accordingly, no penalty is incurred and the ball or the ball-marker must be replaced. If the spot where the ball or ball-marker lay is not known, it must be placed as near as possible to where it lay but not nearer the hole (Rule 20-3c).

20-1/7 Ball-Marker Moved by Opponent's Caddie Accidentally

Q. A player's caddie accidentally kicked his opponent's ball-marker closer to the hole. What is the ruling?

A. In equity (Rule 1-4), the ball-marker should have been replaced as near as possible to the spot where it lay and the player should incur a penalty of one stroke.

Whether Lifting Opponent's Ball-Marker Is Concession of Next Stroke — See 2-4/5.

20-1/8 Ball-Marker Lifted by Player Who Mistakenly Believes He Has Won Hole

Q. A player, mistakenly believing he has won a hole, picks up his ball-marker. What is the ruling?

A. The player incurs a one-stroke penalty — Rule 20-1 — and must replace his ball.

Wrong Information Causes Opponent to Lift His Ball-Marker — See 9-2/5.

Player Who Walks Off Green Under Mistaken Impression Partner Halved Hole Returns and Putts for Half — See 30/4.

20-1/9 Ball-Marker Lifted by Outside Agency

Q. A marked the position of his ball on the putting green while a following match or group was playing through. After the following match or group had played through, A could not find his ball-marker. It apparently had been lifted by one of the players playing through. What is the ruling? 20

A. Under Rule 20-3c, A must place his ball as near as possible to where it lay on the green.

20-1/10 Ball-Marker Moved Off Green by Wind or Casual Water While Play Suspended

Q. While play is suspended due to a rainstorm, a player's ball-marker, which was made of a light- weight material, is moved off a putting green by wind or casual water. What is the procedure?

A. Under Rule 6-8d(iii), the player must place a ball or ball-marker on the spot from which it was moved. If this spot is not determinable, Rule 20-3c would apply.

The fact that the player used a light-weight ball-marker does not affect the result — see Decision 20-1/18. (Revised)

Ball Moved by Wind or Casual Water While Play Suspended — See 18-1/11.

20-1/10.5 Ball-Marker Moved by Wind or Casual Water During Stipulated Round

Q. During a stipulated round, a player marked the position of and lifted his ball under a Rule. Prior to the player replacing his ball, wind or casual water moved his ball-marker. What is the procedure?

A. The ball or ball-marker must be replaced without penalty. If a ball has been lifted under a Rule which requires it to be replaced, it must be placed on the spot from which it was lifted (Rule 20-3a). (New)

20-1/11 Ball-Marker in Position to Assist Another Player

Q. A player marks the position of his ball on the putting green and the ball-marker is so located that it might be of assistance to the opponent or a fellow-competitor in lining up his putt. Accordingly, the player prepares to move his ball-marker one or two clubhead-lengths to the side, but the opponent or fellow-competitor says he wants the ball-marker left where it is. What is the ruling?

A. The player is entitled to move his ball-marker to the side. The opponent or fellow-competitor may not insist on its being left where it is in view of the purposes of Rules 8-2b and 22a.

20-1/12 Marking Position of Ball with Toe of Club

Q. A player, prior to lifting his ball under a Rule, marked the position of the ball by placing the toe of a club at the side of, or behind, the ball. Is this permissible?

A. Yes.

20-1/13 Ball Accidentally Kicked by Player Asked to Lift It Due to Interference

Q. A requests B to lift his (B's) ball because it interferes with A's play. As B is walking up to his ball to lift it, he accidentally kicks it. What is the ruling?

A. B incurs a penalty stroke under Rule 18-2a because the movement of the ball was not directly attributable to the specific act of marking the position of or lifting the ball. B must replace his ball.

Player Kicks Ball While Probing for it in Water in Water Hazard — See 12-1/5.

20-1/14 Ball Moved by Putter Dropped by Player Approaching Ball to Lift It

Q. A player, approaching his ball on the putting green to lift it, dropped his putter on his ball and moved it. Is it correct that there is no penalty in view of Rule 20-1 under which a player incurs no penalty if he accidentally moves his ball in the process of lifting it?

A. No. The player incurred a penalty stroke under Rule 18-2a because the movement of the ball was not directly attributable to the specific act of marking the position of or lifting the ball.

20-1/15 Meaning of "Directly Attributable" in Rules 20-1 and 20-3a

Q. What is meant by the phrase "directly attributable to the specific act" in Rules 20-1 and 20-3a? 20

A. In Rule 20-1 the phrase means the specific act of placing a ball-marker behind the ball, placing a club to the side of the ball, or lifting the ball such that the player's hand, the placement of the ball-marker, or the club, or the lifting of the ball causes the ball or the ball-marker to move.

In Rule 20-3a the phrase means the specific act of placing or replacing a ball in front of a ball-marker, placing a club to the side of the ball-marker, or lifting the ball-marker such that the player's hand, the placement of the ball or the club, or the lifting of the ball-marker causes the ball or the ball-marker to move.

Under either Rule, any accidental movement of the ball or the ball-marker which occurs before or after this specific act, such as dropping the ball or ball-marker, regardless of the height from which it was dropped, is not considered to be "directly attributable" and would result in the player incurring a penalty stroke. (New)

Ball Moved in Removing Ball-Marker After Replacing Ball — See 20-3a/1.

Position of Ball Marked Before Obstruction Removed; Ball Moves When Ball-Marker Removed — See 24-1/5.

20-1/15.5 Lie Altered By Act of Marking Position of Ball

Q. A player marks the position of his ball, and as a result of the act of marking, there is a change in the lie of the ball. Is the player required to restore the lie he had before marking the position of the ball?

A. No. The act of placing a marker may result in some change in the lie of the ball, for example, from grass being depressed by the weight of the marker, or grains of sand being moved in the placement or removal of a marker. Such occurrences may improve or worsen the lie of the ball, and the player must accept the result.

If the player attempted to restore the lie under these circumstances, or if the lie was improved from actions which exceeded what was necessary to the process of marking, he would be subject to penalty under Rule 13-2. (New)

Position of Ball Worsened When Obstruction Removed; Player Replaces Obstruction — See 13-2/15.5.

20-1/16 Marking Position of Ball by Scratching Line on Putting Green

Q. Is it permissible to mark the position of a ball on the putting green by scratching a line on the green with a tee?

A. Yes, provided the surface of the putting green is not tested (Rule 16-1d) and the scratched line does not indicate a line for putting (Rule 8-2b). However, this practice is not recommended due to the possibility of damage to the putting surface. Rather, the position of a ball should be marked by placing a ball-marker, a small coin or other similar object immediately behind the ball — see Note under Rule 20-1.

20-1/17 Tee Marking Position of Player's Ball Deflects Opponent's Ball

Q. In a match, B used a wooden tee to mark the position of his ball. A's ball was deflected by the tee. What is the ruling?

A. The tee was not B's equipment — see Definition of "Equipment." There is no penalty. A must play his ball as it lies.

A should have requested B to move the tee one or more clubhead-lengths to the side or to mark the position of his ball with a ball-marker, a small coin or other similar object — see Note under Rule 20-1.

20-1/18 Position of Ball Marked with Daisy

Q. A player plucked a daisy and marked the position of his ball with it. Is this permissible?

A. Yes. However, it is inadvisable to mark the position of a ball with something, such as a daisy, that might be blown away.

Rotating Ball on Putting Green Without Marking Position — See 18-2a/33.

20-1/19 Placing Object Marking Position of Ball Other Than Behind Ball

Q. When marking the position of a ball, must the ball-marker be placed behind the ball, or may it also be placed to the side of or in front of the ball?

A. There is no restriction. However, if a player positions his ball-marker in front of the ball on the putting green and in the process does something to the green which might influence the movement of the ball when played, *e.g.*, presses down a raised tuft of grass, he is in breach of Rule 1-2.

Placing a ball-marker in front of the ball is not recommended but it is not a breach of Rule 16-1a because this Rule permits touching the line of putt in lifting a ball, and marking the position of the ball is part of the lifting process.

20-1/20 Player Places Ball-Marker Approximately Two Inches Behind Ball

Q. A player consistently places his ball-marker approximately two inches behind the ball on the green. He says that he does so to ensure that he does not accidentally move the ball. Does such a procedure comply with the Rules?

A. No. A player who places a ball-marker two inches behind his ball cannot be considered to have marked the position of the ball with sufficient accuracy. Accordingly, each time he does so, the player incurs a penalty of one stroke, as provided in Rule 20-1, and must place the ball as near as possible to the spot from which it was lifted — Rule 20-3c.

The player's action was unnecessary because Rule 20-1 states that no penalty is incurred if a ball is accidentally moved in the process of marking or lifting it under a Rule.

20-1/21 Position of Ball Not Marked But Player Able to Replace Ball Because of Adjacent Blemish

Q. There is a distinct blemish immediately behind a ball lying on a putting green. The player claims he may lift his ball without marking its position because the blemish effectively marks the position. Is the player correct?

A. No. Under Rule 20-1, the position of a ball must be marked before the ball is lifted. Using a blemish as a ball-marker is not acceptable.

Position of Ball Lifted for Identification Not Marked, Intention to Lift Not Announced and Ball Cleaned Beyond Extent Necessary to Identify It — See 21/4.

20-1/22 Knocking Ball Aside After Marking Position Instead of Lifting

Q. A player, whose ball is on the putting green, marks the position of his ball and knocks the ball aside with his putter instead of lifting it. What is the ruling?

A. Knocking the ball aside was the equivalent of lifting it under Rule 20-1. There would be no penalty unless the act was for the purpose of testing the putting surface (Rule 16-1d) or playing a practice stroke (Rule 7-2).

20-2a/1 Penalty When Ball Dropped in Other Than Prescribed Manner

Q. If a ball is dropped in a manner other than that prescribed in Rule 20-2a and the error is not corrected, it is stated in that Rule that the penalty is one stroke. However, the general penalty for a breach of Rule 20-2 is loss of hole in match play or two strokes in stroke play. Which penalty applies?

A. The one-stroke penalty specifically prescribed in Rule 20-2a applies.

20-2a/2 Spinning Ball When Dropping

Q. A player puts spin on a ball purposely when dropping it. What is the ruling?

A. The player incurs a penalty of one stroke under Rule 20-2a for dropping the ball in an improper manner, unless he corrects his mistake as permitted by Rule 20-6.

Dropped Ball Accidentally Deflected by Opponent or His Caddie — See 19-3/2.

20-2a/3 Ball Dropped in Improper Manner and in Wrong Place

Q. A player obtaining relief from ground under repair dropped a ball in a manner not conforming with Rule 20-2a and in a wrong place. What is the ruling?

A. If the player corrected the errors before playing his next stroke, there was no penalty — Rule 20-6.

If the player failed to correct the errors before playing his next stroke:

(a) In match play, he lost the hole for playing from a wrong place — Rule 20-7a.

(b) In stroke play, he incurred a penalty of three strokes — one stroke for dropping in an improper manner (Rule 20-2a) and two strokes for a breach of Rule 25-1b (see Rule 20-7b).

20-2a/4 Ball Dropped in Improper Manner Moves When Addressed; Player Then Lifts Ball and Drops It in Proper Manner

Q. A player drops his ball other than in the manner prescribed in Rule 20-2a. He addresses the ball and the ball moves. He then is advised that he dropped his ball improperly. So, as permitted by Rule 20-6, he lifts the ball, drops it properly and plays. According to Rule 20-6, the player incurs no penalty for the improper drop. Does he incur a penalty stroke under Rule 18-2b because the ball moved after it was addressed, even though the ball was subsequently lifted and re-dropped?

A. Yes. The ball was in play when it was first dropped, even though it was dropped in an improper manner (Rule 20-4). When it moved after being addressed, the penalty prescribed in Rule 18-2b was applicable.

Other Decisions relating to Rule 20-2a:

Pitch-Mark in Dropping Area Repaired Before Ball Dropped — See 13-2/10.

Removing Sand or Loose Soil from Dropping Area — See 13-2/11.

Removal of Loose Impediments from Area in Which Ball to Be Dropped — See 23-1/6.

Who Drops Ball in Foursome Competition — See 29/4.

20-2a/5 Caddie Holds Back Tree Branch to Prevent Branch from Deflecting Dropped Ball

Q. May a player have his caddie hold back a tree branch that is waist high and situated at the spot at which the player wishes to drop his ball under a Rule?

If the branch is not held back, the dropped ball might lodge in the branch or, in any case, the branch will be likely to deflect the dropped ball.

A. No. Such an act would be exerting influence on the position or movement of the ball, contrary to Rule 1-2.

Dropped Ball Strikes Tree Branch Then Ground; Whether Re-Drop Required — See 20-2c/1.3.

20-2a/6 Ball Dropped Under One Option of Unplayable Ball Rule Strikes Player; Player Wishes to Change Relief Option

Q. A player declares his ball unplayable and elects to proceed under Rule 28b, by dropping a ball within two club-lengths of the spot where it lay. The dropped ball strikes the player's foot, so he is required by Rule 20-2a to re-drop. May the player change his relief option and, for example, proceed under Rule 28c?

A. No. A player may not change his relief option when re-dropping a ball under Rule 20-2a.

Changing Relief Option When Re-Dropping Required — See 20-2c/5.

Changing Relief Option After Ball Dropped in a Wrong Place — See 20-6/2.

Player Declares Ball Unplayable a Second Time and Wishes to Proceed Under Stroke and Distance After Dropping a Ball Under Other Unplayable Option — See 28/6.5.

20-2b/1 Dropped Ball Never Strikes Ground

Q. A player drops a ball where the applicable Rule requires. It lodges in a bush without striking the ground. What is the ruling?

A. The ball is in play. It struck a part of the course where required by the applicable Rule and did not roll into a position requiring it to be re-dropped under Rule 20-2c.

20-2b/2 Measuring Club-Lengths

20

When measuring a distance of one club-length (Rules 24 or 25) or two club-lengths (Rules 26-1c or 28), a player is entitled to measure directly across a ditch or through a fence, a tree or a wall made of earth or artificial materials.

Club to be Used in Measuring Club-Length — See 20/1.

20-2c/0.5 Ball Dropped from Ground Under Repair Area Rolls to Position Where Area Interferes with Stance; Whether Re-Drop Required

Q. A player's ball lies in ground under repair through the green. The player elects to take relief and drops the ball in accordance with Rule 25-1b(i). The ball remains outside the ground under repair area but it rolls to a position where the player would have to stand in the area to play his stroke. Must the player re-drop the ball?

A. Yes. The ball has rolled and come to rest "in a position where there is interference by the condition from which relief was taken" — see Rule 20-2c(v). The same applies if a player is taking relief from an immovable obstruction. (Revised)

Competitor Drops One Ball in Accordance with Two Different Rules Instead of Playing Second Ball; Dropped Ball Rolls Back into the Condition from Which Relief Taken— See 3-3/12.

20-2c/0.7 Ball Dropped from Immovable Obstruction Rolls Nearer Obstruction than Nearest Point of Relief; Whether Re-Drop Required If Player Changes Clubs and Obstruction No Longer Interferes

Q. A player's ball lies behind a tree and he would play a low shot with a 4-iron, under the tree's branches, except that a protective fence interferes with the area of his intended swing. He determines the nearest point of relief using his 4-iron and measures a one club-length area within which to drop the ball. After he drops the ball in accordance with the Rules, the ball rolls and comes to rest nearer the fence than the nearest point of relief. Therefore, there is still interference by the fence for the intended stroke with the 4-iron. However, the ball is now in a position where it would be reasonable for the player to play his next shot over the tree with a pitching-wedge, and the fence would not interfere with this stroke. May the player play the dropped ball or must it be re-dropped?

20

A. The ball must be re-dropped because it came to rest at a point where the player still had interference from the fence for a stroke with the club used to determine the nearest point of relief - see Rule 20-2c(v).

Club Used to Determine "Nearest Point" Not Used for Next Stroke— See 24-2b/4.

20-2c/0.8 Player Takes Relief from an Area of Ground Under Repair; Whether Re-Drop Required if Condition Interferes for Stroke with Club Not Used to Determine "Nearest Point of Relief"

Q. A player finds his ball in heavy rough approximately 230 yards from the green. He selects a wedge to play his next shot and finds that his stance touches a line defining an area of ground under repair. He determines the nearest point of relief and drops the ball within one club-length of this point. The ball rolls into a good lie from where he believes he can play a 3-wood for his next stroke. If the player used a wedge for his next stroke he would not have interference from the ground under repair, but adopting a normal stance with the 3-wood, he again touches the ground under repair with his foot. Must the player re-drop his ball under Rule 20-2c?

A. No. The player proceeded in accordance with Rule 25-1b by determining his nearest point of relief using the club with which he expected to play his next stroke and he would only be required to re-drop the ball under Rule 20-2c if interference still existed for a stroke with this club — see analogous Decision 20-2c/0.7.

As it was expedient for the player to play his next stroke with another club, which resulted in interference from the condition, he would have the option of playing the ball as it lies or proceeding again under Rule 25-1b. (New)

Club Used to Determine Nearest Point of Relief Not Used for Next Stroke — See 24-2b/4.

20-2c/1 Dropped Ball Rolling Out of Prescribed Dropping Area

Q. A player taking relief under the Rules sometimes appears to obtain more relief than he is entitled to because the relevant Rule allows him some latitude within which to drop and the dropped ball then rolls some distance from the place where it was dropped. When a Rule prescribes an area within which a ball must be dropped, *e.g.*, within one or two club-lengths of a particular point, should it be re-dropped if it rolls outside the area so prescribed?

A. No, not necessarily. Provided the ball has been correctly dropped (Rule 20-2a) and does not roll into any of the positions listed in Rule 20-2c, it is in play and must not be re-dropped. In particular, under Rule 20-2c(vi), the ball may roll up to two club-lengths from the point where it first struck a part of the course when dropped, and this may result in its coming to rest an appreciable distance farther from the condition from which relief is being taken. For example:

(a) a ball dropped within two club-lengths of the margin of a lateral water hazard may come to rest almost four club-lengths from the hazard margin without the player being required to re-drop it under Rule 20-2c; and

(b) a ball dropped away from an immovable obstruction within one club-length of the nearest point of relief may come to rest almost three club-lengths from the nearest point of relief without the player being required to re-drop it under Rule 20-2c.

20-2c/1.3 Dropped Ball Strikes Tree Branch Then Ground; Whether Re-Drop Required

Q. A player drops a ball within the area prescribed by the applicable Rule. It bounces off a tree branch and as a result strikes the ground outside that area. What is the ruling?

A. The ball struck a part of the course (the branch) where the applicable Rule requires (Rule 20-2b). Therefore, provided it does not roll into any of the positions listed in Rule 20-2c, it is in play and must not be re-dropped. In measuring the two club lengths to determine if a re-drop is required under Rule 20-2c(vi), the point on the ground immediately below the spot where the ball first struck a part of the course (the branch) shall be used for measuring purposes.

20-2c/1.5 Ball Rolls Towards Hole When Dropped at Spot from Which Previous Stroke Played

Q. A player is required or elects to play his next stroke at the spot from which his previous stroke was played. He is able to identify that specific spot by reference to the divot hole which his previous stroke made. He drops a ball immediately behind that divot hole. The ball rolls nearer the hole than the spot from which the previous stroke was played, but not more than two club-lengths from where it first struck the ground. What is the ruling?

A. Rule 20-2c(vii)(a) requires a ball to be re-dropped if it rolls and comes to rest nearer the hole than "its original position or estimated position . . . unless otherwise permitted by the Rules." The original position is the spot from which the previous stroke was played. Since the dropped ball rolled nearer the hole than that spot, it must be re-dropped.

However, in many such cases the player cannot determine exactly the spot from which his previous stroke was played. In those cases, the player has satisfied the requirements of the Rule if he uses his best endeavors to estimate the spot. The estimated spot is treated as the specific spot (see Rule 20-2b) and the ball must be re-dropped if it rolls nearer the hole than the estimated spot.

The same principle applies if the spot where a ball is to be placed is not determinable and the player is required, under Rule 20-3c, to drop the ball as near as possible to the spot where it lay. (Revised)

20-2c/1.7 Whether Re-Drop Required if Ball Dropped Under Rule 24-2b Rolls Nearer Hole Than Nearest Point of Relief but Not Nearer Than Where it Originally Lay

Q. A player's ball comes to rest on a cart path such that his nearest point of relief is behind the obstruction. He properly determines this point and lifts and drops the ball in accordance with Rule 24-2b. The ball rolls and comes to rest nearer the hole than the nearest point of relief, but not nearer the hole than where it lay originally on the path. Must the ball be re-dropped?

A. Yes — see Rule 20-2c(vii)(b). (New)

20-2c/2 Ball Dropped Third Time When Placement Required After Second Drop

Q. A player dropped his ball twice under a Rule and each time the ball rolled nearer the hole. He then dropped the ball a third time instead of placing it as required by Rule 20-2c. What is the ruling?

A. Before playing a stroke, the player may lift the ball and place it as prescribed in Rule 20-2c, without penalty (Rule 20-6). If he fails to do so and plays the ball, he incurs a penalty of loss of hole in match play or two strokes in stroke play for a breach of Rule 20-2c.

20-2c/3 Placing Ball Instead of Dropping When Obvious Dropped Ball Will Roll into Hazard, Etc.

Q. A player is required to drop a ball. However, it is obvious that the ball when dropped will roll into a hazard, more than two club-lengths, etc., in which case it must be re-dropped and then placed under Rule 20-2c. In such a case, is it permissible to waive the dropping requirement and allow the player initially to place the ball?

A. No. Dropping and then re-dropping are necessary to resolve any doubt as to whether the ball will roll into a hazard, etc., and to establish the spot at which the ball must be placed, if necessary.

20-2c/3.5 Dropped Ball Comes to Rest and Then Rolls Out of Bounds

Q. A player's ball comes to rest against a boundary stake. He declares the ball unplayable and drops it within two club-lengths of where the ball originally lay, as prescribed by Rule 28b. After the ball has been at rest, it rolls and comes to rest out of bounds. What is the ruling?

A. If a dropped ball comes to rest, but subsequently moves, the ball shall be played as it lies (see Note to Rule 20-2). In this case the ball is out of bounds and the player must proceed under Rule 27-1. Since the ball was at rest before moving, Rule 20-2c is not applicable. (Revised)

20-2c/4 Caddie Stops Dropped Ball Before It Comes to Rest; When Penalty Incurred

There is no penalty if a player's caddie deliberately stops a ball dropped by the player after the ball has rolled to a position from which the player would be required to re-drop it under Rule 20-2c, provided it is reasonable to assume that the ball would not return to a position at which Rule 20-2c would be inapplicable. However, if a player's caddie acts prematurely and stops a dropped ball before it has reached such a position, the player incurs a penalty of loss of hole in match play or two strokes in stroke play under Rule 1-2 — see reference to Rule 1-2 under Rule 20-2a — and must drop the ball as near as possible to the spot where it was when the caddie stopped it.

20-2c/5 Changing Relief Option When Re-Dropping Required

Q. A player declares his ball unplayable. Of the three options available under Rule 28, he elects Rule 28b and drops the ball within two club-lengths of the spot where it lay. The ball rolls and comes to rest nearer the hole than its original position, so the player is required by Rule 20-2c to re-drop. May the player now proceed under a different option, *e.g.*, Rule 28c?

A. No. If the player did so, he would be in breach of Rule 20-2c. The same principles would apply when proceeding under Rule 26-1.

Ball Dropped Under One Option of Unplayable Ball Rule Strikes Player; Player Wishes to Change Relief Option — See 20-2a/6.

Changing Relief Option After Ball Dropped in a Wrong Place — See 20-6/2.

Player Declares Ball Unplayable a Second Time and Wishes to Proceed Under Stroke and Distance After Dropping a Ball Under Other Unplayable Option — See 28/6.5.

20-2c/6 Ball Moved in Measuring to Determine If Re-Drop Required

Q. A player drops his ball in accordance with the Rules. The ball rolls and the player is uncertain whether it has come to rest more than two club-lengths from where it first struck a part of the course. The player measures to determine whether he must re-drop under Rule 20-2c(vi) and in doing so accidentally causes the ball to move. What is the ruling if (a) the ball had rolled more than two club-lengths or (b) the ball had not rolled more than two club-lengths?

A. In equity (Rule 1-4) and by analogy with Rule 10-4, no penalty is incurred in either case. If the ball had rolled more than two club-lengths, it must be re-dropped. If the ball had not rolled more than two club-lengths, it must be replaced.

20-2c/7 Player Takes Relief from Area of Casual Water and Ball Comes to Rest in a Position Where Another Area of Casual Water Interferes; Whether Re-Drop Required

Q. Through the green, there are two areas of casual water which are close together. There is interference from one area and the player elects to take relief. He drops the ball in accordance with Rule 25-1b(i) and it rolls to a position where interference no longer exists from the first area of casual water, but there is interference from the second area. Does Rule 20-2c(v) require the player to re-drop the ball?

A. No, the ball is in play. The player may play the ball as it lies or take relief from the second area in accordance with Rule 25-1b(i).

The same procedure applies to ground under repair or a hole, cast or runway made by a burrowing animal, a reptile or a bird.

Nearest Point of Relief from Cart Path is in Casual Water; Nearest Point of Relief from Casual Water is Back on Cart Path — See 1-4/8.

Other Decisions relating to Rule 20-2c:

Changing Relief Option After Ball Dropped in a Wrong Place — See 20-6/2.

20 **After Relief Taken from Obstruction for Stroke Towards Green, Obstruction Interferes with Stance for Necessary Sideways Stroke** — See 24-2b/9.5.

Ball Dropped from Casual Water in Bunker at Point of Maximum Relief Rolls Elsewhere — See 25-1b/6.

Permissible Dropping Area So Narrow Player Has Difficulty Dropping Within It — See 26-1/19.

20-3a/0.5 Whether Player Himself Must Place or Replace Ball

Q. Rule 20-3a states: "A ball to be placed under the Rules shall be placed by the player or his partner. If a ball is to be replaced, the player, his partner or the person who lifted or moved it shall place it on the spot from which it was lifted or moved." On the other hand, other Rules, *e.g.*, Rules 15-2 and -3 and 18-2b and -2c state that the player shall place or replace the ball. Does Rule 20-3a override other Rules which imply that the player himself must place or replace the ball?

A. Yes.

20-3a/1 Ball Moved in Removing Ball-Marker After Replacing Ball

Q. A player replaces his ball under a Rule and, in the act of removing the object marking its position, accidentally moves the ball. What is the ruling?

A. Removal of the ball-marker is part of the replacement process. Accordingly, under Rule 20-3a, no penalty is incurred, and the ball must be replaced.

Meaning of "Directly Attributable" in Rules 20-1 and 20-3a — See 20-1/15.

20-3a/2 Trademark Aimed Along Line of Putt When Ball Replaced

Q. When a player is replacing his ball, is it permissible for him to position the ball so that the trademark is aimed along the line of putt to indicate the line of play?

A. Yes.

Other Decisions relating to Rule 20-3a:

Player Returns Ball to Spot from Which Lifted by Rolling It with Putter — See 16-1d/3.

Ball-Marker Moved by Wind or Casual Water During Stipulated Round — See 20-1/10.5.

Ball Replaced at Wrong Place on Putting Green and Holed — See 20-7b/1.

Removal of Loose Impediments from Spot on Which Ball to Be Placed — See 23-1/6.5.

Placing Ball on Bank of Water Hazard Instead of Dropping to Prevent Ball Rolling into Water — See 26-1/10.

Penalty for Repeatedly Replacing Ball Nearer Hole on Green — See 33-7/6.

20-3b/1 Lie of Lifted Ball in Bunker Altered by Another Player's Stroke

Q. The balls of A and B are in the same heel mark in a bunker. B's ball is farther from the hole. A lifts his ball under Rule 22, and B plays and obliterates the heel mark. What should A do?

A. Under Rule 20-3b, A is required to recreate his original lie as nearly as possible, including the heel mark, and place his ball in that lie.

20-3b/2 Lie in Bunker Changed by Another Player Taking His Stance

Q. In playing from a bunker, B, in taking his stance, pushed up a mound of sand behind A's ball, which had not been lifted. What is the ruling?

A. Since A's ball did not move when B took his stance, Rule 20-3b does not apply. In equity (Rule 1-4), A's original lie should be restored as nearly as possible by removing the mound of sand.

20-3b/3 Lie Changed by Removal of Gallery-Control Stake

Q. A ball comes to rest adjacent to a gallery-control stake. A marshal, without the sanction of the player, removes the stake and in so doing raises the turf in front of the ball. Is the player entitled to proceed under Rule 20-3b?

A. No. Since the ball did not move when the gallery-control stake was removed, Rule 20-3b does not apply.

However, if the original lie could be easily restored, in equity (Rule 1-4), the raised turf should be pressed down so that the original lie is restored as nearly as possible.

If the original lie could not be easily restored, in equity (Rule 1-4), the player should place his ball, without penalty, in the nearest lie most similar to that which it originally occupied, but not more than one club-length from the original lie, not nearer the hole and not in a hazard.

Lie or Line of Play Affected by Pitch-Mark Made by Partner's, Opponent's or Fellow-Competitor's Ball — See 13-2/8.

Player's Lie Affected by Sand from Partner's, Opponent's or Fellow-Competitor's Stroke from Bunker — See 13-2/8.5.

[20-3b/4 Reserved]

20-3b/5 Lie of Ball to Be Replaced Altered and Spot Where Ball Originally Lay Not Determinable

Q. In stroke play, B plays A's ball and in the process removes a divot. The original lie of A's ball has been altered and it is impossible to determine the spot where A's ball originally lay. Should A proceed under Rule 20-3b or Rule 20-3c?

A. Since the lie of A's ball was altered, Rule 20-3b applies.

Lie of Ball Embedded in Hazard Altered When Ball Lifted to Determine Whether Unfit for Play — See 5-3/5.

Lie Altered When Player Presses Oscillating Ball into Surface of Putting Green — See 18-2a/6.

Ball Moved Accidentally and Original Lie Altered; Player Places Ball in Wrong Place and Plays — See 18-2a/21.3.

Decisions relating to Rule 20-3c:

Ball Lodged in Tree Knocked Down from Unknown Place by Outside Agency — See 18-1/9.

Ball Moved Accidentally; Spot Where Ball Originally Lay Not Determinable; Player Places Ball Instead of Dropping It — See 18-2a/21.5.

Ball Dislodged from Tree by Player; Spot Where Ball Lay Not Determinable — See 18-2a/29.

Ball-Marker Moved Accidentally by Player — See 20-1/5.5

Ball-Marker Moved Accidentally by Player in Process of Marking Position of Ball — See 20-1/6.

Ball-Marker Lifted by Outside Agency — See 20-1/9.

Ball-Marker Moved Off Green by Wind or Casual Water — See 20-1/10.

Lie of Ball to Be Replaced Altered and Spot Where Ball Originally Lay Not Determinable — See 20-3b/5.

20-3d/1 Placed Ball Rolls into Hole

Q. A replaces his ball on the putting green. As he is about to address the ball, it rolls into the hole. Should the ball be replaced or is A deemed to have holed out with his previous stroke?

A. The answer depends on whether the ball, when replaced, came to rest on the spot on which it was placed before it started rolling. If it did, A is deemed to have holed out with his previous stroke. If not, A is required to replace the ball (Rule 20-3d).

Ball Overhanging Hole Is Lifted, Cleaned and Replaced; Ball Then Falls into Hole — See 16-2/0.5.

Ball Dislodged from Tree by Player; Ball Fails to Remain on Correct Spot When Replaced — See 18-2a/29.

20-3d/2 Ball in Bunker Moves Closer to Hole When Obstruction Removed and Ball Will Not Remain at Rest When Replaced; All Other Parts of Bunker Are Nearer Hole

Q. A ball came to rest against a movable obstruction, a rake, in a bunker. When the rake was moved the ball rolled nearer the hole. According to Rule 24-1, the ball had to be replaced. Due to the slope and the fact that the sand was firm, the ball, when replaced, rolled closer to the hole.

Under Rule 20-3d, if a ball will not come to rest on the spot where it originally lay, it must be placed at the nearest spot not nearer the hole where it can be placed at rest. The spot where the ball originally lay was farther from the hole than any other part of the bunker. Thus, there was nowhere to place the ball at rest in the bunker which was not nearer the hole. What is the proper procedure if:

1. The only way the ball would remain at rest at the spot where it lay would be to press it lightly into the sand?
2. The sand is so hard that it is impossible to replace the ball?

20 A. There is nothing in the Rules of Golf permitting a player to press his ball lightly into the sand or ground to make it remain at rest. Accordingly, in either case, since the player could not place the ball in conformity with the Rules, he should, in equity (Rule 1-4), have dropped the ball, under penalty of one stroke, outside the bunker, keeping the point where the ball lay directly between the hole and the spot on which the ball is dropped.

Whether Rakes Should be Placed in or Outside Bunkers — See Misc./2.

20-3d/3 Ball In Rough Moves Downward When Addressed; Ball Will Not Remain at Rest When Replaced

Q. A player's ball is sitting up in the rough about three inches above the ground. He addresses the ball. It moves downward about two inches and comes to rest at Point X. The player attempts to replace the ball as required by Rule 18-2b, but the ball falls downward to Point X. Under Rule 20-3d, he again attempts to replace the ball,with the same result. The player must now place the ball at the nearest spot not nearer the hole where it can be placed at rest — Rule 20-3d.

If the nearest spot where the ball will remain at rest is Point X, must the player place the ball there, even though that point is vertically below the original lie?

A. Yes.

20-4/1 Ball Replaced on Putting Green But Ball-Marker Not Removed; Ball Then Moves

Q. A player replaces his ball on the putting green but does not remove his ball-marker. Subsequently the wind moves his ball to a new position. What is the ruling?

A. Under Rule 20-4, a ball is in play when it is replaced, whether or not the object used to mark its position has been removed. Consequently the ball must be played from the new position — see Decision 18-1/12.

20-4/2 Ball Lifted by Player from Putting Green and Placed by Caddie Behind Ball-Marker

Q. A player marks the position of his ball on the putting green by placing a coin immediately behind the ball. He lifts the ball and gives it to his caddie to have it cleaned. The caddie then intentionally places the ball immediately behind the coin, *i.e.*, not in the ball's original position, to allow the player to assess the line of putt from behind the hole. Is the ball in play when the caddie places the ball?

A. No. In these circumstances, the caddie's act in placing the ball on the putting green does not put the ball in play. The ball is not considered to be in play until the player repositions it with the intention of replacing the ball as required by Rule 16-1b. If the player played a stroke with his ball while it was out of play, he would be playing a wrong ball (Rule 15).

Player Lifts Ball, Sets It Aside and Plays It from Where Set Aside — See 15/4.

Other Decisions relating to Rule 20-4:

Original Ball Found Within Five-Minute Search Period After Another Ball Dropped — See 27-1/2.

Ball Dropped Under Unplayable Ball Rule Comes to Rest in Original Position or Another Position at Which Ball Is Unplayable — See 28/3.

20-5/1 Teed Ball Missed Then Hit Out of Bounds

Q. A player plays a stroke from a teeing ground and misses the ball. He plays a second stroke and hits the ball out of bounds. In proceeding under Rule 27-1, may he tee a ball anywhere within the teeing ground or must he drop a ball where the original ball was teed?

A. The player may tee a ball anywhere within the teeing ground.

20-6/1 Ball Placed When Required to Be Dropped or Dropped When Required to Be Placed; Correction of Error

Q. A player placed a ball when he should have dropped it or dropped it when he should have placed it. Before playing a stroke, may the player lift the ball, without penalty, under Rule 20-6 and proceed correctly?

A. Yes. Otherwise the player would lose the hole in match play or incur a penalty of two strokes in stroke play for a breach of the applicable Rule.

Ball Dropped Third Time When Placement Required After Second Drop; Correction of Error — See 20-2c/2.

20-6/2 Changing Relief Option After Ball Dropped in a Wrong Place

Q. A player declares his ball unplayable and elects to take relief under Rule 28c. He drops the ball in a wrong place and is advised of this fact. He then lifts his ball under Rule 20-6 and states that he wishes to proceed under Rule 28b. Is the player entitled to proceed under Rule 28b?

A. Yes. Decisions 20-2a/6 and 20-2c/5 suggest a different conclusion. However, in those cases Rules 20-2a and 20-2c are invoked and those Rules imply that a ball to be re-dropped must be re-dropped under the option originally invoked.

Player Unaware Ball in Water Hazard Takes Relief from Interference by Burrowing Animal Hole — See 25-1b/26.

Player Declares Ball Unplayable a Second Time and Wishes to Proceed Under Stroke and Distance After Dropping a Ball Under Other Unplayable Option — See 28/6.5.

20-6/3 Ball Mistakenly Substituted When Dropped; Correction of Error

Q. A player's ball lies on a paved cart path. In taking relief from the obstruction, he mistakenly drops a ball other than the original ball. He discovers his error before playing his next stroke. How should he proceed?

A. The player is not entitled to substitute a ball when proceeding under Rule 24-2b, unless the ball is not immediately recoverable. Therefore, the player must lift the substituted ball, without penalty, and drop the original ball in accordance with the Rules.

20-7/1 Ball Played from Spot Where Original Ball Deflected Out of Bounds by Maintenance Vehicle

Q. A player's tee shot travels about 175 yards and, while still in motion, is deflected out of bounds by a golf course maintenance vehicle. The player, claiming the vehicle should not have been there, dropped a ball near the spot where the vehicle deflected the original ball, completed play of the hole and stated that he had incurred no penalty. Was the player correct?

A. No. A maintenance vehicle is an outside agency. The original ball would have been played as it lay, without penalty, if it had been in bounds — Rule 19-1. Since the ball was out of bounds, the player was obliged to proceed under Rule 27-1.

The player, in dropping a ball near where the original ball was deflected and playing it, played from a wrong place.

In match play, he incurred a penalty of loss of hole — Rule 20-7a.

In stroke play, he incurred the stroke-and-distance penalty prescribed by Rule 27-1 and an additional penalty of two strokes for a breach of that Rule. Since the breach was a serious one, he was subject to disqualification unless he corrected the error as prescribed in the second paragraph of Rule 20-7b.

Ball Moved Accidentally and Original Lie Altered; Player Places Ball in Wrong Place and Plays — See 18-2a/21.3.

Casual Water Mistaken for Water Hazard; Original Ball Played Under Water Hazard Rule — See 25-1b/12.

Player Plays Second Shot, Declares Ball Unplayable and Returns to Tee — See 28/6.

Player Plays from a Wrong Place on Basis of Incorrect Ruling — See 34-3/3.

20-7/2 Ball Declared Unplayable in Water Hazard Is Dropped in Hazard and Played

Q. A player declares his ball unplayable in a water hazard and drops the ball in the water hazard, thinking that Rule 28b or c is applicable, and plays it. He then realizes that it is not permissible to declare a ball unplayable in a water hazard. What is the ruling?

A. The player played the ball from a wrong place, *i.e.*, a place not permitted by Rule 26-1, the water hazard relief Rule.

In match play, the player loses the hole (Rule 20-7a).

In stroke play, if a serious breach of the water hazard Rule was not involved, the player, in addition to incurring the penalty stroke provided for in Rule 26-1, incurs a two-stroke penalty for playing from a wrong place and must play out the hole with the ball played out of the water hazard — see first paragraph of Rule 20-7b and Rule 26-1.

If a serious breach of the water hazard Rule was involved, the player must, before playing from the next teeing ground, play a ball in accordance with Rule 26-1 and add two penalty strokes to the score with that ball; otherwise the player is disqualified — see second and third paragraphs of Rule 20-7b.

20-7b/0.5 Meaning of "Serious Breach"

Q. When is playing from a wrong place a "serious breach?"

A. A serious breach has occurred when a player proceeds otherwise than in accordance with the Rules and, in the opinion of the Committee, either gains a significant advantage or negotiates a significant distance without making a stroke.

Procedure If Both Original and Second Balls Dropped in Wrong Place and Played — See 3-3/5.5.

Water Hazard Treated as Lateral Water Hazard — See 26-1/11.

Example of Serious Breach of Lateral Water Hazard Rule — See 26-1/21.

Ball Dropped in Area Where Original Ball Lost; Ball Then Played — See 27-1/3.

Significant Advantage Gained When Player Plays Stroke from Environmentally-Sensitive Area Defined as Water Hazard — See 33-8/44.

20-7b/1 Ball Replaced at Wrong Place on Putting Green and Holed

Q. In stroke play, a competitor in replacing his ball on the putting green inadvertently put the ball in a wrong place nearby and holed out. The error was then discovered and the competitor put his ball in the right place and holed out. What is the ruling?

A. The score with the ball played from the wrong place counts and the competitor must add two penalty strokes to that score (Rule 16-1b or 20-3a and Rule 20-7b).

The competitor incurs no penalty for having putted from the right place after holing out from a wrong place.

20-7b/2 Ball Putted from Wrong Place Lifted and Putted from Right Place

Q. In stroke play, A mistakenly replaced his ball in front of B's ball-marker (which was near A's ball-marker) and putted. The ball came to rest about one foot from the hole. The error was then discovered and A lifted his ball without marking its position, placed it in front of his own ball-marker and finished the hole. What is the ruling?

A. When A replaced his ball in front of B's ball-marker and putted, he played from a wrong place and incurred a penalty of two strokes; the ball was in play — Rule 20-7b.

When A then lifted his ball from where it lay about one foot from the hole without marking its position and did not replace it, he incurred the general penalty (two strokes) for a breach of Rule 20-1 — see second paragraph of Rule 20-1.

Thus, A incurred a total penalty of four strokes.

20-7b/3 Ball Believed to Be Lost in Bunker; Competitor Drops Another Ball in Bunker and Plays It; Original Ball Then Found Outside Bunker

Q. In stroke play, A played a long shot to the green and the ball appeared to have come to rest in a bunker beside the green. The ball was not found in the bunker. A dropped a ball in the bunker and played it onto the green. A then discovered his original ball behind the green. What is the ruling?

A. When A dropped another ball in the bunker, it became the ball in play under penalty of stroke and distance and the original ball was lost.

Since the place where the ball was dropped was well in advance of the spot from which the original ball was last played, A was guilty of a serious breach of the relevant Rule (Rule 27-1) in failing to go back to that spot. He should have been disqualified unless he rectified the breach as prescribed in Rule 20-7b, in which case he would incur an additional penalty of two strokes.

Ball Knocked Out of Bunker by Fellow-Competitor's Stroke at Own Ball Not Replaced — See 18-4/2.

Ball Dropped Outside Bunker Under Option of Unplayable Ball Rule Requiring Drop in Bunker — See 28/10.

[20-7b/4 Reserved]

20-7b/5 Competitor's Ball Played by Fellow-Competitor; Competitor Substitutes Another Ball at Wrong Place, Plays It and Then Abandons It and Plays Out Original Ball from Right Place

Q. In stroke play, A, B, and C hit their tee shots into the same area. After B and C have played their second shots, A discovers that the remaining ball is not his and assumes that his ball has been played by B. Since his (A's) original ball is not immediately recoverable, A substitutes another ball as permitted by Note 1 under Rule 18, places it on the spot from which B played his second shot and plays it to the green. There it is discovered that it was C, not B, who wrongly played A's ball and that A has therefore played the substituted ball from a wrong place. A accepts a two-stroke penalty under the relevant Rule (Rule 18-1), but he then abandons the substituted ball, thinking he must correct his error. A picks up his original ball, goes back to the spot where C played his second shot, plays it from there on to the putting green and takes two putts to hole out. A then drives from the next tee. What is the ruling, and what did A score on the hole?

A. A's procedure was correct up to the point when he abandoned the substituted ball. The substituted ball, albeit played from a wrong place, was now A's ball in play, and his original ball was out of play. Instead of abandoning the substituted ball, A should have played out the hole with it in accordance with Rule 20-7b, adding to his score the two-stroke penalty he had correctly accepted under Rule 18-1. When A went back and played his original ball from the right place (i.e., from where C had wrongly played it), he was substituting a ball for his ball in play in breach of Rule 15-1 as well as playing from the wrong place. Therefore, he incurred an additional penalty of four strokes (Rules 15-1 and 20-7b) for a total of six penalty strokes. A's score for the hole was 11. (Revised)

20-7b/6 Competitor Plays Second Ball Under Rule 20-7b; Clarification of "Penalty Strokes Incurred Solely by Playing the Ball Ruled Not to Count"

The Note under Rule 20-7b permits a player who has played a second ball to disregard penalty strokes incurred solely in playing a ball ruled not to count, such as accidentally causing the ball to move (Rule 18-2a) or proceeding under the water hazard Rule (Rule 26-1). However, a player cannot disregard a breach of the Rules which might apply to either ball, such as a breach of the practice Rule (Rule 7-2), the advice Rule (Rule 8-1) or playing a wrong ball (Rule 15-3). (Revised)

Wrong Ball Played in Belief It Is Provisional or Second Ball — See 15/7.

Other Decisions relating to Rule 20-7b:

Guidelines for Which Ball Counts When Player Proceeds Under Rule 3-3 — See 3-3/0.5.

Ball Dropped in Wrong Place and Played; Rule 3-3 Then Invoked and Second Ball Dropped in Right Place; Both Balls Played Out — See 3-3/3.

Ball Dropped in Wrong Place But Not Played; Rule 3-3 Then Invoked and Second Ball Dropped in Right Place; Both Balls Played Out — See 3-3/4.

Whether Score with Second Ball Counts If Ball Dropped in Wrong Place and Played — See 3-3/5.

Competitor's Ball Moved by Fellow-Competitor's Ball Not Replaced — See 18-5/3.

Ball Dropped in Improper Manner and in Wrong Place — See 20-2a/3.

Point Where Ball Last Crossed Margin of Lateral Water Hazard Determined and Ball Dropped and Played; Point Then Proves to Be Wrong Point — See 26-1/17.

Provisional Ball Lifted Subsequently Becomes Ball in Play; Competitor Then Plays from Wrong Place — See 27-2b/10.

Rule 21. Cleaning Ball

A ball on the *putting green* may be cleaned when lifted under Rule 16-1b. Elsewhere, a ball may be cleaned when lifted except when it has been lifted:

a. To determine if it is unfit for play (Rule 5-3);

b. For identification (Rule 12-2), in which case it may be cleaned only to the extent necessary for identification; or

c. Because it is interfering with or assisting play (Rule 22).

If a player cleans his ball during play of a hole except as provided in this Rule, he shall incur a penalty of one stroke and the ball, if lifted, shall be replaced.

If a player who is required to replace a ball fails to do so, he shall incur the penalty for breach of Rule 20-3a, but no additional penalty under Rule 21 shall be applied.

Exception: If a player incurs a penalty for failing to act in accordance with Rule 5-3, 12-2 or 22, no additional penalty under Rule 21 shall be applied.

21/1 Removing Lime from Ball

Q. Lime has been used to mark lines on the ground for gallery-control purposes. A ball lands on such a line and some lime adheres to the ball. May the player remove the lime?

A. No, unless the ball is in a position from which it may be lifted under the Rules and cleaned under Rule 21.

21/2 Removing Grass Adhering to Ball

Q. Through the green, is it permissible to remove cut grass adhering to a ball?

A. No. Such action is prohibited by Rule 21. Anything adhering to a ball is not a loose impediment — see Definition of "Loose Impediments."

Removal of Insect on Ball — See 23-1/5.

21/3 Whether Ball Cleaned Through Act of Caddie Throwing It to Player

Q. A caddie, with authority of the player, lifts the player's ball because it interferes with the play of another player and throws the ball to the player, who catches it. It is not permissible to clean a ball lifted because of interference. Does the act of throwing and catching the ball constitute cleaning it?

A. Whether or not a ball is cleaned is a question of fact. The action described could result in a ball being cleaned. Any doubt should be resolved against the player.

21/4 Position of Ball Lifted for Identification Not Marked, Intention to Lift Not Announced and Ball Cleaned Beyond Extent Necessary to Identify It

Q. A player lifted his ball for identification purposes without announcing his intention to his opponent, marker or a fellow-competitor. Thus, he was in breach of Rule 12-2. He also failed to mark the position of the ball before he lifted it in breach of Rule 20-1 and cleaned the ball more than was necessary for it to be identified, a breach of Rule 21. The penalty for breach of each of these Rules is one stroke. Does the player incur a penalty of three strokes?

A. No. The player incurs a penalty of one stroke for failing to act in accordance with Rule 12-2. An additional penalty under Rule 20-1 or Rule 21 is not justified — see Rule 12-2 and Exception under Rule 21.

Other Decisions relating to Rule 21:

Ball in Ground Under Repair Thought to be Unfit for Play Lifted and Cleaned — See 5-3/6.

Ball Lifted Without Authority and Cleaned — See 18-2a/13.

Rule 22. Ball Interfering with or Assisting Play

Any player may:

a. Lift his ball if he considers that the ball might assist any other player or

b. Have any other ball lifted if he considers that the ball might interfere with his play or assist the play of any other player,

but this may not be done while another ball is in motion. In stroke play, a player required to lift his ball may play first rather than lift. A ball lifted under this Rule shall be replaced.

PENALTY FOR BREACH OF RULE:
Match play - Loss of hole;
Stroke play - Two strokes.

Note: Except on the *putting green*, the ball may not be cleaned when lifted under this Rule — see Rule 21.

22/1 Mental Interference by Another Ball

Q. In order for A to be entitled to have B's ball lifted because of interference, does B's ball have to be on or near A's line of play and thus in a position to interfere physically with A's ball? Or may A also have B's ball lifted if it is off his line of play but catches his eye and thus constitutes mental interference?

A. A player may, under Rule 22, have another ball lifted if the ball interferes either physically or mentally with his play.

22/2 Player Claims That Another Ball Lying 30 Yards Away Interferes with His Play

Q. B's ball is three feet from the green on a direct line to the hole with A's ball which is 30 yards from the green. May A require B to lift his ball, on the ground that the ball interferes with his play?

A. Yes.

22/3 Player Requests Another Player to Lift His Ball in Absence of Reasonable Possibility Ball Might Interfere or Assist

Q. A's ball is on the putting green. B's ball is 100 yards from the green. B requests A to lift his ball under Rule 22 as it might interfere with his (B's) play. This happens several times during the round. Is such procedure permissible?

A. Rule 22 is intended to cover situations where there is a reasonable possibility that one ball might assist or interfere with another ball. If the Rule is being abused, as in this case, the Committee would be justified in penalizing B for undue delay — Rule 6-7.

[22/4 Reserved]

22/5 Assisting Ball Lifted by Opponent Replaced on Request; Player's Ball Then Strikes Opponent's Ball and Opponent Lodges Claim

Q. In a match between A and B, A's ball is near the hole in a position to serve as a backstop for B's ball. A lifts his ball to clean it. B requests A to replace his ball before he (B) putts. A protests but B insists that, under the Rules, A must replace his ball immediately. A replaces his ball but disputes B's right to require him to do so and claims the hole. B putts and his ball strikes A's ball and stops very close to the hole. A replaces his ball and holes out for a 4. B then holes out for a 4. The match continues and the claim is later referred to the Committee. How should the Committee rule?

A. The hole stands as played. The Rules do not require A to replace his ball, but B was not in breach of the Rules by asking A to replace it — see Rule 22.

22/6 Competitor Requests That Ball in Position to Assist Him Should Not Be Lifted

Q. In stroke play, B's ball lies just off the putting green. A's ball lies near the hole in a position to serve as a backstop for B's ball. B requests A not to lift his ball. Is such a request proper?

A. No. If a competitor and a fellow-competitor were to agree to exclude the operation of Rule 22, both should be disqualified under Rule 1-3.

Competitor Not Given Opportunity to Lift Ball Assisting Fellow-Competitor — See 3-4/1.

Ball-Marker in Position to Assist Another Player — See 20-1/11.

Request to Lift Ball That Might Assist Partner Not Honored — See 30-3f/11.

Player Requested to Lift Ball Due to Interference Plays Out of Turn Instead — See 10-1c/2.

22/7 Ball Assisting Fellow-Competitor on Putting Green; Procedure for Committee Member If Competitor Does Not Lift Ball

Q. In stroke play, a competitor's ball is in a position to assist the play of a fellow-competitor and the competitor is in a position to lift the ball under Rule 22 without delaying the fellow-competitor's play. However, the competitor does not take any action to invoke the Rule. Would a Committee member be justified in intervening and requesting the competitor to invoke the Rule to protect himself and the rest of the field?

A. Yes. If the competitor were to object, there would be strong evidence of an agreement to exclude the operation of Rule 22 in contravention of Rule 1-3. The Committee member would be justified in so advising the competitors involved and warning that any further such evidence might result in disqualification of both under Rule 1-3.

Other Decisions relating to Rule 22:

Two Balls Lie Together in Hazard and Neither Is Identifiable — See 1-4/6.

Interfering Ball in Bunker Lifted; Lie Altered by Another Player's Stroke — See 20-3b/1.

Abandoned Ball Interferes with Play — See 24-1/2.

Rule 23. Loose Impediments

Definition

"Loose impediments" are natural objects such as stones, leaves, twigs, branches and the like, dung, worms and insects and casts or heaps made by them, provided they are not fixed or growing, are not solidly embedded and do not adhere to the ball.

Sand and loose soil are *loose impediments* on the *putting green* but not elsewhere.

Snow and natural ice, other than frost, are either *casual water* or *loose impediments,* at the option of the player. Manufactured ice is an *obstruction.*

Dew and frost are not *loose impediments.*

23-1. Relief

Except when both the *loose impediment* and the ball lie in or touch the same *hazard,* any *loose impediment* may be removed without penalty. If the ball *moves,* see Rule 18-2c.

When a ball is in motion, a *loose impediment* which might influence the movement of the ball shall not be removed.

PENALTY FOR BREACH OF RULE:
Match play — Loss of hole;
Stroke play — Two strokes.

(Searching for ball in *hazard* — see Rule 12-1.)

(Touching *line of putt* — see Rule 16-1a.)

23/1 When Loose Impediment Transformed into Obstruction

Loose impediments may be transformed into obstructions through processes of construction or manufacturing. For example, a log (loose impediment) which has been split and had legs attached has been changed by construction into a bench (obstruction); or a piece of coal (loose impediment) is an obstruction when manufactured into a charcoal briquet.

23/2 Meaning of "Solidly Embedded" in Definition of "Loose Impediments"

Q. The Definition of "Loose Impediments" states that a stone is a loose impediment if it is not "solidly embedded." When is a stone solidly embedded?

A. If a stone is partially embedded and may be picked up with ease, it is a loose impediment. When there is doubt as to whether a stone is solidly embedded or not, it should not be removed.

23/3 Half-Eaten Pear

Q. A half-eaten pear lies directly in front of a ball in a bunker and there is no pear tree in the vicinity of the bunker. In the circumstances, is the pear an obstruction rather than a loose impediment, in which case the player could remove it without penalty?

A. No. A pear is a natural object. When detached from a tree it is a loose impediment. The fact that a pear has been half-eaten and there is no pear tree in the vicinity does not alter the status of the pear.

23/4 Fruit Skins

Q. Is a banana skin or other fruit skin a loose impediment?

A. Yes.

23/5 Ant Hill

Q. Is an ant hill a loose impediment?

A. Yes. A player is entitled to remove an ant hill under Rule 23-1.

23/6 Dead Land Crab

Q. A ball lodges against a dead land crab in a bunker. May the crab be removed without penalty?

A. No. A dead land crab is a natural object and thus a loose impediment and not an obstruction. Removal of the crab would be a breach of Rule 13-4.

Dead Snake — See 18/4.

23/7 Fallen Tree

Q. Is a fallen tree a loose impediment?

A. If it is still attached to the stump, no; if it is not attached to the stump, yes.

23/8 Worm Partially Underground

Q. Is a worm, when half on top of the surface of the ground and half below, a loose impediment which may be removed? Or is it fixed or solidly embedded and therefore not a loose impediment?

A. A worm which is half underground is not "fixed or growing" or "solidly embedded" within the meaning of those terms in the Definition of "Loose Impediments." Accordingly, such a worm may be removed under Rule 16-1a(i) or Rule 23.

23/9 Embedded Acorn

Q. Is an embedded acorn a loose impediment?

A. Not if the acorn is solidly embedded — see Definition of "Loose Impediments."

Club Touches Partially Embedded Pine Needle on Backswing in Bunker — See 13-4/32.

Player Repairs Depression on Line of Putt Created When Partially Embedded Acorn Removed — See 16-1a/7.

23/10 Ball Embedded in Fruit

Q. A ball is embedded in an orange lying under an orange tree. What is the ruling?

A. The player must play the ball as it lies or declare it unplayable. Since the orange was adhering to the ball, it was not a loose impediment.

Grass Adhering to Ball — See 21/2.

23/11 Loose Soil Remaining When Molehill Swept Flat

Q. Decision 25/23 states that a molehill, when swept flat, loses its status as such and relief under Rule 25 is no longer available. Is the loose soil remaining a loose impediment?

A. No, unless it is on the putting green — see Definition of "Loose Impediments."

23/12 Aeration Plugs

Q. Are plugs of compacted soil produced through aeration of fairways loose impediments?

A. Yes. Loose soil is not a loose impediment. However, such plugs, since they consist of compacted soil, are loose impediments.

23/13 Clod of Earth

Q. Is a loose clod of earth a loose impediment?

A. Yes. Loose soil is not a loose impediment except on the putting green. However, a clod of earth is not loose soil.

23/14 Gravel Used to Surface Road

Q. A player hits his ball onto a gravel-covered road. Even though he is entitled to relief from this obstruction, he prefers to play the ball from the road. May he remove gravel that might interfere with his stroke?

A. Yes. Gravel is a loose impediment and a player may remove loose impediments under Rule 23-1. This right is not cancelled by the fact that, when a road is covered with gravel, it becomes an artificially-surfaced road and thus an obstruction.

Status of Moss or Creepers in Tree — See 13-2/37.

Grass Cuttings — See 25/11.

23-1/1 Means by Which Loose Impediments May Be Removed

Q. Worm casts are loose impediments. By what means may such casts be removed?

A. Except on the line of putt, loose impediments may be removed by any means.

In removing loose impediments on the line of putt, the player must not touch the line of putt except in the process of picking up or brushing aside the loose impediments with his hand or a club without pressing anything down (Rule 16-1a).

23-1/2 Large Stone Removable Only with Much Effort

Q. A player's ball lies in the rough directly behind a loose stone the size of a watermelon. The stone can be removed only with much effort. Is it a loose impediment which may be removed?

A. Yes. Stones of any size (not solidly embedded) are loose impediments and may be removed, provided removal does not unduly delay play (Rule 6-7).

23-1/3 Assistance in Removing Large Loose Impediment

Q. May spectators, caddies, fellow-competitors, etc., assist a player in removing a large loose impediment?

A. Yes.

23-1/4 Breaking Off Part of Large Loose Impediment

Q. If part of a large branch which has fallen from a tree (and thus is a loose impediment) interferes with a player's swing, may the player break off the interfering part rather than move the whole branch?

A. Yes.

Bending Grass in Removal of Loose Impediment — See 13-2/13.

Determining Whether Natural Object Interfering with Area of Intended Swing Is Loose Impediment — See 13-2/26.

23-1/5 Removal of Insect on Ball

Q. A live insect is stationary or crawling on a player's ball which is lying through the green. May the player remove the insect with his fingers or blow the insect off the ball?

A. Yes, in both cases, under Rule 23-1. A live insect is not considered to be adhering to the ball and therefore is a loose impediment — see Definition of "Loose Impediments."

23-1/5.5 Status of Insect on Ball in Bunker

Q. With regard to Decision 23-1/5, what is the ruling if the ball was in a bunker?

23

A. The insect is considered to be in the bunker and because it is, by definition, a loose impediment, the player may not touch or physically remove the insect from the ball (Rule 13-4c). However, as the insect is animate and capable of moving on its own, the player may take action, such as waving his hand or a club or towel, to encourage the insect to move. If the insect moves, there is no penalty provided the player has not touched the insect or the ground in the bunker, or moved another loose impediment in the bunker. (New)

Flying Insect in Water Hazard — See 13-4/16.5.

23-1/6 Removal of Loose Impediments from Area in Which Ball to Be Dropped

Q. Through the green, is it permissible for a player to remove loose impediments from the area in which he is preparing to drop his ball?

A. Yes.

23-1/6.5 Removal of Loose Impediments from Spot on Which Ball to Be Placed

Q. A player taking relief under a Rule drops his ball and it rolls more than two club-lengths. He re-drops under Rule 20-2c, with the same result. He must now place the ball as near as possible to the spot where it first struck the ground when re-dropped — Rule 20-2c. Before he places the ball, may he remove loose impediments on or around the spot on which the ball is to be placed?

A. Yes.

23-1/7 Loose Impediment Affecting Lie Moved When Ball Lifted

Q. A loose impediment affecting a player's lie is moved when the player lifts his ball under a Rule which requires him to replace the ball. In equity (Rule 1-4), should the player be required to replace the loose impediment?

A. Yes.

23-1/8 Loose Impediments Affecting Lie Removed While Ball Lifted

Q. A player's ball lies in an area through the green where there are a number of loose impediments, including a tree branch against which the ball has come to rest. It appears likely that the ball will move if the player moves the tree branch. The player wishes to lift the ball under Rule 5-3 (Ball Unfit for Play) or Rule 12-2 (Identifying Ball), or he is requested to lift it under Rule 22 (Ball Interfering with or Assisting Play). He lifts the ball but, before replacing it, he removes the loose impediments in the area, including the tree branch against which the ball was resting. Is this permissible?

A. No. Under Rule 18-2c, through the green a player incurs a penalty if his ball moves after a loose impediment within one club-length of it has been touched. It would circumvent Rule 18-2c if, before a ball is replaced, it was permissible to remove loose impediments which affected the player's lie before the ball was lifted. In equity (Rule 1-4), the player should be penalized one stroke.

In such circumstances, if a player wishes to remove loose impediments affecting his lie, he should do so either before lifting the ball or after replacing it. If his ball then moves, under Rule 18-2c the player incurs a penalty stroke and must replace the ball.

Removing Sand or Loose Soil from Dropping Area — See 13-2/11.

Ball Declared Unplayable in Bunker; Player Removes Loose Impediment from Bunker While Ball Lifted — See 13-4/35.7.

Loose Impediments Within One Club-Length Removed; Ball Lifted and Replaced; Ball Moves Before Address — See 18-2c/3.

23-1/9 Removal of Loose Impediment Lying Out of Bounds

Q. A loose impediment lying out of bounds interferes with a player's stance. May the player remove the impediment?

A. Yes.

Ball in Hazard Moves After Loose Impediment Outside Hazard Moved — See 18-2c/4.

Other Decisions relating to Rule 23-1:

Player Removes Loose Impediments Affecting Opponent's Lie in Hazard — See 1-2/6.

Removal of Obstruction in Hazard Would Move Loose Impediment — See 1-4/5.

Replacing or Removing Undetached Divot — See 13-2/5.

Ball Outside Bunker; Stone in Bunker on Line of Play Pressed Down or Removed — See 13-2/31.

Accidentally Moving Loose Impediment in Hazard — See 13-4/13.

Player Accidentally Kicks Pine Cone into Bunker and Picks It Up — See 13-4/14.

Ball in Hazard Moves When Loose Impediment Removed — See 13-4/15.

Removal of Loose Impediment in Water Hazard Covering Wrong Ball — See 13-4/16.

Loose Impediment Removed from Water Hazard; Player Then Decides Not to Play from Hazard — See 13-4/17.

Ball Touched Accidentally in Removing Loose Impediment — See 18-2a/31.

Ball Touched with Fir Cone or Stick to Prevent Movement When Loose Impediment Removed — See 18-2a/32.

Pine Needles Piled for Removal Interfere with Line of Play After Ball Dropped Away — See 25-1b/17.

Player Lifts Loose Impediment in Bunker When His Ball and Partner's Ball in Bunker — See 30-3f/1.

Competitor Lifts Loose Impediment in Bunker When His Ball and Partner's Ball in Bunker — See 31-8/1.

23-1/10 Removal of Loose Impediments Affecting Player's Play

Q. A player with a downhill putt picks up loose impediments between his ball and the hole but leaves some behind the hole. The opponent or fellow-competitor wants to remove the impediments behind the hole as they may serve as a backstop, but the player objects. May the opponent or fellow-competitor remove the loose impediments behind the hole?

A. No. When it is the player's turn to play, his opponent or a fellow-competitor has no right to remove loose impediments affecting the player's play if the player requests the opponent or fellow-competitor not to do so. If the opponent or fellow-competitor ignores the request, he is in breach of Rule 1-2.

In the absence of a request not to remove loose impediments affecting the player's play, an opponent or fellow-competitor who does so incurs no penalty.

In either instance, if the player replaces the loose impediments he is in breach of Rule 1-2.

Removal of Dew or Frost from Line of Putt — See 16-1a/3.

Loose Impediments Removed from Line of Putt with Cap or Towel — See 16-1a/8.

Brushing Loose Impediments Off Line of Putt with Palm of Hand — See 16-1a/9.

Loose Impediments Brushed Along Line of Putt Rather Than to Side — See 16-1a/10.

Determining Whether Natural Object on Line of Putt Is Loose Impediment — See 16-1a/11.

Opponent or Fellow-Competitor Removes Obstruction Affecting Player's Play — See 24/16.

Other Decisions relating to Rule 23-1:

Ball Moved Accidentally by Foot During Removal of Loose Impediment on Putting Green — See 18-2c/1.

Competitor Seeks Help in Removal of Loose Impediment to Avoid Penalty — See 33-7/7.

23

Rule 24. Obstructions

Definitions

The *"nearest point of relief"* is the reference point for taking relief without penalty from interference by an immovable *obstruction* (Rule 24-2), an *abnormal ground condition* (Rule 25-1) or a *wrong putting green* (Rule 25-3).

It is the point on the *course,* nearest to where the ball lies, which is not nearer the *hole* and at which, if the ball were so positioned, no interference (as defined) would exist.

Note: The player should determine his *nearest point of relief* by using the club with which he expects to play his next *stroke* to simulate the address position and swing for such *stroke.*

An *"obstruction"* is anything artificial, including the artificial surfaces and sides of roads and paths and manufactured ice, except:

a. Objects defining *out of bounds,* such as walls, fences, stakes and railings;

b. Any part of an immovable artificial object which is *out of bounds;* and

c. Any construction declared by the *Committee* to be an integral part of the *course.*

An *obstruction* is a movable *obstruction* if it may be moved without unreasonable effort, without unduly delaying play and without causing damage. Otherwise it is an immovable *obstruction.*

Note: The *Committee* may make a Local Rule declaring a movable *obstruction* to be an immovable *obstruction.*

24-1. Movable Obstruction

A player may obtain relief from a movable *obstruction* as follows:

a. If the ball does not lie in or on the *obstruction,* the *obstruction* may be removed. If the ball *moves,* it shall be replaced, and there is no penalty provided that the movement of the ball is directly attributable to the removal of the *obstruction.* Otherwise, Rule 18-2a applies.

b. If the ball lies in or on the *obstruction,* the ball may be lifted, without penalty, and the *obstruction* removed. The ball shall *through the green* or in a *hazard* be dropped, or on the *putting green* be placed, as near as possible to the spot directly under the place where the ball lay in or on the *obstruction,* but not nearer the *hole.*

The ball may be cleaned when lifted under Rule 24-1.

When a ball is in motion, an *obstruction* which might influence the movement of the ball, other than an attended *flagstick* or *equipment* of the players, shall not be removed.

(Exerting influence on ball — see Rule 1-2.)

Note: If a ball to be dropped or placed under this Rule is not immediately recoverable, another ball may be substituted.

24-2. Immovable Obstruction

a. Interference

Interference by an immovable *obstruction* occurs when a ball lies in or on the *obstruction,* or so close to the *obstruction* that the obstruction interferes with the player's *stance* or the area of his intended swing. If the player's ball lies on the *putting green,* interference also occurs if an immovable *obstruction* on the *putting green* intervenes on his *line of putt.* Otherwise, intervention on the *line of play* is not, of itself, interference under this Rule.

b. Relief

Except when the ball is in a *water hazard* or a

lateral water hazard, a player may obtain relief from interference by an immovable *obstruction*, without penalty, as follows:

(i) *Through the Green*: If the ball lies *through the green*, the *nearest point of relief* shall be determined which is not in a *hazard* or on a *putting green*. The player shall lift the ball and drop it within one club-length of and not nearer the *hole* than the *nearest point of relief* on a part of the *course* which avoids interference (as defined) by the immovable *obstruction* and is not in a *hazard* or on a *putting green*.

(ii) In a *Bunker*: If the ball is in a *bunker*, the player shall lift and drop the ball in accordance with Clause (i) above, except that the *nearest point of relief* must be in the *bunker* and the ball must be dropped in the *bunker*.

(iii) On the *Putting Green*: If the ball lies on the *putting green*, the player shall lift the ball and place it at the *nearest point of relief* which is not in a *hazard*. The *nearest point of relief* may be off the *putting green*.

The ball may be cleaned when lifted under Rule 24-2b.

(Ball rolling to a position where there is interference by the condition from which relief was taken — see Rule 20-2c(v).)

Exception: A player may not obtain relief under Rule 24-2b if (a) it is clearly unreasonable for him to play a *stroke* because of interference by anything other than an immovable *obstruction* or (b) interference by an immovable *obstruction* would occur only through use of an unnecessarily abnormal *stance*, swing or direction of play.

Note 1: If a ball is in a *water hazard* (including a *lateral water hazard*), the player is not entitled to relief without penalty from interference by an immovable *obstruction*. The player shall play the ball as it lies or proceed under Rule 26-1.

Note 2: If a ball to be dropped or placed under this Rule is not immediately recoverable, another ball may be substituted.

Note 3: The *Committee* may make a Local Rule stating that the player must determine the *nearest point of relief* without crossing over, through or under the *obstruction*.

c. Ball Lost

It is a question of fact whether a ball lost after having been struck toward an immovable *obstruction* is lost in the *obstruction*. In order to treat the ball as lost in the *obstruction*, there must be reasonable evidence to that effect. In the absence of such evidence, the ball must be treated as a *lost ball* and Rule 27 applies.

If a ball is *lost* in an immovable *obstruction*, the spot where the ball last entered the *obstruction* shall be determined and, for the purpose of applying this Rule, the ball shall be deemed to lie at this spot.

(i) *Through the Green*: If the ball last entered the immovable *obstruction* at a spot *through the green*, the player may substitute another ball without penalty and take relief as prescribed in Rule 24-2b(i).

(ii) In a *Bunker*: If the ball last entered the immovable *obstruction* at a spot in a *bunker*, the player may substitute another ball without penalty and take relief as prescribed in Rule 24-2b(ii).

(iii) In a *Water Hazard* (including a *Lateral Water Hazard*): If the ball last entered the immovable *obstruction* at a spot in a *water hazard*, the player is not entitled to relief without penalty. The player shall proceed under Rule 26-1.

(iv) On the *Putting Green*: If the ball last entered the immovable *obstruction* at a spot on the *putting green*, the player may substitute another ball without penalty and take relief as prescribed in Rule 24-2b(iii).

PENALTY FOR BREACH OF RULE:
Match play — Loss of hole;
Stroke play — Two strokes.

24/1 Stile Attached to Boundary Fence

Q. Is a stile attached to a boundary fence an obstruction?

A. Yes, unless the Committee declares it to be an integral part of the course under Rule 33-2a(iv).

Exposed Water Pipe Adjacent and Parallel to Boundary Fence — See 33-2a/1.

24/2 Angled Supports or Guy Wires Supporting Boundary Fence

Q. Angled supports or guy wires support a boundary fence or a protective net above such a fence. If the angled supports or guy wires extend onto the course, are they obstructions?

A. Any part of such an angled support or guy wire which is in bounds is an obstruction.

24/3 Concrete Bases of Boundary Fence Posts

Q. Posts of a boundary fence have been set in concrete bases 14 inches in diameter. Are the parts of the bases within the boundary of the course obstructions?

A. No. Such a base is part of the fence and thus no part of it is an obstruction — see Definition of "Obstructions." If such bases are at or below ground level, the boundary line is the inside points of the fence posts at ground level. If they are above ground level, the Committee should clarify the location of the boundary line.

24/4 Part of Boundary Fence Within Boundary Line

Q. Part of a boundary fence is bowed towards the course so that it is inside the boundary line formed by the fence posts. A player's ball comes to rest against this part of the fence. Is the player entitled to relief under Rule 24-2b?

A. No. A fence defining out of bounds is not an obstruction even if part of it is inside the boundary line formed by the fence posts — see Definitions of "Obstructions" and "Out of Bounds."

Improving Position of Ball by Bending Boundary Fence — See 13-2/18.

Gate in Boundary Fence — See 27/18.

Displaced Boundary Stake — See 33-2a/20.

24/5 Boundary Stakes Having No Significance in Play of Hole Being Played

Q. White stakes installed between the 7th and 8th holes define out of bounds during play of the 7th hole, but they have no significance during play of the 8th hole. Are such stakes obstructions during play of the 8th hole?

A. No, the Definition of "Out of Bounds" states that such stakes are not obstructions. However, in this case it is recommended that, by Local Rule, the stakes be deemed immovable ostructions during play of the 8th hole. (Revised)

Removal of Boundary Stake Interfering with Swing — See 13-2/17.

24/6 Stone Broken Away from Retaining Wall in Water Hazard

Q. A player's ball in a water hazard is in a playable lie but it is directly behind a stone which has broken away from a retaining wall in the hazard. The wall is an immovable obstruction from which the player is not entitled to relief without penalty. Is the stone which has broken away a movable obstruction, in which case the player may remove it before playing a stroke?

A. Yes.

24/7 Stone Serving as Part of Drain in Bunker

Q. A large stone has been placed at the entrance to a drain in a bunker to prevent sand from washing into the drain. What is the status of such a stone?

A. The stone is an immovable obstruction since it serves as part of the drain which is itself an immovable obstruction. The status of such a stone should be clarified by the Committee.

24/8 Parked Car

Q. A player's ball lies under a parked car.What is the procedure?

A. If the car is readily movable, it should be treated as

a movable obstruction and moved — see Rule 24-1.

If the car is not readily movable, it should be treated as an immovable obstruction and the player is entitled to relief as provided in Rule 24-2b.

24/9 Artificially-Surfaced Road or Path

Q. An artificially-surfaced road or path is an obstruction. What constitutes artificial surfacing?

A. A road or path to which any foreign material, *e.g.*, concrete, tar, gravel, wood chips, etc., has been applied is artificially surfaced and thus an obstruction.

Gravel Used to Surface Road — See 23/14.

24/10 Paved Area

Q. Is a paved area, such as a paved car park or parking lot, an obstruction?

A. Yes. A paved area has the same status as an artificially-surfaced road.

24/11 Wooden Planks

Q. Is wood which has been manufactured into planks an obstruction?

A. Yes.

Ball Lying on Obstruction in Bunker — See 13/5.

When Loose Impediment Transformed into Obstruction — See 23/1.

Half-Eaten Pear — See 23/3.

Tree Basins — See 33-2a/10.5.

24/12 Wooden or Earthen Steps

Wooden steps which have been constructed on a steep bank are obstructions — see Decision 23/1.

Steps which have been cut into a steep bank but which have not been covered with any artificial material such as wooden planks are not obstructions.

[24/13 Reserved]

24/14 Turf Raised by Underground Pipe

Q. A water pipe is partly underground and partly

above ground. In some areas where the pipe is underground it has raised the turf. Is such turf, which has been raised by an obstruction, considered part of the obstruction?

A. No.

Probing Near Ball for Immovable Obstruction — See 13-2/27.

[24/15 Reserved]

24/16 Opponent or Fellow-Competitor Removes Obstruction Affecting Player's Play

Q. An opponent or a fellow-competitor removes an obstruction which affects the player's play. What is the ruling?

A. If the obstruction was movable and the player had asked him not to remove it, the opponent loses the hole, or the fellow-competitor incurs a two-stroke penalty (Rule 1-2); otherwise, there is no penalty.

If the obstruction was immovable, the opponent loses the hole, or the fellow-competitor incurs a two-stroke penalty (Rule 1-2).

[24-1/1 Reserved]

24-1/2 Abandoned Ball

Q. A player's ball comes to rest against an abandoned ball. What is the procedure?

A. An abandoned ball is a movable obstruction. The player may remove it under Rule 24-1.

Rule 22, which deals specifically with one ball interfering with another, does not apply. It applies only if a ball in play interferes with another ball in play.

24-1/3 Movable Artificial Object Lying Out of Bounds

Q. A movable artificial object lying out of bounds interferes with a player's stance. May the player remove it?

A. Yes. Rule 24-1 applies.

24-1/4 Holding Ball in Place While Removing Obstruction

Q. During removal of a movable obstruction, may a player hold his ball to prevent it from moving?

A. No. Such procedure would be a breach of Rule 18-2a. There is no penalty if a ball moves during removal of a movable obstruction provided the movement of the ball is directly attributable to the removal of the obstruction.

24-1/5 Position of Ball Marked Before Obstruction Removed; Ball Moves When Ball-Marker Removed

Q. A player's ball lies against a movable obstruction. Before removing the obstruction, the player marks the position of his ball so that he will be able to replace the ball precisely if the ball moves when the obstruction is removed. The player removes the obstruction and the ball does not move. However, the ball moves when the ball-marker is removed. What is the ruling?

A. The ball-marker is itself a movable obstruction. Accordingly, under Rule 24-1, the player incurs no penalty and he must replace the ball.

Other Decisions relating to Rule 24-1:

Flagstick Lying on Putting Green Removed by Player to Prevent Another Player's Ball from Striking It — See 1-2/3.

Removal of Obstruction in Hazard Would Move Loose Impediment — See 1-4/5.

Position of Ball Worsened When Obstruction Removed; Player Replaces Obstruction — See 13-2/15.5.

Ball in Plastic Bag Moves When Bag Blown to New Position by Wind — See 18-1/7.

Ball in Bunker Moves Closer to Hole When Obstruction Removed and Ball Will Not Remain at Rest When Replaced; All Other Parts of Bunker Are Nearer Hole — See 20-3d/2.

[24-2/1 Reserved]

[24-2/2 Reserved]

24-2a/1 Mental Interference by Obstruction

Q. A player's ball lies several inches to the side of a sprinkler head. The sprinkler head does not physically interfere with the player's stance or the area of his intended swing. However, the sprinkler head bothers the player mentally. Is the player entitled to relief under Rule 24-2b?

A. No. See Rule 24-2a.

[24-2a/2 Reserved]

24-2a/3 Interference by Immovable Obstruction Within Teeing Ground

Q. A player's tee shot strikes a tree, resulting in his ball coming to rest within the teeing ground of the hole being played. His ball now lies in such a position that a sprinkler head interferes with his stance. Is the player entitled to relief?

A. The Rules of Golf do not contemplate such a situation. In equity (Rule 1-4), the player is entitled to relief without penalty and must follow the procedure prescribed in Rule 24-2b(i) for a ball which lies through the green.

The same principle would apply if there was interference by casual water, ground under repair, etc. (Rule 25-1b(i)) or if the player's ball was embedded in its own pitch-mark (Rule 25-2).

[24-2b/1 Reserved]

[24-2b/2 Reserved]

[24-2b/3 Reserved]

24-2b/3.5 Player Unable Physically to Determine Nearest Point of Relief

24 **Q.** In proceeding under Rule 24-2b(i) or 25-1b(i), "the nearest point of relief" is, according to the Definition of "Nearest Point of Relief," determined by using the club with which the player would expect to play the next stroke. What is the procedure if a player is unable physically to determine the nearest point of relief because that point is within the trunk of a tree or a large bush?

A. The nearest point of relief within the tree or bush must be estimated and the player must drop the ball within one club-length of the estimated point. (Revised)

24-2b/4 Club Used to Determine "Nearest Point of Relief" Not Used for Next Stroke

Q. The Note to the Definition of "Nearest Point of Relief" states: "The player should determine his nearest point of relief by using the club with which he expects to play his next stroke to simulate the address position and swing for such stroke." If the subsequent lie of the ball were such that it was expedient for the player to play his next stroke with some other club, may the player use the other club?

A. Yes. (Revised)

Dropped Ball Rolls Nearer Obstruction Than Nearest Point; Whether Re-Drop Required if Player Changes Clubs and Obstruction No Longer Interferes — See 20-2c/0.7.

Player Takes Relief from an Area of Ground Under Repair; Whether Re-Drop Required if Condition Interferes for Stroke with Club Not Used to Determine "Nearest Point of Relief" — See 20-2c/0.8.

[24-2b/4.5 Reserved]

[24-2b/5 Reserved]

24-2b/6 Relief from Immovable Obstruction Incidentally Results in Relief from Boundary Fence

Q. A player's ball is in such a position that a boundary fence and an immovable obstruction near the fence both interfere with the area of the player's intended swing. It is reasonable for him to play the stroke despite the interference from the boundary fence. If the player takes relief from the obstruction under Rule 24-2b, he will incidentally get relief from the fence. Is the player entitled to invoke Rule 24-2b in such circumstances?

A. Yes.

24-2b/7 Relief from Obstruction Interfering with Swing Incidentally Gives Relief from Intervention on Line of Play

Q. A player's ball lies behind an immovable obstruction. The obstruction interferes with the player's swing and also intervenes on his line of play. In obtaining relief from interference with his swing, must the player drop the ball in such a position that intervention on the line of play is maintained?

A. No. Since the obstruction interferes with the player's swing, the player is entitled to relief under Rule 24-2b. If, in proceeding under this Rule, the player could drop the ball in a place which would also avoid intervention on his line of play, he is entitled to do so.

24-2b/8 Dropping from Rough to Fairway in Obtaining Relief from Obstruction

Q. A player whose ball lies in the rough close to the fairway is entitled to relief from an immovable obstruction. In obtaining relief under Rule 24-2b(i), may the player drop the ball on the fairway?

A. Yes. There is no distinction in the Rules between fairway and rough; both are covered by the term "through the green."

24-2b/9 After Relief from Obstruction Second Obstruction Interferes

Q. A player obtaining relief from an immovable obstruction drops his ball in such a position that another immovable obstruction interferes with his swing. What is the procedure?

A. The player is entitled to relief from the second obstruction as provided in Rule 24-2b.

Player Takes Relief from Area of Casual Water and Ball Comes to Rest in a Position Where Another Area of Casual Water Interferes; Whether Re-Drop Required — See 20-2c/7.

24-2b/9.5 After Relief Taken from Obstruction for Stroke Towards Green, Obstruction Interferes with Stance for Necessary Sideways Stroke

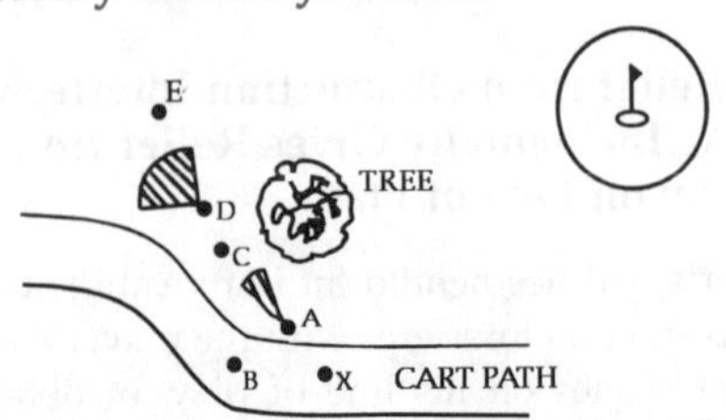

Q. With regard to the illustration above, Point X is the original position of the ball and Point A is the nearest point of relief from the obstruction (cart path). The player drops his ball within one club-length of Point A (within the shaded area) and it comes to rest on the cart path at Point B. He re-drops as required by Rule 20-2c, again dropping within one club-length of Point A and the ball comes to rest at Point C.

At Point C there is no interference by the cart path for a stroke towards the green. However, the player cannot play towards the green from Point C because of intervention by the tree. His only reasonable stroke is sideways to the fairway, and his stance for such a stroke would be on the cart path. Is the player now required to place the ball as near as possible to the spot where it first struck the ground when re-dropped under the penultimate paragraph of Rule 20-2c?

A. No. The player is not entitled to place the ball because at Point C there is no interference by the cart path for a stroke towards the green, the intended direction of play when relief was taken. However, as a result of the tree, the player has a new situation. He is entitled to take relief under Rule 24-2b(i) for the sideways stroke since this is not an unnecessarily abnormal direction of play — see Exception under Rule 24-2b — and his nearest point of relief would be Point D. After the ball is dropped within one club-length of Point D (within the shaded area) and it comes to rest at Point E, the player may play in any direction he wishes.

Nearest Point of Relief from Cart Path Is in Casual Water; Nearest Point of Relief from Casual Water Is Back on Cart Path — See 1-4/8.

Ball Lying on Immovable Obstruction Is Dropped Away; Ball Rolls to Position Where Player Would Have to Stand on Obstruction; Whether Re-Drop Required — See 20-2c/0.5.

24

24-2b/10 Obstruction in Ground Under Repair Interferes with Player's Swing

Q. An immovable obstruction situated within an area defined as ground under repair interferes with the area of the player's intended swing. May the player take relief from the obstruction under Rule 24-2b, drop his ball in the ground under repair and then have the option of playing the ball as it lies or proceeding under Rule 25-1b which provides relief from ground under repair?

A. Yes.

Player Entitled to Relief from Obstruction Lifts Ball; Player Then Replaces Ball and Plays It from Original Position — See 18-2a/12.

Player Entitled to Relief Without Penalty from Condition Lifts Ball; Chooses Not to Take Relief and Wishes to Proceed Under the Unplayable Ball Rule — See 18-2a/12.5.

Ball in Casual Water Within Ground Under Repair; Whether Player Entitled to Take Relief from Both Conditions in Single Procedure — See 25-1b/11.5.

24-2b/11 Ball Lying on Elevated Obstruction

Q. A ball comes to rest on a bridge over a deep hollow. What is the ruling?

A. Under Rule 24-2b, the player may drop the ball within one club-length of the point on the ground in the hollow directly beneath where the ball lay on the bridge, *i.e.*, vertical distance is disregarded.

24-2b/12 Ball in Drainpipe Under Course; Entrance to Drainpipe Is Out of Bounds

Q. A ball enters an underground drainpipe the entrance to which is out of bounds. The ball is found in the drainpipe under an area which is through the green. What is the ruling?

A. Under Rule 24-2b(i), the player is entitled to drop the ball, without penalty, within one club-length of the spot on the ground immediately above its resting place in the drainpipe, but not nearer the hole and not in a hazard or on a putting green. A boundary line extends vertically upwards and downwards — see Definition of "Out of Bounds."

24

If the player cannot find or identify the ball and there is reasonable evidence that the ball is lost in the drainpipe within the boundaries of the course, the player may invoke Rule 24-2c(i). As that part of the drainpipe situated off the course is not an obstruction (see Definition of "Obstruction") the ball "last entered the immovable obstruction" where the underground drainpipe coincides with the boundary line. Therefore, as stated above, the player may drop a ball, without penalty, within one club-length of the spot on the ground immediately above where the drainpipe coincides with the boundary line, on a part of the course which is not nearer the hole, not in a hazard or on a putting green.

In the absence of reasonable evidence he must proceed under Rule 27-1. (Revised)

Ball Lost in Underground Drainpipe — See 24-2c/1.

[24-2b/13 Reserved]

24-2b/14 Window of Clubhouse Opened and Ball Played Through Window

Q. A competitor hit a ball into a clubhouse which was not out of bounds and had not been declared an integral part of the course. In order to play it out, he opened a window, claiming that it was a movable (or partially movable) obstruction. Was this permissible?

A. Yes. The clubhouse was an immovable obstruction. However, any part of it designed to be movable, such as a window or door, may be moved to any position if this can be done without undue delay.

The same principle would apply if the clubhouse had been declared an integral part of the course.

Improving Line of Play by Removing Stone from Wall — See 13-2/32.

Improving Line of Play by Removing Part of Fence — See 13-2/32.5.

Outside Agency Removes Immovable Obstruction on Player's Line of Play — See 13-2/33.

24-2b/15 Opening Barn Doors to Play Shot Through Barn

Q. May a player open the doors of a barn to enable him to play a shot through the barn?

A. Yes. A barn is an immovable obstruction, but the doors are movable and may be opened. See also Decision 24-2b/14.

24-2b/15.3 Status of Movable Part of Drainage Hose

Q. In a water hazard, a player's swing is interfered with by a drainage hose. One end of the hose is immovable, *i.e.*, it is anchored in the ground. However, that part of the hose interfering with the player's swing can readily be moved to one side or the other. Is the player entitled to move the hose to the side so that is does not interfere with his swing?

A. Yes, since the part of the hose interfering with player's swing is designed to be movable.

Area of Intended Swing Improved by Removing Immovable Obstruction — See 13-2/15.

Stake Supporting Tree Broken in Attempt to Remove It — See 13-2/16.

24-2b/16 Obstruction Interferes But Ball Unplayable Due to Some Other Condition

Q. A player's ball lies between two exposed tree roots. The ball is clearly unplayable due to the roots. An immovable obstruction is so located that it would interfere with the player's backswing if the player could play the ball. The player claims he is entitled to relief, without penalty, under Rule 24-2b(i). Is the player correct?

A. No. See Exception under Rule 24-2b. The player must invoke Rule 28.

24-2b/17 Obstruction Interferes with Abnormal Stroke; Abnormal Stroke Reasonable in Circumstances

Q. A right-handed player's ball is so close to a boundary fence on the left of a hole that the player, in order to play towards the hole, must play left-handed. In playing a left-handed stroke, the player's backswing would be interfered with by an immovable obstruction. Is the player entitled to relief from the obstruction?

A. The player is entitled to relief since employment of an abnormal (left-handed) stroke is necessary in the circumstances — see Exception under Rule 24-2b.

The proper procedure is for the player to take relief for a left-handed stroke in accordance with Rule 24-2b(i).

The player may then use a normal right-handed swing for his next stroke. If the obstruction interferes with the swing or stance for the right-handed stroke, the player may take relief for the right-handed stroke in accordance with Rule 24-2b(i).

24-2b/18 Obstruction Interferes with Abnormal Stroke; Abnormal Stroke Not Reasonable in Circumstances

Q. A right-handed player's ball is in a poor lie. A nearby immovable obstruction would not interfere with a normal right-handed swing but it would interfere with a left-handed swing. The player says he wishes to play his next stroke left-handed and, since the obstruction would interfere with such a stroke, he is entitled to proceed under Rule 24-2b. May the player invoke Rule 24-2b?

A. No. If the only reason for the player to use a left-handed stroke is to escape a poor lie, use of an abnormal (left-handed) stroke is not justifiable and the player is not entitled to invoke Rule 24-2b — see Exception under Rule 24-2b.

24-2b/19 Stroke at Ball Not Reasonable Due to Interference by Immovable Obstruction and Casual Water

Q. A player's ball lies against an immovable obstruction in casual water. It is clearly unreasonable for him to play a stroke because of interference by either of them. The Exceptions to Rule 24-2b and Rule 25-1b appear to preclude free relief from either because of interference by the other. Is this correct?

A. No. The player may take relief without penalty under either Rule 24-2b or Rule 25-1b. The purpose of the Exception to each of these Rules is to prevent the player from fortuitously obtaining free relief when it is clearly unreasonable for him to play a stroke because of interference by something from which free relief is not available.

24-2b/20 Interference by Line or Mark on Ground Consisting of Lime or Paint

Q. A ball comes to rest on a line or other mark on the ground consisting of lime or paint which has been drawn for gallery-control purposes or for providing fixed reference points relating to yardage. Is the player entitled to relief under Rule 24-2b?

A. No. Such lines or marks are not obstructions.

24-2b/21 Interference by Immovable Artificial Object Situated Out of Bounds

Q. An immovable artificial object situated out of bounds interferes with a player's swing. May the player obtain relief as provided in Rule 24-2b?

A. No. Immovable artificial objects off the course are not obstructions (see Definition of "Obstructions"); therefore, the Rules provide no relief without penalty.

Part of Fence Off Course Leans Across Boundary and Interferes with Swing — See 13-2/20.

24-2c/1 Ball Lost in Underground Drainpipe

Q. A player's ball goes into an underground drainpipe, but he cannot reach or identify it. What is the ruling?

A. An underground drainpipe or culvert is an obstruction. If there is reasonable evidence that the ball is lost in the immovable obstruction, the player may invoke Rule 24-2c. Under Rule 24-2c the ball is deemed to lie at the spot where it last entered the obstruction.

24 If the entrance to the underground drainpipe or culvert is in a water hazard, Rule 24-2c(iii) applies and the player is not entitled to relief without penalty and must proceed under Rule 26-1.

If the entrance to the underground drainpipe or culvert is out of bounds, in the absence of reasonable evidence that the ball is lost within the boundaries of the course, the player must proceed under Rule 27-1 — see Decision 24-2b/12. (Revised)

Rule 25. Abnormal Ground Conditions and Wrong Putting Green

Definitions

An *"abnormal ground condition"* is any *casual water, ground under repair* or hole, cast or runway on the *course* made by a *burrowing animal,* a reptile or a bird.

A *"burrowing animal"* is an animal that makes a hole for habitation or shelter, such as a rabbit, mole, ground hog, gopher or salamander.

Note: A hole made by a non-*burrowing animal,* such as a dog, is not an *abnormal ground condition* unless marked or declared as *ground under repair.*

"Casual water" is any temporary accumulation of water on the *course* which is visible before or after the player takes his *stance* and is not in a water hazard. Snow and natural ice, other than frost, are *casual water* or *loose impediments,* at the option of the player. Manufactured ice is an *obstruction.* Dew and frost are not *casual water.* A ball is in *casual water* when it lies in or any part of it touches the *casual water.*

"Ground under repair" is any part of the *course* so marked by order of the *Committee* or so declared by its authorized representative. It includes material piled for removal and a hole made by a greenkeeper, even if not so marked.

All ground and any grass, bush, tree or other growing thing within the *ground under repair* is part of the *ground under repair.* The margin of *ground under repair* extends vertically downwards, but not upwards. Stakes and lines defining *ground under repair* are in such ground. Such stakes are *obstructions.* A ball is in *ground under repair* when it lies in or any part of it touches the *ground under repair.*

Note 1: Grass cuttings and other material left on the *course* which have been abandoned and are not intended to be removed are not *ground under repair* unless so marked.

Note 2: The *Committee* may make a Local Rule prohibiting play from *ground under repair* or an environmentally-sensitive area which has been defined as *ground under repair.*

The *"nearest point of relief"* is the reference point for taking relief without penalty from interference by an immovable *obstruction* (Rule 24-2), an *abnormal ground condition* (Rule 25-1) or a *wrong putting green* (Rule 25-3).

It is the point on the *course,* nearest to where the ball lies, which is not nearer the *hole* and at which, if the ball were so positioned, no interference (as defined) would exist.

Note: The player should determine his *nearest point of relief* by using the club with which he expects to play his next *stroke* to simulate the address position and swing for such *stroke.*

A *"wrong putting green"* is any *putting green* other than that of the hole being played. Unless otherwise prescribed by the *Committee,* this term includes a practice *putting green* or pitching green on the *course.*

25-1. Abnormal Ground Condition

a. Interference

25

Interference by an *abnormal ground condition* occurs when a ball lies in or touches the condition or when such a condition interferes with the player's *stance* or the area of his intended swing. If the player's ball lies on the *putting green,* interference also occurs if such condition on the *putting green* intervenes on his *line of putt.* Otherwise, intervention on the *line of play* is not, of itself, interference under this Rule.

Note: The *Committee* may make a Local Rule denying the player relief from interference with his *stance* by an *abnormal ground condition.*

b. Relief

Except when the ball is in a *water hazard* or a *lateral water hazard,* a player may obtain relief from interference by an *abnormal ground condition* as follows:

(i) *Through the Green*: If the ball lies *through the green,* the *nearest point of relief* shall be determined which is not in a *hazard* or on a *putting green.* The player shall lift the ball and drop it without penalty within one club-length of and not nearer the *hole* than the *nearest point of relief,* on a part of the *course* which avoids interference (as defined) by the condition and is not in a *hazard* or on a *putting green.*

(ii) In a *Bunker*: If the ball is in a *bunker,* the player shall lift and drop the ball either:

(a) Without penalty, in accordance with Clause (i) above, except that the *nearest point of relief* must be in the *bunker* and the ball must be dropped in the *bunker,* or if complete relief is impossible, in the *bunker* as near as possible to the spot where the ball lay, but not nearer the *hole,* on a part of the *course* which affords maximum available relief from the condition; or

(b) Under penalty of one stroke, outside the *bunker* keeping the point where the ball lay directly between the *hole* and the spot on which the ball is dropped, with no limit to how far behind the *bunker* the ball may be dropped.

(iii) On the *Putting Green*: If the ball lies on the *putting green,* the player shall lift the ball and place it without penalty at the *nearest point of relief* which is not in a *hazard,* or if complete relief is impossible, at the nearest position to where it lay which affords maximum available relief from the condition, but not nearer the *hole* nor in a *hazard*. The *nearest point of relief* or maximum available relief may be off the *putting green*.

The ball may be cleaned when lifted under Rule 25-1b.

(Ball rolling to a position where there is interference by the condition from which relief was taken — see Rule 20-2c(v)).

Exception: A player may not obtain relief under Rule 25-1b if (a) it is clearly unreasonable for him to play a *stroke* because of interference by anything other than a condition covered by Rule 25-1a or (b) interference by such a condition would occur only through use of an unnecessarily abnormal *stance*, swing or direction of play.

Note 1: If a ball is in a *water hazard* (including a *lateral water hazard*), the player is not entitled to relief without penalty from interference by an *abnormal ground condition*. The player shall play the ball as it lies (unless prohibited by Local Rule) or proceed under Rule 26-1.

Note 2: If a ball to be dropped or placed under this Rule is not immediately recoverable, another ball may be substituted.

c. Ball Lost

It is a question of fact whether a ball *lost* after having been struck toward an *abnormal ground condition* is *lost* in such condition. In order to treat the ball as *lost* in the *abnormal ground condition*, there must be reasonable evidence to that effect. In the absence of such evidence, the ball must be treated as a *lost ball* and Rule 27 applies.

If a ball is *lost* in an *abnormal ground condition*, the spot where the ball last entered the condition shall be determined and, for the purpose of applying this Rule, the ball shall be deemed to lie at this spot.

(i) *Through the Green*: If the ball last entered the *abnormal ground condition* at a spot *through the green*, the player may substitute another ball without penalty and take relief as prescribed in Rule 25-1b(i).

(ii) In a *Bunker:* If the ball last entered the *abnormal ground condition* at a spot in a *bunker,* the player may substitute another ball without penalty and take relief as prescribed in Rule 25-1b(ii).

(iii) In a *Water Hazard* (including a *Lateral Water Hazard*): If the ball last entered the *abnormal ground condition* at a spot in a *water hazard,* the player is not entitled to relief without penalty. The player shall proceed under Rule 26-1.

(iv) On the *Putting Green:* If the ball last entered the *abnormal ground condition* at a spot on the *putting green,* the player may substitute another ball without penalty and take relief as prescribed in Rule 25-1b(iii).

25-2. Embedded Ball

A ball embedded in its own pitch-mark in the ground in any closely-mown area *through the green* may be lifted, cleaned and dropped, without penalty, as near as possible to the spot where it lay but not nearer the *hole.* The ball when dropped must first strike a part of the *course through the green.* "Closely-mown area" means any area of the *course,* including paths through the rough, cut to fairway height or less.

25-3. Wrong Putting Green

a. Interference

Interference by a *wrong putting green* occurs when a ball is on the *wrong putting green.*

Interference to a player's *stance* or the area of his intended swing is not, of itself, interference under this Rule.

b. Relief

If a player has interference by a *wrong putting green,* the player must take relief, without penalty, as follows:

The *nearest point of relief* shall be determined which is not in a *hazard* or on a *putting green.* The player shall lift the ball and drop it within one club-length of and not nearer the *hole* than the *nearest point of relief*, on a part of the *course* which avoids interference (as defined) by the *wrong putting green* and is not in a *hazard* or on a *putting green*. The ball may be cleaned when so lifted.

PENALTY FOR BREACH OF RULE:
Match play — Loss of hole;
Stroke play — Two strokes.

25/1 Soft, Mushy Earth

Q. Is soft, mushy earth casual water?

A. No. Soft, mushy earth is not casual water unless water is visible on the surface before or after the player takes his stance — see Definition of "Casual Water."

25/2 Overflow from Water Hazard

Q. If a pond (water hazard) has overflowed, is the overflow casual water?

A. Yes. Any overflow of water from a water hazard which is outside the margin of the hazard is casual water.

Ball Lost in Either Water Hazard or Casual Water Overflowing Hazard — See 1-4/7.

25/3 Pitch-Mark Filled with Casual Water

Q. A player's ball plugged deeply in short rough. No casual water was visible on the surface, but the pitch-mark in which the ball came to rest filled with water. Was the player's ball in casual water?

A. Yes.

25/4 Water Visible as Result of Undue Effort with Feet

Q. In a wet area, casual water is not visible before or after the player takes his normal stance. However, by pressing down hard with one foot, the player causes water to appear around the sole of his shoe. Is the player entitled to relief under Rule 25-1b?

A. No. Water visible through undue effort with the feet is not casual water — see Definition of "Casual Water."

25/5 Casual Water on Putting Green Visible When Player Walks Beside Line of Putt But Not Visible Elsewhere

Q. A player's ball lies on a putting green. Casual water is not visible on the green. However, when the player walks beside his line of putt, casual water is visible around the player's feet. Is the player entitled to relief?

A. Not unless there is casual water visible around the player's feet when he takes his stance — see Definition of "Casual Water."

[25/6 Reserved]

Other Decisions relating to Rule 25:

Mopping Up Casual Water on Line of Play — See 13-2/34.

Brushing Aside or Mopping Up Casual Water on Line of Putt — See 16-1a/1.

Ball Moved by Wind or Casual Water While Play Suspended — See 18-1/11.

Ball-Marker Moved Off Green by Wind or Casual Water — See 20-1/10.

Removal of Casual Water on Putting Green by Committee — See 33/1.

25/7 Fallen Tree in Process of Being Removed

Q. A greenkeeper is in the process of sawing up a fallen tree and stacking the wood. What is the status of such a tree?

A. The tree in its entirety is ground under repair as it constitutes "material piled for removal" — see Definition of "Ground Under Repair."

25/8 Tree Stump

Q. Do the Rules provide relief without penalty from a tree stump?

A. No, not unless it has been marked as ground under repair or it is in the process of being unearthed or cut up for removal, in which case it is "material piled for removal" and thus automatically ground under repair — see Definition of "Ground Under Repair."

A tree stump which the Committee intends to remove, but which is not in the process of being removed, is not automatically ground under repair.

25/9 Fallen Tree Attached to Stump

Q. A tree has fallen onto a fairway due to a windstorm and is still attached to the stump. Does it constitute ground under repair?

A. No. However, a player could request relief from the Committee and the Committee would be justified in declaring the area covered by the tree to be ground under repair.

Other Decisions relating to Rule 25:

Damage to Line of Putt Caused by Fellow-Competitor's Caddie — See 16-1a/14.

Declaring Area as Ground Under Repair During Competition Round — See 33-2a/2.

Extensive Damage Due to Heavy Rain and Traffic — See 33-2a/3.

Referee's Authority to Declare Ground Under Repair — See 34-2/1.

25/10 Ball Lost in Tree in Ground Under Repair

Q. A ball is lost in a tree rooted in an area marked as ground under repair. Is the player entitled to relief without penalty under Rule 25-1c?

A. As all ground and any grass, bush, tree or other growing thing within ground under repair is considered to be part of the ground under repair (see Definition of "Ground Under Repair"), the ball is lost in ground under repair and the player is entitled to relief under Rule 25-1c.

In this case, the reference point for taking relief is the spot where the ball last entered the area of ground under repair. (Revised)

25/10.5 Ball in Tree in Ground Under Repair

Q. A player's ball is found through the green in a tree rooted in an area marked as ground under repair. The spot on the ground directly under where the ball lies is outside the white-lined area defining the ground under repair. Is the player entitled to relief under Rule 25-1b(i)?

A. Yes, because the ball lies in or touches the ground under repair — see Definition of "Ground Under Repair." In this case, the reference point for taking relief is the spot on the ground immediately below the place where the ball lay in the tree. (New)

Ball Outside Ground Under Repair Area But High Grass Within Area Interferes With Swing — See 25-1a/1.

25/11 Grass Cuttings

Grass cuttings are only ground under repair if they have been piled for removal — see Note 1 under Definition of "Ground Under Repair." If cuttings piled for removal interfere with a player's stance or swing, the player is entitled to relief under Rule 25-1b.

Grass cuttings are loose impediments (see Definition of "Loose Impediments"), whether or not they are piled for removal, and may be removed by the player — Rule 23-1.

25/12 Cracks in Earth

Q. Are cracks in the earth which occur in hot and dry conditions ground under repair? Do the Rules of Golf provide relief?

A. No. However, a player whose ball is in a large crack would be justified in requesting the Committee to declare the crack to be ground under repair, and the Committee would be justified in doing so.

25/13 Bunker Totally Under Repair

If an entire bunker is being renovated, it does not lose its status as a hazard. However, it is recommended that the Committee should, during the renovation period, define the bunker as ground under repair and classify it as through the green. If such a bunker has been defined as ground under repair but has not been classified as through the green, the player may, under Rule 25-1b(ii):

(a) drop the ball without penalty in the bunker as near as possible to the spot where the ball lay, but not nearer the hole, on ground which affords maximum available relief, *i.e.*, ground which is most nearly normal, or

(b) drop the ball under penalty of one stroke behind the bunker, keeping the point where the ball lay between the hole and the spot on which the ball is dropped.

25/14 Explanation of "Hole Made by Greenkeeper" in Definition of "Ground Under Repair"

Q. What constitutes a "hole made by greenkeeper"?

A. A "hole made by a greenkeeper" is usually ground temporarily dug up in connection with course maintenance, such as a hole made in removing turf or a tree stump, laying pipelines, etc.

25/15 Aeration Holes

Q. Is an aeration hole a hole made by a greenkeeper within the meaning of that term in the Definition of "Ground Under Repair"?

A. No.

25/16 Rut Made by Tractor

Q. Is a rut made by a tractor considered a hole made by a greenkeeper and thus ground under repair? If not, should the Committee declare such a rut to be ground under repair?

A. Such a rut is not a hole made by a greenkeeper. The Committee would be justified in declaring a deep rut to be ground under repair, but not a shallow indentation made by greenkeeping equipment.

Competitor Announces Intention to Play Two Balls; Plays Original Ball Before Dropping Second Ball; Elects Not to Play Second Ball — See 3-3/7.5.

Ball in Rut; Competitor Drops One Ball in Accordance with Rules for Ground Under Repair and Unplayable Ball — See 3-3/11.

25/17 Sunken Hole Plug

Q. Is an old hole plug which has sunk below the level of the surface of the putting green a hole made by a greenkeeper and therefore ground under repair?

A. No. Rule 16-1c applies.

Hole on Putting Green Not in Use — See 16/7.

25/18 Hole of Removed Stake Defining Water Hazard

Q. A stake defining the margin of a water hazard is removed. Is the hole in which the stake was previously located a "hole made by a greenkeeper" and thus ground under repair?

A. Yes. However, such a hole is in a water hazard (see Definition of "Water Hazard") and a player would not be entitled to relief from the hole if his ball was in the water hazard — see first paragraph of Rule 25-1b. (Revised)

[25/19 Reserved]

25/19.5 Footprint of Burrowing Animal, Reptile or Bird

Q. Is the footprint of a burrowing animal, a reptile or a bird a "hole, cast or runway" within the meaning of these terms in the Definition of "Abnormal Ground Conditions"?

A. No. A footprint is an irregularity of surface from which there is no relief without penalty. (Revised)

[25/20 Reserved]

25/21 Lifting Ball to Determine Whether It Lies in Burrowing Animal Hole

Q. May a player whose ball lies in a depression, other than in a water hazard, lift his ball to determine if it is in a hole made by a burrowing animal?

A. In equity (Rule 1-4), the player may lift the ball, without penalty, provided he announces his intention in advance to his opponent in match play or his marker or a fellow-competitor in stroke play, marks the position of the ball, and gives his opponent, marker or fellow-competitor an opportunity to observe the lifting. If the ball is in a burrowing animal hole, he is entitled to relief under Rule 25-1b. Otherwise, the ball must be replaced and the opponent, marker or fellow-competitor given an opportunity to observe the replacement. If the player fails to comply with this procedure, he shall incur a penalty of one stroke, but no additional penalty under Rule 20-1 shall be applied. A ball so lifted may not be cleaned unless it is found to be lying in a burrowing animal hole and the player elects to take relief under Rule 25.

Ball Found in Burrowing Animal Hole After Five-Minute Search — See 27/7.

[25/22 Reserved]

25/23 Molehills

Q. Molehills are casts made by a burrowing animal. If the greenkeeping staff have swept them flat, but the surface is still irregular, do molehills cease to be classified as casts made by a burrowing animal?

25 A. If it is established that mounds of soil are casts (or remains of casts) made by moles, relief is permissible under Rule 25-1b. However, when such a mound has been swept flat, it becomes an irregularity of surface and there is no relief without penalty.

25-1/1 Ball in Casual Water Difficult to Retrieve

Q. There is reasonable evidence that a player's ball came to rest in a large puddle of casual water. A ball is visible in the casual water, but the player cannot retrieve it or identify it as his ball without unreasonable effort. The player abandons the ball and proceeds under Rule 25-1c, which provides relief for a ball lost in casual water. Was the player justified in doing so?

A. Yes. A player is not obliged to use unreasonable effort to retrieve a ball in casual water, for identification purposes.

However, if it would not take unreasonable effort to retrieve a ball in casual water, the player must retrieve it. If it turns out to be the player's ball and he elects to take relief, he must proceed under Rule 25-1b(i); otherwise, he must proceed under Rule 25-1c(i).

25-1a/1 Ball Outside Ground Under Repair Area But Tree Within Area Interferes with Swing

Q. The margins of ground under repair do not extend vertically upwards. If the ball lies outside ground under repair and a tree rooted within the ground under repair interferes with a player's swing, but there is no interference with his stance, is the player entitled to relief?

A. Yes. The Definition of "Ground Under Repair" states: "All ground and any grass, bush, tree or other growing thing within the ground under repair is part of the ground under repair." Therefore, the player may take relief under Rule 25-1 as the tree within the ground under repair interferes with the area of his intended swing. (Revised)

Ball in Tree in Ground Under Repair — See 25/10.5.

25-1a/2 Casual Water on Putting Green Intervenes Between Ball Off Green and Hole

Q. A player's ball lies just off the putting green and casual water on the green intervenes between the ball and the hole. Is the player entitled to relief?

25

A. No. In addition, Rule 13-2 prohibits the player from removing casual water from his line of play. (Revised).

Casual Water on Putting Green; Whether Player Entitled to Relief for Intervention if Ball is on Green and Nearest Point of Relief is off Green — See 25-1b/10.5.

[25-1b/1 Reserved]

25-1b/2 Diagrams Illustrating "Nearest Point of Relief"

The following diagrams illustrate the term "nearest point of relief" in Rule 25-1b(i) in the case of both a right-handed and left-handed player.

The "nearest point of relief" must be strictly interpreted. A player is not permitted to choose on which side of the ground under repair he will drop the ball, unless there are two equidistant nearest points of relief. Even if one side of the ground under repair is fairway and the other is bushes, if the nearest point of relief is in the bushes then the player, if taking relief, must drop the ball within one club-length of that point, even though he may have to drop the ball in a virtually unplayable lie.

The same procedure applies under Rule 24-2b dealing with immovable obstructions. (Revised)

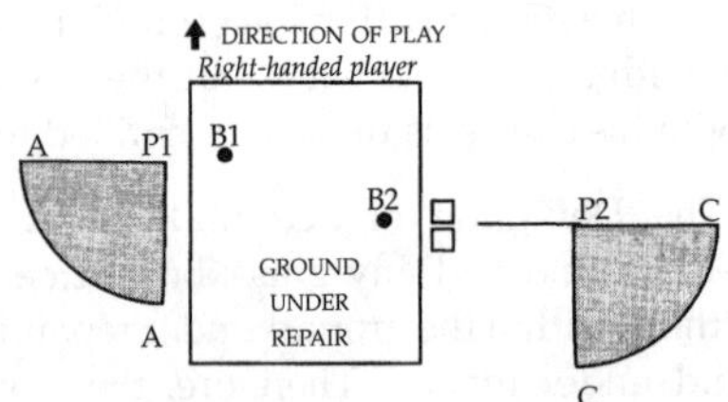

B1 = position of ball in ground under repair, etc.
P1 = nearest point of relief
P1-A-A = shaded area within which ball to be dropped, radius of one club-length from P1 measured with any club
B2 = position of ball in ground under repair, etc.
□□ — = notional stance required to play ball at P2 with club with which player would expect to play the stroke
P2 = nearest point of relief
P2-C-C = shaded area within which ball to be dropped, radius of one club-length from P2, measured with any club

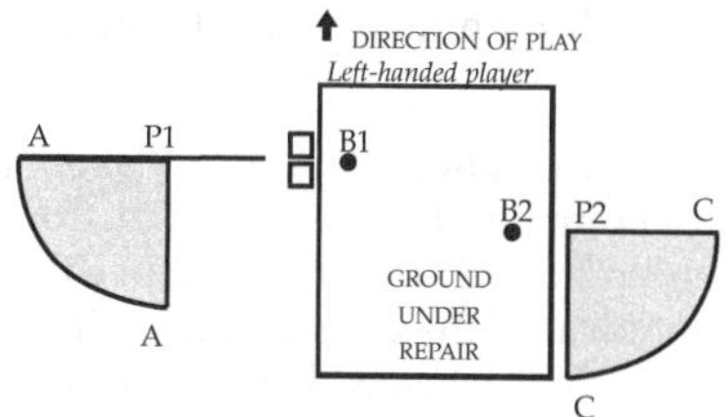

B1 and B2 are the positions of the ball in ground under repair, etc.
P1 is the nearest point of relief B1
P2 is the nearest point of relief B2

Shaded area P1-A-A = dropping area for ball at B1
Shaded area P2-C-C = dropping area for ball at B2

□□— = player's notional stance to play ball at P1

25-1b/3 Improving Line of Play When Taking Relief from Abnormal Ground Conditions

Q. In certain circumstances, in complying with Rule 25-1b, it is possible for a player incidentally to improve his line of play, *e.g.*, avoid playing over a bunker or a tree. Is this permissible?

A. Yes. If a player's ball is in one of the conditions covered by Rule 25 and if, in taking relief in accordance with the procedure laid down in Rule 25-1b, his line of play is improved, this is his good fortune.

Player Entitled to Relief from Abnormal Ground Condition Lifts Ball; Player Then Replaces Ball and Plays It from Original Position — See 18-2a/12.

Player Entitled to Relief Without Penalty from Condition Lifts Ball; Chooses Not to Take Relief and Wishes to Proceed Under the Unplayable Ball Rule — See 18-2a/12.5.

25-1b/4 Casual Water Covering Teeing Ground

Q. After several groups have played a particular hole, a player arrives at the teeing ground of that hole which has become completely covered with casual water. What is the procedure?

A. In such a case, the matter should be brought to the attention of the Committee. Rule 25-1 is not applicable since the player's ball is not in play — see Definition of "Ball in Play."

In match play, the Committee may relocate the teeing ground.

In stroke play, if the conditions are such that removal of the casual water might be possible, the Committee should suspend play and attempt to remove the casual water. If the removal of the casual water is impossible, the Committee may (1) suspend play until the teeing ground is playable or cancel the round (Rule 33-2d) or (2) relocate the teeing ground if this could be done without giving any competitor an undue advantage or disadvantage. (Revised)

Interference by Casual Water Within Teeing Ground — See 24-2a/3.

Hole Surrounded by Casual Water — See 33-2d/2.

25-1b/5 Explanation of "Maximum Available Relief" from Casual Water in Bunker

Q. In a bunker completely covered by casual water, is the place providing "maximum available relief" the spot which will provide the most relief for both lie and stance or just lie?

A. The term applies to both lie and stance. The spot providing "maximum available relief" might be such that the ball will be in shallower water than the player's feet after he takes his stance, or vice versa.

25-1b/6 Ball Dropped from Casual Water in Bunker at Point of Maximum Relief Rolls Elsewhere

Q. A player whose ball lies in a bunker completely covered by casual water drops his ball under Rule 25-1b(ii) at a spot where there is 1/4 inch of casual water. This spot is the nearest spot providing maximum available relief. The ball rolls into a spot where there is about 1/2 inch of casual water. What is the ruling?

A. In equity (Rule 1-4), and under the principle of Rule 20-2c(v), the player may re-drop and, if the ball so rolls again, place the ball where it first struck a part of the course when re-dropped.

25-1b/7 Ball to Be Dropped in Bunker Dropped Outside Bunker and Rolls into Bunker

Q. A player's ball lies in casual water in a bunker. The player elects to proceed under Rule 25-1b(ii)(a) and determines that the nearest point of relief in the bunker is close to the back of the bunker. The player drops his ball within one club-length of the nearest point of relief on a slope outside the bunker because he fears it will plug in the sand. The ball rolls down the slope and comes to rest in the bunker not nearer the hole than the nearest point of relief. Is the player subject to penalty?

A. Yes, unless he lifts the ball and proceeds correctly, as provided in Rule 20-6. Under Rule 25-1b(ii)(a), the player is required to drop the ball in the bunker. If the player, although proceeding under this Rule, drops the ball outside the bunker and plays it, he is in breach of Rule 25 and the penalty is loss of hole in match play or two strokes in stroke play. (Revised)

25-1b/8 Player's Options When Bunker Completely Covered by Casual Water

Q. If a player's ball lies in a bunker completely covered by casual water, what are his options?

A. The player may play the ball as it lies or:

(1) drop the ball in the bunker without penalty at the nearest point, not nearer the hole, where the depth of the casual water is least — Rule 25-1b(ii)(a); or

(2) drop the ball behind the bunker under penalty of one stroke — Rule 25-1b(ii)(b); or

(3) declare the ball unplayable and proceed in accordance with Rule 28. (Revised)

25-1b/9 Player Who Invokes First Option of Rule 25-1b(ii) Then Wishes to Invoke Second Option

25

Q. A player's ball is in a bunker completely covered by casual water. Under the first option of Rule 25-1b(ii), he drops the ball on ground in the bunker affording maximum available relief. He then decides he would have been better off to invoke the second option and drop behind the bunker. May he invoke the second option?

A. No. Rule 25-1b(ii) permits the player to proceed under one of two options. He is not entitled to invoke one option and then, if he does not like the result, invoke the other. Therefore, as Rule 25-1 no longer applies, the player must play the ball as it lies or proceed under the unplayable ball Rule, incurring the penalty stroke prescribed by that Rule. (Revised)

25-1b/10 Casual Water on Putting Green; Nearest Point of Relief Is Off Green

Q. A player whose ball is on a putting green is entitled to relief from casual water. However, the nearest position affording complete relief which is not nearer the hole or in a hazard is off the green in the rough. If the player opts to take relief, must he place the ball in the rough?

A. Yes. See Rule 25-1b(iii). (Revised)

25-1b/10.5 Casual Water on Putting Green; Whether Player Entitled to Relief for Intervention If Ball Is On Green and Nearest Point of Relief Is Off Green

Q. In Illustration X, a player's ball lies at Point 1 in casual water on the putting green. In Illustration Y, a player's ball lies at Point 1 on the putting green with casual water intervening on his line of putt.

Under Rule 25-1b(iii), the player is not entitled to place the ball at Point 4, which is on the green, because Point

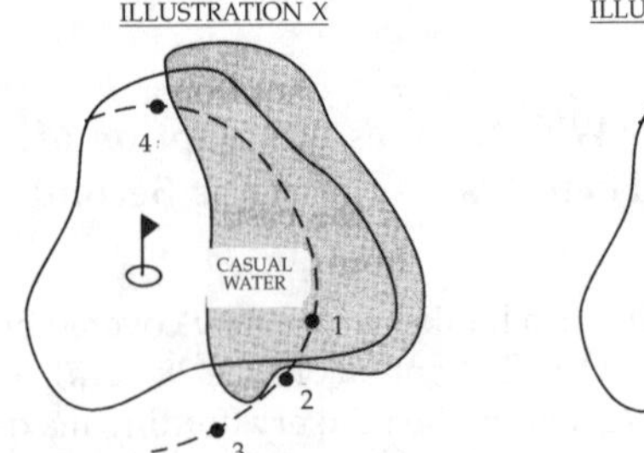

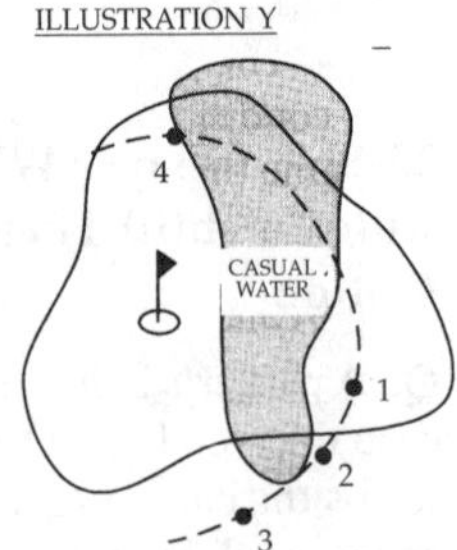

4 is farther from Point 1 than either Point 2 or Point 3, both of which are off the green. It would seem that Point 2 may be the correct point because there is no relief if a ball lies off the green and casual water on the green intervenes on the line of play. In taking relief, must the player place the ball at Point 2 or Point 3?

A. Since, in both illustrations, the ball lies on the putting green, the player is entitled to relief with respect to the lie of the ball and intervention on his line. Accordingly, in either case the player must place the ball at Point 3, the nearest point which affords complete relief with respect to both situations. (Revised)

25-1b/11 Ball in Casual Water Within Ground Under Repair

Q. A ball lies in casual water within an area defined as ground under repair. May a player take relief from the casual water under Rule 25-1b, drop the ball in the ground under repair, and then either play the ball as it lies or take relief from the ground under repair under Rule 25-1b?

A. Yes.

25-1b/11.5 Ball in Casual Water Within Ground Under Repair; Whether Player Entitled to Take Relief from Both Conditions in Single Procedure

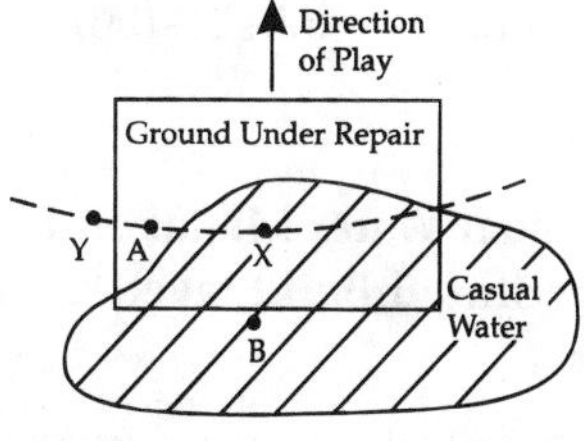

Q. The illustration above shows a player's ball which lies in casual water, at Point X, within an area of ground under repair. May the player, in a single procedure, drop the ball at Point Y, the nearest point of relief from both conditions?

A. No. The player has the option of taking relief from each condition in separate stages but not from both at the same time.

The player may take relief from the casual water at Point A and then may take relief from the ground under repair.

Alternatively, he may take relief from ground under repair at Point B and then may take relief from the casual water.

Nearest Point of Relief from Cart Path Is in Casual Water; Nearest Point of Relief from Casual Water Is Back on Cart Path — See 1-4/8.

Player Takes Relief from Area of Casual Water and Ball Comes to Rest in a Position Where Another Area of Casual Water Interferes; Whether Re-Drop Required — See 20-2c/7.

25-1b/12 Casual Water Mistaken for Water Hazard; Original Ball Played Under Water Hazard Rule

Q. A player whose ball is in casual water mistakes the casual water for a water hazard. He retrieves his original ball, drops it 10 yards behind the casual water in accordance with the water hazard Rule and plays it. His error is then discovered. What is the ruling?

A. The player did not follow the procedure prescribed in Rule 25-1b(i) for dropping a ball from casual water; he dropped the ball in a wrong place. In match play, he loses the hole — Rule 20-7a. In stroke play, he incurs a penalty of two strokes — Rules 25-1b(i) and 20-7b.

25-1b/13 Casual Water Mistaken for Water Hazard; Substituted Ball Played Under Water Hazard Rule

Q. A player whose ball is in casual water mistakes the casual water for a water hazard. The player does not retrieve his original ball, although he could have done so without unreasonable effort — see Decision 25-1/1. Rather, he drops another ball 10 yards behind the casual water in accordance with the water hazard Rule and plays it. His error is then discovered. What is the ruling?

A. Since the player could retrieve the ball without unreasonable effort, he was not permitted to substitute a ball in taking relief from the casual water. Additionally, as a result of proceeding under the water hazard Rule, he dropped the ball in a wrong place.

In match play, the player loses the hole (Rules 15-1, 25-1b(i) and 20-7a).

In stroke play, he incurs a total penalty of four strokes — two for wrongly substituting a ball (Rule 15-1) and two for playing from a wrong place (Rules 25-1b(i) and 20-7b).

[25-1b/14 Reserved]

25-1b/14.5 Ball Declared Unplayable Dropped in Ground Under Repair from Which Play Prohibited; Ball Then Dropped Under Ground Under Repair Rule

Q. A player declared his ball unplayable. In proceeding under Rule 28b or c, the player dropped his ball in an area of ground under repair from which play was prohibited by Local Rule. He then took the mandatory relief under Rule 25-1b. Is this procedure permitted?

A. Yes.

Ball in Ground Under Repair Thought to be Unfit for Play Lifted and Cleaned — See 5-3/6.

Obstruction in Ground Under Repair Interferes with Player's Swing — See 24-2b/10.

Ball Embedded in Ground Under Repair in Closely Mown Area — See 25-2/4.

25-1b/15 Measuring Across Ground Under Repair in Obtaining Relief

Q. A player obtaining relief from a narrow strip of ground under repair through the green determines his nearest point of relief (Point A) which is not in a hazard or on a putting green. Point A is on the right-hand side of the ground under repair. Within one club-length of Point A is a point (Point B) on the left side of the ground under repair which meets the requirements of Rule 25-1b(i). May the player drop his ball at Point B?

A. Yes. There is nothing in Rule 25-1b prohibiting measuring the one club-length across ground under repair in obtaining relief. (Revised)

Ball Dropped from Ground Under Repair Area Rolls to Position Where Area Interferes with Stance; Whether Re-Drop Required — See 20-2c/0.5.

25-1b/16 Ball Equidistant From Two Points Which Meet Requirements of Ground Under Repair Rule

Q. Through the green, the player's ball lies in ground under repair and he opts for relief under Rule 25-1b(i). There is no single nearest point of relief. Rather, there are two such points equidistant from the spot where the ball lies. May the player drop within one club-length of either point?

A. Yes. (Revised)

After Declaring Ball Unplayable and Lifting It, Player Discovers That Ball Was in Ground Under Repair — See 28/13.

25-1b/17 Pine Needles Piled for Removal Interfere with Line of Play After Ball Dropped Away

Q. A player whose ball lies in pine needles piled for removal drops away under Rule 25-1b. The ball comes to rest in such a position that the pile of pine needles intervenes on his line of play. May the player remove the pine needles from his line of play?

25

A. Yes. Pine needles piled for removal are loose impediments or ground under repair. Initially, the player was entitled to remove the pine needles under Rule 23-1 (Loose Impediments) or drop away, as he did, under Rule 25-1b.

After the player dropped away a new situation existed and he was no longer entitled to invoke Rule 25-1b. However, he was not prohibited from removing the pine needles under Rule 23-1.

Ball Played from Ground Under Repair Picked Up and Relief Taken Under Ground Under Repair Rule — See 18-2a/8.

25-1b/18 Crawfish Mound Interferes with Stance or Swing

Q. When a crawfish digs a hole, it creates a sizable mound of mud. If such a mound interferes with a player's stance or swing, does he get relief under Rule 25-1b?

A. Yes, provided the player's ball does not lie in a water hazard — see first paragraph of Rule 25-1b. A crawfish is a burrowing animal. (Revised)

Touching Mound Made by Burrowing Animal with Backswing in Bunker — See 13-4/5.

25-1b/19 Ball Lies on Mound Made by Burrowing Animal; Unreasonable to Play Stroke Due to Bush

Q. A player's ball lies under a bush and it is clearly unreasonable for the player to play a stroke at it. However, the ball lies on a mound made by a burrowing animal. Is the player entitled to relief without penalty under Rule 25-1b?

A. Under the Exception to Rule 25-1b a player may not obtain relief from an abnormal ground condition if it is clearly unreasonable for him to play a stroke due to interference by something other than such a condition. Therefore, in the circumstances described, the player is not entitled to relief. (Revised)

Stroke at Ball Not Reasonable Due to Interference by Immovable Obstruction and Casual Water — See 24-2b/19.

25-1b/20 Stance Interfered with by Burrowing Animal Hole; Unreasonable to Play Stroke Because of Other Condition

Q. A player's ball is in an indentation at the base of a tree in such a position that it is clearly unreasonable for him to play a stroke. Despite this, the player claims relief without penalty under Rule 25-1 because his stance for a stroke at the ball in the indentation would be on a burrowing animal hole. Is the player entitled to relief without penalty under Rule 25-1b?

A. Under the Exception to Rule 25-1b a player may not obtain relief from an abnormal ground condition if it is clearly unreasonable for him to play a stroke due to interference by something other than such a condition. In the circumstances described above, the player's ball is unplayable as it lies in an indentation at the base of a tree. Therefore, the player is not entitled to relief under Rule 25-1 from the burrowing animal hole. (Revised)

25-1b/21 Cast of Burrowing Animal Interferes with Stroke Towards Green; Tree Prevents Such Stroke

Q. A player's ball is immediately behind a tree. A cast behind the ball made by a burrowing animal would interfere with the player's backswing for a stroke towards the green, but not with a sideways stroke, which is the only reasonable stroke. If the player says he intends to play towards the green into the tree, may he take relief without penalty under Rule 25-1b?

A. Under the Exception to Rule 25-1b a player may not obtain relief from an abnormal ground condition if interference from such a condition would only occur through the player using an unnecessarily abnormal direction of play. Therefore, in the circumstances described above, the player is not entitled to relief. (Revised)

25-1b/22 Cast of Burrowing Animal Interferes with Sideways Stroke; When Relief Granted

Q. A ball is behind a tree so that a sideways stroke is the only reasonable stroke for the player. However, a cast made by a burrowing animal interferes with the backswing for a sideways stroke. Is the player entitled to relief under Rule 25-1b?

A. Yes, and if relief gets the player out from behind the tree, he is entitled to play towards the green.

25-1b/23 Ball Enters Burrowing Animal Hole Out of Bounds and Comes to Rest in Bounds

Q. The entrance to a burrowing animal hole is out of bounds, but most of the burrow is in bounds under the course. A ball enters the hole from out of bounds and comes to rest in bounds under ground classified as through the green. What is the procedure?

A. Under Rule 25-1b, the player may drop the ball, without penalty, within one club-length of the point on the ground directly above its position in the burrow. In such cases, vertical distance is disregarded in applying the Rules.

25-1b/24 Ball Enters Burrowing Animal Hole in Bounds and Comes to Rest Out of Bounds

Q. A player's ball entered a rabbit hole, the mouth of which was in bounds but only about a foot from a boundary fence. The rabbit hole sloped steeply down below the fence, so that the ball came to rest beyond the boundary line. What is the ruling?

A. Whether or not a ball is out of bounds depends on where it lies in relation to the boundary of the course and this must be measured vertically upwards or downwards — see Definition of "Out of Bounds."

In the case cited, the ball was lying out of bounds and Rule 27-1 applied. Relief could not be obtained under Rule 25-1, *i.e.*, from a hole made by a burrowing animal.

25-1b/25 Ball Enters Burrowing Animal Hole in Bunker and Comes to Rest Underneath Putting Green

Q. A ball enters a burrowing animal hole in a greenside bunker and comes to rest beneath the putting green. As the ball is not in the bunker or on the putting green, is relief taken in accordance with Rule 25-1b(i), *i.e.*, through the green?

A. Yes.

25-1b/26 Player Unaware Ball in Water Hazard Takes Relief from Interference by Burrowing Animal Hole

Q. A player, unaware that his ball is in a dry water hazard, drops a ball under Rule 25-1b(i) believing he is entitled to relief from a hole made by a burrowing animal. After dropping the ball in the hazard, he discovers his mistake. What is the ruling?

A. As the player's ball lay in a water hazard, he was not entitled to relief, without penalty, from a hole made by a burrowing animal — see first paragraph of Rule 25-1b. However, as his ball lay in a water hazard, he is not precluded from taking relief under Rule 26.

In this situation, he may lift the dropped ball (Rule 20-6) and;

1. replace the ball where it originally lay in the water hazard, in which case he incurs a penalty stroke under Rule 18-2a — see Decision 18-2a/12; or

2. proceed under Rule 26-1. He incurs a penalty of one stroke under Rule 26-1, but no additional penalty is incurred. (Revised)

25-1c/1 Meaning of "Reasonable Evidence" in Rule 25-1c

Q. An area of casual water preceded by high rough is in a hollow not visible from the tee. A ball driven into this area is lost. The ball may be lost in the casual water or it may be lost in the high rough. Is there reasonable evidence that the ball is lost in the casual water?

A. No. In such circumstances, there is not reasonable evidence that the ball is lost in casual water. The player must proceed under Rule 27-1.

25-1c/2 Ball Dropped and Played Under Ground Under Repair Rule in Absence of Reasonable Evidence Original Ball Lost in Ground Under Repair

Q. A player, after a search of less than one minute, considers that his ball is lost in ground under repair, although there is not reasonable evidence to that effect.

He drops a ball under Rule 25-1c and plays it. His original ball is then found beyond the ground under repair area. What is the ruling?

A. When the player dropped another ball under Rule 25-1c, it became the ball in play and the original ball was lost.

In the absence of reasonable evidence that the ball had been lost in ground under repair, the player was required to put another ball into play under Rule 27-1. In playing the ball dropped under Rule 25-1c, the player played from a wrong place.

In match play, he incurred a penalty of loss of hole (Rule 20-7a).

In stroke play, he incurred the stroke-and-distance penalty prescribed by Rule 27-1 and an additional penalty of two strokes for a breach of that Rule. If the breach was a serious one, he was subject to disqualification unless he corrected the error as provided in the second paragraph of Rule 20-7b.

Ball Played Under Rule for Ball Lost in Ground Under Repair After Another Ball Played Under Stroke-and-Distance Procedure — See 15/8.

25-1c/3 Ball Played in Ground Under Repair Area Lost in Same Area

Q. A player plays a stroke at his ball which is lying in a large area of ground under repair. The player advances the ball but not far enough to get it out of the ground under repair. The ball cannot be found. What is the ruling?

A. The player may drop a ball outside the ground under repair area, without penalty, as provided in Rule 25-1c.

Alternatively, the player may, under penalty of one stroke, drop a ball in the ground under repair as nearly as possible at the spot from which his original ball was last played — Rule 27-1 (Ball Lost).

Another Decision relating to Rule 25-1c:

Whether Provisional Ball Becomes Ball in Play If Original Ball Lost in Ground Under Repair — See 27-2c/1.5.

25-2/1 Ball Bounces Out of Its Pitch-Mark and Spins Back into It

Q. A player's ball lands in soft ground in a closely mown area through the green, bounces out of its pitch-mark and then spins back into the pitch-mark. Is the player entitled to relief under Rule 25-2?

A. Yes. If a ball spins back into its pitch-mark, it is embedded in the pitch-mark.

25-2/2 Dropped Ball Embeds

Q. A player takes relief under an applicable Rule and drops a ball on a fairway. The ball embeds on impact. Is the player entitled to relief under Rule 25-2?

A. Yes.

25-2/2.5 Dropped Ball Embeds; Procedure If Ball Again Embeds When Re-Dropped

Q. According to Decision 25-2/2, if a ball dropped on a fairway embeds on impact, the player is entitled to relief under Rule 25-2. What is the proper procedure if a ball embeds each time it is dropped?

A. If a ball embeds when dropped and embeds again when re-dropped, the player may, in equity (Rule 1-4), place the ball as near as possible to the spot where it embedded when re-dropped, but not nearer the hole.

If the player drops the ball more than twice, the ball embeds each time and he then becomes aware that he was entitled to place the ball after the second drop, he may place the ball as near as possible to the spot where it embedded on the second drop.

[25-2/3 Reserved]

25-2/4 Ball Embedded in Ground Under Repair in Closely Mown Area

Q. A player's ball is embedded in ground under repair in a closely mown area through the green. May the player drop the ball within the ground under repair under Rule 25-2 (Embedded Ball) and then elect whether to play the ball as it lies or take relief from the ground under repair under Rule 25-1b?

A. Yes.

Ball in Casual Water Within Ground Under Repair; Whether Player Entitled to Take Relief from Both Conditions in Single Procedure — See 25-1b/11.5.

25-2/5 Ball Embedded in Grass Bank or Face of Bunker

Q. Are grass banks or faces of bunkers considered to be "closely mown areas" under Rule 25-2 (Embedded Ball) and may relief be taken from them under that Rule?

A. No, not unless they are cut to fairway height or less.

Ball Completely Embedded in Lip of Bunker — See 13/4.

Local Rule for Bunker Faces Consisting of Stacked Turf — See 33-8/39.

25-2/6 Ball on Steep Bank Driven Straight into Ground

Q. A player's ball lies on a steep bank in the fairway. He plays a stroke and drives the ball straight into the bank, *i.e.*, the ball is never airborne. Is the player entitled to relief without penalty under Rule 25-2?

A. No. Under Rule 25-2, relief is provided if a ball is embedded in its own pitch-mark. The word "pitch-mark" implies that the ball has become airborne.

25-2/7 Lifting Ball to Determine Whether It Is Embedded

Q. A player's ball lies on a fairway and he believes the ball may be embedded in its own pitch-mark. Is the player entitled to lift the ball to determine whether it is embedded?

A. In equity (Rule 1-4), the player may lift the ball, without penalty, provided he announces his intention in advance to his opponent in match play or his marker or a fellow-competitor in stroke play, marks the position of the ball, and gives his opponent, marker or fellow-competitor an opportunity to observe the lifting. If the ball is embedded in the ground, he is entitled to relief under Rule 25-2. Otherwise, the ball must be replaced and the opponent, marker or fellow-competitor given an opportunity to observe the replacement. If the player fails to comply with this procedure, he shall incur a penalty of one stroke, but no additional penalty under Rule 20-1 shall be applied. A ball so lifted may not be cleaned unless it is found to be embedded in the ground and the player elects to take relief under Rule 25-2.

Other Decisions Relating to Rule 25-2:

Pitch-Mark in Dropping Area Repaired Before Ball Dropped — See 13-2/10.

Ball Embedded Within Teeing Ground — See 24-2a/3.

25-3/1 Status of Half of Double Green Serving Hole Not Being Played

Q. One half of a U-shaped putting green serves as the 11th green and the other half serves as the 17th green. In play of the 17th hole, if a ball comes to rest on the part of the green serving the 11th hole, does Rule 25-3 (Wrong Putting Green) apply?

A. No, not unless the Committee divides the green by use of stakes or a line and declares one part to be the green of the 11th hole and the other part to be the green of the 17th hole. The Definition of "Putting Green" gives a Committee this right.

Rule 26. Water Hazards (Including Lateral Water Hazards)

Definitions

A "*water hazard*" is any sea, lake, pond, river, ditch, surface drainage ditch or other open water course (whether or not containing water) and anything of a similar nature.

All ground or water within the margin of a *water hazard* is part of the *water hazard*. The margin of a *water hazard* extends vertically upwards and downwards. Stakes and lines defining the margins of *water hazards* are in the *hazards*. Such stakes are *obstructions*. A ball is in a *water hazard* when it lies in or any part of it touches the *water hazard*.

Note 1: *Water hazards* (other than *lateral water hazards*) should be defined by yellow stakes or lines.

Note 2: The *Committee* may make a Local Rule prohibiting play from an environmentally-sensitive area which has been defined as a *water hazard*.

A "*lateral water hazard*" is a *water hazard* or that part of a *water hazard* so situated that it is not possible or is deemed by the *Committee* to be impracticable to drop a ball behind the *water hazard* in accordance with Rule 26-1b.

That part of a *water hazard* to be played as a *lateral water hazard* should be distinctively marked.

A ball is in a *lateral water hazard* when it lies in or any part of it touches the *lateral water hazard.*

Note 1: *Lateral water hazards* should be defined by red stakes or lines.

Note 2: The *Committee* may make a Local Rule prohibiting play from an environmentally-sensitive area which has been defined as a *lateral water hazard.*

Note 3: The *Committee* may define a *lateral water hazard* as a *water hazard.*

26-1. Ball in Water Hazard

It is a question of fact whether a ball lost after having been struck toward a *water hazard* is lost inside or outside the *hazard.* In order to treat the ball as lost in the *hazard,* there must be reasonable evidence that the ball lodged in it. In the absence of such evidence, the ball must be treated as a *lost ball* and Rule 27 applies.

If a ball is in or is lost in a *water hazard* (whether the ball lies in water or not), the player may under penalty of one stroke:

a. Play a ball as nearly as possible at the spot from which the original ball was last played (see Rule 20-5);

or

b. Drop a ball behind the *water hazard,* keeping the point at which the original ball last crossed the margin of the *water hazard* directly between the *hole* and the spot on which the ball is dropped, with no limit to how far behind the *water hazard* the ball may be dropped;

or

c. As additional options available only if the ball last crossed the margin of a *lateral water hazard,* drop a ball outside the *water hazard* within two club-lengths of and not nearer the *hole* than (i) the point where the original ball last crossed the margin of the *water hazard* or (ii) a point on the opposite margin of the *water hazard* equidistant from the *hole.*

The ball may be cleaned when lifted under this Rule.

(Ball moving in water in a *water hazard* — see Rule 14-6.)

26-2. Ball Played Within Water Hazard

a. Ball Comes To Rest in The Hazard

If a ball played from within a *water hazard* comes to rest in the same *hazard* after the *stroke,* the player may:

(i) proceed under Rule 26-1; or
(ii) under penalty of one stroke, play a ball as nearly as possible at the spot from which the last *stroke* from outside the *hazard* was played (see Rule 20-5).

If the player proceeds under Rule 26-1a, he may elect not to play the dropped ball. If he so elects, he may:

(a) Proceed under Rule 26-1b, adding the additional penalty of one stroke prescribed by that Rule;

or

(b) Proceed under Rule 26-1c, if applicable, adding the additional penalty of one stroke prescribed by that Rule;

or

(c) Add an additional penalty of one stroke and play a ball as nearly as possible at the spot from which the last *stroke* from outside the *hazard* was played (see Rule 20-5).

b. Ball Lost or Unplayable Outside Hazard or Out of Bounds

If a ball played from within a *water hazard* is lost or declared unplayable outside the *hazard* or is *out of bounds,* the player, after taking a penalty of one stroke under Rule 27-1 or 28a, may:

(i) play a ball as nearly as possible at the spot in the *hazard* from which the original ball was last played (see Rule 20-5);or
(ii) proceed under Rule 26-1b, or if applicable Rule 26-1c, adding the additional penalty of one stroke prescribed by the Rule and using as the reference point the point where the original ball last crossed

26

the margin of the *hazard* before it came to rest in the *hazard;* or

(iii) add an additional penalty of one stroke and play a ball as nearly as possible at the spot from which the last *stroke* from outside the *hazard* was played (see Rule 20-5).

Note 1: When proceeding under Rule 26-2b, the player is not required to drop a ball under Rule 27-1 or 28a. If he does drop a ball, he is not required to play it. He may alternatively proceed under Clause (ii) or (iii).

Note 2: If a ball played from within a *water hazard* is declared unplayable outside the *hazard,* nothing in Rule 26-2b precludes the player from proceeding under Rule 28b or c.

PENALTY FOR BREACH OF RULE:
Match play — Loss of hole;
Stroke play — Two strokes.

26/1 When Ball Is in Water Hazard

Q. Is a ball in a water hazard when some part of the ball breaks the plane that extends vertically upwards from the margin of the hazard even though the ball does not touch the ground or grass inside the hazard?

A. Yes, since the Definition of "Water Hazard" provides that "the margin of a water hazard extends vertically upwards."

26/2 Ball Within Natural Margin of Water Hazard But Outside Stakes Defining Margin

Q. Stakes defining the margin of a water hazard were improperly installed. As a result, an area which clearly was part of the water hazard was outside the stakes and,

thus, technically was outside the hazard. A player's ball came to rest in water in this area. The player claimed that, in view of the alignment of the stakes, his ball was in casual water through the green. Was the claim valid?

A. No. The Committee erred in not properly defining the margin of the hazard as required by Rule 33-2a, but a player is not entitled to take advantage of such an error. Since it was clear that the place where the player's ball lay was within the natural boundaries of the water hazard, the claim should not be upheld.

26/3 Unmarked Water Hazard

Q. An unmarked ditch on the left of a hole is in bounds, but the left-hand margin is out of bounds. Accordingly, it is impossible to drop behind the water hazard under Rule 26-1b. A player's ball comes to rest in the ditch. Is the player restricted to playing the ball as it lies or proceeding under Rule 26-1a?

A. It is the responsibility of the Committee to define accurately the margins of water hazards and lateral water hazards — see Rule 33-2a. However, if the Committee has not done so, the ditch is, by definition, a lateral water hazard and the player should be permitted to proceed under Rule 26-1c(i). (Revised)

26/3.5 Lateral Water Hazard Defined as Water Hazard

Q. A body of water which is both in front of and to the right of a putting green is so large that it is impossible to drop behind the water hazard as required by Rule 26-1b. May the Committee define the hazard or parts of the hazard as a water hazard even though it meets the Definition of a "Lateral Water Hazard"?

A. Yes — see Note 3 to the Definition of "Lateral Water Hazard." However, this should only be done when a Committee deems it necessary to preserve the integrity of the hole. In such cases the establishment of a Ball Drop or Dropping Zone as an additional option under the water hazard Rule (Rule 26-1) may be justified. (New)

26/4 Man-Made Reservoir

Q. Is a man-made reservoir considered a water hazard?

A. Yes.

26/5 Unidentifiable Ball Played in Water Hazard and Lost

Q. A player's ball came to rest in a water hazard. He found a ball in the hazard but could not identify it. He played the ball into deep water within the hazard and the ball was lost. May the player assume that the ball he played in the hazard was not his ball, in which case the stroke played in the hazard would not count?

A. No. There was not reasonable evidence that the ball played was other than the player's ball. Lacking such evidence, he must count the stroke. The burden of proof is on the player.

26/6 Ball Assumed to Be in Water Hazard Found Outside Hazard After Another Ball Played Under Stroke-and-Distance Procedure

Q. A player assumes his original ball to be in a water hazard, although there was not reasonable evidence to that effect. Using the option in Rule 26-1a, he plays another ball at the spot from which the original ball was played. He then finds his original ball outside the hazard. What is the ruling?

A. The original ball is lost and the other ball is in play under penalty of stroke and distance — see Decision 27/17.

26/7 Ball Apparently in Water Hazard Found Outside Hazard After Another Ball Played Under Stroke-and-Distance Procedure

Q. A player's ball appears to have come to rest in a water hazard. Without comment, the player plays another ball at the spot from which the original ball was played and then finds his original ball outside the hazard. What is the ruling?

26

A. The original ball is lost and the other ball is in play under penalty of stroke and distance — see Decision 27/17.

Other Decisions relating to Rule 26:

Removal of Obstruction in Hazard Would Move Loose Impediment — See 1-4/5.

Player Who Told Opponent He Would Proceed Under Water Hazard Rule Changes Mind After Opponent Plays — See 9-2/13.

Flying Insect in Water Hazard — See 13-4/16.5.

Player Cleans Clubhead in Water Hazard When Ball Lies in Hazard — See 13-4/40.

Stone Broken Away from Retaining Wall in Water Hazard — See 24/6.

Overflow from Water Hazard — See 25/2.

Hole of Removed Stake Defining Water Hazard — See 25/18.

Player Unaware Ball in Water Hazard Takes Relief from Interference by Burrowing Animal Hole — See 25-1b/26.

Where to Place Lines or Stakes Defining Margin of Water Hazard — See 33-2a/4.

Pond Is Water Hazard from Back Tee and Lateral Water Hazard from Forward Tee — See 33-2a/6.

Deeming Body of Water as Both Water Hazard and Lateral Water Hazard — See 33-2a/7.

Treating Ocean and Beach as Through the Green — See 33-2a/8.

How to Mark Island Green — See 33-2a/10.

26-1/1 Meaning of "Reasonable Evidence" in Rule 26-1

The term "reasonable evidence" in Rule 26-1 is purposely and necessarily broad so as to permit sensible judgments to be reached on the basis of all the relevant circumstances of particular cases. As applied in this context, a player may not deem his ball lost in a water hazard simply because he thinks the ball may be in the hazard. The evidence must be preponderantly in favor of its being in the hazard. Otherwise, the ball must be considered lost outside the hazard and the player must proceed under Rule 27-1. Physical conditions in the area have a great deal to do with it. For example, if a water hazard is surrounded by a fairway on which a ball could hardly be lost, the existence of reasonable evidence that the ball is in the hazard would be more likely than if there was deep rough in the area. Observing a ball splash in a water hazard would not necessarily provide reasonable evidence as splashing balls sometimes skip out of hazards. It would depend on all the circumstances.

Changing Relief Option When Re-Dropping Required — See 20-2c/5.

26-1/2 Player Proceeding Under Water Hazard Rule Drops Ball in Another Hazard

Q. A player's ball lies in a water hazard. In applying Rule 26-1b, the player drops a ball in a bunker or another water hazard. Is this permissible?

A. Yes.

Ball Declared Unplayable Through the Green Dropped in Water Hazard; player Elects Not to Play Ball and Wishes to Proceed Under the Water Hazard Rule — See 28/4.5.

26-1/3 Ball Played Under Water Hazard Rule; Original Ball Then Found Outside Hazard

Q. A player believed his original ball came to rest in a water hazard. He searched for about a minute but did not find his ball. So he dropped another ball behind the hazard under Rule 26-1 and played it. He then found his original ball outside the hazard within five minutes of having begun search for it. What is the ruling?

A. When the player dropped another ball behind the hazard, it became the ball in play and the original ball was lost.

If there was reasonable evidence that the original ball was in the water hazard, the player was entitled to invoke Rule 26-1.

In the absence of reasonable evidence that the original ball was in the water hazard, the player was required to put another ball into play under Rule 27-1. In playing the ball dropped under Rule 26-1, the player played from a wrong place.

In match play, he incurred a penalty of loss of hole (Rule 20-7a).

In stroke play, he incurred the stroke-and-distance penalty prescribed by Rule 27-1 and an additional penalty of two strokes for a breach of that Rule. If the breach was a serious one, he was subject to disqualification unless he corrected the error as provided in the second paragraph of Rule 20-7b.

26-1/4 Ball Played Under Water Hazard Rule Without Reasonable Evidence Original Ball in Hazard; Original Ball Then Found in Hazard

Q. A player's ball carried over a water hazard into some trees. It could not be determined whether the ball bounced back into the hazard or came to rest in the trees. Therefore, there was not reasonable evidence that the ball was in the hazard.

The player did not search for his original ball. He assumed that it was in the hazard, dropped a ball behind the hazard at a spot which conformed with Rule 26-1b and played that ball onto the green. As he was walking to the green, he found his original ball in the hazard. What is the ruling?

A. The first paragraph of Rule 26-1 states in part: "In order to treat the ball as lost in the hazard, there must be reasonable evidence that the ball lodged in it. In the absence of such evidence, the ball must be treated as a lost ball and Rule 27 applies." Therefore, the player was not entitled to assume that his original ball was in the hazard and the fact that it was subsequently found in the hazard is irrelevant. When the player dropped another ball behind the hazard, it became the ball in play and the original ball was lost. The player was required to proceed under Rule 27-1. In playing the ball dropped under Rule 26-1, he played from a wrong place.

In match play, he incurred a penalty of loss of hole (Rule 20-7a).

In stroke play, he incurred the stroke-and-distance penalty prescribed by Rule 27-1 and an additional penalty of two strokes for a breach of that Rule. If the breach was a serious one, he was subject to disqualification unless he corrected the error as provided in the second paragraph of Rule 20-7b.

26-1/5 Ball Dropped and Played Under Water Hazard Rule; Original Ball Then Found in Hazard and Holed Out as Second Ball

Q. In stroke play, a competitor, unable to find his ball in a water hazard, drops another ball behind the hazard under Rule 26-1b and plays it. He then finds his original ball in the hazard. Not being sure of his rights, he plays out both balls under Rule 3-3, opting to score with the original ball. What is the ruling?

A. When the competitor dropped the ball behind the hazard, that ball became the ball in play — see Definition of "Ball in Play." The score with that ball was the competitor's score for the hole. The score with the original ball could not count because that ball was no longer the ball in play. However, the competitor incurs no penalty for playing out with the original ball.

26-1/6 Ball Played Back into Water Hazard from Putting Green Side of Hazard

Q. A player plays his second shot over a water hazard into a bunker behind the green. He skulls his third shot and the ball comes to rest in the water hazard. The ball is not playable. What are the player's options?

A. The player may, under penalty of one stroke:

(a) drop a ball behind the water hazard, keeping the point at which the original ball last crossed the hazard margin between the hole and the spot on which the ball is dropped — Rule 26-1b. This procedure would probably make it necessary for the player to return to the tee side of the hazard and play over the hazard again; or

(b) drop a ball in the bunker at the spot where his second shot came to rest — Rule 26-1a.

26-1/7 Ball Moved Out of Bounds by Flow of Water in Water Hazard

Q. The flow of water in a water hazard carries a ball out of bounds. May the player invoke Rule 26-1?

A. No. Since the ball lies out of bounds, the player must proceed under Rule 27-1. Water is not an outside agency — see Definition of "Outside Agency" — and thus the ball would not be replaced under Rule 18-1.

In a situation where it is likely that a ball will be carried out of bounds by the flow of water in a water hazard, it is suggested that a screen be installed to prevent such an occurrence.

26-1/8 Ball Moved into Bounds by Flow of Water in Water Hazard

Q. A ball lands in a river out of bounds and the flow of water carries the ball into bounds. That part of the river which is in bounds is defined as a water hazard. May the player invoke Rule 26-1?

A. Yes, since the ball lies within the boundaries of the course. The ball should be considered to have last crossed the hazard margin at the boundary line. If it is not possible to drop behind the hazard under Rule 26-1b, which seems likely, the player is entitled to proceed under Rule 26-1c — see Decision 26/3. If that is not possible, the player must proceed under Rule 26-1a, incurring a stroke-and-distance penalty, or play the ball as it lies in the river.

26-1/9 Caddie Lifts Ball in Water Hazard Without Player's Authority

Q. A player's ball lying in a water hazard is lifted by the player's caddie without the player's authority. What is the ruling?

A. The player incurred a one-stroke penalty when his caddie lifted his ball — Rule 18-2a. The player may either replace the ball as required by Rule 18-2a or proceed under Rule 26-1 and incur an additional one-stroke penalty under that Rule.

26-1/10 Placing Ball on Bank of Water Hazard Instead of Dropping to Prevent Ball Rolling into Water

Q. A player's ball lies in a playable position on the bank of a water hazard. The player hits the ball out of bounds. If he proceeds under Rule 27-1 and drops a ball on the bank as nearly as possible at the spot from which the original ball was played, the ball will be likely to roll into deep water. May he place the ball in such circumstances, rather than drop it? 26

A. No. However, the player is not obliged to drop a ball within the hazard in accordance with Rule 27-1. He may take the penalty stroke provided in Rule 27-1 and then, under an additional penalty of one stroke, put a ball into play outside the hazard in accordance with either Rule 26-2b(ii) or 26-2b(iii).

Ball Lost in Either Water Hazard or Casual Water Overflowing Hazard — See 1-4/7.

Players Inadvertently Exchange Balls Recovered from Water Hazard — See 15-1/4.

Ball Declared Unplayable in Water Hazard Is Dropped in Hazard and Played — See 20-7/2.

Casual Water Mistaken for Water Hazard; Original Ball Played Under Water Hazard Rule — See 25-1b/12.

Casual Water Mistaken for Water Hazard; Substituted Ball Played Under Water Hazard Rule — See 25-1b/13.

26-1/11 Water Hazard Treated as Lateral Water Hazard

Q. In stroke play, a competitor played a stroke over a water hazard and the ball spun back into the hazard. The competitor, in error, treated the hazard as a lateral water hazard and dropped a ball under Rule 26-1c(i) within two club-lengths of where it crossed the hazard margin when it spun back into the hazard. He played the ball onto the green and then his procedure was questioned. What is the ruling?

A. The competitor incurred a penalty of one stroke under Rule 26-1. Furthermore, he was guilty of a serious breach of that Rule. He must, under an additional penalty of two strokes, rectify the error as provided in the second paragraph of Rule 20-7b or be disqualified.

Meaning of Serious Breach — See 20-7b/0.5.

26-1/12 Hazard Marked as Water Hazard Where Ball Last Crosses Margin and as Lateral Hazard Where Ball Comes to Rest

26

Q. A body of water is defined in part as a water hazard and in part as a lateral water hazard. A ball last crosses the hazard margin at a spot where it is marked as a water hazard but it comes to rest in that part of the hazard marked as a lateral water hazard. In addition to playing the ball as it lies, what are the player's options?

A. Since the ball last crossed the margin of the hazard where it is defined as a water hazard, the options in Rule 26-1c are not available. Thus, the player is limited to the options in Rules 26-1a and -1b.

26-1/13 Opposite Side of Lateral Water Hazard Defined as Water Hazard

Q. A player hit a ball into a lateral water hazard. The player wanted to drop within two club-lengths of a point on the opposite margin of the hazard equidistant from the hole, as permitted under Rule 26-1c. However, the opposite margin was marked as a water hazard. Was the player entitled to drop a ball within two club-lengths of the point in question on the opposite margin?

A. Yes. In such a case, relief is determined according to the status of the hazard at the point where the ball last crossed the hazard margin.

26-1/14 Clarification of "Opposite Margin" in Rule 26-1c(ii)

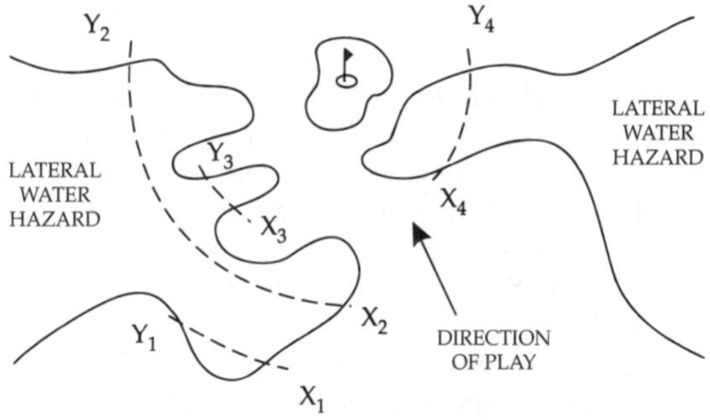

Q. Please clarify the words "opposite margin" in Rule 26-1c. With regard to the above illustration, "X1" indicates where a ball in the hazard last crossed the hazard margin. May the player drop a ball within two club-lengths of "Y1"? And, may a player whose ball last crossed the hazard margin at "X2" drop a ball within two club-lengths of "Y2," and so on?

A. With respect to "X1," "Y1" is "a point on the opposite margin of the water hazard equidistant from the hole." Accordingly, the player would be entitled to drop a ball within two club-lengths of "Y1."

The same applies in the cases of "X3" — "Y3" and "X4" — "Y4," but not in the case of "X2" — "Y2." A "point on the opposite margin" is a point across the hazard from "the point where the original ball last crossed the margin of the hazard." "Y2" is not across the hazard from "X2" because an imaginary straight line from "X2" to "Y2" crosses land outside the hazard.

26-1/15 Procedures for Relief from Lateral Water Hazard

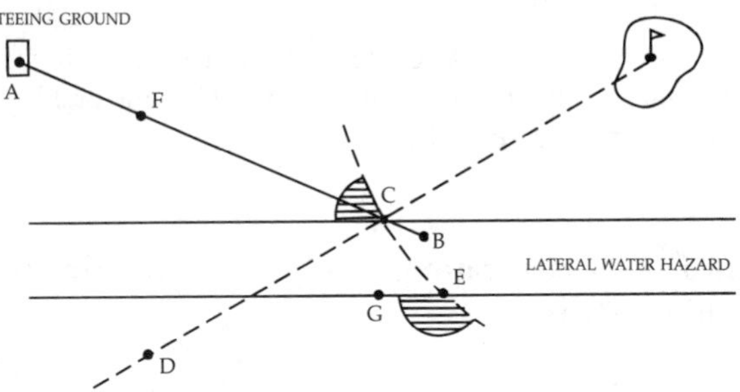

In the above illustration, a player has played a ball from the teeing ground (Point A) into the lateral water hazard at Point B. It last crossed the margin of the hazard at Point C. He may play the ball as it lies or, under penalty of one stroke:

(a) play another ball from the teeing ground — Rule 26-1a;

(b) drop a ball anywhere on the far side of the hazard on the dotted line from the hole through Point C, *e.g.*, Point D — Rule 26-1b;

(c) drop a ball in the shaded area on the near side of the hazard which is all ground within two club-lengths of Point C, but not nearer the hole than Point C — Rule 26-1c(i); or

(d) drop a ball in the shaded area on the far side of the hazard which is all ground within two club-lengths of Point E, but not nearer the hole than Point E — Rule 26-1c(ii).

The player may not drop a ball on the so-called "line-of-flight" at Point F or anywhere else on the line the ball followed from A to B, except in the shaded area on the near side. Nor may he drop a ball within two club-lengths of Point G, the point on the far side of the hazard directly opposite Point C.

26-1/16 Point Where Ball Last Crossed Margin of Lateral Water Hazard Determined and Ball Dropped; Point Then Proves to Be Wrong Point

Q. In stroke play, A's ball goes into a lateral water hazard and is not found. A uses his best judgment in determining the point where the ball last crossed the hazard margin. B, A's marker and a fellow-competitor, agrees with that judgment and A drops a ball in accordance with Rule 26-1c, using the agreed point on the margin as the reference point. Before A plays his next stroke, C, another fellow-competitor, says that A's ball last crossed the hazard margin 20 yards beyond the point judged by A to be the point where the ball last crossed. A's ball is then found where C said it would be. What is the ruling?

A. Since he dropped his ball in a wrong place, A should, under Rule 20-6, lift the dropped ball and drop it in a right place, without penalty. A is precluded from lifting the ball dropped in a wrong place and playing the original ball from the hazard. The original ball was lost when another ball was put into play under Rule 26-1 — see Definition of "Lost Ball."

26-1/17 Point Where Ball Last Crossed Margin of Lateral Water Hazard Determined and Ball Dropped and Played; Point Then Proves to Be Wrong Point

Q. In the circumstances described in Decision 26-1/16, what is the ruling if A, having dropped a ball in a wrong place, plays it before his error is discovered?

A. A must continue play with the ball played from a wrong place, without penalty. Applying a penalty under Rule 26-1 for playing from a wrong place (see Rule 20-7b) is not appropriate. Otherwise, a competitor would risk incurring a penalty every time he makes an honest judgment as to the point where his ball last crosses a water hazard margin and that judgment subsequently proves incorrect.

26-1/18 Impossible to Drop Not Nearer Hole Than Point Where Ball Last Crossed Margin of Lateral Water Hazard

Q. When a ball last crosses the margin of a lateral water hazard at the side of a putting green, it is sometimes impossible to drop a ball within two club-lengths of the point where the ball last crossed the hazard margin without dropping nearer the hole than that point. What is the procedure in such a case?

A. It is usually possible to drop a ball on the near side of a lateral water hazard and conform with Rule 26-1c(i) by dropping the ball close to the hazard margin. Where this is impossible, the player must proceed under one of the other options provided in Rule 26-1.

Part of Lateral Water Hazard Where Impossible to Drop Not Nearer Hole; Procedure for Committee — See 33-2a/9.

26-1/19 Permissible Dropping Area Under Lateral Water Hazard Rule So Narrow Player Has Difficulty Dropping Within It

When a ball comes to rest in a lateral water hazard and relief is taken under Rule 26-1c, the ball must be dropped (1) outside the hazard and (2) not nearer the hole than the point where the ball last crossed the margin of the hazard (Point X). When the lateral water hazard is behind or to the side of the putting green, the permissible dropping area may be very narrow. If the ball, when dropped, first strikes a part of the course in the hazard or nearer the hole than Point X, the drop does not count for the purpose of determining when the ball must be placed under Rule 20-2c. The player must lift the ball and continue to drop it until the ball first strikes a part of the course within the permissible dropping area. Only if the ball has been dropped in the permissible dropping area twice and, each time, either rolls into the hazard or nearer the hole than Point X may it be placed as permitted by Rule 20-2c. If a ball is placed otherwise than as described, and is played, a breach of Rule 26-1c occurs.

Stakes and lines defining the margins of water hazards should be placed along the natural limits of the hazard. However, minor deviation to alleviate the dropping area problem would be appropriate. Alternatively, a Ball Drop (or Dropping Zone) should be established.

26-1/20 Allowing Drop Opposite Spot Where Ball Comes to Rest in Lateral Water Hazard

Q. A lateral water hazard is so situated that it is difficult to determine where a ball lying in the hazard last crossed the hazard margin. Would it be permissible to make a Local Rule to the effect that a player whose ball lies in this hazard may drop a ball, under penalty of one stroke, within two club-lengths of the point on the hazard margin opposite where the original ball came to rest in the hazard, instead of within two club-lengths of where the original ball last crossed the hazard margin, *i.e.*, the Local Rule would modify Rule 26-1c?

A. No. Such modification of Rule 26-1c is not authorized. Moreover, the suggested Local Rule would be inoperable if the player's ball was lost in the hazard.

26-1/21 Example of Serious Breach of Lateral Water Hazard Rule

Q. In stroke play, A and B drive into a lateral water hazard. They determine where their original balls last crossed the hazard margin and elect to proceed under Rule 26-1c, taking a penalty of one stroke. A drops a ball slightly closer to the hole than the spot where his ball last crossed the hazard margin; B drops a ball 50 yards closer to the hole. A and B play their next strokes. What is the ruling?

A. A incurs an additional penalty of two strokes for a breach of Rule 26-1c and must play out the hole with the ball dropped in a wrong place and played — see Rule 20-7b, first paragraph.

B is guilty of a serious breach of Rule 26-1c. He incurs an additional penalty of two strokes and, before playing from the next teeing ground, he must drop another ball in accordance with Rule 26-1c and play out the hole; otherwise B is disqualified — see Rule 20-7b, third paragraph.

Meaning of Serious Breach — See 20-7b/0.5.

26-2/1 Explanation of Options Under Rules 26-2a and -2b

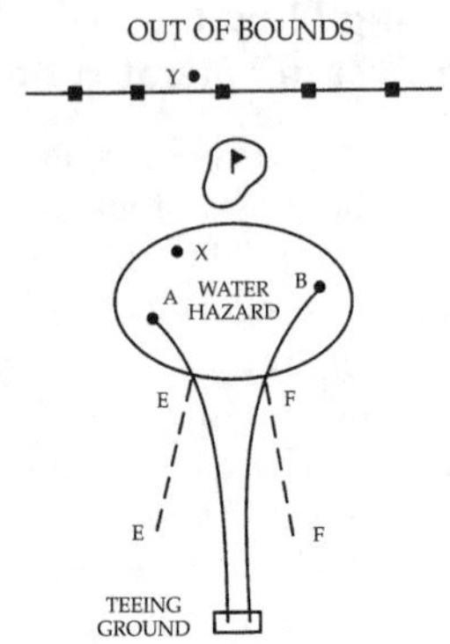

Regarding the above illustration, A and B play from the tee. A's ball comes to rest in the water hazard at Point A. B's ball comes to rest at Point B. Both A and B elect to play from the hazard. A fails to get out of the hazard. He plays to Point X, and his ball is not playable. B plays to Point Y, which is out of bounds.

Under penalty of one stroke, A may:

(a) drop a ball at Point A and play again from there, playing 4 (Rule 26-2a(i)); or

(b) drop a ball anywhere on dotted line E-E and play from there, playing 4 (Rule 26-2a(i)); or

(c) play another ball from the tee, playing 4 (Rule 26-2a(ii)).

26 If A drops a ball at Point A and the ball comes to rest at a spot from which he judges he cannot play, he may, adding an additional penalty of one stroke, either drop a ball anywhere on the dotted line E-E or play another ball from the tee, playing 5.

B, after taking the penalty stroke prescribed in Rule 27-1, may drop a ball at Point B and play again from there, playing 4 (Rule 26-2b(i)).

Alternatively, B, after taking the penalty stroke prescribed in Rule 27-1, may drop a ball at Point B and elect not to play that ball or elect not to drop a ball at Point B. In either case, he shall then:

(a) under an additional penalty of one stroke, drop a ball anywhere on dotted line F-F and play from there, playing 5 (Rule 26-2b(ii)); or

(b) under an additional penalty of one stroke, play another ball from the tee, playing 5 (Rule 26-2b(iii)).

Stroke Played from Environmentally-Sensitive Area Defined as Water Hazard — See 33-8/43.

Rule 27. Ball Lost or Out of Bounds; Provisional Ball

Definitions

A ball is *"lost"* if:

a. It is not found or identified as his by the player within five minutes after the player's *side* or his or their *caddies* have begun to search for it; or

b. The player has put another ball into play under the *Rules*, even though he may not have searched for the original ball; or

c. The player has played any stroke with a *provisional ball* from the place where the original ball is likely to be or from a point nearer the *hole* than that place, whereupon the *provisional ball* becomes the *ball in play*.

Time spent in playing a *wrong ball* is not counted in the five-minute period allowed for search.

"Out of bounds" is beyond the boundaries of the *course* or any part of the *course* so marked by the *Committee*.

When *out of bounds* is defined by reference to stakes or a fence, or as being beyond stakes or a fence, the *out of bounds* line is determined by the nearest inside points of the stakes or fence posts at ground level excluding angled supports.

Objects defining *out of bounds* such as walls, fences, stakes and railings, are not *obstructions* and are deemed to be fixed.

When *out of bounds* is defined by a line on the ground, the line itself is *out of bounds*.

The *out of bounds* line extends vertically upwards and downwards.

A ball is *out of bounds* when all of it lies *out of bounds.*

A player may stand *out of bounds* to play a ball lying within bounds.

A *"provisional ball"* is a ball played under Rule 27-2 for a ball which may be *lost* outside a *water hazard* or may be *out of bounds.*

27-1. Ball Lost or Out of Bounds

If a ball is *lost* or is *out of bounds,* the player shall play a ball, under penalty of one stroke, as nearly as possible at the spot from which the original ball was last played (see Rule 20-5).

Exceptions:

1. If there is reasonable evidence that the original ball is *lost* in a *water hazard,* the player shall proceed in accordance with Rule 26-1.
2. If there is reasonable evidence that the original ball is *lost* in an immovable *obstruction* (Rule 24-2c) or an *abnormal ground condition* (Rule 25-1c) the player may proceed under the applicable *Rule.*

PENALTY FOR BREACH OF RULE 27-1:
Match play — Loss of hole;
Stroke play — Two strokes.

27-2. Provisional Ball

a. Procedure

If a ball may be *lost* outside a *water hazard* or may be *out of bounds,* to save time the player may play another ball provisionally in accordance with Rule 27-1. The player shall inform his opponent in match play or his *marker* or a *fellow-competitor* in stroke play that he intends to play a *provisional ball,* and he shall play it before he or his *partner* goes forward to search for the original ball.

27

If he fails to do so and plays another ball, such ball is not a *provisional ball* and becomes the *ball in play* under penalty of stroke and distance (Rule 27-1); the original ball is deemed to be *lost*.

(Order of play from *teeing ground*— see Rule 10-3.)

b. When Provisional Ball Becomes Ball in Play

The player may play a *provisional ball* until he reaches the place where the original ball is likely to be. If he plays a *stroke* with the *provisional ball* from the place where the original ball is likely to be or from a point nearer the *hole* than that place, the original ball is deemed to be *lost* and the *provisional ball* becomes the *ball in play* under penalty of stroke and distance (Rule 27-1).

If the original ball is *lost* outside a *water hazard* or is *out of bounds,* the *provisional ball* becomes the *ball in play,* under penalty of stroke and distance (Rule 27-1).

If there is reasonable evidence that the original ball is *lost* in a *water hazard,* the player shall proceed in accordance with Rule 26-1.

Exception: If there is reasonable evidence that the original ball is *lost* in an immovable *obstruction* (Rule 24-2c) or an *abnormal ground condition* (Rule 25-1c) the player may proceed under the applicable Rule.

c. When Provisional Ball to Be Abandoned

If the original ball is neither *lost* nor *out of bounds,* the player shall abandon the *provisional ball* and continue play with the original ball. If he fails to do so, any further *strokes* played with the *provisional ball* shall constitute playing a *wrong ball* and the provisions of Rule 15 shall apply.

Note: *Strokes* taken and *penalty strokes* incurred solely in playing a *provisional ball* subsequently abandoned under Rule 27-2c shall be disregarded.

27/1 Player Directs Caddie Not to Search for His Ball Until Others Can Assist

Q. A hits a long drive into heavy rough. B hits a short drive into heavy rough. A's caddie starts walking towards the area where A's ball may be to search for A's ball. Everyone else, including A, walks towards the area where B's ball may be to look for B's ball. A directs his caddie also to look for B's ball and delay search for his (A's) ball until everyone else can assist. Is such procedure permitted?

A. Yes.

27/1.5 Time Permitted for Search for Lost Ball if Play Suspended During Search

Q. A player has been searching for his ball for three minutes when play is suspended. How much time is he allowed for further search?

A. The player may continue searching for two more minutes. The suspension of play has no effect on the five-minute search period. Thus, even if the player searches for his ball during the suspension of play, he is still only permitted a total of five minutes to search for his ball. (New)

27/2 Time Permitted for Search for Lost Ball After Wrong Ball Played

Q. In stroke play, a competitor searches for his ball for three minutes, finds a ball, plays it and then discovers he has played a wrong ball. He returns to the area from which the wrong ball was played and resumes search for his ball. How much time is he allowed for further search — two minutes or five minutes?

A. Two minutes — see Definition of "Lost Ball."

27/3 Time Permitted for Search When Lost Ball Found and Then Lost Again

Q. A player finds his ball in high rough after a two-minute search, leaves the area to get a club and, when he returns, is unable to find the ball. Is he allowed three minutes or five minutes to find his ball?

A. Three minutes.

27/4 Time Permitted for Search for Original Ball and Provisional Ball

Q. Is a player allowed five minutes to search for his original ball and five more minutes to search for his provisional ball, or just a total of five minutes?

A. If the two balls are so close together that, in effect, both balls would be searched for simultaneously, a total of five minutes for search is allowed. Otherwise, the player is allowed to search five minutes for each ball.

27/5 Player Searching for Ball Mistakes His Ball for Opponent's

Q. In a match, A begins to search for his ball and after two minutes finds a ball which he believes to be his opponent's ball and resumes his search. The five-minute search period elapses and thereafter it is discovered that the ball which he found and believed to be his opponent's was in fact his ball. What is the ruling?

A. Once a ball has been found a player has an opportunity to identify it as his. In this case, the player had every opportunity to identify the ball as his within the five-minute search period and failed to do so. Therefore, the ball is, by definition, "lost." (Revised)

27/5.5 Original Ball Found Within Five-Minute Search Period Not Identified Until After Period Has Elapsed

Q. A player plays a second shot, searches for his ball for just over four minutes and then starts to walk back down the fairway to play another ball under Rule 27-1. A ball is then found within the five-minute search period, but as the player is now a considerable distance away, he is unable to identify the ball as his before the search period has elapsed. What is the ruling?

A. As a ball was found within five minutes of beginning search, the player is allowed enough time to reach the area in order to identify it. If the player identifies the ball as his, it is not a "lost ball" even though the identification takes place after the five-minute search period has elapsed. (New)

27/6 Player Unable to Find His Ball Because Another Player Played It

Q. A and B hit their tee shots into the same general area. A found a ball and played it. B went forward to look for his ball and could not find it. After a few minutes, B started back to the tee to put another ball into play. On the way, he found A's ball and knew then that A had played his (B's) ball in error. What is the ruling?

A. In match play, A lost the hole (Rule 15-2).

In stroke play, A incurred a penalty of two strokes for playing a wrong ball and must then play his own ball (Rule 15-3). A's ball was not lost even if A and B had been searching for more than five minutes because A had not "begun to search for it (his ball)"; the searching had been for B's ball — see Definition of "Lost Ball."

On the other hand, B began to search for his ball as soon as he went forward to look for it. If less than five minutes had elapsed before B found A's ball, B should have placed a ball on the spot from which A had wrongly played his (B's) ball and continued play, without penalty — see last paragraph of Rule 15-3. However, if five minutes had expired, B's original ball was lost and he was obliged to put another ball into play under penalty of stroke and distance (Rule 27-1).

27/7 Ball Found in Burrowing Animal Hole After Five-Minute Search

Q. A player's tee shot comes to rest in an area containing heavy rough and a large burrowing animal hole. After a search of five minutes, the players in the group determine that there is not reasonable evidence that the ball is lost in the burrowing animal hole. The player returns to the tee to put another ball into play under Rule 27-1. As the player is returning to the tee, the ball is found in the burrowing animal hole. May the player now proceed under Rule 25-1 on the basis that reasonable evidence did exist?

A. No. When five minutes elapsed and there was not reasonable evidence that the ball was lost in the burrowing animal hole, the ball was lost and Rule 27-1 was applicable. (Revised)

Ball Lost in Underground Drainpipe — See 24-2c/1.

27/8 Ball Found After Search Exceeding Five Minutes Is Then Played

Q. A player searches for his ball for five minutes and does not find it. He continues to search, finds the ball and plays it. What is the ruling?

A. The ball was lost and therefore out of play when the five-minute period allowed for search expired — see Definitions of "Ball in Play" and "Lost Ball." When the player played a stroke with a ball out of play, he played a wrong ball — see Definition of "Wrong Ball" — and incurred a penalty of loss of hole in match play or two strokes in stroke play — Rules 15-2 and -3. In stroke play, he was disqualified if he did not correct the error by proceeding under Rule 27-1 before playing from the next tee — Rule 15-3.

27/9 Player Searches for Lost Ball After Putting Another Ball into Play

Q. According to Rule 27, if a player hits his tee shot into the woods and tees up and plays another ball without announcing it as a provisional ball, the second ball becomes the ball in play and the original ball is lost. In such a case, is the player precluded from searching for his original ball?

A. No. But the player may not play the ball if he finds it and must not unduly delay play.

27/10 Player Unable to Distinguish His Ball from Another Ball

Q. A and B hit their tee shots into the same area. Both balls were found but, because A and B were playing identical balls and neither had put an identification mark on his ball, they could not determine which ball was A's and which was B's. What is the ruling?

A. Since neither player could identify a ball as his ball, both balls were lost — see Definition of "Lost Ball." 27

This incident underlines the advisability of the player putting an identification mark on his ball — see Rules 6-5 and 12-2, Preamble.

27/11 Provisional Ball Not Distinguishable from Original Ball

A player entitled to play a provisional ball from the tee plays it into the same area as his original ball. The balls have identical markings and the player cannot distinguish between them. Following are various situations and the solutions, which are based on equity (Rule 1-4), when the above circumstances exist:

Situation 1: One ball is found in a water hazard and the other ball is not found.

Solution 1: The ball which was found must be presumed to be the provisional ball.

Situation 2: Both balls are found in a water hazard.

Solution 2: The player must return to the tee and play another ball; he would be playing 3.

Situation 3: One ball is found in a water hazard and one ball is found in the rough.

Solution 3: The player must return to the tee and play another ball; he would be playing 3.

Situation 4: One ball is found in bounds and the other ball is lost or found out of bounds.

Solution 4: The ball in bounds must be presumed to be the provisional ball.

Situation 5: Both balls are found in bounds and (1) both balls are playable, (2) one ball is playable and the other unplayable or (3) both balls are unplayable.

Solution 5: One could argue that both balls are lost. It would be inequitable to require the player to return to the tee, playing 5, when the player has found both balls but does not know which is the original and which the provisional. Accordingly, the player must select one of the balls, treat it as his provisional and abandon the other.

27/12 Identification of Ball Through Testimony of Spectator

Q. A's ball and B's ball came to rest close together. Neither A nor B could identify one of the balls as his ball because they were using balls with identical markings. A spectator who saw both shots land was able to state which ball belonged to A and which one belonged to B. May his testimony be accepted, or should both balls be deemed lost because they could not be identified by A and B?

A. If the Committee determined that, based on information given by the spectator, A and B were able to identify their balls, the balls should not be deemed lost. Otherwise, they would have to proceed under Rule 27-1.

27/13 Refusal to Identify Ball

Q. A player purposely refuses to identify a ball as his. What can the opponent or a fellow-competitor do in such a case?

A. An opponent or fellow-competitor has the right to be satisfied about the identification of a player's ball.

If a player has dishonestly not identified his ball, the opponent or fellow-competitor may refer the dispute to the Committee — Rule 34-3. In such a case, the Committee would be justified in imposing a penalty of disqualification under Rule 33-7.

Identifying Ball by Brand and Number Only — See 12-2/1.

27/14 Ball in Tree Identified But Not Retrieved

Q. A player's ball is lodged high in a tree. He identifies it with the aid of binoculars but is unable to retrieve it. Is the ball lost, in which case the player must invoke Rule 27-1?

A. No. Since the ball was identified, it was not lost — see Definition of "Lost Ball." The player may invoke the unplayable ball Rule (Rule 28).

27/15 Ball in Tree Visible But Not Identifiable

Q. A player is certain that his ball is lodged high in a tree. He can see a ball in the tree, but he cannot identify it as his ball. Is the player's ball lost, in which case he must proceed under Rule 27-1?

A. Yes.

27/16 Ball Declared Lost Is Found Before Another Ball Put into Play

Q. A player searched for his ball for two minutes, declared it lost and started back to play another ball at the spot from which the original ball was played. Before he put another ball into play, his original ball was found within the five-minute period allowed for search. What is the ruling?

A. A player cannot render a ball lost by a declaration — see Definition of "Lost Ball." The original ball remained in play — see Definition of "Ball in Play."

Searching Ten Minutes for Lost Ball — See 6-7/2.

27/17 Status of Original Ball If Another Ball Played Under Stroke-and-Distance Procedure

In general, if a player after playing a stroke plays another ball under a stroke-and-distance procedure, the original ball is lost and the other ball is the ball in play under penalty of stroke and distance.

Such a position is supported by:

(a) the Definition of "Ball in Play," which provides that a ball substituted for the ball in play becomes the ball in play, whether or not such substitution is permitted;

(b) the Definition of "Lost Ball," which provides that a ball is lost if the player has put another ball into play under the Rules, *i.e.*, played another ball under a stroke-and-distance procedure; and

27 (c) Rule 27-2a, which provides: "The player shall inform his opponent in match play or his marker or a fellow-competitor in stroke play that he intends to play a provisional ball, and he shall play it before he

or his partner goes forward to search for the original ball. If he fails to do so and plays another ball, such ball is not a provisional ball and becomes the ball in play under penalty of stroke and distance (Rule 27-1); the original ball is deemed to be lost."

Original Ball Found and Played After Another Ball Put into Play — See 15/5.

27/18 Gate in Boundary Fence

Q. A gate in a boundary fence swings onto the course. Sometimes the gate is open and sometimes it is closed. If the gate is open, may a player close it if it interferes with his swing?

A. A gate in a boundary fence, when closed, is part of the boundary fence, is not an obstruction (see Definition of "Obstructions") and may not be moved.

A gate in a boundary fence, if open, is not covered by the Rules. In equity (Rule 1-4), a player who finds a gate in a boundary fence open may leave it as he finds it or close it, but he must not move it to any other position.

Removal of Boundary Stake Interfering with Swing — See 13-2/17.

Improving Position of Ball by Bending Boundary Fence — See 13-2/18.

Improving Area of Intended Swing by Moving Growing or Fixed Object Situated Out of Bounds — See 13-2/19.

Part of Fence Off Course Leans Across Boundary and Interferes with Swing — See 13-2/20.

Player Removes Boundary Post on Line of Play But Replaces It Before Playing — See 13-2/25.

Stroke Played with Ball Lying Out of Bounds — See 15/6.

Ball Lifted and Dropped Away from Boundary Stake Under Obstruction Rule — See 18-2a/3.

27/19 When Ball Inside Boundary Fence Is Out of Bounds

Q. In view of the Definition of "Out of Bounds," is it correct to say that, if the posts of a boundary fence are on the golf course side of the fence, the diameter of the posts is greater than the diameter of a golf ball and the fence is straight, a ball lying against the inside of the fence would be out of bounds?

A. Yes.

Stile Attached to Boundary Fence — See 24/1.

Angled Supports or Guy Wires Supporting Boundary Fence — See 24/2.

Concrete Bases of Boundary Fence Posts — See 24/3.

Part of Boundary Fence Within Boundary Line — See 24/4.

Ball Moved Out of Bounds by Flow of Water in Water Hazard — See 26-1/7.

Ball Moved into Bounds by Flow of Water in Water Hazard — See 26-1/8.

Exposed Water Pipe Adjacent and Parallel to Boundary Fence — See 33-2a/1.

27/20 Public Road Defined as Out of Bounds Divides Course; Status of Ball Crossing Road

Q. A public road defined as out of bounds divides a course. A ball crosses the road and comes to rest on the part of the course on the other side of the road. Is the ball out of bounds?

A. No. Since the ball lies on the course, it is in bounds unless a Local Rule provides otherwise. However, because it is unfair that a ball on the road is out of bounds and a ball beyond it is in bounds, it is suggested that the following Local Rule should be adopted:

> "A ball which crosses a public road defined as out of bounds and comes to rest beyond that road is out of bounds, even though it may lie on another part of the course."

Boundary Stakes Having No Significance in Play of Hole Being Played — See 24/5.

Tee Decreed to Be in Bounds for Tee Shot and Out of Bounds Thereafter — See 33-2a/13.

27 **Internal Out of Bounds Applying to Stroke from Teeing Ground Only** — See 33-2a/14.

Establishing Boundary Line Inside Fence on Property Line — See 33-2a/15.

Deeming Ball in Bounds Until Beyond Boundary Wall — See 33-2a/16.

Boundary Altered by Unauthorized Removal of Boundary Stake — See 33-2a/19.

Displaced Boundary Stake — See 33-2a/20.

27-1/1 Original Ball Found Within Five-Minute Search Period After Another Ball Teed

Q. A player plays from the teeing ground, searches briefly for his ball and then goes back and tees another ball. Before he plays the teed ball, and within the five-minute search period, the original ball is found. May the player abandon the teed ball and play the original ball?

A. Yes. The teed ball was not in play since the player had not yet made a stroke at it — see Definition of "Ball in Play."

27-1/2 Original Ball Found Within Five-Minute Search Period After Another Ball Dropped

Q. A player plays his second shot, searches for his ball briefly and then goes back and drops another ball under Rule 27-1. Before he plays the dropped ball, and within the five-minute search period, the original ball is found. May the player abandon the dropped ball and play the original ball?

A. No. The dropped ball was in play (Rule 20-4) and the original ball was lost.

27-1/2.5 Lost Ball Treated as Moved by Outside Agency in Absence of Reasonable Evidence to That Effect

Q. A player who is unable to find his ball treats it as moved by an outside agency, rather than lost, although there is no reasonable evidence to that effect. Accordingly, he drops a ball where he thinks his original ball came to rest (Rule 18-1) and plays it, rather than taking a stroke-and-distance penalty for relief for a lost ball (Rule 27-1). What is the ruling?

A. In the absence of reasonable evidence that the ball had been moved by an outside agency, the player was required to put another ball into play under Rule 27-1. In playing the ball dropped under Rule 18-1, the player played from a wrong place.

In match play, he incurred a penalty of loss of hole (Rule 20-7a).

In stroke play, he incurred the stroke-and-distance penalty prescribed by Rule 27-1 and an additional penalty of two strokes for a breach of that Rule. Because the breach was a serious one, he was subject to disqualification unless he corrected the error as provided in the second paragraph of Rule 20-7b.

Original Ball Found and Played After Another Ball Put into Play — See 15/5.

Ball Believed to Be Lost in Bunker; Competitor Drops Another Ball in Bunker and Plays It; Original Ball Then Found Outside Bunker — See 20-7b/3.

Ball Lost in Tree in Ground Under Repair — See 25/10.

27-1/3 Ball Dropped in Area Where Original Ball Lost; Ball Then Played

Q. A player, unable to find his ball, drops another ball in the area where his original ball was lost and plays that ball. What is the ruling?

A. In match play, the player loses the hole — Rule 20-7a.

In stroke play, the player incurs the stroke-and-distance penalty prescribed by Rule 27-1 and an additional penalty of two strokes for a breach of that Rule. If the breach was a serious one, he must rectify the error as provided in the second paragraph of Rule 20-7b; otherwise, he is disqualified.

Meaning of Serious Breach — See 20-7b/0.5.

Other Decisions relating to Rule 27-1:

Ball Played from Outside Teeing Ground Goes Out of Bounds — See 11-4b/6.

Stroke Played with Ball Lying Out of Bounds — See 15/6.

Ball Thrown into Bounds by Outside Agency and Played; Caddie Aware of Action of Outside Agency — See 15/9.

Ball Thrown into Bounds by Outside Agency and Played; Neither Player Nor His Caddie Aware of Action of Outside Agency — See 15/10.

Ball Wrongly Thought to Be Out of Bounds Lifted; Competitor Proceeds Under Rule 27-1 — See 18-2a/11.

Ball Moved Accidentally by Backward Movement of Club After Stroke Misses; Ball Comes to Rest Out of Bounds — See 18-2a/22.

Ball Moves After Address and Comes to Rest Out of Bounds — See 18-2b/9.

Opponent's Caddie Lifts Player's Ball Which May or May Not Have Been Out of Bounds — See 18-3b/5.

Player's Ball Strikes Own Caddie and Comes to Rest Out of Bounds — See 19-2/2.

Player's Ball Strikes Own Caddie Standing Out of Bounds and Comes to Rest on Course — See 19-2/3.

Player's Ball Strikes Own Caddie Standing Out of Bounds and Comes to Rest Out of Bounds — See 19-2/4.

Ball Strikes Opponent Standing Out of Bounds and Comes to Rest Out of Bounds — See 19-3/1.

Dropped Ball Comes to Rest and Then Rolls Out of Bounds — See 20-2c/3.5.

Teed Ball Missed Then Hit Out of Bounds — See 20-5/1.

Ball Played from Spot Where Original Ball Deflected Out of Bounds by Maintenance Vehicle — See 20-7/1.

Ball Enters Burrowing Animal Hole Out of Bounds and Comes to Rest in Bounds — See 25-1b/23.

Ball Enters Burrowing Animal Hole in Bounds and Comes to Rest Out of Bounds — See 25-1b/24.

Ball Played in Ground Under Repair Area Lost in Same Area — See 25-1c/3.

Tee Shot Out of Bounds in Mixed Foursome in Which Different Tees Used by Men and Women — See 29/2.

27-2/1 Provisional Ball Serving as Ball in Play If Original Ball Unplayable or in Water Hazard

Q. May a player announce that a second ball he is going to play is both (a) a provisional ball in case the original ball is lost outside a water hazard or out of bounds and (b) the ball in play in case the original ball is unplayable or in a water hazard? 27

A. No.

27-2/2 Member of Committee Finds Player's Original Ball; Player Prefers to Continue with Provisional Ball

Q. Is a member of the Committee or a forecaddie obliged to inform a player that his original ball has been found, even if it is clear that the player does not plan to search for it because he would prefer to continue play with the provisional ball he has played?

A. Yes.

Other Decisions relating to Rule 27-2:

Provisional Ball Used as Second Ball When Not Determinable Whether Original Ball Is Out of Bounds — See 3-3/1.

Condition Requiring Use of Ball on List of Conforming Golf Balls; Ball Not on List Played as Provisional Ball — See 5-1/3.

Wrong Ball Played in Belief It Is Provisional Ball — See 15/7.

Provisional Ball Moves After Being Addressed — See 15/7.

Original Ball Struck by Provisional Ball — See 18-5/2.

Provisional Ball Struck by Original Ball — See 19-5/5.

Who Plays Provisional Ball in Foursome — See 29-1/3.

Provisional Ball Played by Wrong Member of Side in Foursome — See 29-1/4.

27-2a/1 Announcement of Provisional Ball

Q. A player hits his ball into an area where it may be lost outside a water hazard or out of bounds. The player then drops another ball and plays it. The player intends the dropped ball to be a provisional ball, but he does not inform his opponent, marker or fellow-competitor that he is "playing a provisional ball." In such a situation, can a player's actions constitute announcement that he is playing a provisional ball?

A. No. Rule 27-2a specifically provides that the player must inform his opponent, marker or fellow-competitor that he intends to play a provisional ball.

27

The player's statement must specifically mention the words "provisional ball" or must make it clear that he is proceeding under Rule 27-2a. Therefore, a player who says nothing has put another ball into play.

The following are examples of statements that do not satisfy the requirement of announcing a provisional ball:

(a) "That might be lost. I am going to re-load."
(b) "That might be out of here."
(c) "I'd better hit another one."
(d) "I will never find that one. I'll play another."

27-2a/1.5 Meaning of "Goes Forward to Search"

Q. With respect to Rule 27-2a, when has a player gone forward to search for the original ball such that a provisional ball cannot be played?

A. The sole purpose of Rule 27-2 is to enable the player to save time. The only way he can effectively do so is to play the provisional ball before going forward for the purpose of searching for the original ball. However, this provision should not be so narrowly interpreted to preclude a player from playing a provisional ball even though he has proceeded from where he last played in the direction of the original ball, e.g., in retrieving a ball or a different club to play the provisional ball. The Committee must consider all of the relevant facts in determining if the player did in fact go forward to search for the original ball. (New)

27-2a/2 Provisional Ball Played Solely in Belief Original Ball Might Be in Water Hazard

Q. A player's tee shot might be in a water hazard, but clearly it is not lost outside a water hazard or out of bounds. The player announces that, since his ball might be in the hazard, he is going to play a provisional ball and he does so. Rule 27-2a seems to prohibit a provisional ball in the circumstances. What is the ruling?

A. The player did not play a provisional ball which, according to the Definition of "Provisional Ball," is a ball played under Rule 27-2 for a ball which may be lost outside a water hazard or may be out of bounds. The second ball from the tee was in play since it was not a provisional ball.

27-2a/2.5 Player Plays Provisional Ball in Belief Original Might Be Lost Outside Water Hazard Then Discovers There Is No Possibility of Its Being Lost Outside Water Hazard

Q. A player's tee shot is struck towards an area of trees, bushes and tall grass. Believing his ball might be lost outside a water hazard, the player announces his intention to play a provisional ball and plays a ball from the tee. When he arrives at the area, he finds that the area in question is wetlands that has been defined as a lateral water hazard and that there is reasonable evidence that his ball is lost in it. What is the ruling?

A. As the player played the second ball from the tee in the belief that his original ball might be lost outside a water hazard, that ball was a provisional ball. The subsequent discovery that the area in question is in fact a lateral water hazard is irrelevant. Therefore, the player must abandon the provisional ball and proceed under Rule 26-1 — see Rule 27-2c. (New)

27-2a/3 Play of Provisional Ball in Absence of Reasonable Possibility Original Ball Is Lost or Out of Bounds

Q. In the absence of reasonable possibility that a ball is lost outside a water hazard or is out of bounds, may the player play a provisional ball?

A. No. If a player plays a ball under such circumstances, the ball is not a provisional ball but the ball in play — see Decision 27-2a/2.

27-2a/4 Play of a Second Provisional Ball

Q. If a player properly plays a provisional ball and believes that it may be out of bounds, may he play a second provisional ball before going forward to look for the original ball and the first provisional ball?

A. Yes. The second provisional ball bears to the first provisional ball the same relationship as the first provisional ball bears to the original ball.

27-2b/1 Continuation of Play with Provisional Ball Without Searching for Original Ball

Q. At a par-3 hole, a player hits his tee shot into dense woods. He then hits a provisional ball which comes to rest near the hole. In view of the position of the provisional ball, the player does not wish to find his original ball. He does not search for it and walks directly towards his provisional ball to continue play with it. His opponent (or fellow-competitor) believes it would be beneficial to him if the original ball were found. May the opponent (or fellow-competitor) search for the player's ball?

A. Yes. In equity (Rule 1-4) he may search for five minutes provided that in the meantime the player does not play a stroke with the provisional ball, it being nearer the hole than the place where the original ball is likely to be. The player is entitled to play such a stroke. If he does, the original ball is then lost under Rule 27-2b and further search for it would serve no purpose. In match play, if the player so proceeds and his provisional ball is closer to the hole than his opponent's ball, his opponent may recall the stroke (Rule 10-1c). However, recalling the stroke would not change the status of the original ball, which was lost when the provisional ball was played out of turn. See also Decision 27-2c/2. (Revised)

27-2b/2 When Provisional Ball Holed Becomes Ball in Play

Q. At a short hole, A's tee shot may be out of bounds or lost, so he plays a provisional ball, which he holes. A does not wish to look for his original ball. B, A's opponent or a fellow-competitor, goes to look for the original ball. When does the provisional ball become the ball in play?

A. In equity (Rule 1-4) the provisional ball becomes the ball in play as soon as A picks it out of the hole, provided his original ball has not already been found in bounds within five minutes of B starting to search for it. (Revised)

27-2b/3 Original Ball Is Beyond Provisional Ball; Player Searches Briefly for Original Ball, Plays Provisional Ball and Then Finds Original Ball

Q. A player's provisional ball comes to rest short of where the original ball is likely to be. After a two-minute search for the original ball, the player goes back, plays a second stroke with the provisional ball and then his original ball is found within the five-minute time limit. What is the ruling?

A. The player must continue play with the original ball. Play of a provisional ball does not render the original ball lost until it has been played from the place where the original ball is likely to be or from a point nearer the hole than that place — Rule 27-2b.

27-2b/4 Provisional Ball Played from Beyond Where Original Ball Likely to Be But Not Beyond Where Original Ball Found

Q. A player, believing his tee shot might be lost or in a road defined as out of bounds, played a provisional ball. He searched for his original ball but did not find it. He went forward and played his provisional ball. Then he went further forward and found his original ball in bounds. The original ball must have bounced down the road and then come back into bounds, because it was found much farther from the tee than anticipated. Was the original ball still the ball in play?

A. No. The player played a stroke with the provisional ball from a point nearer the hole than the place where the original ball was likely to be. When he did so, the provisional ball became the ball in play and the original ball was lost — Rule 27-2b.

The place where the original ball in fact lay was irrelevant.

27

27-2b/5 Original Ball Played After Provisional Ball Played from Point Nearer Hole Than Original Ball Is Likely to Be

Q. A player, unable to find his original ball, goes forward and plays a second stroke with his provisional ball from a point nearer the hole than the place where the original ball is likely to be. His original ball is then found and he plays it. What is the ruling?

A. When the player played his second stroke with the provisional ball, the original ball was out of play and the provisional ball was in play — Rule 27-2b. In playing a stroke with a ball out of play (the original ball), the player played a wrong ball — see Definition of "Wrong Ball" — and was subject to penalty as prescribed in Rule 15.

27-2b/6 Player Abandons Original Ball and Walks Forward to Play Provisional Ball; Original Ball Then Found

Q. A player, having searched for a minute for his original ball, abandoned it and walked forward to continue play with his provisional ball. Before he played the provisional ball, some spectators found the original ball before the five-minute search period expired. What is the ruling?

A. The original ball remained the ball in play since it was found within five minutes after search for it had begun and the player had not played a stroke with the provisional ball from the place where the original ball was likely to be or from a point nearer the hole than that place — Rule 27-2b.

Player Discovers Original Ball in Hole After Searching Five Minutes and Then Continuing Play with Provisional Ball — See 1-1/3.

27-2b/6.5 Player Declares Provisional Ball Unplayable and Drops Ball; Original Ball Then Found

Q. A player hits his tee shot into heavy rough approximately 150 yards from the teeing ground and, since his ball may be lost outside a water hazard, he plays a provisional ball. After searching briefly for his original ball he goes forward to play his provisional ball which is in a bush approximately 200 yards from the teeing ground. He declares his provisional ball unplayable and drops it within two club-lengths of where it lay under Rule 28b. Before playing the provisional ball, the player's original ball is found by a spectator within five minutes of the player having begun to search for it. What is the ruling?

A. The original ball remained the ball in play since it was found within five minutes after search for it had begun and the player had not played a stroke with the provisional ball (see Rule 27-2b). The fact that the player lifted and dropped the provisional ball under Rule 28b is irrelevant. (New)

Player Declares First Ball from Tee Unplayable, Abandons Provisional Ball and Claims He is Lying Three With Third Ball — See 28/2.

27-2b/7 Provisional Ball Played in Erroneous Belief It Is Original Ball

Q. A player, believing his original ball may be out of bounds, plays a provisional ball which comes to rest in the same area. He finds a ball which he believes is his original ball, plays it and then discovers that the ball he played was his provisional ball. What is the ruling?

A. If a player reaches the place where his original ball is likely to be and plays another stroke with a provisional ball, the provisional ball is in play and the original ball is lost — Rule 27-2b.

27-2b/8 Provisional Ball Lifted in Erroneous Belief Original Ball Is in Bounds

Q. A player, believing his original ball might be out of bounds, played a provisional ball which came to rest short of where the original ball came to rest. He walked forward, saw his original ball and, believing the original ball to be in bounds, picked up the provisional ball. He then discovered that the original ball was out of bounds. What is the ruling?

A. Since the original ball was out of bounds, the provisional ball was in play — Rule 27-2b. When the player lifted the ball in play (provisional ball) without authority under the Rules, he incurred a penalty stroke and was required to replace it — Rule 18-2a.

27-2b/9 Provisional Ball Lifted Subsequently Becomes Ball in Play

Q. In stroke play, a competitor, believing his tee shot might be lost, plays a provisional ball. He finds a ball he believes is his original ball, plays a stroke at it, picks up his provisional ball and then discovers that the ball he played was not his original ball, but rather a wrong ball. He resumes search for his original ball but cannot find it. What is the ruling?

A. The competitor lifted a ball which was to become the ball in play, *i.e.*, the provisional ball — see Rule 27-2b. Accordingly, the competitor incurred a stroke-and-distance penalty under Rule 27-1 as a result of losing his original ball, a two-stroke penalty under Rule 15-3 for playing a wrong ball and a one-stroke penalty under Rule 18-2a for picking up his provisional ball. He is required to replace and play out the provisional ball. The competitor would be playing his seventh stroke.

27-2b/10 Provisional Ball Lifted Subsequently Becomes Ball in Play; Competitor Then Plays from Wrong Place

Q. With regard to Decision 27-2b/9, what is the ruling if the competitor returns to the tee with the provisional ball and puts it into play again?

A. When the competitor played again from the tee rather than replacing and playing the provisional ball from where it was lifted, he incurred the general penalty of two strokes for a breach of Rule 18 (in accordance with Rule 20-7b), rather than a one-stroke penalty under Rule 18-2a. The competitor would be playing his eighth stroke from the tee.

27-2c/1 Possibility That Original Ball Is in Water Hazard May Not Preclude Play of Provisional Ball

Q. Is it true that, if a player's original ball may have come to rest in a water hazard, the player is precluded from playing a provisional ball?

A. No. Even though the original ball may be in a water hazard, the player is entitled to play a provisional ball if the original ball might also be lost outside the water hazard or out of bounds. In such a case, if the original ball is found in the water hazard, the provisional ball must be abandoned — Rule 27-2c.

27-2c/1.5 Whether Provisional Ball Becomes Ball in Play If Original Ball Lost in Ground Under Repair

Q. A player hits his tee shot into an area of tall rough and, since the ball may be lost, he plays a provisional ball. During search for the original ball, the player discovers that the Committee has marked a large area of the rough as ground under repair. It is established that there is reasonable evidence that the original ball is lost in the ground under repair. Does the provisional ball automatically become the ball in play since the original ball was lost outside a water hazard?

A. No. The player may continue play with the provisional ball under Rule 27-2b or he may proceed under Rule 25-1c(i) as his ball was lost in ground under repair — see Exception to Rule 27-2b. (Revised)

27-2c/2 Original Ball Found; Player Wishes to Ignore It and Continue Play with Provisional Ball

Q. At a par-3 hole, a player hits his tee shot into a heavy thicket and, since his ball may be lost, he hits a provisional ball, which comes to rest near the hole. In the circumstances, it is advantageous to the player not to find his original ball, in which case the provisional ball would become the ball in play. Accordingly, the player does not search for the original ball; he walks directly towards his provisional ball. While the player is on his way to his provisional ball, his original ball is found by a member of the Committee, a forecaddie, his opponent or a fellow-competitor. The player is advised that his original ball has been found. May the player ignore the original ball and continue play with the provisional ball?

A. No. The player must inspect the ball which has been found and, if it is the player's original ball, he must continue play with it (or proceed under the unplayable ball Rule). The provisional ball must be abandoned — Rule 27-2c. See also Decision 27-2b/1.

27-2c/3 Provisional Ball Played from Point Nearer Hole Than Original Ball Because Player Erroneously Thought Original Ball, Which Was Visible, Was Out of Bounds

Q. A player's ball came to rest 20 yards over a green and beyond a white stake which the player's caddie said was a boundary stake. The player played a provisional ball which came to rest short of the green, but closer to the hole than his original ball. The player played the provisional ball onto the green. At that point, he walked behind the green towards his original ball, which had been visible all along, and discovered that the white stake was not a boundary stake and that his original ball was in bounds. What is the ruling?

A. The player should have determined the status of his original ball before playing a second stroke with the provisional ball and, since the original ball was not out of bounds, he should have abandoned the provisional ball. When he failed to do so, the second stroke with the provisional ball was a stroke with a wrong ball — Rule 27-2c.

In match play, the player lost the hole (Rule 15-2).

In stroke play, he incurred a two-stroke penalty (Rule 15-3) and was required to hole out with the original ball.

27-2c/4 Original Ball and Provisional Ball Found Out of Bounds

Q. A player finds both his original ball and his provisional ball out of bounds. The balls were played from the tee. When the player returns to the tee and plays another ball, has he taken 3 strokes or 5?

A. The player will have taken 5 strokes when he plays the third ball from the tee. A stroke played with a provisional ball and any penalty related to it are not disregarded unless the provisional ball is abandoned as provided in Rule 27-2c.

Rule 28. Ball Unplayable

The player may declare his ball unplayable at any place on the *course* except when the ball is in a *water hazard*. The player is the sole judge as to whether his ball is unplayable.

If the player deems his ball to be unplayable, he shall, under penalty of one stroke:

a. Play a ball as nearly as possible at the spot from which the original ball was last played (see Rule 20-5);

or

b. Drop a ball within two club-lengths of the spot where the ball lay, but not nearer the *hole;*

or

c. Drop a ball behind the point where the ball lay, keeping that point directly between the *hole* and the spot on which the ball is dropped, with no limit to how far behind that point the ball may be dropped.

If the unplayable ball is in a *bunker,* the player may proceed under Clause a, b or c. If he elects to proceed under Clause b or c, a ball must be dropped in the *bunker.*

The ball may be cleaned when lifted under this Rule.

PENALTY FOR BREACH OF RULE:
Match play — Loss of hole;
Stroke play — Two strokes.

28/1 When Necessary to Find and Identify Ball Declared Unplayable

Q. A player hits his tee shot into a deep canyon. The player immediately declares the ball unplayable and plays another ball from the tee under the stroke-and-distance option of Rule 28. May a player declare unplayable a ball which has not been found?

A. Yes. A player may proceed under the stroke-and-distance option (Rule 28a) without finding his ball.

However, since Rules 28b and c require reference to where the ball lay, the player must find and identify his ball in order to proceed under either of these options.

28/2 Player Declares First Ball from Tee Unplayable, Abandons Provisional Ball and Claims He Is Lying Three with Third Ball

Q. A player hit his tee shot deep into the woods on the right. The player then hit a provisional ball into the same woods. The player did not search for either ball.

The player declared his first ball unplayable, said he was abandoning his provisional ball and hit a third ball from the tee. The player maintained that his third ball was in play and that he was lying 3. He based his argument on Rule 28, which states that the player is the sole judge as to whether his ball is unplayable, and on Decision 28/1, which says in effect that a player may proceed under the stroke-and-distance option of the unplayable ball Rule without finding his ball. The Committee ruled that the player's stroke with the third ball was his fifth stroke, but the wording of Decision 28/1 leaves a little doubt. Did the Committee rule correctly?

A. Yes. The player may not declare the first ball from the tee unplayable, disregard the provisional ball and put another ball into play under a stroke-and-distance penalty because, having played the provisional ball, he must find the original ball before he can declare it unplayable. Unless the original ball was found, the provisional ball would automatically become the ball in play.

This case differs from Decision 28/1. No provisional ball was played in that case.

Player Declares Provisional Ball Unplayable and Drops Ball; Original Ball Then Found — See 27-2b/6.5.

28/3 Ball Dropped Under Unplayable Ball Rule Comes to Rest in Original Position or Another Position at Which Ball Is Unplayable

Q. A player declared his ball unplayable and, under Rule 28b, dropped his ball within two club-lengths of the spot where it lay. The ball came to rest in the original position or another position at which the ball was unplayable. What is the ruling?

A. The ball was in play when it was dropped — Rule 20-4. Thus, if the ball came to rest in the original position, the player must again invoke the unplayable ball Rule, incurring an additional penalty stroke, unless he decides to play the ball as it lies. The same applies if the ball came to rest in another position at which it was unplayable, assuming that the ball did not roll into a position covered by Rule 20-2c, in which case re-dropping without penalty would be required.

28/4 Ball Declared Unplayable Through the Green Dropped in Hazard

Q. A player's ball lies through the green. The player declares the ball unplayable. In proceeding under Rule 28b or c, the player drops a ball in a hazard. Is this permissible?

A. Yes.

Ball Declared Unplayable Dropped in Ground Under Repair from Which Play Prohibited; Ball Then Dropped Under Ground Under Repair Rule — See 25-1b/14.5.

Ball Declared Unplayable in Water Hazard Is Dropped in Hazard and Played — See 20-7/2.

28/4.5 Ball Declared Unplayable Through the Green Dropped in Water Hazard; Player Elects Not to Play Ball and Wishes to Proceed Under the Water Hazard Rule

Q. With regard to Decision 28/4, if the player drops a ball into a lateral water hazard and the ball rolls into a position where the player is unable to play the ball, how should he proceed?

A. The player's only option is to proceed under Rule 26-1a.

As the player deliberately dropped the ball directly into the water hazard "the point at which the original ball last crossed the margin of the water hazard" cannot be identified. Therefore, in the absence of this reference point, neither Rule 26-1b nor 26-1c can be applied.

Player Proceeding Under Water Hazard Rule Drops Ball in Another Hazard — See 26-1/2.

28/5 Regression Under Unplayable Ball Rule

Q. A player plays a stroke from Point A to Point B. Point B is in an area from which it is very difficult to extricate a ball. The player considers declaring the ball unplayable but this would result in a stroke-and-distance penalty (Rule 28a). Dropping behind under Rule 28c is impossible due to a boundary fence and dropping within two club-lengths under Rule 28b is not feasible because it would require a considerable number of such drops to escape the area. The player plays from Point B and moves the ball a few feet to Point C, where the ball is clearly unplayable. Under Rule 28a, may the player:

(a) declare the ball unplayable at Point C and drop a ball under penalty of one stroke at Point B, and then
(b) declare the ball unplayable at Point B and drop a ball, under an additional penalty of one stroke, at Point A?

A. No. Under Rule 28a, the player would be entitled to drop a ball only at the place from which he played his last stroke (Point B).

In the circumstances, the player's only alternative is to invoke Rule 28b a sufficient number of times (starting at Point C and dropping the ball sideways within two club-lengths each time) to get the ball into a playable position.

28/6 Player Plays Second Shot, Declares Ball Unplayable and Returns to Tee

Q. With regard to Decision 28/5, if Point A is the teeing ground and Point B is the spot from which the second shot was played, what is the penalty if the player, having declared his ball unplayable at Point C, returns to the tee and plays out the hole from there?

A. The player was entitled to drop and play a ball at Point B under Rule 28a, but not Point A. When he played a ball from Point A, he played from a wrong place.

In match play, the player incurs a penalty of loss of hole for a breach of Rule 28 — see also Rule 20-7a.

In stroke play, a serious breach of Rule 28 is involved. Accordingly, the player is disqualified unless the serious breach is corrected as provided in Rule 20-7b.

Except in the special circumstances covered by Rule 26-2, the Rules do not allow a player to regress beyond the spot from which his last stroke was played, in this case Point B. Such action generally constitutes a serious breach, as in this case.

Meaning of Serious Breach — See 20-7b/0.5.

28/6.5 Player Declares Ball Unplayable a Second Time and Wishes to Proceed Under Stroke and Distance After Dropping a Ball Under Other Unplayable Option

Q. A player plays a stroke from Point A to Point B. The player declares his ball unplayable and proceeds under either Rule 28b or c. After dropping under penalty of one stroke, the ball comes to rest at Point C. The player declares his ball unplayable for a second time and wishes to proceed under Rule 28a, playing from Point A. Is this permissible?

A. Yes. The player may play from Point A because he did not make a stroke at the ball from either Point B or Point C. Point A was the spot from which the original ball was last played. The player would incur a total of two penalty strokes.

Ball Dropped Under One Option of Unplayable Ball Rule Strikes Player; Player Wishes to Change Relief Option — See 20-2a/6.

Changing Relief Option When Re-Dropping Required — See 20-2c/5.

Changing Relief Option After Ball Dropped in Wrong Place — See 20-6/2.

28/7 Player Misses Ball and Declares It Unplayable

Q. A player's tee shot comes to rest in tree roots. He makes a stroke, fails to move the ball and then declares the ball unplayable. May the player return to the tee, playing 4, under Rule 28a?

A. No. Rule 28a permits the player to play "a ball . . . at the spot from which the original ball was last played." The original ball was last played from the tree roots, not the tee.

28/8 Ball Declared Unplayable; Place from Which Previous Stroke Played Is Nearer Hole

Q. A player's ball strikes a rock and bounces farther away from the hole than the spot from which the stroke was played. The player declares the ball unplayable. May the player invoke the stroke-and-distance option of Rule 28 in the circumstances?

A. Yes.

28/9 Ball Lying on Grass-Covered Ground Within Bunker Declared Unplayable

Q. A player's ball is lying on grass-covered ground within a bunker. The player declares the ball unplayable and elects to drop it under Rule 28c. Must he drop it in the bunker?

A. No. Grass-covered ground within a bunker is not part of the bunker. Accordingly, the player may drop the ball behind the bunker.

28/10 Ball Dropped Outside Bunker Under Option Requiring Drop in Bunker

Q. In stroke play, a competitor declares his ball unplayable in a bunker and, purporting to proceed under Rule 28b or c, drops a ball outside the bunker, whereas both such provisions require that a ball be dropped in the bunker. What is the penalty?

A. Generally, the penalty should be disqualification for a serious breach of Rule 28, unless rectified under Rule 20-7b. However, if the position of the ball after it is dropped out of the bunker is not substantially different from what it would have been if the competitor had invoked the stroke-and-distance option under Rule 28a, he incurs the penalty stroke prescribed by Rule 28 and an additional penalty of two strokes for a breach of that Rule, rather than disqualification.

28/11 Ball Unplayable in Tree and Player Opts to Drop Within Two Club-Lengths

Q. A player's ball is eight feet off the ground, lodged in a tree. The player declares the ball unplayable. May the player proceed under option b of Rule 28 which permits him to drop a ball within two club-lengths of where his ball lay unplayable?

A. Yes. The player would be entitled to drop a ball within two club-lengths of the point on the ground immediately below the place where the ball lay in the tree. In some instances this may allow the player to drop a ball on a putting green.

Ball Unplayable in Tree Dislodged by Shaking Tree or Throwing Club — See 18-2a/27.

Ball in Tree Identified But Not Retrieved Declared Unplayable — See 27/14.

28/12 Ball Unplayable at Base of Cliff and Player Wishes to Drop Within Two Club-Lengths of Point Above Ball

Q. Under Decision 28/11, if a ball in a tree is declared unplayable, the player may, under Rule 28b, drop a ball within two club-lengths of the spot on the ground directly beneath where the ball lies.

Suppose a player declares unplayable a ball lying at the base of a cliff and wishes to proceed under Rule 28b. May the player drop a ball within two club-lengths of a point directly above where the ball lies in order to get himself onto the top of the cliff?

A. No.

In Decision 28/11, the player was permitted to ignore vertical distance in taking relief under Rule 28b only because his ball was off the ground. In this case, the ball at the base of the cliff is on the ground.

28/13 After Declaring Ball Unplayable and Lifting It, Player Discovers Ball Was in Ground Under Repair

Q. A player lifts his ball after declaring it unplayable and then discovers that the ball was lying in ground under repair. Does the declaration and the lifting of the ball commit the player to proceeding under Rule 28?

A. No. Provided the player has not put a ball into play under Rule 28, he is not precluded by that Rule from taking relief, without penalty, under the ground under repair Rule (Rule 25). (Revised)

Player Entitled to Relief Without Penalty from Condition Lifts Ball; Chooses Not to Take Relief and Wishes to Proceed Under the Unplayable Ball Rule — See 18-2a/12.5.

28/14 Wrong Ball Declared Unplayable Played Under Stroke-and-Distance Procedure; Original Ball Then Found

Q. A player finds a stray ball, which he mistakenly thinks is his, in a bad lie. He declares it unplayable and decides to adopt the procedure in Rule 28a. After going back, he plays the stray ball under penalty of stroke and distance at the spot from which his original ball was played. He then finds his original ball in a playable position. What is the ruling?

A. The original ball is lost and the stray ball played under penalty of stroke and distance is in play — see Decision 27/17.

The ruling would have been different if the player had decided to proceed under either Rule 28b or 28c — see Decision 28/15.

28/15 Wrong Ball Declared Unplayable, Dropped Within Two Club-Lengths and Played Before Error Discovered

Q. A player finds a stray ball, which he mistakenly thinks is his, in a bad lie. He declares it unplayable and decides to adopt the procedure in Rule 28b. He drops the stray ball within two club-lengths of the spot where it lay and plays it. He then finds his original ball in a playable position.

In Decision 28/14 the basic situation is exactly the same, but in that case the player elected to proceed under Rule 28a and it was ruled that the stray ball played under penalty of stroke and distance was in play.

What is the ruling in this case?

A. The procedures in Rules 28b and 28c cannot be applied except with reference to the position of the player's ball in play, and this must first be found and identified — see Decision 28/1. In the present case, the stray ball dropped and played by the player was not his original ball. Nor was it a substituted ball, as the player believed that he was proceeding with his original ball. It was, therefore, a wrong ball — see Definitions of "Ball in Play" and "Wrong Ball." The player incurred a penalty of loss of hole in match play or two strokes in stroke play (Rule 15). In stroke play, he must continue play with his original ball.

The ruling in Decision 28/14 is different because, when a player plays a ball under the stroke-and-distance procedure, the location of his original ball is irrelevant and it need not even have been found and identified.

Wrong Ball Dropped Under Unplayable Ball Rule But Not Played — See 15/13.

Other Decisions Relating to Rule 28:

Ball Declared Unplayable in Bunker; Player Removes Loose Impediment from Bunker While Ball Lifted — See 13-4/35.7.

Caddie on Own Initiative Lifts Ball Considering It Unplayable — See 18-2a/15.

OTHER FORMS OF PLAY

Rule 29. Threesomes and Foursomes

Definitions

Threesome: A match in which one plays against two, and each side plays one ball.

Foursome: A match in which two play against two, and each side plays one ball.

29-1. General

In a threesome or a foursome, during any *stipulated round* the *partners* shall play alternately from the *teeing grounds* and alternately during the play of each hole. *Penalty strokes* do not affect the order of play.

29-2. Match Play

If a player plays when his *partner* should have played, his *side* shall lose the hole.

29-3. Stroke Play

If the *partners* play a *stroke* or *strokes* in incorrect order, such *stroke* or *strokes* shall be cancelled and the *side* shall incur a penalty of two strokes. The *side* shall correct the error by playing a ball in correct order as nearly as possible at the spot from which it first played in incorrect order (see Rule 20-5). If the *side* plays a *stroke* from the next *teeing ground* without first correcting the error or, in the case of the last hole of the round, leaves the *putting green* without declaring its intention to correct the error, the *side* shall be disqualified.

29/1 Changing Partners After Driving from First Tee

Q. A and B are to play C and D in a foursome match in which the conditions of the competition permit substitutions. D is absent at the time the match is to start. Accordingly, E is substituted for D. C plays the first stroke for side C-E. At that point, D arrives. May D be reinstated in the match since E has not played a stroke?

A. No. Once any player in a foursome match has played from the first tee, the composition of neither side may be changed.

29/2 Mixed Foursome in Which Different Tees Used by Men and Women; Tee Shot Out of Bounds

Q. In a mixed foursome in which the men play from the back tees and the women play from the forward tees, a man hits a tee shot out of bounds. Does his partner play the next stroke from the back tee or the forward tee?

A. The partner must play from the back tee.

29/3 Player in Foursome Match Practices Putts on Previous Green After Partner Has Driven from Next Tee

Q. A and B are partners in a foursome match. A was practicing putts on the 11th green after B drove off the 12th tee. Was A playing practice strokes during the play of a hole?

A. Yes. A and B lost the 12th hole for a breach of Rule 7-2.

29/4 Dropping Ball in Foursome Competition

Q. Rule 20-2a provides that "the player himself" must drop a ball. Under the Definition of "Partner," it is stated that, in the case of threesomes and foursomes, the term "player" includes his partner where the context so admits. When a side in a foursome is required to drop a ball, may either member of the side drop it?

A. No. In view of the requirement of Rule 20-2a that the player himself shall drop the ball, the member of the side whose turn it is to play next must drop the ball.

29/5 Hitting Sand in Bunker with Club After Failing to Extricate Ball; Foursome Match

Q. In a foursome match, A and B are partners. A plays a bunker shot, fails to get the ball out and takes a swing with his club into the sand. This action does not improve the position of the ball in the bunker.

Rule 13-4 provides that, when a ball lies in a hazard, the *player* "shall not touch the ground in the hazard ... with a club." When A took the swing, it was B's turn to play the next stroke for side A-B. So, presumably, B was the "player" insofar as the Rules were concerned. Accordingly, it would appear A-B would incur no penalty under Rule 13-4 as a result of A's swing. Is this correct?

A. No. In a foursome, the word "player" includes his partner — see Definition of "Partner." A-B incur a penalty of loss of hole for a breach of Rule 13-4 — see Decision 13-4/35.

29/6 Signing of Score Card in Foursome Stroke Play

Q. Rule 31-4 dealing with scoring in four-ball stroke play states: "Only one of the partners need be responsible for complying with Rule 6-6b." What is the ruling in this regard in foursome stroke play?

A. Although Rule 29 is silent on the matter, in foursome stroke play only one of the partners need be responsible for complying with Rule 6-6b.

Competitor Records Incorrect Handicap for Partner in Foursome Stroke Play Competition; Error Discovered After Competition Closed — See 6-2b/2.5.

Competitors in Foursome Competition Fail to Record Individual Handicaps on Score Card — See 6-2b/4.

29-1/1 Ball Played from Outside Teeing Ground in Foursome Match

Q. A and B are playing C and D in a foursome match. A plays from outside the teeing ground and Side A-B is required by C and D to replay the stroke. Should A or B replay it?

A. A must replay the stroke. The original stroke does not count.

29-1/2 Competitor Plays from Outside Teeing Ground in Foursome Stroke Play; Partner Replays Stroke

Q. In foursome stroke play A plays in correct order but from outside the teeing ground. B, his partner, then plays from within the teeing ground, whereas A should have done so. What is the ruling?

A. The side is penalized two strokes for playing from outside the teeing ground (Rule 11-4) and two strokes for playing in incorrect order (Rule 29-3). A must now play another ball from within the teeing ground. Otherwise, the side is disqualified.

29-1/3 Who Plays Provisional Ball in Foursome

Q. A and B are partners in a foursome. A drives and there is doubt whether the ball is out of bounds. They decide to play a provisional ball. Who plays it?

A. The provisional ball is played by B.

29-1/4 Provisional Ball Played by Wrong Member of Side in Foursome

Q. A and B were partners in a foursome competition. A drove from the tee and, since the ball might be lost, A-B elected to play a provisional ball. A played the provisional ball, whereas, under Rule 29, B should have played it. What is the ruling?

A. If the original ball was found in bounds and thus the provisional ball did not become the ball in play, there was no penalty.

If the original ball was lost and the provisional ball became the ball in play, A-B lost the hole in match play (Rule 29-2) or incurred a penalty of two strokes in stroke play (Rule 29-3). In stroke play, the provisional ball would have to be abandoned and B would have to play from the tee — Rule 29-3.

29-1/5 Order of Play If Player Accidentally Moves Ball After Address

Q. In a foursome match, a player accidentally moves the ball after addressing it and incurs a penalty of one stroke under Rule 18-2b. The ball is replaced. Does the player or his partner play the next stroke?

A. The player must play the next stroke. Penalty strokes do not affect the order of play (Rule 29-1).

29-1/6 Player Misses Ball Accidentally When Making Stroke

Q. In a foursome event, A and B are partners. A attempts to strike the ball and misses. Whose turn is it to play?

A. An accidental miss is a stroke — see Definition of "Stroke." It is B's turn to play.

29-1/7 Player Misses Ball Purposely So Partner Would Play Ball Over Water

Q. A and B, partners in a foursome competition, were faced with a difficult shot over a pond. A, a poor player, swung but purposely missed the ball. B, an expert player, then played the ball to the green. Is this permissible?

A. No. Since A had no intention of moving the ball, he did not play a stroke — see Definition of "Stroke" — and it remained his turn to play.

When B played instead of A, A and B incurred a penalty of loss of hole in match play or two strokes in stroke play — Rules 29-2 and -3. In stroke play, A must play a ball at the spot from which B played. If A did not do so before the side played from the next teeing ground, A and B were disqualified — Rule 29-3.

29-1/8 Order of Play in Foursome Stroke Play When Wrong Ball Played

Q. In foursome stroke play, A played a wrong ball. Who plays the next shot, A or his partner, B?

A. A must play the next stroke. In a foursome competition, penalty strokes do not affect the order of play — see Rule 29-1. The side A-B incurs a penalty of two strokes — Rule 15-3.

29-1/9 Both Player and Partner Drive at Same Tee in Foursome Play

Q. A and B are partners in foursome play. At the 5th hole, forgetting that they were playing a foursome, A and then B drive. What is the ruling:
(a) if it was A's turn to drive?
(b) if it was B's turn to drive?

A. (a) If it was A's turn to drive, B's ball would be the side's ball in play and would be lying 3 — see Decision 27/17.

(b) If it was B's turn to drive, the side loses the hole in match play or incurs a penalty of two strokes in stroke play (Rules 29-2 and -3). In stroke play, the side must continue with B's ball which lies 3.

Restriction on Which Partner in Foursome Competition May Play from 1st Tee — See 33-1/3.5.

29-2/1 Wrong Partners Drive for Both Sides in Foursome Match

29

Q. A and B are playing C and D in a foursome match. A and C drive off at a hole at which B and D should have driven. The error is then discovered. What is the ruling?

A. The side which drove first loses the hole under Rule 29-2.

29-2/2 Side Drives for Three Holes in Wrong Order and Then Claim Is Made

Q. In a foursome match, A and B are playing C and D. A drives at the 9th hole and again, in error, at the 10th hole. B drives at the 11th and A drives at the 12th. The error is then discovered. C and D claim the 10th, 11th and 12th holes, and the matter is referred to the Committee. What is the ruling?

A. A and B lose the 12th hole under Rule 29-2.

C and D's claim of the 10th and 11th holes could have been considered only if C and D had been given wrong information by A and B and the claim had been based on facts previously unknown to C and D. A and B are deemed to have given wrong information to C and D—see first paragraph of Rule 9-2. However, C and D must have seen A and B play out of order on all three holes. Therefore, the claim was not based on facts previously unknown to C and D.

Rule 30. Three-Ball, Best-Ball and Four-Ball Match Play

Definitions

Three-Ball: A match play competition in which three play against one another, each playing his own ball. Each player is playing two distinct *matches.*

Best-Ball: A match in which one plays against the better ball of two or the best ball of three players.

Four-Ball: A match in which two play their better ball against the better ball of two other players.

30-1. Rules of Golf Apply

The Rules of Golf, so far as they are not at variance with the following special Rules, shall apply to three-ball, best-ball and four-ball *matches.*

30-2. Three-Ball Match Play

a. Ball at Rest Moved by an Opponent

Except as otherwise provided in the *Rules,* if the player's ball is touched or *moved* by an opponent, his *caddie* or *equipment* other than during search, Rule 18-3b applies. That opponent shall incur a *penalty stroke* in his match with the player, but not in his match with the other opponent.

b.Ball Deflected or Stopped by an Opponent Accidentally

If a player's ball is accidentally deflected or stopped by an opponent, his *caddie* or *equipment*, no penalty shall be incurred. In his match with that opponent the player may play the ball as it lies or, before another *stroke* is played by either *side*, he may cancel the *stroke* and play a ball without penalty as nearly as possible at the spot from which the original ball was last played (see Rule 20-5). In his match with the other opponent, the ball shall be played as it lies.

Exception: Ball striking person attending *flagstick* — see Rule 17-3b.

(Ball purposely deflected or stopped by opponent — see Rule 1-2.)

30-3. Best-Ball and Four-Ball Match Play

a. Representation of Side

A *side* may be represented by one *partner* for all or any part of a match; all *partners* need not be present. An absent *partner* may join a match between holes, but not during play of a hole.

b. Maximum of Fourteen Clubs

The *side* shall be penalized for a breach of Rule 4-4 by any *partner.*

c. Order of Play

Balls belonging to the same *side* may be played in the order the *side* considers best.

d. Wrong Ball

If a player plays a *stroke* with a *wrong ball* except in a *hazard,* he shall be disqualified for that hole, but his *partner* incurs no penalty even if the *wrong ball* belongs to him. If the *wrong ball* belongs to another player, its owner shall place a ball on the spot from which the *wrong ball* was first played.

e. Disqualification of Side

(i) A *side* shall be disqualified for a breach of any of the following by any *partner:*

Rule 1-3 — Agreement to Waive Rules.
Rule 4-1 or -2 — Clubs.
Rule 5-1 or -2 — The Ball.
Rule 6-2a — Handicap (playing off higher handicap).
Rule 6-4 — *Caddie.*
Rule 6-7 — Undue Delay; Slow Play (repeated offense).
Rule 14-3 — Artificial Devices and Unusual *Equipment.*

(ii) A *side* shall be disqualified for a breach of any of the following by all *partners:*

Rule 6-3 — Time of Starting and Groups.
Rule 6-8 — Discontinuance of Play.

f. Effect of Other Penalties

If a player's breach of a *Rule* assists his *partner*'s play or adversely affects an opponent's play, the *partner* incurs the applicable penalty in addition to any penalty incurred by the player.

In all other cases where a player incurs a penalty for breach of a *Rule,* the penalty shall not apply to his *partner.* Where the penalty is stated to be loss of hole, the effect shall be to disqualify the player for that hole.

g. Another Form of Match Played Concurrently

In a best-ball or four-ball match when another form of match is played concurrently, the above special Rules shall apply.

30/1 Caddie Shared by Members of Opposite Sides in Four-Ball Match Moves Ball

Q. A caddie shared by A and C, who were on opposite sides in a four-ball match, moves A's ball. What is the ruling?

A. If the caddie was not acting upon directions of C, A is penalized one stroke — see Definition of "Caddie" and Rule 18-2a.

If the caddie was acting upon directions of C, C is penalized one stroke under Rule 18-3b.

30/2 Caddie Shared by Opponents' Side in Four-Ball Match Moves Player's Ball

Q. A and B are playing C and D in a four-ball match. A caddie shared by C and D accidentally moves A's ball. Who is penalized?

A. Rule 18-3b provides that, if a player's ball is moved by an opponent's caddie, that opponent incurs a penalty stroke. However, when opponents share a caddie, there is no fair way of assigning the penalty to one member of the side. Accordingly, in equity (Rule 1-4), both C and D incur a penalty stroke.

A must replace his ball — Rule 18-3b.

30/2.5 Player Touches Putting Green in Pointing Out Line for Putting for Partner and Incidentally Touches Own Line of Putt

Q. In a four-ball match, A and B are partners and their balls lie on the putting green. A touches the green in pointing out a line for putting for B. Incidentally, the spot which A touches is on his (A's) line of putt.

B is disqualified for the hole under Rule 8-2b. Is A disqualified for the hole under Rule 16-1a?

A. No.

Player Who Has Holed Out Touches Partner's Line of Putt — See 1-2/3.5.

30/3 Determination of Honor in Four-Ball Match in Which Points Awarded for Both Better-Ball and Aggregate Scores

Q. In a four-ball match, one point is awarded for the better-ball score at each hole and one point is awarded for the aggregate score at each hole. How is the honor determined?

A. The Rules of Golf do not cover such a match — see Definition of "Sides and Matches." It is recommended that the honor be determined by the better-ball score only.

30/4 Player Who Walks Off Green Under Mistaken Impression Partner Halved Hole Returns and Putts for Half

Q. A and B are playing C and D in a four-ball match. At one hole C and D hole out and their better-ball score is 4. A, who had marked the position of his ball and lifted it, has a putt for a 4 but he mistakenly thinks B has scored a 4. Accordingly, A walks off the green, leaving his ball-marker on the green. B immediately advises A that he (B) scored a 5. So A returns to the green, replaces his ball and holes out for a 4.

C and D claim the hole on the ground that A cannot come back and putt after walking off the green, thinking his partner had halved the hole. Are C and D correct?

A. No. Since A had not waived his turn to putt and there was no undue delay, A was entitled to proceed as he did. If, however, A had not left his ball-marker on the green, and therefore the position of his ball was no longer marked, he would have incurred a penalty stroke under Rule 20-1 and would no longer have had a putt for the half.

30/5 In Four-Ball Match Player with Putt for Half Picks Up in Error at Suggestion of Opponent Based on Misunderstanding

Q. A and B are playing C and D in a four-ball match. A has holed out in 4, the better ball for his side. When C holes out, A remarks: "Nice 4, C. D, you may pick your ball up." C does not correct A by stating he had a 5 and allows his partner D to pick his ball up although D still has a putt for a half.

Upon leaving the putting green, it occurs to C that he has allowed D to pick up when D had an opportunity to halve the hole. In the circumstances, could A's remark be construed as a concession of D's putt?

A. No. A's suggestion that D might pick up D's ball was based on A's mistaken impression that C had scored a 4 and that therefore D's putt could have no bearing on the result.

C should have corrected A's mistaken impression before D picked up his ball. Since C failed to do so and

30

D did not finish the hole, C's score of 5 for the hole was C-D's better-ball score. Thus, C and D lost the hole.

30/6 Player Plays Practice Putt After He and Partner Have Holed Out But Before Opponents Hole Out

Q. In a four-ball match, A plays a practice putt after he and his partner have holed out but before the opponents have holed out. Was A in breach of Rule 7-2?

A. No. Rule 7-2 prohibits practicing during play of a hole. A did not practice during play of the hole because he and his partner had completed it. However, A was guilty of a breach of etiquette.

Another Decision relating to Rule 30:

Flagstick Attended by Partner Without Express Authority of Player; Ball Strikes Flagstick or Partner — See 17-3/4.

30-1/1 Side Plays Out of Turn from Tee; Opponents Require One Member of Side to Replay But Not Other

Q. A and B are playing C and D in a four-ball match. At one hole A and B drive out of turn. C and D require that A abandon his ball and replay in correct order and that B continue with his original ball. A and B maintain that if A is required to drive again then B must also do so. What is the ruling?

A. Rule 10-1c states in part: "… the opponent may immediately require the player to abandon the ball so played …" In this context, "immediately" means before anyone else plays.

Accordingly, if A and B played in that order, C and D could not require A to replay his stroke after B had played, but they could require B to replay.

If A and B played in the order B-A, A could be required to replay, but not B.

30-2/1 Player Plays Out of Turn from Tee in Three-Ball Match; One Opponent Requests Replay and Other Does Not

Following are the rulings in a three-ball match if A, B and C are scheduled to play in that order from the tee, B inadvertently drives first and A and C disagree on whether B should be required to replay the stroke under Rule 10-1c:

(a) If A wants B to replay the stroke but C does not, B must complete the hole with two balls. He must replay the stroke in his match with A, and continue with his original ball in his match with C.

(b) If C wants B to replay the stroke but A does not, B must continue with his original ball in both matches. B did not play out of turn with respect to C. Accordingly, C has no right to require B to replay the stroke.

If A, B and C are scheduled to play in that order from the tee, C inadvertently drives first and A and B disagree on whether C should be required to replay, C must complete the hole with two balls. He must replay his stroke in his match with the opponent who requires him to replay and continue with his original ball in his match with the other opponent.

30-3a/1 Absent Partner Joins Match During Play of Hole

Q. Rule 30-3a states in part: "An absent partner may join a match between holes, but not during play of a hole." If A and B are to play C and D in a four-ball match and A is absent when the match begins, what is the ruling if A joins the match during play of a hole?

A. A incurs the general penalty prescribed in Rule 2-6 and thus is disqualified for the hole. If any of A's strokes assisted B's play, B also is disqualified for the hole — Rule 30-3f.

30-3a/2 Absent Partner Gives Advice Before Joining Match

Q. A and B are to play C and D in a four-ball match. A is absent when the match begins. A arrives just after B, C and D have teed off at the 3rd hole. According to Decision 30-3a/1, A is prohibited from joining the match until the 4th hole. Is it permissible for A to give B advice during the play of the 3rd hole?

A. Yes.

30-3a/3 Determination of Handicap Allowances in Four-Ball Match If One Player Unable to Compete

Q. In a four-ball handicap match, the player with the lowest handicap is unable to play. Should the absent player be disregarded in determining the handicap allowances?

A. No. Under Rule 30-3a, a side may be represented by one partner for all or any part of the match. In determining handicap allowances, the handicaps of the three players should be reduced by the handicap of the absent player.

If a wrong handicap is declared for the absent player, Rule 6-2a applies.

30-3c/1 Player Putting First When Partner Farther from Hole Stands on Partner's or Opponent's Line of Putt

Q. A and B are partners in a four-ball match. A's ball is closer to the hole than any other ball and it is B's turn to play. A-B decide that A shall putt before B — Rule 30-3c. However, in doing so A would be standing on B's line of putt or the line of putt of an opponent. What is the ruling?

A. A would be entitled to putt first even if he would be standing on B's line. Rule 30-3c takes precedence over Rule 16-1a which prohibits touching the line of putt.

A would also be entitled to putt first if he would be standing on an opponent's line of putt. However, it would be a sporting gesture by A-B if they relinquished A's right to putt first in these circumstances.

30-3c/2 Waiving Turn to Putt in Four-Ball Match

Q. In a four-ball match, A and B are playing C and D. All four balls are on the green in three strokes. The balls of A and C are about ten feet from the hole; B's ball is two feet away and D's is three feet away. C picks up his ball. A leaves his ball on the green, but tells B and D to "battle it out." D putts first and holes; B then putts and misses. May A then putt for a half?

A. No. A and B abandoned A's right to complete the hole by allowing D to putt before A and B when it was A-B's turn to play. Under Rule 30-3c, A-B could have opted for B to putt before A. However, if B had done so and missed, it would then have been A's turn to play.

The answer is different if B's ball is three feet away, D's is two feet away and B putts and misses. In these circumstances, A may putt, provided he does so before D putts.

Waiving Turn to Play in Four-Ball Stroke Play — See 31-5/1.

30-3d/1 Player Plays Partner's Ball

Q. A and B are partners in a four-ball match. By mistake, A putts B's ball and A is disqualified for the hole under Rule 30-3d for playing a wrong ball. B replaces his ball as required by Rule 30-3d and holes his putt. The opponents then claim that B also is disqualified for the hole under Rule 30-3f because A's act of putting B's ball assisted B in determining how much his putt would break, etc. Is the claim valid?

A. No. Rule 30-3d specifically provides that B incurs no penalty. Rule 30-3f is not applicable.

30-3d/2 Player Wins Hole with Wrong Ball and Partner Picks Up; Error Discovered at Next Hole

Q. In a four-ball match, Side A-B holed out for a 4. C, a member of Side C-D, then holed a putt for a 3 and his partner, D, picked up what he thought was his ball. After playing from the next tee, it was discovered that C had putted out at the previous hole with D's ball. Side A-B claimed the hole. What is the ruling?

A. C gave wrong information to Side A-B when he did not inform Side A-B as soon as practicable that he had incurred a penalty for playing a wrong ball — see Rule 9-2. Accordingly, a belated claim by Side A-B was valid — Rule 2-5.

The Committee should have ruled that C was disqualified for the hole — Rule 9-2 or Rule 30-3d — and, since D did not complete the hole, Side A-B won the hole. (Revised)

30-3d/3 Players on Opposite Sides Exchange Balls During Play of Hole and Their Partners Pick Up; Error Discovered at Next Hole

Q. A and B were playing C and D in a four-ball match. At the 2nd hole, by mistake A played C's ball and then C played A's. C holed out with A's ball, scoring 5. A holed out C's ball, scoring 4. B and D picked up. Thus, A and B "won" the hole. The error was discovered during play of the 3rd hole, and Side C-D lodged a claim. What is the ruling?

A. A and C were disqualified for the 2nd hole for playing wrong balls. They should have informed their opponents as soon as practicable, which in this case was as soon as they had the opportunity to discover that they had done so, *i.e.*, when they reached the balls wrongly played to play them again. Because they failed to do so, they gave wrong information (Rule 9-2) and, under Rule 2-5, a belated claim that A (and C as well) was disqualified for the 2nd hole for a breach of Rule 30-3d should be upheld.

It could be argued that B and D's play of the 2nd hole was adversely affected (in that they picked up) and that accordingly Rule 30-3f applies. However, Rule 30-3d specifically provides that the "partner incurs no penalty." This applies even if play of the wrong ball would have assisted the partner — See Decision 30-3d/1 — and by implication it applies in the related case of an adverse effect on an opponent's play.

Furthermore, applying Rule 30-3f for the breaches of Rule 9-2 would not have been proper because those breaches were the direct result of the penalties incurred under Rule 30-3d.

Accordingly, if B picked up before D, Side C-D won the hole. If D picked up before B, Side A-B won the hole. If the order in which B and D picked up was not determinable, the Committee should have ruled that the 2nd hole was halved.

30-3d/3.5 Player Plays Partner's Ball; Error Discovered After Opponents Have Played Next Strokes

Q. A and B are playing C and D in a four-ball match. At the 2nd hole, after the tee shots A mistakenly plays B's ball. The error is discovered after C and D play their second strokes, and C and D claim the hole. What is the ruling?

A. A is disqualified for the hole because he played a wrong ball (Rule 30-3d). B incurs no penalty for A having played his ball (Decision 30-3d/1) and players B, C and D should continue play of the hole. (Revised)

30-3f/1 Player Lifts Loose Impediment in Bunker When His Ball and Partner's Ball in Bunker

Q. A and B are partners in a four-ball match. A's ball and B's ball are in the same bunker. A lifts a loose impediment lying in the bunker. A is disqualified for the hole for a breach of Rule 13-4. Does B incur a penalty?

A. If A's infringement assisted B's play, B also is disqualified for the hole — Rule 30-3f. Otherwise, B incurs no penalty.

30-3f/2 Hitting Sand in Bunker with Club After Failing to Extricate Ball; Partner's Ball in Same Bunker

Q. In a four-ball match A and B were partners. A played a stroke in a bunker and failed to get the ball out of the bunker. He then swung his club into the sand in the bunker, but this action did not affect his new lie in the bunker:

(a) What is the ruling if B's ball lay in the same bunker when A swung his club into the sand?
(b) What is the ruling if B's ball lay elsewhere?

A. In either case, A is disqualified for the hole (Rule 13-4 and Decision 13-4/35). The penalty does not apply to B unless A's action assisted B's play or adversely affected an opponent's play (Rule 30-3f).

30-3f/3 Player's Ball Resting Against Flagstick Lifted Before Being Holed; Others in Match Pick Up Mistakenly Believing Player Won Hole

Q. In a four-ball match, A's ball rested against the flagstick but it was not holed in terms of the Definition of "Holed." Instead of proceeding under Rule 17-4, A picked up the ball without marking its position. The other three players, believing that A had won the hole, picked up. Before anyone played from the next tee, a spectator pointed out that A's ball had not been holed. The players immediately asked the Committee for a ruling. What would be the correct ruling?

A. A incurred a penalty stroke under Rule 20-1 when he lifted his ball without marking its position. Since A did not inform the opponents about the penalty before they picked up, A was disqualified for the hole for giving wrong information — Rule 9-2. Since A's infringement adversely affected the opponents, *i.e.*, caused them to pick up, A's partner was also disqualified for the hole — Rule 30-3f. Thus, the opponents won the hole.

30-3f/4 Wrong Information Given by Player Out of Contention in Four-Ball Match

Q. A and B are playing C and D in a four-ball match, and the situation is as follows:

A's ball is on the green; he lies 3.

B's ball is in a bunker; he lies 5 and it is his turn to play.

C's ball is on the green; he lies 4.

D has picked up.

After B addresses his ball in the bunker, the ball moves and B incurs a penalty stroke under Rule 18-2b. B does not inform anyone that he has incurred a penalty stroke. B then replaces his ball and plays onto the green.

A then holes out for a 5 and C does likewise.

B is disqualified for the hole under Rule 9-2 for failing to inform C or D, before C played his next stroke, that he (B) had incurred a penalty stroke. Is A also disqualified for the hole under Rule 30-3f on the ground that B's failure to inform C or D of his (B's) penalty stroke adversely affected C's play?

A. No. B was clearly out of contention, and the result of the hole was dependent upon A and C alone. Accordingly, B's failure to inform C or D about the penalty could not have adversely affected C's play.

30-3f/5 Player Attending Flagstick for Opponent Struck by Ball of Opponent's Partner Who Played Out of Turn

Q. A and B are playing C and D in a four-ball match. It is B's turn to play and C is attending the flagstick at B's request. A, whose ball is in a deep bunker in such position that he cannot see C, plays out of turn and his ball strikes C. What is the ruling?

A. B authorized C to attend the flagstick which is the equivalent of A having authorized attendance of the flagstick. See Definition of "Partner," which provides that in a four-ball match, where the context so admits, the word "player" includes his partner.

Accordingly, A is disqualified for the hole (Rule 17-3b), but the penalty does not apply to B (Rule 30-3f).

30-3f/6 Player Plays Away from Hole to Assist Partner

Q. In a four-ball competition, a player purposely putts away from the hole to a position slightly farther from the hole than the spot where his partner's ball lies and on the same line to the hole as his partner's ball. The player then putts towards the hole, and the roll of his ball is helpful to his partner in determining how much his putt will break, etc. Is such procedure contrary to the Rules?

A. Such procedure is contrary to the spirit of the game. In match play, in equity (Rule 1-4), the player should be disqualified for the hole and, since his action assisted his partner's play, the partner should incur the same penalty — Rule 30-3f.

In stroke play, the player should incur a penalty of two strokes and, under Rule 31-8, the partner should incur the same penalty.

Putting Out After Concession of Stroke; Act Assists Partner — See 2-4/6.

Advice Given on Request of Opponent in Four-Ball Match — See 8-1/25.

Player Plays Partner's Ball; Act Assists Partner — See 30-3d/1.

30-3f/7 Player After Picking Up Drops Ball Where Partner's Ball Lies and Plays Practice Stroke

Q. In four-ball play, A and B are partners. A hits his tee shot out of bounds and decides not to complete play of the hole. B was undecided on club selection for his second shot, so A drops a ball near B's ball and hits a shot towards the green. What penalties were incurred?

A. Since the side, *i.e.*, both A and B, had not completed the play of the hole, A was practicing during play of the hole and thus was in breach of Rule 7-2.

Since it must be assumed that the breach assisted B, he would also be penalized — Rules 30-3f and 31-8.

30-3f/8 Player Disqualified for Next Hole Plays That Hole

Q. In a four-ball match, A practices chip shots to the 18th green between play of the 9th and 10th holes. Thus, A is disqualified for the 10th hole under Rule 7-2. If A plays the 10th hole, is B, A's partner, also subject to disqualification for the 10th hole if A's play of the hole assists B's, *e.g.*, with regard to club selection?

A. Since A was disqualified for the 10th hole, the strokes played by him on that hole were practice strokes. Therefore, A was in breach of Rule 7-2 each time he played a stroke on the 10th and, if B was assisted by any such stroke, B incurred the applicable penalty.

Absent Partner Joins Match During Play of Hole — See 30-3a/1.

30-3f/9 Player's Ball Moved by Partner in Playing His Own Ball

Q. In four-ball match play, A and B are partners. In playing his own ball, B accidentally strikes A's ball with his club and causes it to move. What is the procedure?

A. A incurs a penalty stroke under Rule 18-2a and must replace his ball. Assuming the infringement did not assist B, B incurs no penalty — Rule 30-3f.

30-3f/10 Player's Ball Lifted Without Authority by Opponent in Four-Ball Match

Q. In a four-ball match, an opponent lifted a player's ball on the putting green after marking its position. He did this without the authority of the player. Is the opponent subject to penalty?

A. Yes. Rule 20-1 prohibits such action. Accordingly, the opponent incurs a penalty stroke under Rule 18-3b, but the penalty does not apply to his partner — see Rule 30-3f. The player must replace his ball.

30-3f/11 Request to Lift Ball That Might Assist Partner Not Honored

Q. A and B are playing C and D in a four-ball match. B's ball is near the hole in a position to serve as a backstop for A's ball. C requests B to lift his ball. B does not comply. A putts and his ball strikes B's ball. What is the ruling?

A. B is disqualified for the hole for failing to comply with Rule 22. Since the infringement assisted A, he is also disqualified for the hole — Rule 30-3f.

Rule 31. Four-Ball Stroke Play

In four-ball stroke play two *competitors* play as *partners*, each playing his own ball. The lower score of the *partners* is the score for the hole. If one *partner* fails to complete the play of a hole, there is no penalty.

31-1. Rules of Golf Apply

The Rules of Golf, so far as they are not at variance with the following special Rules, shall apply to four-ball stroke play.

31-2. Representation of Side

A *side* may be represented by either *partner* for all or any part of a *stipulated round;* both *partners* need not be present. An absent *competitor* may join his *partner* between holes, but not during play of a hole.

31-3. Maximum of Fourteen Clubs

The *side* shall be penalized for a breach of Rule 4-4 by either *partner.*

31-4. Scoring

The *marker* is required to record for each hole only the gross score of whichever *partner*'s score is to count. The gross scores to count must be individually identifiable; otherwise the *side* shall be disqualified. Only one of the *partners* need be responsible for complying with Rule 6-6b.

(Wrong score — see Rule 31-7a.)

31-5. Order of Play

Balls belonging to the same *side* may be played in the order the *side* considers best.

31-6. Wrong Ball

If a *competitor* plays a *stroke* or *strokes* with a *wrong ball* except in a *hazard*, he shall add two *penalty strokes* to his score for the hole and shall then play the correct ball. His *partner* incurs no penalty even if the *wrong ball* belongs to him.

If the *wrong ball* belongs to another *competitor*, its owner shall place a ball on the spot from which the *wrong ball* was first played.

31-7. Disqualification Penalties

a. Breach by One Partner

A *side* shall be disqualified from the competition for a breach of any of the following by either *partner*:

Rule 1-3 — Agreement to Waive Rules.
Rule 3-4 — Refusal to Comply with Rule.
Rule 4-1 or -2 — Clubs.
Rule 5-1 or -2 — The Ball.
Rule 6-2b — Handicap (playing off higher handicap; failure to record handicap).
Rule 6-4 — *Caddie.*
Rule 6-6b — Signing and Returning Card.
Rule 6-6d — Wrong Score for Hole, i.e., when the recorded score of the *partner* whose score is to count is lower than actually taken. If the recorded score of the *partner* whose score is to count is higher than actually taken, it must stand as returned.
Rule 6-7 — Undue Delay; Slow Play (repeated offense).
Rule 7-1 — Practice Before or Between Rounds.
Rule 14-3 — Artificial Devices and Unusual *Equipment*.
Rule 31-4 — Gross Scores to Count Not Individually Identifiable.

b. Breach by Both Partners

A *side* shall be disqualified:

(i) for a breach by both *partners* of Rule 6-3 (Time of Starting and Groups) or Rule 6-8 (Discontinuance of Play), or

(ii) if, at the same hole, each *partner* is in breach of a *Rule* the penalty for which is disqualification from the competition or for a hole.

c. For the Hole Only

In all other cases where a breach of a *Rule* would entail disqualification, the *competitor* shall be disqualified only for the hole at which the breach occurred.

31-8. Effect of Other Penalties

If a *competitor*'s breach of a *Rule* assists his *partner*'s play, the *partner* incurs the applicable penalty in addition to any penalty incurred by the *competitor*.

In all other cases where a *competitor* incurs a penalty for breach of a *Rule*, the penalty shall not apply to his *partner*.

Decisions relating to Rule 31:

Competitor Who Has Holed Out Touches Partner's Line of Putt — See 1-2/3.5.

Flagstick Attended by Partner Without Express Authority of Competitor; Ball Strikes Flagstick or Partner — See 17-3/4.

Decision relating to Rule 31-3:

Breach of 14-Club Rule in Stroke Play Discovered at 8th Hole; Where Penalty Strokes Applied — See 4-4a/10.

31-4/1 Gross Score of Partner with Better Net Score Omitted from Card

Q. In four-ball stroke play on handicap, partners A and B both holed out in 4 at the 8th hole; partner A did not receive a handicap stroke at the hole, but partner B did. The marker, who was a fellow-competitor, recorded a gross score of 4 for A, who did not receive a stroke, and no gross score for B. However, the marker also recorded a net 3 in the better-ball column.

On completion of the round, the card, in all other respects correct, was signed and returned to the Committee. Both the marker and the partners were interviewed, and it was established that in fact both partners had gross scores of 4 at the 8th hole. What is the ruling?

A. Under Rules 6-6b and 31-4, it was the responsibility of one of the partners to check the side's better-ball gross score for each hole before countersigning the card.

When checking the card, the partner concerned should have noticed that there was no gross score recorded for B at the 8th hole and should have corrected this mistake. As he did not do so, A's gross 4 was the side's score for the hole. It is the responsibility of the Committee — and not the competitor — to record the better-ball net score for each hole.

31-5/1 Player Waives Turn to Play; Circumstances Under Which He May Complete Hole

Q. A and B are partners in four-ball stroke play. A's tee shot at a par-3 entirely over water comes to rest in the water hazard. As B's tee shot comes to rest on the putting green, A elects not to play a ball under Rule 26-1 and proceeds to the green. B four putts and scores 5 for the hole. May A return to the tee and put another ball into play under Rule 26-1?

A. Yes. However, he may be subject to penalty under Rule 6-7 for unduly delaying play.

31-5/2 Extent to Which Side May Play in Order It Considers Best

Rule 31-5, which is an exception to Rule 10-2 (Order of Play), permits a side to play in the order it considers best. Generally, a side will exercise its right under Rule 31-5 for strategic reasons. However, in doing so, the side must not unduly delay play (Rule 6-7).

The following are examples of a side (competitors A and B) playing in an order other than that set forth in Rule 10-2b and whether a penalty under Rule 6-7 would be appropriate:

(a) A's ball is on the putting green five feet from the hole and he plays before B, whose ball is on the putting green 20 feet from the hole — no penalty.

(b) A's ball is in an awkward lie in a hazard 30 yards from the hole and he plays before B, whose ball is in the fairway 50 yards from the hole — no penalty.

(c) A's ball is 220 yards from the hole on a par-5 hole and he plays his second stroke before B, whose ball is 240 yards from the hole plays — no penalty.

(d) In situation (c) above, A's ball comes to rest 30 yards from the green. The side then elects to have A play his third stroke before B plays his second stroke — B is penalized two strokes for a breach of Rule 6-7.

31-7a/1 Competitor Records Score for Hole Not Completed

Q. A and B are partners in four-ball stroke play. At the 10th hole, A picks up and B holes out in 5 strokes. The marker records a score of 6 for A and a score of 5 for B. The card is returned with these scores recorded. Is any penalty incurred because A-B returned a card containing a score for A at a hole which A did not complete?

A. No. Rule 31-7a provides that disqualification of a side under Rule 6-6d applies only when the recorded score of the partner whose score is to count is lower than actually taken. The score recorded for A was not A-B's lower score for the 10th hole. Accordingly, no penalty is applicable.

Side's Scores Transposed at a Hole in Handicap Competition But Not to Side's Advantage — See 32-2a/1.

31-7a/2 Lower Gross Score Attributed to Wrong Partner

Q. A and B were partners in four-ball stroke play. At the 11th hole, A picked up and B holed out in 4 strokes. The marker inadvertently recorded a score of 4 for A. The card was returned. What is the ruling?

A. It was A's recorded score of 4 which was the side's gross score to count. As this was lower than the score actually taken by A, the side is disqualified under Rule 31-7a.

Side's Scores Transposed at a Hole in Handicap Competition to Side's Advantage — See 32-2a/2.

31-8/1 Competitor Lifts Loose Impediment in Bunker When His Ball and Partner's Ball Are in Bunker

Q. A and B are partners in a four-ball stroke play competition. A's ball and B's ball are in the same bunker. A lifts a loose impediment lying in the bunker. A is penalized two strokes for a breach of Rule 13-4. Does B incur a penalty?

A. If A's infringement assisted B's play, B also is penalized two strokes — Rule 31-8. Otherwise, B incurs no penalty.

Other Decisions relating to Rule 31-8:

Competitor Plays Away from Hole to Assist Partner — See 30-3f/6.

Competitor After Picking Up Drops Ball Where Partner's Ball Lies and Plays Practice Stroke — See 30-3f/7.

Rule 32. Bogey, Par and Stableford Competitions

32-1. Conditions

Bogey, par and Stableford competitions are forms of stroke competition in which play is against a fixed score at each hole. The Rules for stroke play, so far as they are not at variance with the following special Rules, apply.

a. Bogey and Par Competitions

The reckoning for bogey and par competitions is made as in match play. Any hole for which a *competitor* makes no return shall be regarded as a loss. The winner is the *competitor* who is most successful in the aggregate of holes.

The *marker* is responsible for marking only the gross number of *strokes* for each hole where the *competitor* makes a net score equal to or less than the fixed score.

Note 1: Maximum of 14 clubs — Penalties as in match play — see Rule 4-4.

Note 2: Undue delay; slow play (Rule 6-7) — The player's score shall be adjusted by deducting one hole from the overall result.

b. Stableford Competitions

The reckoning in Stableford competitions is made by points awarded in relation to a fixed score at each hole as follows:

Hole Played In	Points
More than one over fixed score or no score returned	0
One over fixed score	1

Fixed score 2
One under fixed score 3
Two under fixed score 4
Three under fixed score 5
Four under fixed score 6

The winner is the *competitor* who scores the highest number of points.

The *marker* shall be responsible for marking only the gross number of *strokes* at each hole where the *competitor*'s net score earns one or more points.

Note 1: Maximum of 14 clubs (Rule 4-4) — Penalties applied as follows: From total points scored for the round, deduction of two points for each hole at which any breach occurred; maximum deduction per round: four points.

Note 2: Undue delay; slow play (Rule 6-7) — The player's score shall be adjusted by deducting two points from the total points scored for the round.

32-2. Disqualification Penalties

a. From the Competition

A *competitor* shall be disqualified from the competition for a breach of any of the following:

Rule 1-3 — Agreement to Waive Rules.
Rule 3-4 — Refusal to Comply with Rule.
Rule 4-1 or -2 — Clubs.
Rule 5-1 or -2 — The Ball.
Rule 6-2b — Handicap (playing off higher handicap; failure to record handicap).
Rule 6-3 — Time of Starting and Groups.
Rule 6-4 — *Caddie.*
Rule 6-6b — Signing and Returning Card.
Rule 6-6d — Wrong Score for Hole, except that no penalty shall be incurred when a breach of this Rule does not affect the result of the hole.
Rule 6-7 — Undue Delay; Slow Play (repeated offense).
Rule 6-8 — Discontinuance of Play.
Rule 7-1 — Practice Before or Between Rounds.
Rule 14-3 — Artificial Devices and Unusual *Equipment*.

b. For a Hole

In all other cases where a breach of a *Rule* would entail disqualification, the *competitor* shall be disqualified only for the hole at which the breach occurred.

32-1/1 Competing Simultaneously in Bogey or Stableford Competition and Stroke Play Competition

Q. Is it permissible for a player to compete simultaneously in a bogey or Stableford competition and a stroke play competition?

A. Yes, since bogey and Stableford competitions are forms of stroke play competition.

32-1/2 Omitting Holes in Bogey or Stableford Competition

Q. In a bogey or Stableford competition, may a player omit two holes of the round and return a score for 16 holes?

A. Yes. Under Rule 32-1a, any hole for which a competitor makes no return in a bogey competition is regarded as a loss. Under Rule 32-1b, if no score is returned on a hole in a Stableford competition, the competitor scores no points for that hole.

32-1/3 Determination of Honor in Handicap Stableford Competition

Q. In a Stableford competition the reckoning is made as in match play and strokes are taken according to the handicap stroke table. If B has the honor at a hole, and A and B have the same gross score at that hole but A receives a handicap stroke, who has the honor at the next hole?

A. A has the honor because of a better net score.

32-2a/1 Four-Ball Stableford Competition on Handicap Basis; Side's Scores Transposed at a Hole But Not to Side's Advantage

Q. A and B were partners in a four-ball Stableford competition on a handicap basis. At a hole where A, but not B, received a handicap stroke, A scored a 4 (net 3) and B scored a 5. The marker inadvertently transposed the scores, recording a 5 (net 4) for A and a 4 for B. The card was returned with these scores recorded. What is the ruling?

A. There is no penalty. Although B's recorded score of 4 was lower than actually taken by him, since it was not lower than the recorded score of net 4 for A (which was higher than actually taken by A), there was no breach of Rule 31-7a. Nor was there a breach of Rule 32-2a, since the error did not affect the result of the hole.

The same ruling would apply in a four-ball bogey or par competition on a handicap basis.

32-2a/2 Four-Ball Stableford Competition on Handicap Basis; Side's Scores Transposed at a Hole to Side's Advantage

Q. A and B were partners in a four-ball Stableford competition on a handicap basis. At a hole, A scored 4 (net 3) and B scored 5 (net 4). The marker inadvertently transposed the scores, recording a 5 (net 4) for A and a 4 (net 3) for B. The card was returned with these scores recorded. What is the ruling?

A. B's recorded score of 4 (net 3) was the lower recorded score. As this was lower than the score actually taken by B and was also lower than A's recorded score of 5 (net 4), the result of the hole was affected and the side is disqualified under Rule 32-2a for a breach of Rule 31-7a.

The same ruling would apply in a four-ball bogey or par competition on a handicap basis.

32-2a/3 Handicap Stableford Competition; Recording of Lower Gross Score Affects Result of Hole

Q. In a handicap Stableford competition against a fixed score of par, a competitor inadvertently returns his score card to the Committee with a score of 6 at the 9th hole when his score for the hole was actually 7. The 9th hole is a par 4 at which the competitor receives a handicap stroke. What is the ruling?

A. As the recording of the lower score affected the result of the hole, i.e., the competitor would be awarded 1 point for the hole when he should have received no points, the competitor is disqualified under Rule 32-2a for a breach of Rule 6-6d. (New)

32-2a/4 Handicap Stableford Competition; Recording of Lower Gross Score Does Not Affect Result of Hole

Q. In a handicap Stableford competition against a fixed score of par, a competitor inadvertently returns his score card to the Committee with a score of 6 at the 11th hole when his score for the hole was actually 7. The 11th hole is a par 4 at which the competitor receives no handicap strokes. What is the ruling?

A. As the recording of the lower score did not affect the result of the hole, i.e., the competitor would be awarded no points for the hole despite recording a 6 instead of a 7, there is no penalty (Rule 32-2a). (New)

32-2a/5 Handicap Bogey or Par Competition; Recording of Lower Gross Score Does Not Affect Result of Hole

Q. In a handicap bogey or par competition, a competitor inadvertently returns his score card to the Committee with a score of 3 at the 10th hole when his score for the hole was actually 4. The 10th hole is a par 4 at which the competitor receives a handicap stroke. What is the ruling?

A. As the recording of the lower score did not affect the result of the hole, i.e., the competitor would be awarded the hole despite recording a 3 instead of a 4, there is no penalty (Rule 32-2a). (New)

32-2b/1 Breach of Rule by Both Partners at Same Hole in Four-Ball Stableford

Q. A and B are partners in a four-ball Stableford competition. During the play of a hole, A and B find they have exchanged balls at the previous hole. What is the ruling?

A. A and B are not disqualified from the competition but only for the hole at which they exchanged balls, for which they score no points.

ADMINISTRATION

Rule 33. The Committee

33-1. Conditions; Waiving Rule

The *Committee* shall lay down the conditions under which a competition is to be played.

The *Committee* has no power to waive a Rule of Golf.

Certain special rules governing stroke play are so substantially different from those governing match play that combining the two forms of play is not practicable and is not permitted. The results of *matches* played and the scores returned in these circumstances shall not be accepted.

In stroke play the *Committee* may limit a *referee*'s duties.

33-2. The Course

a. Defining Bounds and Margins

The *Committee* shall define accurately:

(i) the *course* and *out of bounds,*
(ii) the margins of *water hazards* and *lateral water hazards,*
(iii) *ground under repair,* and
(iv) *obstructions* and integral parts of the *course.*

b. New Holes

New *holes* should be made on the day on which a stroke competition begins and at such other times as the *Committee* considers necessary, provided all *competitors* in a single round play with each *hole* cut in the same position.

Exception: When it is impossible for a damaged *hole* to be repaired so that it conforms with the Definition, the *Committee* may make a new *hole* in a nearby similar position.

Note: Where a single round is to be played on more than one day, the *Committee* may provide in the conditions of a competition that the *holes* and *teeing grounds* may be differently situated on each day of the competition, provided that, on any one day, all *competitors* play with each *hole* and each *teeing ground* in the same position.

c. Practice Ground

Where there is no practice ground available outside the area of a competition *course,* the *Committee* should lay down the area on which players may practice on any day of a competition, if it is practicable to do so. On any day of a stroke competition, the *Committee* should not normally permit practice on or to a *putting green* or from a *hazard* of the competition *course.*

d. Course Unplayable

If the *Committee* or its authorized representative considers that for any reason the *course* is not in a playable condition or that there are circumstances which render the proper playing of the game impossible, it may, in match play or stroke play, order a temporary suspension of play or, in stroke play, declare play null and void and cancel all scores for the round in question. When a round is cancelled, all penalties incurred in that round are cancelled.

(Procedure in discontinuing play—see Rule 6-8.)

33-3. Times of Starting and Groups

The *Committee* shall lay down the times of starting and, in stroke play, arrange the groups in which *competitors* shall play.

When a match play competition is played over an extended period, the *Committee* shall lay down the limit of time within which each round shall be completed. When players are allowed to arrange the date of their match within these limits, the *Committee* should announce that the match must be played at a stated time on the last day of the period unless the players agree to a prior date.

33-4. Handicap Stroke Table

The *Committee* shall publish a table indicating the order of holes at which handicap strokes are to be given or received.

33-5. Score Card

In stroke play, the *Committee* shall issue for each *competitor* a score card containing the date and the *competitor*'s name or, in foursome or four-ball stroke play, the *competitors*' names.

In stroke play, the *Committee* is responsible for the addition of scores and application of the handicap recorded on the card.

In four-ball stroke play, the *Committee* is responsible for recording the better-ball score for each hole and in the process applying the handicaps recorded on the card, and adding the better-ball scores.

In bogey, par and Stableford competitions, the *Committee* is responsible for applying the handicap recorded on the card and determining the result of each hole and the overall result or points total.

33-6. Decision of Ties

The *Committee* shall announce the manner, day and time for the decision of a halved match or of a tie, whether played on level terms or under handicap.

A halved match shall not be decided by stroke play. A tie in stroke play shall not be decided by a match.

33-7. Disqualification Penalty; Committee Discretion

A penalty of disqualification may in exceptional individual cases be waived, modified or imposed if the *Committee* considers such action warranted.

Any penalty less than disqualification shall not be waived or modified.

33-8. Local Rules

a. Policy

The *Committee* may make and publish Local Rules for abnormal conditions if they are consistent with the policy set forth in Appendix I.

b. Waiving Penalty

A Rule of Golf shall not be waived by a Local Rule. However, if a *Committee* considers that local abnormal conditions interfere with the proper playing of the game to the extent that it is necessary to make a Local Rule which modifies the Rules of Golf, the Local Rule must be authorized by the USGA.

33/1 Removal of Casual Water on Putting Green by Committee

Q. If casual water accumulates on a putting green during a round, would it be appropriate for the Committee to remove the casual water by mopping it up with a towel or by other means?

A. Yes, and the Committee may also enlist the help of players to do so. However, a player would be in breach of Rule 13-2 if he were to mop up casual water on his line of play or line of putt without the Committee's permission. (Revised)

Casual Water Covering Teeing Ground — See 25-1b/4.

Dividing Double Green — See 25-3/1.

[33/2 Reserved]

33/3 Match Play Finalists Both Disqualified

If both finalists in a match play competition are disqualified, the event must conclude without a winner.

33/4 Direction Posts

If direction posts may interfere with the line of play, they should, where practicable, be installed so as to be movable.

33/5 Distance Markers

Q. May a Committee install markers on a hole to indicate distances to the green?

A. Yes.

33/6 Map of Putting Green Indicating Hole Position Displayed at Tee

Q. At the teeing ground of each hole, a Committee has displayed a map of the putting green. The position of the hole on the green is indicated on each map. Is this proper?

A. Yes. Displaying such maps is not contrary to the Rules.

33/7 Whether Player Disqualified in Match Play Event Entitled to Prize Won Prior to Disqualification

Q. If a player in a match play event is disqualified, should he be entitled to any prize he had previously won in the event?

A. Yes.

Other Decisions relating to Rule 33:

Indicating Hole Numbers on Teeing Grounds — See 11-5/2.

Artificial Limbs — See 14-3/15.

Ball Assisting Fellow-Competitor on Putting Green; Procedure for Committee Member If Competitor Does Not Lift Ball — See 22/7.

Preventing Ball from Being Carried Out of Bounds by Flow of Water in Water Hazard — See 26-1/7.

Player's Ball Found by Committee Member; Player Prefers to Continue with Provisional Ball — See 27-2/2.

33-1/1 Altering Conditions After Competition Starts

Q. A condition of a stroke play competition provided that scores must be returned by 7:30 P.M. At 5:00 P.M., a member of the Committee extended the deadline to accommodate four late-arriving competitors. Is such action proper?

A. No. Once a competition has started, the conditions should be altered only in very exceptional circumstances. In this case, no such circumstances existed.

Players Exclude Operation of Condition — See 1-3/7.

33-1/2 Number of Holes of Stroke Play Competition Reduced During the Competition

Q. A 72-hole stroke play competition is scheduled over four consecutive days. Eighteen holes are to be played each day. On the third day, all competitors finish the first nine holes but a number of competitors are still playing the second nine holes. At that point, the course becomes unplayable due to heavy rain and play is suspended. The rain continues and it is impossible to resume play that day. What are the Committee's options?

A. Under Rules 33-1 and 33-2d, the Committee has the following choices:

(a) resume play the next day and finish the third round, and then play the last 18 holes that day or on a subsequent day,

(b) cancel the third round, replay it on a subsequent day and then play the last 18 holes that day or on a subsequent day,

(c) reduce to three the number of rounds of the competition and finish the suspended third round on a subsequent day, or cancel the third round and replay it on a subsequent day, or

(d) cancel the third and fourth rounds and declare the leader after 36 holes to be the winner.

The third and fourth choices are undesirable. It is preferable not to reduce the number of rounds of a competition when the competition is in progress.

The Committee does not have the authority to reduce the number of holes of a stipulated round once play has commenced in that round.

33-1/3 Starting Players from 1st and 10th Tees

Q. May the Committee start play in a competition from both the 1st and the 10th tees?

A. Yes. See Definition of "Stipulated Round," which says that the holes are to be played in correct sequence unless otherwise authorized by the Committee.

33-1/3.5 Restriction On Which Partner in Foursome Competition May Play from 1st Tee

Q. Rule 29-1 states that in a foursome "the partners shall play alternately from the teeing grounds and alternately during the play of each hole." However, it is a matter of personal choice which partner drives at the first tee.

May a Committee, in the conditions of a foursome competition, stipulate which partner must play from the first tee?

A. Yes.

33-1/4 Match Decided by Wrong Form of Play by Agreement of Players

Q. The four participants in a first-round match thought the competition was a foursome competition, whereas it was in fact a four-ball competition. They played the first hole on a foursome basis and then learned of their error. Rather than go back and begin again on a four-ball basis, they agreed (1) to continue playing a foursome and (2) that in the four-ball competition the side losing the foursome match would default to the winning side.

The matter came to the Committee's attention after the side receiving the default reached the semi-finals of the four-ball event. What should the Committee do?

A. The side should be disqualified under Rule 1-3 for agreeing to decide a match other than as prescribed in the conditions, and the Committee should decide how the competition should be concluded.

Wrong Form of Play Used in Match Play Event — See 6-1/1.

33-1/5 Competitor in Stroke Play Event Plays with Two Players Engaged in Match

33

Q. A competitor in a stroke play competition had no other competitor with whom to play. So he joined two players engaged in a match and one of those players served as his marker. Is such procedure considered combining stroke play and match play, contrary to Rule 33-1?

A. No. The competitor was playing stroke play only and the other two players were playing match play only. The Committee should retrospectively appoint the player concerned as the competitor's marker — see Definition of "Marker."

33-1/6 One Player in Match Competes Concurrently in Stroke Play Competition

Q. A and B played a match. A concurrently competed in a stroke play competition. What should the Committee do?

A. Under Rule 33-1, both the result of the match and the score returned by A in the stroke play event were unacceptable.

If the match was to be played on any day in a prescribed period, A and B must replay the match within the prescribed period. If it was too late for A and B to replay the match within the period, A and B are disqualified, unless one concedes the match to the other — see Rule 2-4.

It would not be proper to allow A to replay the round in the stroke play competition. A had already competed in that competition, and his score was unacceptable.

Competing Simultaneously in Bogey or Stableford Competition and Stroke Play Competition — See 32-1/1.

33-1/7 Making Competitors Responsible for Adding Scores

Q. May the Committee make it a condition of a competition that competitors are responsible for the addition of scores?

A. No. Such a condition would modify Rule 33-5.

Requirement That Alteration on Score Card Be Initialed — See 6-6a/6.

Requirement That Score Be Entered Into Computer — See 6-6b/8.

33-1/8 Use of Golf Carts in Competition

Q. May a player use a golf cart during a competition?

A. Yes, unless such equipment is prohibited in the conditions of the competition (Rule 33-1).

33-1/9 Breach of Condition Prohibiting Golf Carts

Q. A condition of a competition prohibits the use of golf carts. If a player infringes this condition, what is the penalty?

A. If no penalty is stated, the general penalty applies at each hole where the cart is used, *i.e.*, loss of hole in match play (Rule 2-6) or two strokes in stroke play (Rule 3-5).

Who May Serve as Caddie — See 6-4/2.

33-1/9.5 Breach of Transportation Condition by Caddie

Q. The Committee has adopted the Transportation Condition in Appendix I as a condition of competition. During the stipulated round, a player's caddie accepts a ride on a golf cart without the authority of the Committee. Is the player penalized for the caddie's breach of the condition?

A. Yes. The player is responsible for any breach of a Rule or condition of competition by his caddie and he incurs the applicable penalty (Rule 6-4). (New)

33-1/10 Banning Caddies

Q. May a Committee, as a condition of a competition, ban the use of caddies?

A. Yes. However, since the Rules make specific provision for the employment of a caddie by a player, such a condition is not recommended.

33-1/11 Restriction on Caddies

Q. May a Committee, in the conditions of a competition, restrict a player in his choice of a caddie? For example, may a Committee for a junior competition prohibit a player from employing a parent as a caddie?

A. Yes.

Prohibiting Employment of Umbrella Carrier — See 6-4/5.

33-1/11.5 Status of Team Captain or Coach

Q. May a Committee, in the conditions of a team competition, specify that, during the stipulated round, the team captain or coach is part of the match or part of the competitor's side, *i.e.*, he is not an outside agency?

A. Yes. If such a condition is adopted, the player(s) or, in some circumstances, the team would be responsible for any breach of the Rules by the captain or coach.

Team Captain Gives Advice While Playing — See 8/2.
Advice Given by Team Coach or Captain — See 8-1/24.

33-1/12 Wrong Handicap Used Due to Committee Misinformation

Q. The players in a four-ball match were unsure as to the handicaps to which they were entitled under the conditions of the competition. They consulted a member of the Committee who wrongly advised them as to the condition regarding handicaps. This resulted in Player A receiving one less handicap stroke than he was entitled to receive. Player A's side lost the match, 4 and 3. The Committee representative's error was then discovered. What should the Committee do?

A. The Committee should resolve the matter in whatever manner it considers most equitable. The Committee could let the result stand or require a replay of the match.

All players except Player A received the correct number of handicap strokes and Player A received only one less stroke than he should have received. In view of this fact and the rather one-sided result, it is recommended that the fairest solution would be to let the result stand.

33-1/13 Competitor Disqualified from Handicap Event Claims Gross Prize

Q. In a stroke play event, a competitor played off a higher handicap than that to which he was entitled. Although the event was primarily a handicap one, there was also a gross prize, and the competitor concerned had the lowest gross score.

The competitor was disqualified from the handicap competition under Rule 6-2b, but he claimed the gross prize. Should he receive the gross prize?

A. Yes.

33-1/14 Condition Regarding Footwear

Q. May a Committee, in the conditions of a competition, prohibit the use of shoes with metal or traditionally designed spikes?

A. Yes. (New)

Other Decisions relating to Rule 33-1:

Condition Requiring Use of Ball on List of Conforming Golf Balls; Penalty for Breach — See 5-1/2.

Permitting Players to Discontinue Play for Refreshment — See 6-8a/2.5.

33-2a/1 Exposed Water Pipe Adjacent and Parallel to Boundary Fence Causes Problems; Suggested Procedure

Q. An exposed water pipe (obstruction) which is parallel to, and about six inches inside, a boundary fence is causing a problem. If a ball lies near the boundary fence, the prohibition against free relief from the fence is effectively negated because in most cases the player would be entitled to drop away from the fence by taking free relief from the water pipe under Rule 24-2b. Is there a solution to this dilemma?

A. It is suggested that the water pipe be declared an integral part of the course and thus not an obstruction

— see Definition of "Obstructions" — in which case the player would have to play the ball as it lies or declare it unplayable. (Revised)

Stone Serving as Part of Drain in Bunker — See 24/7.

33-2a/2 Declaring Area as Ground Under Repair During Competition Round

Q. A's ball is in a poor lie in a washed-out area which warrants being marked as ground under repair but is not so marked. He declares the ball unplayable and proceeds under Rule 28, incurring a one-stroke penalty. Subsequently, in the same competition round, B's ball is in the same area. B requests the Committee to declare the area ground under repair. Would the Committee be justified in declaring the area ground under repair in such circumstances?

A. Yes; this applies in either match or stroke play. However, it is preferable that all areas which warrant marking as ground under repair should be so marked before the start of a competition.

33-2a/3 Extensive Damage Due to Heavy Rain and Traffic

When heavy rains have resulted in many areas of unusual damage to the course (such as deep ruts caused by vehicles or footprints by spectators) and it is not feasible to define them with stakes or lines, a notice to players along the following lines is suggested:

> "Ground under repair may include areas of unusual damage, including areas where spectators or other traffic have combined with wet conditions to affect materially the ground surface, but only when so declared by a Committee member."

Without such notice, Committee members have authority to declare unusual damage to be ground under repair, if so authorized. However, a notice has the advantage of advising all players that relief from unusual damage might be given.

Line of Putt Damaged by Fellow-Competitor's Caddie — See 16-1a/14.

Old Hole Plug Sunk or Raised on Line of Putt — See 16-1c/3.

Fallen Tree Attached to Stump — See 25/9.

Cracks in Earth — See 25/12.

Rut Made by Tractor — See 25/16.

Marking Environmentally-Sensitive Areas — See 33-8/41.

33-2a/4 Where to Place Lines or Stakes Defining Margin of Water Hazard

Lines and stakes defining the margins of a water hazard should be placed as nearly as possible along the natural limits of the hazard, *i.e.*, where the ground breaks down to form the depression containing the water. See also Decision 26-1/19.

Ball Within Natural Margin of Water Hazard But Outside Stakes Defining Margin — See 26/2.

[33-2a/5 Reserved]

33-2a/6 Pond Is Water Hazard from Back Tee and Lateral Water Hazard from Forward Tee

Q. A pond on a par-3 hole meets the Definition of a lateral water hazard in play from the forward tee but not from the back tee. How should the Committee handle this situation?

A. The pond should be defined as a water hazard with yellow stakes or a yellow line and there should be a Local Rule to the effect that the hazard is a lateral water hazard in play from the forward tee.

33-2a/7 Deeming Body of Water as Both Water Hazard and Lateral Water Hazard

A given part of body of water must not be defined as both a water hazard and a lateral water hazard in play of a particular hole, except in the circumstances described in Decision 33-2a/6.

A given part of a body of water may be defined as a water hazard in play of one hole and a lateral water hazard in play of another hole.

A given part of a body of water may be defined as a water hazard and another part of the same body of water as a lateral water hazard.

33-2a/8 Treating Ocean and Beach as Through the Green

There is no authority in the Rules for a Committee to treat the ocean and adjoining beach and rocks as through the green. Such treatment results in a more severe penalty in many instances than is the case if the ocean, beach and rocks are properly defined as a water hazard or lateral water hazard.

Permissible Dropping Area Under Lateral Water Hazard Rule So Narrow Player Has Difficulty Dropping Within It — See 26-1/19.

33-2a/9 Part of Lateral Water Hazard Where Impossible to Drop Not Nearer Hole

If part of a lateral water hazard at the side of a putting green is so configured that it may be impossible to drop a ball within two club-lengths of the point where the ball last crossed the hazard margin without dropping nearer the hole than that point, the following is suggested: (1) the part of the hazard where the situation exists should be distinctively marked; (2) one or two Ball Drops (or Dropping Zones) should be established; and (3) a Local Rule should state that, if a ball in the lateral water hazard last crossed the margin of the hazard in the marked area, the player may, under penalty of one stroke, drop a ball in the Ball Drop or, if two Ball Drops are established, in the nearer of the two Ball Drops.

33-2a/10 How to Mark Island Green

Q. A putting green is situated on an island in a lake. The water between the tee and the green is defined as a water hazard. The water on each side is marked as a lateral water hazard. How should the water behind the island be marked?

A. The Committee would be justified in marking the water behind the island as a lateral water hazard.

Alternatively, the Committee might consider defining the entire lake as a water hazard, establishing a Ball Drop (or Dropping Zone) and adopting a Local Rule giving a player whose ball lies in the hazard the option of dropping a ball in the Ball Drop, under penalty of one stroke.

33-2a/10.5 Status of Tree Basins

Q. What is the status under the Rules of tree wells or tree basins?

A. There is no relief under the Rules from tree basins which are not made of artificial materials.

If a tree basin has an artificial wall, the wall is an obstruction unless the Committee deems it to be an integral part of the course under Rule 33-2a.

33-2a/11 River Forming Part of Course Boundary

Q. When a river forms part of the boundary of a course, should it be defined as a lateral water hazard or as out of bounds?

A. It is up to the Committee to decide (Rule 33-2a).

33-2a/12 Internal Boundary Between Holes

Q. It is proposed to install boundary stakes between two holes as a safety measure. It would prevent players playing a dog-leg hole from driving onto the fairway of another hole in order to cut the "dog-leg." Is it permissible to establish such a boundary?

A. Yes. For the recommended status of such boundary stakes, see Decision 24/5.

33-2a/13 Tee Decreed to Be in Bounds for Tee Shot and Out of Bounds Thereafter

Q. A Committee has decreed that ground surrounding a certain teeing ground is in bounds for tee shots and out of bound thereafter. Is this permissible?

A. No. In play of a particular hole, an area cannot be both in bounds and out of bounds.

33-2a/14 Internal Out of Bounds Applying to Stroke from Teeing Ground Only

A Committee may make a Local Rule under Rule 33-2a declaring part of an adjoining hole to be out of bounds when playing a particular hole, but it is not permissible for a Committee to make a Local Rule placing an area of the course out of bounds to a stroke played from the teeing ground only.

33-2a/15 Establishing Boundary Line Inside Fence on Property Line

Q. Along a fence on our property line, *i.e.*, the fence is a boundary fence, there are flower beds. To save time and protect the flowers, it is proposed to move the boundary line inward several feet by establishing white stakes along the inside edge of the flower bed. Is this permitted by the Rules?

A. Yes.

Stile Attached to Boundary Fence — See 24/1.

Concrete Bases of Boundary Fence Posts — See 24/3.

33-2a/16 Deeming Ball in Bounds Until Beyond Boundary Wall

Q. Because a boundary wall is in disrepair and the inside face is irregular, the Committee has declared by Local Rule that a ball is not out of bounds until it is beyond the wall. Is this permissible or must the inside face of the wall serve as the boundary line?

A. Such procedure is permissible. There is nothing in the Rules stating that, in the case of a boundary wall, the inside face of the wall serves as the boundary line.

[33-2a/17 Reserved]

[33-2a/18 Reserved]

33-2a/19 Boundary Altered by Unauthorized Removal of Boundary Stake

In stroke play, a boundary line has been altered through unauthorized removal of a boundary stake, and therefore there is an area (Area X) which is in bounds if the removed stake is disregarded and out of bounds if the removed stake is replaced.

Q1. A's ball comes to rest in Area X. A is aware that the boundary has been altered. He asks the Committee for a ruling. What is the ruling?

A1. The Committee should replace the removed stake, *i.e.*, restore the original boundary line and require A to proceed under Rule 27-1, unless the Committee knows that one or more preceding competitors had, in ignorance of the fact that a stake has been removed, played from Area X. In that case, the Committee should allow the altered boundary line to stand for the remainder of the competition, and A would play his ball as it lay.

Q2. What would be the ruling if the Committee determined that one or more competitors had, in ignorance of the fact that a stake was missing, played from Area X and one or more other competitors had treated Area X as out of bounds and proceeded under Rule 27-1?

A2. If the inconsistent treatment of Area X could significantly affect the result of the competition, the round should be cancelled and replayed. Otherwise, the round should stand.

33-2a/20 Displaced Boundary Stake

Q. A boundary stake has fallen down, or has been removed without authority of the Committee. The stake is lying several feet from the hole in which it had been situated. It is obvious that the stake had been displaced.

A player's ball comes to rest in bounds near the hole in which the boundary stake had been situated. The ball is in such a position that, if the boundary stake were reinstalled, it would interfere with the player's swing.

Is the player required to replace the stake before playing his next stroke?

33 **A.** No. If a boundary fence or stake is leaning towards the course and as a result interferes with a player's swing, the player is not allowed to straighten the fence or the stake — see Decision 13-2/18. It follows that, if a boundary fence or stake is leaning away from the course, the player is not allowed to straighten it.

A displaced boundary stake is a movable obstruction. Therefore, the player may replace it but he is not required to do so.

Another Decision relating to Rule 33-2a:

Marking Environmentally-Sensitive Areas — See 33-8/41.

33-2b/1 Holes Relocated and/or Tee-Markers Moved During Stroke Play Round

Q. During a round in a stroke play competition, one or more holes were relocated and/or tee-markers moved. What is the proper procedure?

A. If this was authorized by the Committee, the round should be declared null and void. In stroke play, the Committee is prohibited from relocating a hole and from moving tee-markers except as provided in the Exception and Note to Rule 33-2b or in circumstances such as those in Decision 25-1b/4.

If this was done without the authority or sanction of the Committee, generally the round should be declared null and void. However, if the course has not been altered significantly and no competitor has been given an undue advantage or disadvantage, the Committee would be justified in letting the round stand.

33-2d/1 Guidelines on Whether to Cancel Round

Q. In stroke play, in what circumstances should a Committee cancel a round?

A. There is no hard-and-fast rule. The proper action depends on the circumstances in each case and must be left to the judgment of the Committee.

Generally, a round should be cancelled only in a case where it would be grossly unfair not to cancel it. For example, if some competitors begin a round under extremely adverse weather conditions, conditions subsequently worsen and further play that day is impossible, it would be unfair to the competitors who started not to cancel the round.

Number of Holes of Stroke Play Competition Reduced During the Competition — See 33-1/2.

33-2d/2 Hole Surrounded by Casual Water

If all the area around the hole contains casual water, in stroke play the course should be considered unplayable and the Committee should suspend play under Rule 33-2d. In match play, the Committee should relocate the hole.

Casual Water Covering Teeing Ground — See 25-1b/4.

33-2d/3 Competitor Refuses to Start or Picks Up Because of Weather Conditions; Round Subsequently Cancelled

Q. In stroke play, A refuses to start at the time arranged by the Committee because of inclement weather, and B picks up during the round for the same reason. Subsequently, the course becomes unplayable and the Committee cancels the round and reschedules it for the next day. Are A and B entitled to play the next day?

A. Yes. When a round is cancelled all penalties incurred in the round are cancelled — see Rule 33-2d.

Player Unable to Resume Suspended Match at Scheduled Time — See 6-8b/4.

33-2d/4 Match Begun in Ignorance That Course Closed

Q. Two players began a match at 10 A.M. After the players had played two holes, a member of the Committee arrived and advised them that the course had been closed since 9 A.M., but no notice to this effect had been posted at the 1st tee. Should the match be replayed entirely or resumed at the 3rd hole?

A. The match should be replayed entirely. Play on the course while it was closed should be considered null and void.

Replacement of Club Broken on Practice Ground While Play Suspended — See 4-3/11.

Ball Moved by Wind or Casual Water While Play Suspended — See 18-1/11.

33-3/1 Status of Starting Time Fixed by Players

Q. It was a condition of a match play competition that each match must be played on the day and at the time published unless the players agreed to a prior date and time. A and B agreed to play their match at a specified time on a prior date. However, B arrived late. Was B subject to disqualification under Rule 6-3a?

A. Yes. The starting time agreed by A and B had the same status as a starting time fixed by the Committee.

33-3/2 Player Not Present at Time of Starting; Course Closed at the Time

Q. A and B were scheduled to play a match at 9:00 A.M., at which time the course was closed due to weather conditions. A was present at the appointed time. B, assuming the course would be closed, was not present. B arrived at noon, at which time the course was still closed. A claimed the match because B was not present at 9:00 A.M. Was the claim valid?

A. No. As the course was closed, and it was impossible for A and B to start at the appointed time or within a reasonable time thereafter, a new starting time for the match should be arranged.

33-3/3 Competitors Determining Own Groupings and Starting Times

Q. May a Committee permit competitors in a stroke play competition to determine their own groupings and starting times?

A. Yes. Rule 33-3 does not prohibit such an arrangement.

Postponement of Final Match Due to Injury of Player — See 6-3a/1.

All Competitors Must Be Present at Time of Starting — See 6-3a/2.

33-3/4 Groupings for Stroke Play Play-Off

Q. Is there any Rule limiting the number of competitors in a group in a stroke play play-off? For example, if 11 competitors are in a play-off, should they be separated into a group of five and a group of six? Or should they be separated into two groups of four and one group of three?

A. There is no Rule. The matter is up to the Committee. However, it is suggested that normally there should be no more than five competitors in any group.

33-4/1 Alteration of Handicap Stroke Table

Q. As provided in the Definition of a "Stipulated Round," the Committee has authorized certain matches to begin at the 6th hole. The higher-handicapped player in such matches is disadvantaged because, under the Handicap Stroke Table, the first handicap stroke is allocated to the 5th hole and, thus, it is not used if a match is concluded in less than 18 holes. Would it be permissible to alter the Handicap Stroke Table for such matches?

A. Yes.

Other Decisions relating to Rule 33-4:

Handicap Stroke Given at Incorrect Hole in Error — See 6-2a/2.

33-5/1 Score Cards in Sudden-Death Play-Off

Q. Must competitors involved in a sudden-death play-off in stroke play return score cards to the Committee?

A. Yes, but only if the Committee has issued a score card for each competitor in accordance with Rule 33-5. Otherwise, the competitors should not be penalized if they fail to return score cards.

33-5/2 Wrong Handicap Applied by Committee Results in Player Not Receiving Prize

Q. In a stroke play competition, A returns a card showing the handicap to which he is entitled and the Committee applies the wrong handicap or miscalculates the correct net score. This results in another competitor receiving a prize to which A was entitled. The error is discovered after the competition has closed. What is the ruling?

A. The Committee should correct its error by retrieving the prize and awarding it to A. There is no time limit for correcting such an error. Rule 34-1b is not applicable since it deals with penalties and not with Committee errors.

33-5/3 Misapplication of Handicap Affects Match Play Draw

Q. Misapplication of a player's handicap by the Committee on a score card for the qualifying round of a match play event results in an incorrect draw. The error is discovered during the first round of match play. What should the Committee do?

A. The Committee should deal with the matter in the fairest way possible. The Committee should consider amending the draw and canceling the matches affected by the amendment if this is practicable.

Other Decisions relating to Rule 33-5:

Total Score Recorded by Competitor Incorrect — See 6-6d/2.

Competitors Made Responsible for Adding Scores — See 33-1/7.

[33-6/1 Reserved]

[33-6/2 Reserved]

33-6/3 Determining Winner and Positions in Stroke Play Play-Off

If there is a stroke play play-off between two competitors and one of them is disqualified or concedes defeat, it is not necessary for the other to complete the play-off hole or holes to be declared the winner.

If there is a play-off involving more than two com–petitors and not all of them complete the play-off hole or holes, the order in which the competitors are disqualified or decide to withdraw shall determine their positions in the play-off.

33-6/4 Players Decide Method of Settling Tie When Committee Fails to Do So

Q. A and B, in a club match play event in which the Committee had not prescribed how a halved match would be decided, finished their stipulated round all square. A suggested that the tie be decided by an 18-hole play-off. B reluctantly agreed. A won the play-off. B protested to the Committee. He argued that the match should have been settled by a sudden-death play-off, since that is the customary manner of deciding a tie in club events. What should the Committee do?

A. Since the Committee did not prescribe the method of settling the tie, it was appropriate for the players to determine the method. Since the players agreed to an 18-hole play-off, the match should stand as played.

Groupings for Stroke Play Play-Off — See 33-3/4.

33-7/1 Authority to Waive or Modify Disqualification Penalty

Only the Committee as a whole has authority to waive or modify a penalty of disqualification under Rule 33-7. A referee or an individual member of the Committee may not take such action.

33-7/2 Modifying Penalty for Not Holing Out in Stroke Play

Q. In stroke play, a competitor missed a short putt at the 16th hole, knocked his ball off the green, picked it up and teed off at the next hole without having holed out at the 16th.

After the competitor returned his score card, a fellow-competitor brought the matter to the attention of the Committee. The competitor admitted the error and expressed the view that his fellow-competitors were unsportsmanlike in not calling the error to his attention when the incident occurred.

In such circumstances, would the Committee be justified in modifying to two strokes the disqualification penalty provided in Rule 3-2?

A. No. Rule 33-7 should never be invoked in the case of disqualification for failing to hole out in stroke play. The competitor in such a case has not played the course.

Failure of the fellow-competitors to advise the com–petitor of his error is not a good reason for modifying the penalty. It is the responsibility of the competitor to know the Rules.

Waiving or Modifying Penalty for Carrying Non-Conforming Club — See 4-1/1.

Modifying Penalty for Holing Short Putt with Club Whose Playing Characteristics Changed Other Than in Normal Course of Play — See 4-3/4.

Waiving or Modifying Penalty for Use of Non-Conforming Ball — See 5-1/1.

Circumstances Which Warrant Waiving of Disqualification Penalty Under Rule 6-3a — See 6-3a/3.

When Play Suspended by Committee, Modifying or Waiving Penalty for Resuming Play Other Than at Time Ordered by Committee — See 6-8b/6.

When Play Suspended by Committee and Immediate Discontinuance of Play Required; Waiving or Modifying Penalty for Failure to Discontinue Play Immediately — See 6-8b/7.

33-7/3 Competitor's Failure to Countersign Card Blamed on Lack of Time Provided by Committee

Q. In a 36-hole stroke play competition played in one

day over two courses, a competitor returned his first-round score card to the Committee but he failed to countersign it. After the second round the Committee informed him that he was disqualified. The competitor blamed the Committee for the error. He said the Committee, in attempting to get him to leave promptly for the course on which the second round was being played, caused him to return his first-round card hurriedly and that he had been given insufficient time to check and countersign the card. The competitor requested the Committee to waive the penalty under Rule 33-7. Would the Committee be justified in doing so?

A. No. If the competitor did not feel he was given sufficient time to check and sign his first-round card, he should have protested before he returned the card.

33-7/4 Modifying Penalty for Returning Wrong Score

Q. A marker inadvertently recorded a 4 for a competitor on a hole at which the competitor's score was actually 5. The competitor failed to check his score for each hole and therefore did not discover the error. The competitor returned his card to the Committee.

Later, the competitor discovered the error while observing the scoreboard. He immediately reported the error to the Committee. Would it be appropriate in such circumstances to invoke Rule 33-7 and waive or modify the disqualification penalty prescribed in Rule 6-6d?

A. No. A penalty of disqualification may be waived or modified only in exceptional circumstances. Under Rule 6-6d, the competitor is responsible for the correctness of the score recorded for each hole.

33-7/4.5 Competitor Unaware of Penalty Returns Wrong Score; Whether Waiving or Modifying Disqualification Penalty Justified

Q. A competitor returns his score card and the score for one hole is lower than actually taken due to failure to include a penalty of two strokes which he did not know he had incurred. The error is discovered before the competition has closed.

Would the Committee be justified, under Rule 33-7, in waiving or modifying the penalty of disqualification prescribed in Rule 6-6d?

A. No. It is the responsibility of the competitor to know the Rules and their interpretations as contained in "Decisions on the Rules of Golf."

Players Agree Not to Tee Off in Prescribed Order to Save Time; Whether Waiving Penalty of Disqualification Justified — See 1-3/1.

Imposing Disqualification Penalty When Marker Attests Wrong Score Knowingly — See 6-6a/5.

Modifying Penalty for One Practice Stroke on Course Before Stroke Play Round — See 7-1b/1.

Waiving Penalty for Practice on Course — See 7-1b/2.

Waiving Penalty for Competitor Who Practices on Course After Qualifying Round and Is Subsequently in Play-Off on Same Day — See 7-1b/3.

Imposing Disqualification Penalty for Failing to Correct Opponent's Misunderstanding of State of Match — See 9-2/12.

33-7/5 Play of Wrong Ball Not Rectified on Advice of Committee Member

Q. In stroke play, a competitor played a wrong ball at the 14th hole. He discovered the error after holing out. Before teeing off at the 15th, he asked a member of the Committee as to the procedure. The Committee member told the competitor to proceed and consult the Committee when the round was completed, instead of telling him to rectify the error as prescribed in Rule 15-3.

Should the player be disqualified as prescribed in Rule 15-3?

A. No. In the circumstances, the competitor should incur a penalty of two strokes for a breach of Rule 15-3, but the disqualification penalty which he also incurred under that Rule should be waived by the Committee under Rule 33-7.

33-7/6 Competitor Repeatedly Replaces Ball Nearer Hole on Green

Q. On completion of a round in stroke play, a competitor's marker reports that the competitor, after lifting his ball on the putting green, repeatedly placed it nearer the hole than the spot from which it was lifted. The Committee, after gathering all available evidence, concludes that the marker's report is correct. What should the Committee do?

A. The competitor should be disqualified under Rule 33-7.

Imposing Disqualification Penalty for Playing Two Holes Not Included in Stipulated Round — See 3/2.

Imposing Disqualification Penalty for Knowingly Giving Incorrect Information on Rules — See 9/1.

Imposing Disqualification Penalty for Altering Teeing Ground — See 11-2/2.

Imposing Disqualification Penalty for Refusing to Identify Ball — See 27/13.

33-7/7 Competitor Seeks Help from Fellow-Competitor to Avoid Penalty

Q. A competitor's ball is lying through the green. He asks a fellow-competitor to remove a loose impediment lying near the ball because he knows that, if his ball moves after a loose impediment within a club-length is moved by an outside agency, the competitor incurs no penalty. The fellow-competitor removes the loose impediment. What is the ruling?

A. Irrespective of whether or not the ball moves as a result of removing the loose impediment, the action of the competitor is so contrary to the spirit of the game that the Committee should disqualify him under Rule 33-7.

The fellow-competitor incurs no penalty for removing the loose impediment unless the Committee is satisfied that he was aware of the competitor's intention to circumvent a Rule. In that instance, he should also be disqualified under Rule 33-7.

33-8/1 Local Rule for Temporary Putting Green Waives Requirement to Hole Out

33

Q. A course has been going through a period of renovation necessitating the use of temporary putting greens from time to time.

A Local Rule states that a player whose ball lies on a temporary green may either pick up his ball, counting two putts, or putt out.

Is such a Local Rule authorized?

A. No. Rule 1-1 provides: "The Game of Golf consists in playing a ball from the teeing ground into the hole by a stroke or successive strokes in accordance with the Rules." Any Local Rule under which a player would not be required to play the ball into the hole waives this basic Rule and is not authorized.

33-8/2 Local Rule Allows Drop on Green Side of Water Hazard When Ball Fails to Clear Hazard

Q. At two holes a player must hit the ball about 100 yards in order to carry over water hazards. A Local Rule has been adopted to assist golfers who cannot drive over the hazards. The Local Rule states:

> "If a player's first two tee shots do not carry the water hazard, he may drop his ball on the Ball Drop across the hazard, under penalty of two strokes."

Is such a Local Rule authorized?

A. No. Such a Local Rule is contrary to Rule 1-1 which says the game "consists in playing a ball from the teeing ground into the hole by a stroke or successive strokes in accordance with the Rules."

33-8/3 Local Rule Allowing Play of Second Ball in Match Play

Q. May a Committee make a Local Rule allowing play of a second ball in match play when a player is in doubt as to his rights?

A. No. Rule 3-3 specifically restricts the play of a second ball to stroke play.

33-8/4 Local Rule for Events in Which Motorized Golf Carts Permitted

Q. A competition involving stroke play qualifying followed by match play is to be held. Motorized golf carts will be permitted. Play will be in couples. There are enough carts available to provide each couple with a cart. No caddies will be available. Should a Local Rule clarifying the status of the carts be made?

A. It is suggested that the following Local Rule be adopted:

> "A motorized cart is part of the player's equipment:
> (1) When one cart is shared by two players, the cart and everything in it are deemed to be the equipment of the player whose ball is involved except that, when the cart is being moved by one of the players, the cart and everything in it are deemed to be the equipment of that player.
> (2) A player or players using a cart may appoint someone to drive the cart, in which case the driver is considered to be the caddie of the player or players.
> (3) Use of a cart by anyone other than the player or players using it or the appointed driver is prohibited. Any player allowing unauthorized use of his cart is subject to penalty as follows:
> Match play — At the conclusion of the hole at which the breach is discovered, the state of the match shall be adjusted by deducting one hole for each hole at which a breach occurred. Maximum deduction per round: two holes. Stroke play — Two strokes for each hole at which any breach occurred; maximum penalty per round: four strokes. In the event of a breach between the play of two holes, the penalty applies to the next hole. Use of any unauthorized automotive vehicle shall be discontinued immediately upon discovering that a breach has occurred. Otherwise, the player shall be disqualified."

If some caddies are available, it is suggested that they be assigned in an equitable way and that the above suggested Local Rule be adopted with item (2) amended to read as follows:

"A player or players using a cart may appoint someone to drive the cart if no caddie is available, in which case the driver is considered to be the caddie of the player or players." (Revised)

Status of Person in Shared Golf Cart — See 19/2.

33-8/5 Local Rule Permitting Competitors to Discontinue Play by Agreement in Bad Weather

Q. May the Committee for a stroke play event make a Local Rule permitting competitors to discontinue play by agreement among themselves in bad weather?

A. No. Such a Local Rule would modify Rule 6-8a.

[33-8/6 Reserved]

33-8/7 Local Rule Requiring Player to Play Out of Turn on Putting Green

Q. A proposed Local Rule would require that, on the putting green, a player must play continuously until he has holed out. Would such a Local Rule be acceptable?

A. No. Such a Local Rule would modify Rules 10-1b and -2b, which require that the ball farther from the hole shall be played first.

33-8/8 Local Rule Providing Relief from Tree Roots

Q. May a Committee make a Local Rule providing relief without penalty if a player's stroke is interfered with by exposed tree roots?

A. No. A Local Rule is authorized only if an abnormal condition exists. The existence of exposed tree roots is not abnormal.

33-8/9 Local Rule Providing Relief from Damage to Bunkers Caused by Children

Q. Some holes are accessible to the general public, and

children play in the bunkers leaving footprints, holes and sand castles.

May the Committee make a Local Rule allowing a player, without penalty, either to drop his ball outside a bunker damaged by children or to lift his ball from such damage, smooth out the sand and replace the ball?

A. No. This would be a modification of Rule 13-4.

33-8/10 Local Rule Prohibiting Removal of Flagstick

Q. May a Committee make a Local Rule for winter-time play prohibiting removal of the flagstick? The purpose would be to reduce traffic around the hole in the winter when the putting greens are very soft.

A. No. Such a Local Rule would modify the Rules of Golf.

33-8/11 Local Rule Waiving Penalty for Ball Striking Unattended Flagstick

Q. Is it permissible for a Committee to make a Local Rule for winter play waiving the penalty incurred under Rule 17-3c (Ball Striking Flagstick When Unattended) in order to reduce the damage caused to the area around the hole and to speed up play?

A. No.

33-8/12 Local Rule for Ball Deflected by Sprinkler Head

Q. May a Committee make a Local Rule allowing a player to replay a stroke, without penalty, if his ball has been deflected by a sprinkler head?

A. No. A sprinkler head is an outside agency (see Definition of "Outside Agency"). The deflection of a ball by it is a rub of the green and the ball must be played as it lies — see Rule 19-1.

33-8/13 Local Rule for Ball Deflected by Power Line

33

Q. An overhead power line is so situated that a perfectly played shot can be deflected. Would it be proper for the Committee to make a Local Rule allowing a player whose ball is deflected by this power line to replay the stroke, without penalty, if he wishes?

A. No. However, a Local Rule requiring a player to replay the stroke would be acceptable. The following text is suggested:

> "If a ball strikes the power line at the ____ hole, the player must disregard that stroke, abandon the ball and play another ball as nearly as possible at the spot from which the original ball was played in accordance with Rule 20-5 (Playing Next Stroke from Where Previous Stroke Played)."

33-8/14 Local Rule Deeming Interior Boundary Fence to Be an Obstruction

Q. There is a practice range in the middle of the course. The range is surrounded by a fence which defines the range as out of bounds. Would a Local Rule be authorized under which this particular boundary fence, since it is within the course, is treated as an obstruction?

A. No, such a Local Rule is not authorized. An interior boundary fence is not an abnormal condition.

33-8/15 Local Rule Providing Relief from Interference by Immovable Water Hazard Stake for Ball Lying in Water Hazard

Q. If the stakes defining the margins of water hazards are immovable, may the Committee make a Local Rule providing relief without penalty if a player's ball lies in a water hazard and such a stake interferes with his swing or stance?

A. No. Such stakes are immovable obstructions (see Note to Rule 24).

33-8/16 Local Rule Deeming All Stakes on Course to Be Immovable Obstructions

Q. It is proposed to adopt a Local Rule providing that all stakes on the course, *i.e.*, stakes defining the margins of water hazards, ground under repair, etc., are deemed to be immovable obstructions. The Local Rule would not, of course, apply to boundary stakes since they are not on the course. Is such a Local Rule permissible?

A. Yes.

33-8/17 Local Rule Providing Line-of-Sight Relief from Irrigation-Control Boxes

Q. Irrigation-control boxes, which are about two feet wide and four feet high, have been installed near a number of fairways. Would it be appropriate for a Committee to adopt a Local Rule under which relief would be provided from such boxes when they intervene on the line of play, *i.e.*, line-of-sight relief?

A. No. Providing line-of-sight relief from permanent immovable obstructions is not authorized, except in very unusual circumstances. It is not unusual for irrigation-control boxes to be located near fairways.

33-8/18 Local Rule Providing Line-of-Sight Relief from Protective Fence Near Line of Play

If a wire fence is erected to protect players on the tee of one hole from errant shots played at another hole, and it is relatively close to the line of play of the other hole, it would be permissible to make a Local Rule allowing a player whose ball is in such a position that the fence intervenes on his line of play to drop the ball, without penalty, not nearer the hole in a specified Ball Drop (or Dropping Zone).

33-8/19 Local Rule Permitting Relief on Specified Side of Paved Path

Q. A paved path is parallel to the left side of the 12th hole. If a ball is on the path and the nearest point of relief under Rule 24-2b is on the left side of the path, the player effectively gets no relief as there is a very sharp incline on the left of the path that goes down 30 feet. Would it be appropriate to make a Local Rule giving relief in all cases on the fairway side of this path?

A. No. Rule 33-8 states: "The Committee shall make and publish Local Rules for abnormal conditions." It is not abnormal for areas adjacent to paved paths to have dense underbrush, trees, sharp slopes, etc., thereby providing no practical relief.

Furthermore, it would not be appropriate to establish Ball Drops (or Dropping Zones) on the fairway side of the path to alleviate the problem.

33-8/20 Local Rule Providing Relief from Unsurfaced Road for Tee Shot Only

Q. A road which is not artificially-surfaced crosses a fairway 225 yards from the tee. May the Committee adopt a Local Rule granting relief of the type afforded by Rule 24-2b(i) or Rule 25-1b(i) for tee shots, but not subsequent shots, coming to rest on the road?

A. No. The Committee has authority to provide relief from interference by the road but does not have authority so to limit its application.

[33-8/21 Reserved]

33-8/22 Local Rule Treating Ant Hills as Ground Under Repair

Q. An ant hill is a loose impediment and may be removed, but there is no other relief without penalty. Some ant hills are conical in shape and hard, and removal is not possible, but relief under Rule 25-1b is not available since an ant is not a burrowing animal. If such ant hills interfere with the proper playing of the game, would a Local Rule providing relief be authorized?

A. Yes. A Local Rule stating that such ant hills are to be treated as ground under repair would be justified.

Such a Local Rule is also justified on courses where fire-ants exist. A fire-ants' mound or hill is removable, but its removal will cause the fire-ants to swarm out of the ground. When this occurs, anyone in the vicinity is in danger of being bitten by the ants, and the bite of a fire-ant can cause serious illness.

If a Local Rule giving relief from fire-ants has not been adopted and a ball is so close to a fire-ants' mound that the player is in danger, the player is, in equity, entitled to relief as prescribed in Decision 1-4/10.

33-8/23 Local Rule Denying Relief from Ground Under Repair During Play of Particular Hole

Q. An area of ground under repair is situated on the fairway of the 2nd hole, which is parallel to the 1st hole. Is it permissible to make a Local Rule prohibiting relief from this ground under repair during the play of the 1st hole?

A. No.

33-8/24 Local Rule Permitting Relief from Edging Grooves Around Putting Green

Q. Edging grooves, which are about three inches deep and one-quarter to one-half inch wide, are cut at the perimeters of the putting greens to control the creeping of bermuda grass onto the greens. If a ball comes to rest on such a groove, it is impossible to putt the ball with any degree of accuracy. Would a Local Rule providing relief be authorized?

A. Yes. It would be proper to make a Local Rule giving relief if a ball lies on such a groove, but not solely because a groove might affect the player's stance. The Local Rule should read as follows:

> "If a ball lies on an edging groove around a putting green, the player may, without penalty, lift the ball, clean it and place it out of the groove in the nearest position to where it lay, whether on or off the putting green, which is not nearer the hole."

Local Rule for Mushrooms on Line of Putt — See 16-1a/15.

33-8/25 Local Rule for Ground Under Repair Adjacent to Artificially-Surfaced Cart Path

33

Q. When ground under repair is adjacent to an artificially-surfaced cart path (an obstruction), sometimes a player, after obtaining relief from one condition, is interfered with by the other condition. Thus, another drop under another Rule results. This is cumbersome and could lead to complications. Would it be proper to eliminate the problem by means of a Local Rule under which ground under repair adjacent to an artificially-surfaced cart path would have the same status as the cart path?

A. Yes. If white lines are used to define ground under repair, a Local Rule is suggested as follows:

> "White-lined areas tying into artificially-surfaced roads or paths are declared to have the same status as the roads or paths, *i.e.*, they are obstructions, not ground under repair. Relief, without penalty, is provided under Rule 24-2b(i)."

33-8/26 Local Rule Altering Ground Under Repair Relief Procedure

Q. It is planned to define an area containing young trees as ground under repair. Would it be permissible to make a Local Rule requiring that, if a player elects to take relief from this area, he must drop the ball behind the area, keeping the trees between himself and the hole?

A. No. However, if it is not feasible to proceed in conformity with the ground under repair Rule, establishment of special areas on which balls may be dropped is authorized.

33-8/27 Local Rule Providing Relief Without Penalty from Flooded Bunker

Q. May a Committee make a Local Rule allowing a player to drop out of any bunker filled with casual water, without penalty, notwithstanding Rule 25-1b(ii)?

A. No. Such a Local Rule is not acceptable as it waives a penalty imposed by a Rule of Golf, contrary to Rule 33-8b.

33-8/28 Local Rule Permitting Re-Dropping or Placing When Dropped Ball Embeds in Bunker

Q. Our bunkers frequently have casual water in them. The texture of the sand in the bunkers is such that a ball dropped under Rule 25-1b(ii)(a) embeds itself in the wet sand to the depth of the ball or deeper.

Would it be proper to make a Local Rule permitting a ball that embeds in a bunker after being dropped from casual water in the bunker to be re-dropped or placed?

A. No. It is not abnormal for a ball dropped in a bunker to embed itself in the sand.

33-8/29 Local Rule Requiring Player to Take Relief Under Penalty from Tree Nursery or Plantation

Q. May a Committee make a Local Rule requiring that a ball lying in a tree nursery or plantation be dropped outside it under penalty of one stroke?

A. No. If the Committee wishes to prohibit play in such an area, it may declare it to be ground under repair from which relief without penalty is mandatory. However, a Local Rule imposing a penalty of one stroke is not permitted.

33-8/30 Local Rule Permitting the Repair of Turf Plugs On the Putting Green That are Not 4 1/4 Inches in Diameter

Q. Turf plugs which are not 4 1/4 inches in diameter or are not circular have been cut on some putting greens to repair damaged areas of turf. May a Committee adopt a Local Rule permitting the repair of these plugs?

A. Yes. If such areas exist it is recommended that a Local Rule permitting the repair of these plugs under Rule 16-1c be adopted. Otherwise, the repair of such turf plugs would be contrary to Rule 16-1c.

33-8/31 Local Rule Providing Relief from Accumulations of Leaves Through the Green

The Committee may make a temporary Local Rule declaring accumulations of leaves through the green at certain holes to be ground under repair (see Definition of "Ground Under Repair") and Rule 25-1 will apply.

The Local Rule should be restricted to the hole(s) at which trouble with leaves occurs and it should be withdrawn as soon as conditions permit. Particular attention is drawn to the opening paragraph of Rule 25-1c; unless there is reasonable evidence that a ball which cannot be found is lost in the leaves, it must be treated as lost elsewhere and Rule 27 applies.

For fallen leaves in a bunker — See Decision 13-4/33.

[33-8/32 Reserved]

33-8/32.5 Local Rule Treating Severe Damage by Non-Burrowing Animals as Ground Under Repair

Q. May a Committee make a Local Rule declaring areas severely damaged by non-burrowing animals to be ground under repair without marking them as such?

A. Yes. Furthermore, in some instances a Committee would be justified in denying relief from interference with the player's stance by such a condition — see Note under Rule 25-1a.

33-8/33 Local Rule Prohibiting Dropping on Apron When Ball on Wrong Putting Green

Q. Balls from the 13th tee frequently come to rest on the 15th green, and the point of nearest relief under Rule 25-3 is the closely mown apron of the green. Much damage is being caused to this apron. May the Committee make a Local Rule requiring that a ball be dropped not only clear of the putting surface but also clear of the apron of this green?

A. Yes. The following wording for a Local Rule is suggested:

"For the purpose of Rule 25-3, the putting green of the 15th hole includes the apron surrounding the green."

33-8/34 Local Rule Establishes Ball Drop or Dropping Zone; Procedure for Dropping

Q. The Committee has established a Ball Drop or Dropping Zone for relief from an immovable obstruction, ground under repair or a water hazard or for an unplayable ball (see Appendix I). If the player elects to take relief, what is the procedure for dropping and re-dropping?

A. (a) The player does not have to stand within the Ball Drop when dropping the ball.
(b) The dropped ball must first strike a part of the course within the Ball Drop.
(c) If the Ball Drop is defined by a white line, the line is within the Ball Drop.
(d) The dropped ball does not have to come to rest within the Ball Drop.
(e) The dropped ball must be re-dropped if it rolls into a hazard, onto a putting green, out of bounds or more than two club-lengths from where it first struck a part of the course.
(f) The dropped ball may roll nearer the hole provided it comes to rest within two club-lengths of the spot where it first struck a part of the course within the Ball Drop and not into any of the positions covered by (e).
(g) Subject to the provisions of (e) and (f), the dropped ball may roll and come to rest nearer the hole than its original position or estimated position.

33-8/35 Local Rule Treating Rough as a Lateral Water Hazard

Q. The areas immediately adjacent to the fairways consist of large embedded boulders, thick desert brush and prickly cactus. A player whose ball comes to rest in such areas has no opportunity to play a stroke. Would it be proper to make a Local Rule under which such areas would be treated as lateral water hazards?

A. No. There are many courses where the areas adjacent to the fairways are of such a nature that a ball therein is almost always lost or unplayable. Thus, such a situation is not abnormal.

33-8/36 Local Rule Giving Free Relief for Ball in Water Hazard

Q. A drainage ditch crosses a hole 190 yards from the tee. The Committee has marked that portion of the ditch within the limits of the fairway and a Local Rule allows a player relief, without penalty, if his tee shot lies in the ditch within the fairway limits.

Is this a proper Local Rule?

A. No. A drainage ditch is a water hazard — see Definition of "Water Hazard." Under Rule 26-1, the penalty for relief from a water hazard is one stroke. Rule 33-8b prohibits waiving this penalty by Local Rule.

33-8/37 Local Rule Allowing Drop in Water Hazard Behind Point Where Ball Lies Unplayable in Hazard

Q. A water hazard varies from 100 yards to 250 yards in width, and there is little or no water in it. In most cases a ball in the hazard can be played. However, it sometimes happens that a ball fails by a few yards to carry the hazard and ends up unplayable in water.

Under Rule 26-1, the player must either drop behind the hazard or at the spot from which his previous stroke was played. In either case, the relief point is up to 250 yards away. In such circumstances, may the Committee make a Local Rule permitting a player to drop a ball in the hazard under penalty of one stroke, as well as out of the hazard?

A. No.

Local Rule Allowing Drop Opposite Spot Where Ball Comes to Rest in Lateral Water Hazard — See 26-1/20.

Local Rule When Pond is Water Hazard from Back Tee and Lateral from Forward Tee — See 33-2a/6.

Local Rule for Part of Lateral Water Hazard Where Impossible to Drop Not Nearer Hole — See 33-2a/9.

Local Rule for Island Green — See 33-2a/10.

33-8/38 Local Rule Deeming Out of Bounds Ball Which Crosses Boundary But Comes to Rest on Course

Q. Is it permissible to make a Local Rule that a ball is out of bounds if it crosses a boundary, even if it recrosses the boundary and comes to rest on the same part of the course? The purpose of the Local Rule would be to prevent players from cutting across a "dog-leg."

A. No. A ball is out of bounds only when all of it lies out of bounds — see Definition of "Out of Bounds."

The Local Rule suggested in Decision 27/20 deals with a different situation, *i.e.*, one in which a ball crosses an out of bounds area and comes to rest on a different part of the course.

Local Rule for Boundary Stakes Having No Significance in Play of Hole Being Played — See 24/5.

Local Rule for Public Road Dividing Course Which Is Defined as Out of Bounds — See 27/20.

Local Rule Deeming Ball in Bounds Until Beyond Boundary Wall — See 33-2a/16.

33-8/39 Local Rule for Bunker Faces Consisting of Stacked Turf

Q. The face of a bunker which consists of stacked turf may be grass-covered or earthen. May a Committee make a Local Rule (a) clarifying that any face of a bunker which consists of stacked turf is not part of the bunker, and (b) deeming that such faces are not "closely mown areas" (Rule 25-2)?

A. Yes.

Ball Embedded in Grass Bank or Face of Bunker — See 25-2/5.

[33-8/40 Reserved]

33-8/41 Marking Environmentally-Sensitive Areas

If an appropriate authority prohibits entry into and/or play from an area for environmental reasons, it is the

Committee's responsibility to decide whether an environmentally-sensitive area should be defined as ground under repair, a water hazard or out of bounds.

However, the Committee may not define the area as a water hazard or a lateral water hazard unless it is, by Definition, a water hazard. The Committee should attempt to preserve the character of the hole.

As examples:

(a) A small area of rare plants close to a putting green has been declared an environmentally-sensitive area. The Committee may define the area to be ground under repair or out of bounds, but it may not be defined as a water hazard or lateral water hazard. In view of the area's proximity to a putting green, it should not be defined as out of bounds because a stroke-and-distance penalty would be unduly harsh. It would be more appropriate to define the area as ground under repair.

(b) A large area of sand dunes along the side of a hole has been declared an environmentally-sensitive area. In contrast to (a) above, it should not be defined as ground under repair because the absence of a penalty would be unduly generous. It would be more appropriate to define the area as out of bounds.

(c) A large area of wetlands along the side of a hole has been declared an environmentally-sensitive area. As in (b) above, it could be defined as out of bounds, but it would be more appropriate to define it as a lateral water hazard.

An environmentally-sensitive area should be physically protected to deter players from entering the area (*e.g.* by a fence, warning signs and the like) and it should be marked in accordance with the recommendations in the Rules of Golf (*i.e.* by yellow, red or white stakes, depending on the status of the area). It is recommended that stakes with green tops be used to designate an environmentally-sensitive area.

33-8/42 Player Enters Environmentally-Sensitive Area to Retrieve Ball

Q. A player wrongfully enters an environmentally-sensitive area to retrieve his ball. What is the ruling?

A. There is no penalty under the Rules of Golf, but the player may have broken the law or be subject to other disciplinary action. A Local Rule which imposes a penalty for entering an environmentally-sensitive area is not authorized.

33-8/43 Stroke Played from Environmentally-Sensitive Area

Q. A player played a stroke at his ball in an environmentally-sensitive area from which play is prohibited or took his stance in such an area in playing a stroke. What is the ruling?

A. The answer depends on how the Committee has defined the environmentally-sensitive area.

Ground Under Repair, Water Hazard or Lateral Water Hazard: If the ball was in the environmentally-sensitive area, or if the player took his stance in the environmentally-sensitive area to play a stroke at his ball which was lying outside the environmentally-sensitive area, he loses the hole in match play or he incurs a penalty of two strokes in stroke play for a breach of the Local Rule. In stroke play, he must play out the hole with that ball unless a serious breach of the Local Rule has occurred — see Decision 33-8/44.

Out of Bounds: If the ball was in the environmentally-sensitive area, the player played a wrong ball — see Decision 15/6. Accordingly, in match play, the player loses the hole. In stroke play, he incurs a two stroke penalty and is required to proceed under Rule 27-1, incurring the additional one stroke penalty prescribed by that Rule.

If the player took his stance in the environmentally-sensitive area to play a ball which was in bounds, the ruling would be the same as that for *Ground Under Repair, Water Hazard or Lateral Water Hazard.*

In all cases, the player may have broken the law or be subject to other disciplinary action for having entered the environmentally-sensitive area.

33-8/44 Significant Advantage Gained When Player Plays Stroke from Environmentally-Sensitive Area Defined as Water Hazard

Q. A player plays a stroke at his ball which is lying in an environmentally-sensitive area from which play is prohibited and which has been defined as a water hazard.

The point where his ball last crossed the margin of the water hazard is 150 yards behind the place where he played a stroke at his ball. What is the ruling?

A. In match play, the player loses the hole for a breach of the Local Rule.

In stroke play, a serious breach of the Local Rule is involved. The player must correct his error and follow the procedure outlined in Rule 20-7b by playing a ball in accordance with Rule 26-1, incurring the penalty stroke prescribed by that Rule and an additional penalty of two strokes for a breach of the Local Rule; otherwise the player is disqualified. The stroke played with the original ball from within the environmentally-sensitive area and all subsequent strokes, including penalty strokes, with this ball do not count in the player's score.

Meaning of "Serious Breach" — See 20-7b/0.5.

Rule 34. Disputes and Decisions

34-1. Claims and Penalties

a. Match Play

In match play if a claim is lodged with the *Committee* under Rule 2-5, a decision should be given as soon as possible so that the state of the match may, if necessary, be adjusted.

If a claim is not made within the time limit provided by Rule 2-5, it shall not be considered unless it is based on facts previously unknown to the player making the claim and the player making the claim had been given wrong information (Rules 6-2a and 9) by an opponent. In any case, no later claim shall be considered after the result of the match has been officially announced, unless the *Committee* is satisfied that the opponent knew he was giving wrong information.

There is no time limit on applying the disqualification penalty for a breach of Rule 1-3.

b. Stroke Play

Except as provided below, in stroke play, no penalty shall be rescinded, modified or imposed after the competition has closed. A competition is deemed to have closed when the result has been officially announced or, in stroke play qualifying followed by match play, when the player has teed off in his first match.

Exceptions: A penalty of disqualification shall be imposed after the competition has closed if a *competitor:*

(i) was in breach of Rule 1-3 (Agreement to Waive Rules);or

(ii) returned a score card on which he had recorded a handicap which, before the competition closed, he knew was higher than that to which he was entitled, and this affected the number of strokes received (Rule 6-2b); or

(iii) returned a score for any hole lower than actually taken (Rule 6-6d) for any reason other than failure to include a penalty which, before the competition closed, he did not know he had incurred; or

(iv) knew, before the competition closed, that he had been in breach of any other *Rule* for which the prescribed penalty is disqualification.

34-2. Referee's Decision

If a *referee* has been appointed by the *Committee*, his decision shall be final.

34-3. Committee's Decision

In the absence of a *referee*, any dispute or doubtful point on the Rules shall be referred to the *Committee*, whose decision shall be final.

If the *Committee* cannot come to a decision, it shall refer the dispute or doubtful point to the Rules of Golf Committee of the United States Golf Association, whose decision shall be final.

If the dispute or doubtful point has not been referred to the Rules of Golf Committee, the player or players have the right to refer an agreed statement through the Secretary of the Club to the Rules of Golf Committee for an opinion as to the correctness of the decision given. The reply will be sent to the Secretary of the Club or Clubs concerned.

If play is conducted other than in accordance with the Rules of Golf, the Rules of Golf Committee will not give a decision on any question.

34-1a/1 Player Who Has Reached Third Round of Match Play Disqualified for Agreeing to Waive Rules in First-Round Match

Q. Rule 34-1a provides that there is no time limit on applying the disqualification penalty under Rule 1-3 for agreeing to waive a Rule. If A, who agreed with his opponent to waive a Rule in a first-round match, has advanced to the third round before the Committee becomes aware of the breach of Rule 1-3, what should the Committee do?

A. As A is disqualified, the Committee must rule in accordance with equity (Rule 1-4). For guidelines, see Decision 34-1b/8.

34-1b/1 Omission of Penalty Stroke When Score Returned

Q. In stroke play, a competitor returned an incorrect score for a hole due to failure to include a penalty stroke. After the competition closed the error was discovered. Does Rule 34-1b allow imposition of a disqualification penalty for a breach of Rule 6-6d?

A. As stated in Rule 34-1b, the Committee should impose a penalty of disqualification if the competitor knew, before the competition closed, that he had incurred the penalty but intentionally or unintentionally failed to add the penalty to his score, but not if the competitor did not know he had incurred the penalty.

Omission of Penalty Strokes When Score Returned Is Due to Incorrect Ruling — See 34-3/1.

34-1b/1.5 Competitor Correctly Advised by Fellow-Competitor That He Had Incurred a Penalty Disagrees with Fellow-Competitor and Fails to Include Penalty in His Score; Committee Advised of Incident After Competition Had Closed

Q. In stroke play, A, in ignorance of the Rules and with the concurrence of B, his marker, removed a stone from a water hazard when his ball lay in the hazard. Subsequently, A was advised by C, a fellow-competitor,

that he (A) was in breach of Rule 13-4. A disagreed, failed to settle the doubtful point with the Committee at the end of the round and returned his score card without including a two-stroke penalty for a breach of
34 Rule 13-4.

After the competition had closed, C advised the Committee of the incident. Should A be disqualified?

A. Yes. Rule 34-1b says in effect that a competitor shall be disqualified after the competition has closed if he had returned a score, failing to include a penalty which, before the competition closed, he knew he had incurred. As C pointed out to A that he had proceeded incorrectly and A took no action to check whether he had incurred a penalty before returning his card, the Committee should decide that A knew that he had incurred a penalty.

34-1b/2 Competitor's Failure to Countersign Card Discovered After Competition Closed

Q. Shortly after a stroke play competition had closed, it was found that the card of the winner had not been countersigned. Should the Committee take any action?

A. The Committee must decide whether the competitor knew, before the competition closed, that he was in breach of the Rules by failing to sign his score card (Rule 6-6b). If he knew, he should be disqualified. Otherwise, as provided in Rule 34-1b, no penalty shall be imposed and the result of the competition must stand.

34-1b/3 Play of Wrong Ball in Stroke Play Not Rectified; Error Discovered After Competition Closed

Q. In stroke play, A played a wrong ball at the 5th hole but he did not realize it until he had holed out at that hole. Before teeing off at the 6th hole, A and B, who was A's marker, concluded that A had incurred a two-stroke penalty. Accordingly, B added two penalty strokes to A's score for the 5th hole and A and B teed off at the 6th hole without A having rectified his mistake as required under Rule 15-3. A was not aware that he should have rectified the error.

Before returning his card, A advised the Committee of the incident. The Committee confirmed that the penalty was two strokes but did not ask A whether the error had been rectified.

A won the competition. Several days later the runner-up claimed that A should be disqualified under Rule 15-3. What is the ruling?

A. The competition stands as played, with A the winner. Under Rule 34-1b, a penalty of disqualification may not be imposed after a competition is closed if the competitor did not know he had incurred the penalty.

34-1b/4 Competitor Changes Weight of Club During Round; Breach Discovered After Competition Closed

Q. It was reported a few days after conclusion of a stroke play event that the winner had changed the weight of his putter twice during play. Should he be penalized?

A. The Committee must decide whether the competitor knew he was in breach of the Rules in changing the weight of his putter during the course of the round (Rule 4-2). If he knew, the Committee should disqualify him. Otherwise, as provided in Rule 34-1b, no penalty shall be imposed.

34-1b/5 Disqualification Penalty Wrongly Applied to Winner of Event; Error Discovered After Two Other Competitors Play Off for First Place

Q. In the final round of a stroke play competition, the Committee disqualified A for recording on his score card a total score which was one stroke less than his actual score. A's hole by hole scores were correct. The Committee was in error. A would have won the event if he had not been disqualified.

As a result of A's disqualification, B and C play off for first place and B wins the play-off. Before the result of the competition is announced, the Committee discovers that A should not have been penalized.

Should the Committee rectify its error?

A. Yes. The penalty applied to A should be rescinded and A should be declared the winner — see Rule 34-1b.

34-1b/6 Winner's Score Not Posted Due to Committee Error

Q. In a stroke play event, the winner's prize is awarded to B. The next day A advises the Committee that he had returned a lower score than B. A check reveals that A is correct and that, in error, the Committee had failed to post A's score. What should be done?

A. Rule 34-1b does not apply to Committee errors of this kind. The prize should be retrieved from B and given to A, the rightful winner.

Wrong Handicap Used Due to Error by Committee; Error Discovered Several Days Later — See 6-2b/3.

Wrong Handicap Applied by Committee Results in Player Not Receiving Prize — See 33-5/2.

34-1b/7 Wrong Score in Qualifying Round Discovered During Match Play

Q. On completion of the stroke play qualifying round for a match play competition, a player unintentionally failed to include in his score for a hole a penalty he knew he had incurred. After the player had advanced in the match play phase, the error was discovered. What should be done?

A. The player should be disqualified. Under Rule 34-1b, the penalty for a breach of Rule 6-6d was applicable after the qualifying competition was closed.

Wrong Handicap Used in Stroke Play by Mistake; Error Discovered After Competition Closed — See 6-2b/1.

Wrong Handicap Knowingly Used in Stroke Play; Error Discovered After Competition Closed — See 6-2b/2.

Competitor Records Incorrect Handicap for Partner in Foursome Stroke Play Competition; Error Discovered After Competition Closed — See 6-2b/2.5.

34-1b/8 Player Who Has Advanced in Match Play Is Disqualified for Wrong Score in Qualifying Round

Q. The Committee discovers that by mistake A, who has advanced to the fourth round of a match play competition, returned a score lower than actually taken in the qualifying round. A was disqualified. What is the proper procedure with regard to the players beaten by A?

A. The Committee must determine further procedure in equity (Rule 1-4). The choices are:

(a) cancel the competition;
(b) consider the disqualification penalty applicable only from the time of its discovery, thus giving A's next opponent a default;
(c) reinstate the player last eliminated by A; or
(d) require all players eliminated by A to play off for his position.

34-2/1 Referee's Authority to Declare Ground Under Repair

Q. Does the referee of a match have authority to declare an area ground under repair during the match?

A. Yes.

34-2/2 Referee Authorizes Player to Infringe a Rule

Q. In error, a referee authorized a player to infringe a Rule of Golf. Is the player absolved from penalty in such a case?

A. Yes. Under Rule 34-2, a referee's decision is final, whether or not the decision is correct.

Imposition of Penalty by Referee After Any Player in Match Has Played from Next Tee — See 2-5/12.

34-2/3 Referee Warning Player About to Infringe Rule

Q. If the referee observes a player about to break a Rule, may he warn the player and thus prevent a breach?

A. Yes, but he is under no obligation to do so. If he volunteers information about the Rules, he should do so uniformly to all players.

34-2/4 Disagreement with Referee's Decision

Q. In match play, if a player disagrees with a referee's decision, may the player demand that the matter be considered by the Committee?

A. No. A referee's decision may be referred to the Committee only if the referee consents.

34-2/5 Referee Reverses Ruling Made at Last Hole of Match After Players Leave Putting Green

Q. In a match, A and B are all square playing the last hole. An incident occurs on the putting green and the referee rules incorrectly that A loses the last hole and the match, whereas he should have ruled that B lost the last hole and the match. A and B walk off the putting green without disputing the ruling. Subsequently, the referee learns of his error, reverses his ruling and decided that B lost the last hole and the match. Did the referee act properly in reversing his ruling?

A. No. When the referee made his ruling on the putting green of the last hole, that ruling was final — Rule 34-2. It would not have been final if A or B had disputed the ruling before leaving the last green and the referee had agreed to refer the matter to the Committee.

The referee was in error in subsequently reversing the ruling. The error should have been corrected by reverting to the ruling made on the last green.

Ball Thought to Be Unfit for Play; Committee Involvement When Opponent, Marker or Fellow-Competitor Not Readily Available — See 5-3/7.

Procedure for Referee in Determining Ball Farther from Hole — See 10-1b/1.

Flagstick Attended by Referee — See 17-1/3.

34-3/1 Correction of Incorrect Ruling

Q. During the first round of a 36-hole stroke play competition a competitor plays a wrong ball from a bunker at the 6th hole and the ball comes to rest on the green. The competitor holes out with it. He then realizes that he has played a wrong ball and corrects his mistake. The competitor reports the facts to the Committee before returning his card and is incorrectly advised that he has incurred no penalty since the wrong ball was played from a hazard.

During the second round the Committee realizes that it made a mistake and retrospectively adds to the competitor's first-round score two penalty strokes at the 6th hole, but does not disqualify the competitor under Rule 6-6d.

The competitor objects on the ground that the Committee reached a decision on the matter the previous day and that, as Rule 34-3 states that the Committee's decision is final, it cannot now impose a penalty.

Was the Committee's procedure correct?

A. Yes.

Under Rule 34-3, a Committee's decision is final in that the competitor has no right to appeal. However, Rule 34-3 does not prevent a Committee from correcting an incorrect ruling and imposing or rescinding a penalty provided that no penalty is imposed or rescinded after the competition is closed except in the circumstances set forth in Rule 34-1b.

[34-3/2 Reserved]

34-3/3 Player Proceeds on Basis of Incorrect Ruling

Q. A player obtained a ruling from a member of the Committee and proceeded to play on the basis of that ruling, which involved dropping the ball at and playing from a wrong place. The Committee member then learns that he made an incorrect ruling. Should the Committee require the player to disregard the stroke or strokes played subsequent to the incorrect ruling and proceed correctly?

A. No. The strokes played subsequent to the incorrect ruling must stand. This applies whether or not the player has played from the next tee. The player incurs no penalty for having played from a wrong place.

Play of Wrong Ball Not Rectified Due to Incorrect Advice by Committee Member — See 33-7/5.

34-3/3.5 Player Lifts Ball Without Authority Due to Misunderstanding Committee Member's Instructions

Q. A player's ball comes to rest against a movable obstruction and he seeks relief. A member of the Committee correctly advises him that he may remove the obstruction under Rule 24-1 and that he should mark the position of the ball in case it moves during the removal of the obstruction. The player marks the position of the ball and lifts it before the member of the Committee can stop him. The player was under the misapprehension that, having been requested to mark the position of the ball, he was entitled to lift it before the obstruction was removed. Should the player be penalized under Rule 18-2a in these circumstances?

A. No. Provided the Committee member is satisfied that the player misunderstood the instruction, the ball should be replaced without penalty.

34-3/4 Dispute as to Whether Competitor Played from Outside Teeing Ground

Q. In stroke play, B, A's fellow-competitor and marker, claimed at the completion of the round that A had played from outside the teeing ground at the 15th hole. A stated that he had played from within the teeing ground.

The Committee ruled that the claim was invalid because it was not made at the 15th tee and because A disputed the claim. Was the ruling correct?

A. It is a question of fact whether A played from outside the teeing ground. The matter should be resolved on the basis of the weight of evidence. The timing of a claim is not necessarily a factor.

In this case, it was B's word against A's and the weight of evidence did not favor either competitor. In such a case, the benefit of the doubt should be given to A, the player of the stroke.

34-3/5 True State of Match Not Determinable

Q. On completion of a match, A claims he is 1 up and B claims the match is all square. The matter is referred to the Committee. The Committee gathers all available evidence and is unable to determine the true state of the match. What should the Committee do?

A. It should resolve the matter in the fairest way. An equitable solution would be to order that the match be replayed.

APPENDIX I
LOCAL RULES;
CONDITIONS OF THE COMPETITION

Part A: Local Rules

As provided in Rule 33-8a, the *Committee* may make and publish Local Rules for local abnormal conditions if they are consistent with the policy set forth in this Appendix. In addition, detailed information regarding acceptable and prohibited Local Rules is provided in "Decisions on the Rules of Golf" under Rule 33-8.

If local abnormal conditions interfere with the proper playing of the game and the *Committee* considers it necessary to modify a Rule of Golf, authorization from the United States Golf Association must be obtained.

1. Defining Bounds and Margins

Specifying means used to define *out of bounds, water hazards, lateral water hazards, ground under repair, obstructions* and integral parts of the *course* (Rule 33-2a).

2. Water Hazards

a. *Lateral Water Hazards.* Clarifying the status of *water hazards* which may be *lateral water hazards* (Rule 26).

b. *Provisional Ball.* Permitting play of a *provisional ball* for a ball which may be in a *water hazard* of such character that if the original ball is not found, there is reasonable evidence that it is *lost* in the *water hazard* and it would be impracticable to determine whether the ball is in the *hazard* or to do so would unduly delay play. The ball shall be played provisionally under any of the available options under Rule 26-1 or any applicable Local Rule. In such a case, if a *provisional ball* is played and the original ball is in a *water hazard,* the player may play the original ball as it lies or continue with the *provisional ball* in play, but he may not proceed under Rule 26-1 with regard to the original ball.

3. Areas of the Course Requiring Preservation; Environmentally-Sensitive Areas

Assisting preservation of the *course* by defining areas, including turf nurseries, young plantations and other parts of the *course* under cultivation as "*ground under repair*" from which play is prohibited.

When the *Committee* is required to prohibit play from

environmentally-sensitive areas which are on or adjoin the *course,* it should make a Local Rule clarifying the relief procedure.

4. Temporary Conditions — Mud, Extreme Wetness, Poor Conditions and Protection of Course

a. Lifting an Embedded Ball, Cleaning

Temporary conditions which might interfere with proper playing of the game, including mud and extreme wetness, warranting relief for an embedded ball anywhere *through the green* or permitting lifting, cleaning and replacing a ball anywhere *through the green* or on a closely-mown area *through the green.*

b. "Preferred Lies" and "Winter Rules"

Adverse conditions, including the poor condition of the *course* or the existence of mud, are sometimes so general, particularly during winter months, that the *Committee* may decide to grant relief by temporary Local Rule either to protect the *course* or to promote fair and pleasant play. Such Local Rule shall be withdrawn as soon as the conditions warrant.

5. Obstructions

a. General

Clarifying status of objects which may be *obstructions* (Rule 24).

Declaring any construction to be an integral part of the *course* and, accordingly, not an *obstruction,* e.g., built-up sides of *teeing grounds, putting greens* and *bunkers* (Rules 24 and 33-2a).

b. Stones in Bunkers

Allowing the removal of stones in *bunkers* by declaring them to be "movable *obstructions*" (Rule 24-1).

c. Roads and Paths

(i) Declaring artificial surfaces and sides of roads and paths to be integral parts of the *course,* or

(ii) Providing relief of the type afforded under Rule 24-2b from roads and paths not having artificial surfaces and sides if they could unfairly affect play.

d. Fixed Sprinkler Heads

Providing relief from intervention by fixed sprinkler heads on or within two club-lengths of the *putting green* when the ball lies within two club-lengths of the sprinkler head.

e. Protection of Young Trees

Providing relief for the protection of young trees.

f. Temporary Obstructions

Providing relief from interference by temporary *obstructions* (e.g., grandstands, television cables and equipment, etc.).

6. Dropping Zones (Ball Drops)

Establishing special areas on which balls may or shall be dropped when it is not feasible or practicable to proceed exactly in conformity with Rule 24-2b or 24-2c (Immovable *Obstruction*), Rule 25-1b or 25-1c (*Abnormal Ground Conditions*), Rule 25-3 (*Wrong Putting Green*), Rule 26-1 (*Water Hazards* and *Lateral Water Hazards*) or Rule 28 (Ball Unplayable).

Part B: Specimen Local Rules

Within the policy set out in Part A of this Appendix, the *Committee* may adopt a Specimen Local Rule by referring, on a score card or notice board, to the examples given below. However, Specimen Local Rules 3a, 3b, 3c, and 6a and 6b, should not be printed or referred to on a score card as they are all of limited duration.

1. Areas of the Course Requiring Preservation; Environmentally-Sensitive Areas

a. Ground Under Repair; Play Prohibited

If the *Committee* wishes to protect any area of the *course*, it should declare it to be *ground under repair* and prohibit play from within that area. The following Local Rule is recommended:

"The ______________ (defined by ______) is *ground under repair* from which play is prohibited. If a player's ball lies in the area, or if it interferes with the player's *stance* or the area of his intended swing, the player must take relief under Rule 25-1.

PENALTY FOR BREACH OF LOCAL RULE:
Match play — Loss of hole;
Stroke play — Two strokes."

b. Environmentally-Sensitive Areas

If an appropriate authority (i.e., a Government Agency or the like) prohibits entry into and/or play from an area on or adjoining the course for environmental reasons, the *Committee* should make a Local Rule clarifying the relief procedure.

The *Committee* has some discretion in terms of whether the area is defined as *ground under repair,* a *water hazard* or *out of bounds.* However, it may not simply define such an area to be a *water hazard* if it does not meet the Definition of a *"Water Hazard"* and it should attempt to preserve the character of the hole.

The following Local Rule is recommended:

"I. Definition

An environmentally-sensitive area is an area so declared by an appropriate authority, entry into and/or play from which is prohibited for environmental reasons. Such an area may be defined as *ground under repair,* a *water hazard,* a *lateral water hazard* or *out of bounds* at the discretion of the *Committee* provided that, in the case of an environmentally-sensitive area which has been defined as a *water hazard* or a *lateral water hazard,* the area is, by Definition, a *water hazard.*

Note: The *Committee* may not declare an area to be environmentally-sensitive.

II. Ball in Environmentally-Sensitive Area

a. *Ground Under Repair*

If a ball is in an environmentally-sensitive area which is defined as *ground under repair,* a ball must be dropped in accordance with Rule 25-1b.

If there is reasonable evidence that a ball is *lost* within an environmentally-sensitive area which is defined as *ground under repair,* the player may take relief without penalty as prescribed in Rule 25-1c.

b. *Water Hazards* and *Lateral Water Hazards*

If a ball is in or there is reasonable evidence that it is *lost* in an environmentally-sensitive area which is defined as a *water hazard* or *lateral water hazard,* the player must, under penalty of one stroke, proceed under Rule 26-1.

Note: If a ball dropped in accordance with Rule 26 rolls into a position where the environmentally-sensitive area interferes with the player's *stance* or the area of his intended swing, the player must take relief as provided in Clause 3 of this Local Rule.

c. *Out of Bounds*

If a ball is in an environmentally-sensitive area which is defined as *out of bounds,* the player shall play a ball, under penalty of one stroke, as nearly as possible at the spot from which the original ball was last played (see Rule 20-5).

III. Interference with Stance or Area of Intended Swing

Interference by an environmentally-sensitive area occurs when such a condition interferes with the player's *stance* or the area of his intended swing. If interference exists, the player must take relief as follows:

(i) *Through the Green*: If the ball lies *through the green*, the point on the *course* nearest to where the ball lies shall be determined which (a) is not nearer the *hole*, (b) avoids interference by the condition and (c) is not in a *hazard* or on a *putting green*. The player shall lift the ball and drop it without penalty within one club-length of the point thus determined on a part of the course that fulfills (a), (b) and (c) above.

(ii) In a *Hazard*: If the ball is in a *hazard*, the player shall lift the ball and drop it either:

  (a) Without penalty, in the *hazard*, as near as possible to the spot where the ball lay, but not nearer the *hole*, on a part of the *course* which provides complete relief from the condition; or

  (b) Under penalty of one stroke, outside the *hazard*, keeping the point where the ball lay directly between the *hole* and the spot on which the ball is dropped, with no limit to how far behind the *hazard* the ball may be dropped. Additionally, the player may proceed under Rule 26 or 28 if applicable.

(iii) On the *Putting Green*: If the ball lies on the *putting green*, the player shall lift the ball and place it without penalty in the nearest position to where it lay which affords complete relief from the condition, but not nearer the *hole* or in a *hazard*.

The ball may be cleaned when so lifted under Clause 3 of this Local Rule.

Exception: A player may not obtain relief under Clause 3 of this Local Rule if (a) it is clearly unreasonable for him to play a *stroke* because of interference by anything other than a condition covered by this Local Rule or (b) interference by such a condition would occur only through use of an unnecessarily abnormal *stance*, swing or direction of play.

PENALTY FOR BREACH OF LOCAL RULE:
Match play — Loss of hole;
Stroke play — Two strokes.

Note: In the case of a serious breach of this Local Rule, the *Committee* may impose a penalty of disqualification."

2. Protection of Young Trees

When it is desired to prevent damage to young trees, the following Local Rule is recommended:

"Protection of young trees identified by __________ — If such a tree interferes with a player's *stance* or the area of his intended swing, the ball must be lifted, without penalty, and dropped in accordance with the procedure prescribed in Rule 24-2b (Immovable *Obstruction*). If the ball lies in a *water hazard*, the player shall lift and drop the ball in accordance with Rule 24-2b(i) except that the *nearest point of relief* must be in the *water hazard* and the ball must be dropped in the *water hazard* or the player may proceed under Rule 26. The ball may be cleaned when so lifted.

Exception: A player may not obtain relief under this Local Rule if (a) it is clearly unreasonable for him to play a *stroke* because of interference by anything other than such tree or (b) interference by such tree would occur only through use of an unnecessarily abnormal *stance*, swing or direction of play.

PENALTY FOR BREACH OF LOCAL RULE:
Match play — Loss of hole;
Stroke play — Two strokes."

3. Temporary Conditions — Mud, Extreme Wetness, Poor Conditions and Protection of the Course

a. Relief for Embedded Ball; Cleaning Ball

Rule 25-2 provides relief without penalty for a ball embedded in its own pitch-mark in any closely-mown area *through the green*. On the *putting green*, a ball may be lifted and damage caused by the impact of a ball may be repaired (Rules 16-1b and c). When permission to take relief for an embedded ball anywhere *through the green* would be warranted, the following Local Rule is recommended:

"*Through the green*, a ball which is embedded in its own pitch-mark in the ground, other than sand, may be lifted without penalty, cleaned and dropped as near as possible to where it lay but not nearer the *hole*. The ball when dropped must first strike a part of the *course through the green.*

Exception: A player may not obtain relief under this Local Rule if it is clearly unreasonable for him to play a *stroke* because of interference by anything other than the condition covered by this Local Rule.

PENALTY FOR BREACH OF LOCAL RULE:
Match play — Loss of hole;
Stroke play — Two strokes."

Alternatively, conditions may be such that permission to lift, clean and replace the ball will suffice. In such circumstances, the following Local Rule is recommended:

"(Specify area) a ball may be lifted, cleaned and replaced without penalty.

Note: The position of the ball shall be marked before it is lifted under this Local Rule — see Rule 20-1.

PENALTY FOR BREACH OF LOCAL RULE:
Match play — Loss of hole;
Stroke play — Two strokes."

b. "Preferred Lies" and "Winter Rules"

The USGA does not endorse "preferred lies" and "winter rules" and recommends that the Rules of Golf be observed uniformly. *Ground under repair* is provided for in Rule 25 and occasional local abnormal conditions which might interfere with fair play and are not widespread should be defined as *ground under repair.*

However, adverse conditions are sometimes so general throughout a *course* that the *Committee* believes "preferred lies" or "winter rules" would promote fair play or help protect the *course*. Heavy snows, spring thaws, prolonged rains or extreme heat can make fairways unsatisfactory and sometimes prevent use of heavy mowing equipment.

When a *Committee* adopts a Local Rule for "preferred lies" or "winter rules" it should be set out in detail and should be interpreted by the *Committee*, as there is no established code for "winter rules." Without a detailed Local Rule, it is meaningless for a *Committee* to post a notice merely saying "Winter Rules Today."

The following Local Rule would seem appropriate for the conditions in question, but the USGA will not interpret it:

"A ball lying on a closely-mown area *through the green* may, without penalty, be moved or may be lifted, cleaned and placed within (specify area, e.g., six inches, one club-length, etc.) of where it originally lay, but not nearer the *hole* and not in a *hazard* or on a *putting green.* A player may move or place his ball once and after the ball has been so moved or placed, it is in play.

PENALTY FOR BREACH OF LOCAL RULE:
Match play — Loss of hole;
Stroke play — Two strokes."

Before a *Committee* adopts a Local Rule permitting "preferred lies" or "winter rules," the following facts should be considered:

1. Such a Local Rule conflicts with the Rules of Golf and the fundamental principle of playing the ball as it lies.
2. "Winter rules" are sometimes adopted under the guise of protecting the *course* when, in fact, the practical effect is just the opposite — they permit moving the ball to the best turf, from which divots are then taken to injure the *course* further.
3. "Preferred lies" or "winter rules" tend generally to lower scores and handicaps, thus penalizing the players in competition with players whose scores for handicaps are made under the Rules of Golf.
4. Extended use or indiscriminate use of "preferred lies" or "winter rules" will place players at a disadvantage when competing at a *course* where the ball must be played as it lies.

c. Aeration Holes

When a *course* has been aerated, a Local Rule permitting relief, without penalty, from an aeration hole may be warranted. The following Local Rule is recommended:

"*Through the green,* a ball which comes to rest in or on an aeration hole may be lifted without penalty, cleaned and dropped, as near as possible to the spot where it lay but not nearer the *hole.* The ball when dropped must first strike a part of the *course through the green.*

On the *putting green,* the player shall place the ball at the nearest spot not nearer the *hole* which avoids such situation.

PENALTY FOR BREACH OF LOCAL RULE:
Match play — Loss of hole;
Stroke play — Two strokes."

4. Stones in Bunkers

Stones are, by definition, *loose impediments* and, when a player's ball is in a *hazard*, a stone lying in or touching the *hazard* may not be touched or moved (Rule 13-4). However, stones in *bunkers* may represent a danger to players (a player could be injured by a stone struck by the player's club in an attempt to play the ball) and they may interfere with the proper playing of the game.

When permission to lift a stone in a *bunker* would be warranted, the following Local Rule is recommended:

"Stones in *bunkers* are movable *obstructions* (Rule 24-1 applies)."

5. Fixed Sprinkler Heads

Rule 24-2 provides relief without penalty from interference by an immovable *obstruction,* but it also provides that, except on the *putting green,* intervention on the *line of play* is not, of itself, interference under this Rule.

However, on some courses, the aprons of the *putting greens* are so closely mown that players may wish to putt from just off the green. In such conditions, fixed sprinkler heads on the apron may interfere with the proper playing of the game and the introduction of the following Local Rule providing additional relief without penalty from intervention by a fixed sprinkler head would be warranted:

"All fixed sprinkler heads are immovable *obstructions* and relief from interference by them may be obtained under Rule 24-2. In addition, if a ball lies off the *putting green* but not in a *hazard* and such an *obstruction* on or within two club-lengths of the *putting green* and within two club-lengths of the ball intervenes on the *line of play* between the ball and the *hole,* the player may take relief as follows:

The ball shall be lifted and dropped at the nearest point to where the ball lay which (a) is not nearer the *hole,* (b) avoids such intervention and (c) is not in a *hazard* or on a *putting green.* The ball may be cleaned when so lifted.

PENALTY FOR BREACH OF LOCAL RULE:
Match play — Loss of hole;
Stroke play — Two strokes."

6. Temporary Obstructions

When temporary *obstructions* are installed on or adjoining the course, the *Committee* should define the status of such *obstructions* as movable, immovable or temporary immovable *obstructions.*

a. Temporary Immovable Obstructions

If the *Committee* defines such *obstructions* as temporary immovable *obstructions,* the following Local Rule is recommended:

"I. Definition

A temporary immovable *obstruction* is a non-permanent artificial object which is often erected in conjunction with a competition and which is fixed or not readily movable.

Examples of temporary immovable *obstructions* include, but are not limited to, tents, scoreboards, grandstands, television towers and lavatories.

Supporting guy wires are part of the temporary immovable *obstruction* unless the *Committee* declares that they are to be treated as elevated power lines or cables.

II. Interference

Interference by a temporary immovable *obstruction* occurs when (a) the ball lies in front of and so close to the *obstruction* that the *obstruction* interferes with the player's *stance* or the area of his intended swing, or (b) the ball lies in, on, under or behind the *obstruction* so that any part of the *obstruction* intervenes directly between the player's ball and the *hole;* interference also exists if the ball lies within one club-length of a spot where such intervention would exist.

Note: A ball is under a temporary immovable *obstruction* when it is below the outer most edges of the *obstruction,* even if these edges do not extend downwards to the ground.

III. Relief

A player may obtain relief from interference by a temporary immovable *obstruction,* including a temporary immovable *obstruction* which is *out of bounds,* as follows:

(a) *Through the Green:* If the ball lies *through the green,* the point on the *course* nearest to where the ball lies shall be determined which (a) is not nearer the *hole,* (b) avoids interference as defined in Clause 2 and (c) is not in a *hazard* or on a *putting green.* The player shall lift the ball and drop it without penalty within one club-length of the point thus determined on a part of the *course* which fulfills (a), (b) and (c) above.

(b) In a *Hazard*: If the ball is in a *hazard*, the player shall lift and drop the ball either:

(i) Without penalty, in the *hazard*, on the nearest part of the *course* affording complete relief within the limits specified in Clause 3a above or, if complete relief is impossible, on a part of the *course* within the *hazard* which affords maximum available relief; or

(ii) Under penalty of one stroke, outside the *hazard* as follows: the point on the *course* nearest to where the ball lies shall be determined which (a) is not nearer the *hole*, (b) avoids interference as defined in Clause 2 and (c) is not in a *hazard*. The player shall drop the ball within one club-length of the point thus determined on a part of the *course* which fulfills (a), (b) and (c) above.

The ball may be cleaned when lifted under Clause 3.

Note 1: If the ball lies in a *hazard*, nothing in this Local Rule precludes the player from proceeding under Rule 26 or Rule 28, if applicable.

Note 2: If a ball to be dropped under this Local Rule is not immediately recoverable, another ball may be substituted.

Note 3: A *Committee* may make a Local Rule (a) permitting or requiring a player to use a dropping zone or ball drop when taking relief from a temporary immovable *obstruction* or (b) permitting a player, as an additional relief option, to drop the ball on the opposite side of the *obstruction* from the point established under Clause 3, but otherwise in accordance with Clause 3.

Exceptions:

If a player's ball lies in front of or behind the temporary immovable *obstruction* (not in, on or under the *obstruction*) he may not obtain relief under Clause 3 if:

1. It is clearly unreasonable for him to play a *stroke* or, in the case of intervention, to play a *stroke* such that the ball could finish on a direct line to the *hole*, because of interference by anything other than the temporary immovable *obstruction*;
2. Interference by the temporary immovable *obstruction* would occur only through use of an unnecessarily abnormal *stance*, swing or direction of play; or

3. In the case of intervention, it would be clearly unreasonable to expect the player to be able to strike the ball far enough towards the *hole* to reach the temporary immovable *obstruction*.

Note: A player not entitled to relief due to these exceptions may proceed under Rule 24-2.

IV. Ball Lost

If there is reasonable evidence that the ball is *lost* in, on or under a temporary immovable *obstruction*, a ball may be dropped under the provisions of Clause 3 or Clause 5, if applicable. For the purpose of applying Clauses 3 and 5, the ball shall be deemed to lie at the spot where it last entered the *obstruction* (Rule 24-2c).

V. Dropping Zones (Ball Drops)

If the player has interference from a temporary immovable *obstruction*, the *Committee* may permit or require the use of a dropping zone or ball drop. If the player uses a dropping zone in taking relief, he must drop the ball in the dropping zone nearest to where his ball originally lay or is deemed to lie under Clause 4 (even though the nearest dropping zone may be nearer the *hole*).

Note 1: A *Committee* may make a Local Rule prohibiting the use of a dropping zone or ball drop which is nearer the *hole*.

Note 2: If the ball is dropped in a dropping zone, the ball shall not be re-dropped if it comes to rest within two club-lengths of the spot where it first struck a part of the *course* even though it may come to rest nearer the *hole* or outside the boundaries of the dropping zone.

PENALTY FOR BREACH OF LOCAL RULE:
Match play — Loss of hole;
Stroke play — Two strokes."

b. Temporary Power Lines and Cables

When temporary power lines, cables, or telephone lines are installed on the *course*, the following Local Rule is recommended:

"Temporary power lines, cables, telephone lines and mats covering or stanchions supporting them are *obstructions:*

1. If they are readily movable, Rule 24-1 applies.
2. If they are fixed or not readily movable, the player may, if the ball lies *through the green* or in a *bunker*, obtain relief as provided in Rule 24-2b. If the ball lies

in a *water hazard,* the player may lift and drop the ball in accordance with Rule 24-2b(i) except that the *nearest point of relief* must be in the *water hazard* and the ball must be dropped in the *water hazard* or the player may proceed under Rule 26.

3. If a ball strikes an elevated power line or cable, the *stroke* shall be cancelled and replayed, without penalty (see Rule 20-5). If the ball is not immediately recoverable another ball may be substituted.

Note: Guy wires supporting a temporary immovable *obstruction* are part of the temporary immovable *obstruction* unless the *Committee,* by Local Rule, declares that they are to be treated as elevated power lines or cables.

Exception: Ball striking elevated junction section of cable rising from the ground shall not be replayed.

4. Grass-covered cable trenches are *ground under repair* even if not so marked and Rule 25-1b applies."

Part C: Conditions of the Competition

Rule 33-1 provides, "The *Committee* shall lay down the conditions under which a competition is to be played." Such conditions should include many matters such as method of entry, eligibility, number of rounds to be played, etc. which it is not appropriate to deal with in the Rules of Golf or this Appendix. Detailed information regarding such conditions is provided in "Decisions on the Rules of Golf" under Rule 33-1.

However, there are seven matters which might be covered in the Conditions of the Competition to which the *Committee's* attention is specifically drawn by way of a Note to the appropriate Rule. These are:

1. Specification of the Ball (Note to Rule 5-1)

The following two conditions are recommended only for competitions involving expert players:

a. List of Conforming Golf Balls

The USGA periodically issues a List of Conforming Golf Balls which lists balls that have been tested and found to conform. If the *Committee* wishes to require use of a brand of golf ball on the List, the List should be posted and the following condition of competition used:

"The ball the player uses shall be named on the current List of Conforming Golf Balls issued by the United States Golf Association.

PENALTY FOR BREACH OF CONDITION:
Disqualification."

b. One Ball Condition

If it is desired to prohibit changing brands and types of golf balls during a *stipulated round,* the following condition is recommended:

"Limitation on Balls Used During Round: (Note to Rule 5-1)

(i) "One Ball" Condition
During a *stipulated round,* the balls a player uses must be of the same brand and type as detailed by a single entry on the current List of Conforming Golf Balls.

PENALTY FOR BREACH OF CONDITION:
Match Play — At the conclusion of the hole at which the breach is discovered, the state of the match shall be adjusted by deducting one hole for each hole at which a breach occurred; maximum deduction per round: Two holes.
Stroke Play — Two strokes for each hole at which any breach occurred; maximum penalty per round: Four strokes.

(ii) Procedure When Breach Discovered
When a player discovers that he has used a ball in breach of this condition, he shall abandon that ball before playing from the next *teeing ground* and complete the round using a proper ball; otherwise, the player shall be disqualified. If discovery is made during play of a hole and the player elects to substitute a proper ball before completing that hole, the player shall place a proper ball on the spot where the ball used in breach of the condition lay."

2. Time of Starting (Note to Rule 6-3a)

If the *Committee* wishes to act in accordance with the Note, the following wording is recommended:

"If the player arrives at his starting point, ready to play, within five minutes after his starting time, in the absence of circumstances which warrant waiving the penalty of disqualification as provided in Rule 33-7, the penalty for failure to start on time is loss of the first hole to be played in match play or two strokes in stroke play. Penalty for lateness beyond five minutes is disqualification."

3. Pace of Play

The *Committee* may lay down pace of play guidelines to help prevent slow play, in accordance with Note 2 to Rule 6-7.

4. Suspension of Play Due to a Dangerous Situation (Note to Rule 6-8b)

As there have been many deaths and injuries from lightning on golf courses, all clubs and sponsors of golf competitions are urged to take precautions for the protection of persons against lightning. Attention is called to Rules 6-8 and 33-2d. If the *Committee* desires to adopt the condition in the Note under Rule 6-8b, the following wording is recommended:

"When play is suspended by the *Committee* for a dangerous situation, if the players in a match or group are between the play of two holes, they shall not resume play until the *Committee* has ordered a resumption of play. If they are in the process of playing a hole, they shall discontinue play immediately and shall not thereafter resume play until the *Committee* has ordered a resumption of play. If a player fails to discontinue play immediately, **he shall be disqualified** unless circumstances warrant waiving such penalty as provided in Rule 33-7.

The signal for suspending play due to a dangerous situation will be a prolonged note of the siren."

The following signals are generally used and it is recommended that all *Committees* do similarly:

Discontinue Play Immediately: One prolonged note of siren.

Discontinue Play: Three consecutive notes of siren, repeated.

Resume Play: Two short notes of siren, repeated.

5. Practice

a. General

The *Committee* may make regulations governing practice in accordance with the Note to Rule 7-1, Exception (c) to Rule 7-2, Note 2 to Rule 7 and Rule 33-2c.

b. Practice Between Holes (Note 2 to Rule 7)

It is recommended that a condition of competition prohibiting practice putting or chipping on or near the *putting green* of the hole last played be introduced only in stroke play competitions. The following wording is recommended:

"A player shall not play any practice *stroke* on or near the *putting green* of the hole last played. If a practice *stroke* is played on or near the *putting green* of the hole last played, the player shall incur a penalty of two strokes at the next hole, except that in the case of the last hole of the round, he incurs the penalty at that hole."

6. Advice in Team Competitions

If the *Committee* wishes to act in accordance with the Note under Rule 8, the following wording is recommended:

"In accordance with the Note to Rule 8 of the Rules of Golf, each team may appoint one person (in addition to the persons from whom *advice* may be asked under that Rule) who may give advice to members of that team. Such person *(if it desired to insert any restriction on who may be nominated insert such restriction here)* shall be identified to the *Committee* before giving *advice*."

7. New Holes

The *Committee* may provide, in accordance with the Note to Rule 33-2b, that the *holes* and *teeing grounds* for a single round competition, being held on more than one day, may be differently situated on each day.

Other conditions of the competition might include:

Transportation

If it is desired to require players to walk in a competition, the following condition is recommended:

"Players shall walk at all times during a *stipulated round*.

PENALTY FOR BREACH OF CONDITION:
Match play — At the conclusion of the hole at which the breach is discovered, the state of the match shall be adjusted by deducting one hole for each hole at which a breach occurred.
Maximum deduction per round: Two holes.
Stroke play — Two strokes for each hole at which any breach occurred; maximum penalty per round: Four strokes. In the event of a breach between the play of two holes, the penalty applies to the next hole.

Match or stroke play — Use of any unauthorized form of transportation shall be discontinued immediately upon discovery that a breach has occurred. Otherwise, the player shall be disqualified."

How to Decide Ties

Rule 33-6 empowers the *Committee* to determine how and when a halved match or a stroke play tie shall be decided. The decision should be published in advance.

The USGA recommends:

Match Play

A match which ends all square should be played off hole by hole until one *side* wins a hole. The play-off should start on the hole where the match began. In a handicap match, handicap strokes should be allowed as in the prescribed round.

Stroke Play

(a) In the event of a tie in a scratch stroke play competition, a play-off is recommended. Such a play-off may be over 18 holes or a smaller number of holes as specified by the *Committee.* If that is not feasible or there is still a tie, a hole-by-hole play-off is recommended.

(b) In the event of a tie in a handicap stroke play competition, a play-off with handicaps is recommended. Such a play-off may be over 18 holes or a smaller number of holes as specified by the *Committee.* If the play-off is less than 18 holes the percentage of 18 holes to be played should be applied to the players' handicaps to determine their play-off handicaps. Handicap stroke fractions of one-half stroke or more should count as a full stroke and any lesser fraction should be disregarded.

(c) In either a scratch or handicap stroke play competition, if a play-off of any type is not feasible, matching score cards is recommended. The method of matching cards should be announced in advance. An acceptable method of matching cards is to determine the winner on the basis of the best score for the last nine holes. If the tying players have the same score for the last nine, determine the winner on the basis of the last six holes, last three holes and finally the 18th hole. If such a method is used in a handicap stroke play competition, one-half, one-third, one-sixth, etc. of the handicaps should be deducted. Fractions should not be disregarded. If such a method is used in a competition with a multiple tee start, it is recommended that the "last nine holes, last six holes, etc." is considered to be holes 10-18, 13-18, etc.

(d) If the conditions of the competition provide that ties shall be decided over the last nine, last six, last three and last hole, they should also provide what will happen if this procedure does not produce a winner.

Draw for Match Play

Although the draw for match play may be completely blind or certain players may be distributed through different quarters or eighths, the General Numerical Draw is recommended if matches are determined by a qualifying round.

General Numerical Draw

For purposes of determining places in the draw, ties in qualifying rounds other than those for the last qualifying place shall be decided by the order in which scores are returned, with the first score to be returned receiving the lowest available number, etc. If it is impossible to determine the order in which scores are returned, ties shall be determined by a blind draw.

UPPER HALF	LOWER HALF	UPPER HALF	LOWER HALF
64 QUALIFIERS		32 QUALIFIERS	
1 vs. 64	2 vs. 63	1 vs. 32	2 vs. 31
32 vs. 33	31 vs. 34	16 vs. 17	15 vs. 18
16 vs. 49	15 vs. 50	8 vs. 25	7 vs. 26
17 vs. 48	18 vs. 47	9 vs. 24	10 vs. 23
8 vs. 57	7 vs. 58	4 vs. 29	3 vs. 30
25 vs. 40	26 vs. 39	13 vs. 20	14 vs. 19
9 vs. 56	10 vs. 55	5 vs. 28	6 vs. 27
24 vs. 41	23 vs. 42	12 vs. 21	11 vs. 22
4 vs. 61	3 vs. 62	16 QUALIFIERS	
29 vs. 36	30 vs. 35	1 vs. 16	2 vs. 15
13 vs. 52	14 vs. 51	8 vs. 9	7 vs. 10
20 vs. 45	19 vs. 46	4 vs. 13	3 vs. 14
5 vs. 60	6 vs. 59	5 vs. 12	6 vs. 11
28 vs. 37	27 vs. 38	8 QUALIFIERS	
12 vs. 53	11 vs. 54	1 vs. 8	2 vs. 7
21 vs. 44	22 vs. 43	4 vs. 5	3 vs. 6

APPENDICES II and III

Any design in a club or ball which is not covered by Rules 4 and 5 and Appendices II and III, or which might significantly change the nature of the game, will be ruled on by the United States Golf Association.

The dimensions contained in Appendices II and III are referenced in imperial measurements. A metric conversion is also referenced for information, calculated using a conversion rate of 1 inch = 25.4 mm. In the event of any dispute over the conformity of a club or ball, the imperial measurements shall take precedence.

APPENDIX II
Design of Clubs

A player in doubt as to the conformity of a club should consult the United States Golf Association.

A manufacturer should submit to the United States Golf Association a sample of a club which is to be manufactured for a ruling as to whether the club conforms with the *Rules*. If a manufacturer fails to submit a sample before manufacturing and/or marketing the club, the manufacturer assumes the risk of a ruling that the club does not conform with the *Rules*. Any sample submitted to the United States Golf Association will become its property for reference purposes.

The following paragraphs prescribe general regulations for the design of clubs, together with specifications and interpretations.

Where a club, or part of a club, is required to have some specific property, this means that it must be designed and manufactured with the intention of having that property. The finished club or part must have that property within manufacturing tolerances appropriate to the material used.

1. Clubs

a. General

A club is an implement designed to be used for striking the ball and generally comes in three forms: woods, irons and putters distinguished by shape and intended use. A putter is a club with a loft not exceeding ten degrees designed primarily for use on the *putting green*.

The club shall not be substantially different from the traditional and customary form and make. The club shall be composed of a shaft and a head. All parts of the club shall be fixed so that the club is one unit, and it shall have no external attachments except as otherwise permitted by the *Rules*.

b. Adjustability

Woods and irons shall not be designed to be adjustable except for weight. Putters may be designed to be adjustable for weight and some other forms of adjustability are also permitted. All methods of adjustment permitted by the *Rules* require that:

(i) the adjustment cannot be readily made;

(ii) all adjustable parts are firmly fixed and there is no reasonable likelihood of them working loose during a round; and

(iii) all configurations of adjustment conform with the *Rules*.

The disqualification penalty for purposely changing the playing characteristics of a club during a *stipulated round* (Rule 4-2a) applies to all clubs including a putter.

c. Length

The overall length of the club shall be at least 18 inches (457.2 mm) measured from the top of the grip along the axis of the shaft or a straight line extension of it to the sole of the club.

d. Alignment

When the club is in its normal address position the shaft shall be so aligned that:

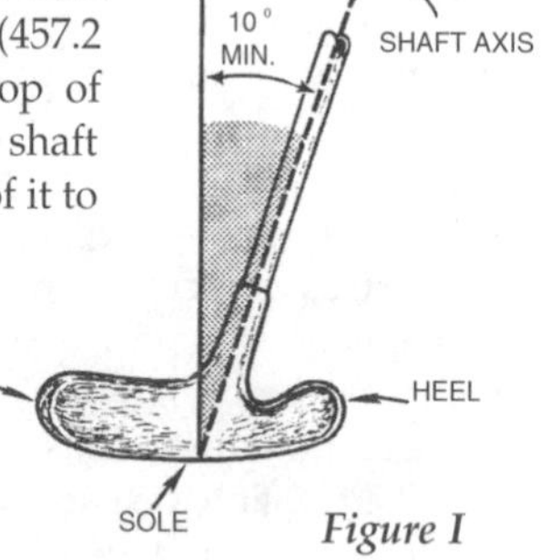

Figure I

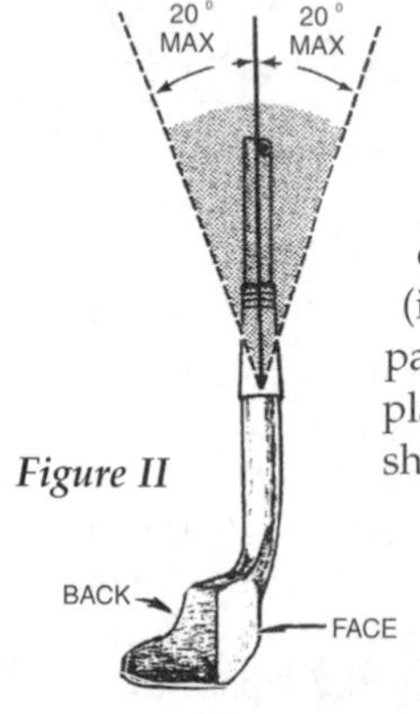

Figure II

(i) the projection of the straight part of the shaft on to the vertical plane through the toe and heel shall diverge from the vertical by at least 10 degrees (see Fig I);

(ii) the projection of the straight part of the shaft on to the vertical plane along the intended line of play shall not diverge from the vertical by more than 20 degrees (see Fig. II).

Except for putters, all of the heel portion of the club shall lie within 0.625 inches (15.88 mm) of the plane containing the axis of the straight part of the shaft and the intended (horizontal) line of play (see Fig. III).

2. Shaft

a. Straightness

The shaft shall be straight from the top of the grip to a point not more than 5 inches (127 mm) above the sole, measured from the point where the shaft ceases to be straight along the axis of the bent part of the shaft and the neck and/or socket (see Fig. IV).

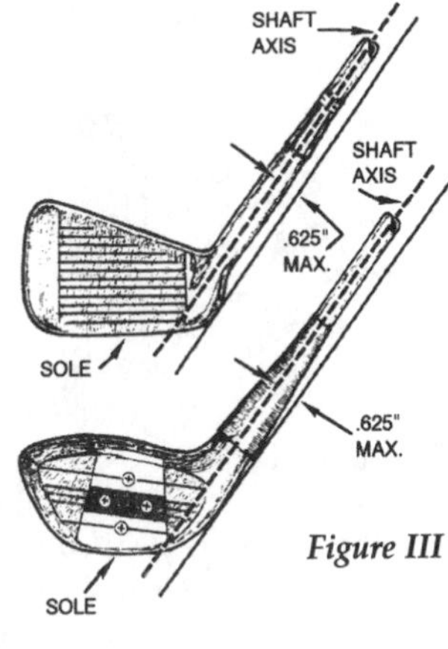

Figure III

b. Bending and Twisting Properties

At any point along its length, the shaft shall:

(i) bend in such a way that the deflection is the same regardless of how the shaft is rotated about its longitudinal axis; and

(ii) twist the same amount in both directions.

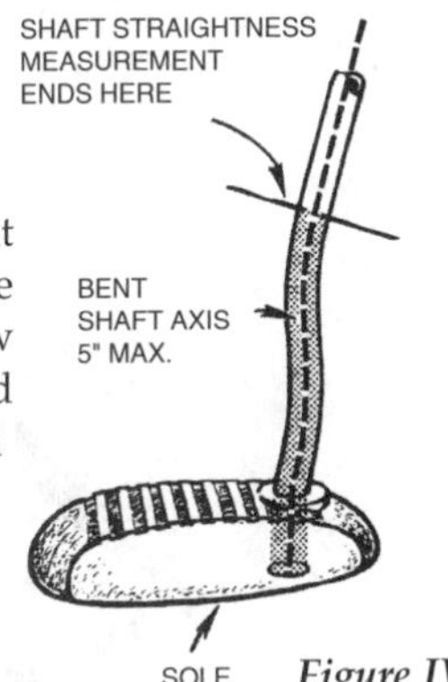

Figure IV

c. Attachment to Clubhead

The shaft shall be attached to the clubhead at the heel either directly or through a single plain neck and/or socket. The length from the top of the neck and/or socket to the sole of the club shall not exceed 5 inches (127 mm), measured along the axis of, and following any bend in, the neck and/or socket (see Fig. V).

Exception for Putters: The shaft or neck or socket of a putter may be fixed at any point in the head.

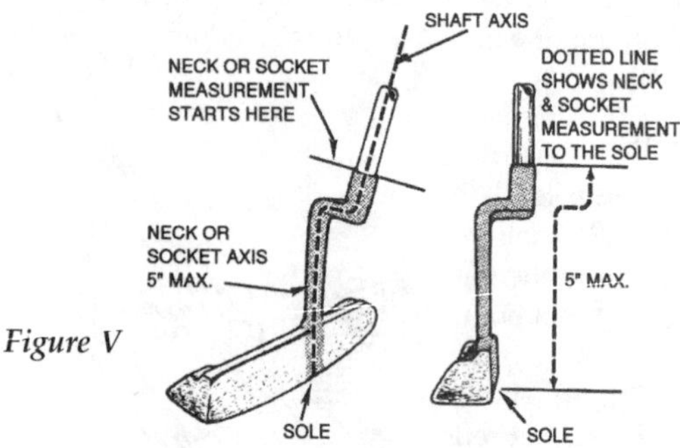

Figure V

3. Grip (see Fig. VI)

The grip consists of material added to the shaft to enable the player to obtain a firm hold. The grip shall be straight and plain in form, shall extend to the end of the shaft and shall not be molded for any part of the hands. If no material is added, that portion of the shaft designed to be held by the player shall be considered the grip.

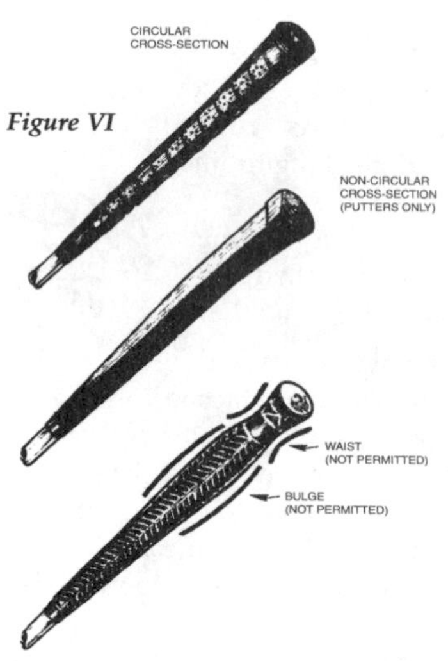

Figure VI

(i) For clubs other than putters the grip must be circular in cross-section, except that a continuous, straight, slightly raised rib may be incorporated along the full length of the grip, and a slightly indented spiral is permitted on a wrapped grip or a replica of one.

(ii) A putter grip may have a non-circular cross-section, provided the cross-section has no concavity, is symmetrical and remains generally similar throughout the length of the grip. (See Clause (v) below).

(iii) The grip may be tapered but must not have any bulge or waist. Its cross-sectional dimension measured in any direction must not exceed 1.75 inches (44.45 mm).

(iv) For clubs other than putters the axis of the grip must coincide with the axis of the shaft.

(v) A putter may have two grips provided each is circular in cross-section, the axis of each coincides with the axis of the shaft, and they are separated by at least 1.5 inches (38.1mm).

4. Clubhead

a. Plain in Shape

The clubhead shall be generally plain in shape. All parts shall be rigid, structural in nature and functional. It is not practicable to define plain in shape precisely and comprehensively but features which are deemed to be in breach of this requirement and are therefore not permitted include:

(i) holes through the head,

(ii) transparent material added for other than decorative or structural purposes,

(iii) appendages to the main body of the head such as knobs, plates, rods or fins, for the purpose of meeting dimensional specifications, for aiming or for any other purpose. Exceptions may be made for putters.

Figure VII

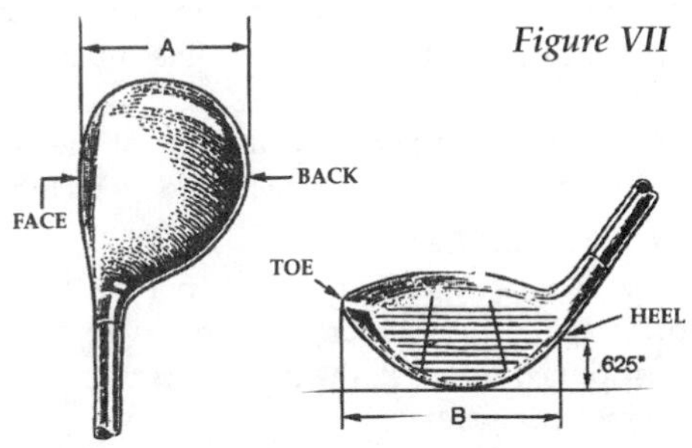

Any furrows in or runners on the sole shall not extend into the face.

b. Dimensions

The distance from the heel to the toe of the clubhead shall be greater than the distance from the face to the back. These dimensions are measured, with the clubhead in its normal address position, on horizontal lines between vertical projections of the outermost points of (i) the heel and the toe and (ii) the face and the back (see Fig VII, dimension A). If the outermost point of the heel is not clearly defined, it is deemed to be 0.625 inches (15.88mm) above the horizontal plane on which the club is resting in its normal address position (see Fig. VII, dimension B).

c. Striking Faces

The clubhead shall have only one striking face, except that a putter may have two such faces if their characteristics are the same, and they are opposite each other.

5. Club Face

a. General

The material and construction of, or any treatment to, the face or clubhead shall not have the effect at impact of a spring (test on file), or impart significantly more spin to the ball than a standard steel face, or have any other effect which would unduly influence the movement of the ball.

The face of the club shall be hard and rigid (some exceptions may be made for putters) and, except for such markings listed below, shall be smooth and shall not have any degree of concavity.

b. Impact Area Roughness and Material

Except for markings specified in the following paragraphs, the surface roughness within the area where impact is intended (the "impact area") must not exceed that of decorative sandblasting, or of fine milling (see Fig. VIII).

The whole of the impact area must be of the same material. Exceptions may be made for wooden clubs.

c. Impact Area Markings

Markings in the impact area must not have sharp edges or raised lips as determined by a finger test. Grooves or punch marks in the impact area must meet the following specifications:

(i) **Grooves.** A series of straight grooves with diverging sides and a symmetrical cross-section may be used (see Fig. IX). The width and cross-section must be consistent

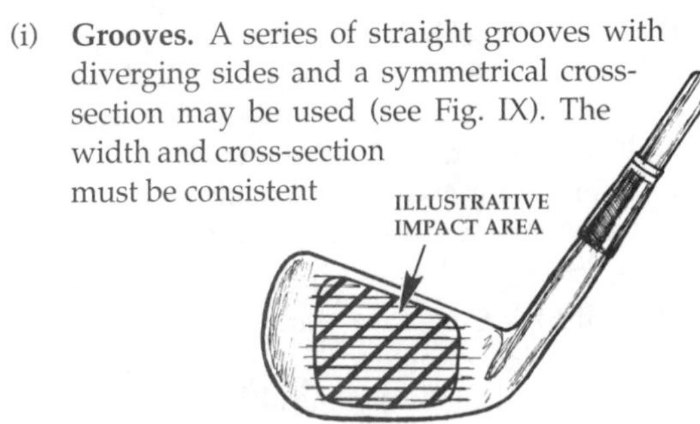

Figure VIII

across the face of the club and along the length of the grooves. Any rounding of groove edges shall be in the form of a radius which does not exceed 0.020 inches (0.508 mm). The width of the grooves shall not exceed 0.035 inches (0.9 mm), using the 30 degree method of measurement on file with the United States Golf Association. The distance between edges of adjacent grooves must not be less than three times the width of a groove, and not less than 0.075 inches (1.905 mm). The depth of a groove must not exceed 0.020 inches (0.508 mm).

Note: Exception — see US Decision 4-1/100.

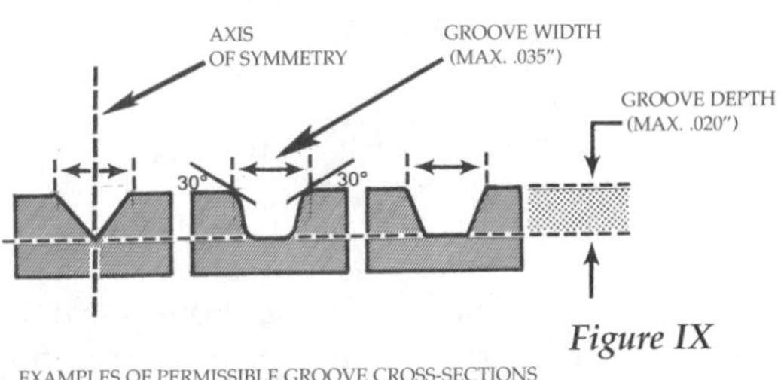

Figure IX

(ii) **Punch Marks.** Punch marks may be used. The area of any such mark must not exceed 0.0044 square inches (2.84 sq. mm). A mark must not be closer to an adjacent mark than 0.168 inches (4.27 mm) measured from center to center. The depth of a punch mark must not exceed 0.040 inches (1.02 mm). If punch marks are used in combination with grooves, a punch mark must not be closer to a groove than 0.168 inches (4.27 mm), measured from center to center.

d. Decorative Markings

The center of the impact area may be indicated by a design within the boundary of a square whose sides are 0.375 inches (9.53 mm) in length. Such a design must not unduly influence the movement of the ball. Decorative markings are permitted outside the impact area.

e. Non-metallic Club Face Markings

The above specifications apply to clubs on which the impact area of the face is of metal or a material of similar hardness. They do not apply to clubs with faces made of other materials and whose loft angle is 24 degrees or less, but markings which could unduly influence the movement of the ball are prohibited. Clubs with this type of face and a loft angle exceeding 24 degrees may have grooves of maximum width 0.040 inches (1.02 mm) and maximum depth 1½ times the groove width, but must otherwise conform to the markings specifications above.

f. Putter Face

The specifications above with regard to roughness, material and markings in the impact area do not apply to putters.

APPENDIX III
The Ball

1. Weight

The weight of the ball shall not be greater than 1.620 ounces avoirdupois (45.93 gm).

2. Size

The diameter of the ball shall not be less than 1.680 inches (42.67mm). This specification will be satisfied if, under its own weight, a ball falls through a 1.680 inches diameter ring gauge in fewer than 25 out of 100 randomly selected positions, the test being carried out at a temperature of 23 ±1°C.

3. Spherical Symmetry

The ball must not be designed, manufactured or intentionally modified to have properties which differ from those of a spherically symmetrical ball.

4. Initial Velocity

The initial velocity of the ball shall not exceed the limit specified (test on file) when measured on apparatus approved by the United States Golf Association.

5. Overall Distance Standard

The combined carry and roll of the ball, when tested on apparatus approved by the United States Golf Association, shall not exceed the distance specified under the conditions set forth in the Overall Distance Standard for golf balls on file with the United States Golf Association.

MISCELLANEOUS DECISIONS

Misc./1 Course Record

The term "course record" is not defined in the Rules of Golf. However, it is generally accepted that a record score should be recognized as the official "course record" only if made in an individual stroke play competition with the holes and tee-markers in their proper medal or championship positions.

It is recommended that a record score should not be recognized as the official "course record" if a Local Rule permitting preferred lies is in operation.

Misc./2 Whether Rakes Should be Placed In or Outside Bunkers

Q. Should rakes be placed in or outside bunkers?

A. There is not a perfect answer for the position of rakes, but on balance it is felt there is less likelihood of an advantage or disadvantage to the player if rakes are placed outside of bunkers.

It may be argued that there is more likelihood of a ball being deflected into or kept out of a bunker if the rake is placed outside the bunker. It could also be argued that if the rake is in the bunker it is most unlikely that the ball will be deflected out of the bunker.

However, in practice, players who leave rakes in bunkers frequently leave them at the side which tends to stop a ball rolling into the flat part of the bunker, resulting in a much more difficult shot than would otherwise have been the case. This is most prevalent at a course where the bunkers are small. When the ball comes to rest on or against a rake in the bunker and the player must proceed under Rule 24-1, it may not be possible to replace the ball on the same spot or find a spot in the bunker which is not nearer the hole — see Decision 20-3d/2.

If rakes are left in the middle of the bunker the only way to position them is to throw them into the bunker and this causes damage to the surface. Also, if a rake is in the middle of a large bunker it is either not used or the player is obliged to rake a large area of the bunker resulting in unnecessary delay.

Therefore, after considering all these aspects, it is recommended that rakes should be left outside bunkers in areas where they are least likely to affect the movement of the ball.

Ultimately, it is a matter for the Committee to decide where it wishes rakes to be placed. (Revised)

DECISIONS APPLICABLE ONLY IN THE UNITED STATES OF AMERICA

US/2-3/100 Player Who Wins First Nine Holes in Nassau Match Withdraws During Second Nine

Q. The "Nassau" System of scoring is used in a team match, *i.e.*, in each match three points are awarded as follows: one point to the winner of the first nine holes, one point to the winner of the second nine and one point to the winner over 18 holes. In one match, a player who had defeated his opponent on the first nine holes withdrew due to illness during the second nine. Should the player retain the point he won on the first nine or, since he withdrew, should he lose all three points?

A. The player should be awarded one point; his opponent won the other two points by default.

US/4-1/100 Clubface Markings

Q. May a player use a golf club with a groove spacing to groove width ratio of 2.3 to 1, if that club was manufactured before March 31, 1990, even though Appendix II 4-1e requires that the groove spacing to groove width ratio must be no less than 3 to 1?

A. Yes. It is, however, the responsibility of the player to provide proof of the date on which the club was manufactured. If the player cannot provide such proof, the club must conform with the specifications described in Appendix II 4-1e.

[US/5-1/100 Reserved]

US/5-1/101 Status of Ball Not on List of Conforming Golf Balls

Brands of balls not appearing on the current List of Conforming Golf Balls fall into three categories:

1. Brands which have never been tested.
2. Brands which appeared on a previous List but which have not been re-submitted for inclusion on the current List, and
3. Brands which have been tested and found not to conform to the Rules and specifications set forth in Appendix III.

Balls in categories 1 and 2 are presumed to conform and the onus of proof is on the person alleging that the ball does not.

All balls of brands in category 3 are deemed to be non-conforming.

US/5-1/102 Status of Ball to Be Removed from List of Conforming Golf Balls

Q. A brand of ball included on the current List of Conforming golf Balls is tested further and found not to conform to the specifications set forth in Appendix III. The brand will therefore be deleted from the next List published. What is the status of the ball in the interim period?

A. Players are entitled to assume that all balls of a brand included on the current List of Conforming Golf Balls conform to the Rules and Appendix III. Accordingly, players may continue to use balls of the brand in question until the publication of the next List, unless by a condition of the competition the Committee has specifically excluded that brand. This applies whether or not it is a condition of the competition that only brands of golf balls on the List of Conforming Golf Balls may be used.

US/6-2a/100 Player in Match Uses Established Handicap But Handicap Too High Due to Player's Failure to Observe Provision of Handicap System

Q. A's handicap is 23 strokes and B's is 31. A and B play a handicap match and B receives 8 strokes, the difference between 31 and 23. B wins the match, 1 up. A questions B's handicap; B admits that he does not adjust his scores under the Equitable Stroke Control provision of the USGA Handicap System. It is determined that, if B had adjusted his scores, his handicap would be 29 strokes. The Committee disqualifies B under Rule 6-2a. Was the Committee correct?

A. Rule 6-2a provides:

> "Before starting a match in a handicap competition, the players should determine from one another their respective handicaps. If a player begins the match having declared a higher handicap which would affect the number of strokes given or received, he shall be disqualified; otherwise, the player shall play off the declared handicap."

B's handicap, although incorrect due to his failure to apply Equitable Stroke Control, was 31. Accordingly, B was not in breach of Rule 6-2a and the match should have stood as played.

As it is impracticable for a Committee conducting a competition to determine whether a player has correctly recorded each score, turned in all scores, etc., for handicap purposes, the Rules of Golf assume that he has done so. The solution to a situation such as this is for the Handicap Committee to take appropriate action against B because of his failure to apply Equitable Stroke Control to the scores he returned for handicap purposes.

US/17/100 Flagstick Dimensions

The USGA recommends that the flagstick be at least seven feet in height and that its diameter be not greater than three-quarters of an inch from a point three inches above the ground to the bottom of the hole.

US/20-1/100 Placing Ball-Marker to Side

Q. If a player is requested to mark the position of his ball to the side of where it lies, must he place a ball-marker behind the ball, measure a clubhead-length to the side of the marker and then move the marker to the side? Or may the player simply measure a clubhead-length from the side of the ball and eliminate one step?

A. The player may measure from the side of the ball, unless the Local Rule entitled "Marking Position of

Lifted Ball" in Appendix I of the Rules book is in effect. That Local Rule requires that a ball-marker be placed behind the ball and then moved to one side, if necessary.

US/29/100 Penalty in "Pinehurst" Foursome Not Related to Ball Holed Out

Q. In a foursome competition played under the so-called "Pinehurst" format, A and B were partners. In accordance with the format, A hit a second shot with B's ball. B then hit a second shot with a ball he thought was A's, but which in fact was a wrong ball. Since B's shot with the wrong ball was a poor one, B picked up the wrong ball and he and A proceeded to play out the hole with B's ball. It was then discovered that the ball B picked up was not A's ball, but rather a wrong ball.

Do A and B incur any penalty because B played a wrong ball in view of the fact that the hole was completed with B's ball which was not related to the play of the wrong ball?

A. The Rules of Golf do not cover this form of play.

It is recommended that a penalty in this form of play should be incurred only if related to the ball ultimately holed out by the side. Thus, as the ball played by B from the tee was ultimately holed out, the side should not have incurred a penalty because B played a stroke with a wrong ball instead of A's ball.

US/33-8/100 Local Rule for Lateral Water Hazard with Bunker Adjacent

Q. The 18th hole at the Pebble Beach Golf Links is bordered along the left side by Carmel Bay, and there is a sea wall which begins more than 100 yards short of the green and extends to the back of the green. There is a bunker approximately 12 feet wide between the sea wall and the fairway for much of this distance.

The bay is a lateral water hazard and the sea wall is the natural margin of the hazard. Accordingly, a player, when dropping a ball under Rule 26-1c(i), must drop in the bunker. The sand at this point is soft and a dropped ball usually plugs.

Would it be permissible to place the line defining the lateral water hazard along the right edge of the bunker, making the bunker part of the lateral water hazard, or alternatively, make a Local Rule to the effect that, when obtaining relief under the lateral water hazard Rule, the player may drop a ball to the right of the bunker?

A. In all cases, the hazard should be marked along its natural boundary, i.e., the sea wall — see Decision 33-2a/4.

If the Committee does not wish to require a player to drop a ball in the bunker when proceeding under the lateral water hazard Rule, the Committee may establish a series of Ball Drops along the right-hand side of the bunker and make a Local Rule stating that a player whose ball comes to rest in the lateral water hazard (having last crossed the hazard margin at a point where, when proceeding under Rule 26-1c(i), the player may drop a ball in the bunker) may drop a ball, under penalty of one stroke, on the nearest Ball Drop which is not nearer the hole. (Revised)

US/33-8/101 Local Rule for Breach of Sportsmanship Code

Q. A high school federation has a sportsmanship code for golfers who compete in high school matches.

May the federation make a Local Rule assessing a penalty for a breach of the code?

A. A Local Rule assessing a penalty for a breach of a sportsmanship code is not authorized. Penalties for a breach of a sportsmanship code should take a more generalized form, *e.g.*, subjection to censure, suspension or revocation of the privilege of playing in events.

[US/33-8/102 Reserved]

US/34-3/100 Committee Intervention in Match Play

In the absence of a referee, a Committee has no authority to intervene in match play unless there is a reason to believe Rule 1-3 is being infringed or a breach of Rule 6-7 is involved. When there is no referee, the players must protect their own rights by invoking Rule 2-5 and by referring to the Committee any dispute they cannot resolve — see Rule 34-3.

US/34-3/101 Committee Intervention in Match Play When Search for Lost Ball Exceeds Five Minutes

Q. Decision US/34-3/100 permits a Committee member to intervene in a match to which a referee has not been assigned in case of a breach of Rule 6-7 (Undue Delay).

Would it be in order for a Committee member to intervene in such a match if he has observed that a player has looked for his ball for five minutes and is continuing to search?

A. Yes. It would be appropriate for a Committee member to intervene and advise the player that the ball is lost under the Rules and, if he does not resume play immediately, a penalty for undue delay will result.

PRINCIPAL CHANGES SINCE 1998-1999 GENERAL

The United States Golf Association and the Royal and Ancient Golf Club of St. Andrews have agreed to a two-year revision cycle for the *Decisions on the Rules of Golf.* Therefore, no existing Decisions will be revised or withdrawn, and no new Decisions will be added to the book until the next edition is published in 2002. Should extraordinary circumstances arise which would warrant amending the *Decisions on the Rules of Golf* in the interim, the United States Golf Association will notify its member clubs, all state and regional golf associations, and appropriate media sources of any change.

NEW DECISIONS

3-3/7.5 **Competitor Announces Intention to Play Two Balls; Plays Original Ball Before Dropping Second Ball; Elects Not To Play Second Ball**

4-1/3 **Status of a Chipper**

4-1/4 **Lead Tape Applied to Clubhead or Shaft Before Start of Round**

4-2/0.5 **Lead Tape Applied to Clubhead or Shaft During Round**

4-3/1 **Meaning of Damage Sustained in "Normal Course of Play"**

4-3/2 **Meaning of "Repair"**
4-3/3 **Club Damaged in Normal Course of Play Breaks into Pieces When Repaired**
5-1/4 **Status of an 'X-out' Ball**
5-1/5 **Whether Player May Borrow Balls from Another Player**
6-2b/5 **Competition in Which Best Two of Four Scores Used to Determine Winners; Competitor Returns Score Card With Higher Handicap**
6-3a/3 **Circumstances Which Warrant Waiving of Disqualification Penalty Under Rule 6-3a**
6-6b/8 **Requirement that Score be Entered Into Computer**
6-8c/1 **Explanation of "Good Reason to Lift"**
6-8d/1 **Resuming Play from Where It was Discontinued; Lie Altered by Natural Causes**
7-2/10 **Match Discontinued by Agreement Cannot be Resumed Until Three Days Later; One Player Wishes to Play on Competition Course Prior to Resumption**
7-2/11 **Match Discontinued by Agreement on the 13th Tee Cannot be Resumed Until the Following Day; May Competitors Play First Twelve Holes Prior to Resuming Match**
8-2a/3 **Player Places Mark to Indicate Distance for Pitch Shot**
9-2/1 **Meaning of "As Soon As Practicable" in Rule 9-2**
12-1/5 **Player Kicks Ball While Probing for It in Water in Water Hazard**
13-4/16.5 **Flying Insect in Water Hazard**
18-2a/13.5 **Ball Lifted and Thrown Into Pond in Anger**
19/2 **Status of Person in Shared Golf Cart**
20/2 **Borrowing Club for Measuring Purposes**
20-1/10.5 **Ball-Marker Moved by Wind or Casual Water During Stipulated Round**
20-1/15 **Meaning of "Directly Attributable" in Rules 20-1 and 20-3a**
20-1/15.5 **Lie Altered By Act of Marking Position of Ball**
20-2c/0.8 **Player Takes Relief from an Area of Ground Under Repair; Whether Re-Drop Required if Condition Interferes for Stroke with Club Not Used to Determine "Nearest Point of Relief"**

20-2c/1.7 **Whether Re-Drop Required if Ball Dropped Under Rule 24-2b Rolls Nearer Hole Than the Nearest Point of Relief but Not Nearer Than Where it Originally Lay**

23-1/5.5 **Status of Insect on Ball in Bunker**

25/10.5 **Ball in Tree in Ground Under Repair**

26/3.5 **Lateral Water Hazard Defined as Water Hazard**

27/1.5 **Time Permitted for Search for Lost Ball if Play Suspended During Search**

27/5.5 **Original Ball Found Within Five-Minute Search Period Not Identified Until After Period Has Elapsed**

27-2a/1.5 **Meaning of "Goes Forward for Search"**

27-2a/2.5 **Player Plays Provisional Ball in Belief Original Ball Might Be Lost Outside Water Hazard then Discovered there is No Possibility of its Being Lost Outside Water Hazard**

27-2b/6.5 **Player Declares Provisional Ball Unplayable and Drops Ball; Original Ball Then Found**

32-2a/3 **Handicap Stableford Competition; Recording of Lower Gross Score Affects Result of Hole**

32-2a/4 **Handicap Stableford Competition; Recording of Lower Gross Score Does Not Affect Result of Hole**

32-2a/5 **Handicap Bogey or Par Competition; Recording of Lower Gross Score Does Not Affect Result of Hole**

33-1/9.5 **Breach of Transportation Condition by Caddie**

33-1/14 **Condition Regarding Footwear**

REVISED DECISIONS

*Denotes Decisions which contain only minor amendments to reflect a change to the Rule under which the Decision is listed.

1-2/1 **Line of Putt Altered Purposely by Opponent or Fellow-Competitor by Stepping on It.** Expanded to clarify that the line of putt can be restored if it is damaged.

1-4/8 **Nearest Point of Relief from Cart Path Is in Casual Water; Nearest Point of Relief from Casual Water Is Back on Cart Path.** Amended to clarify that player may not initially take relief from both conditions in a single procedure.

2-1/2 **Minus or Zero Net Score.** Answer expanded to address four-ball stroke play and Stableford.

2-5/3 **Player Lifts Ball Before Holing Out; Opponent Then Picks Up His Ball Claiming Player Loses Hole.** Amended to clarify that B's claim is valid resulting in A losing the hole.

4-1/2 ***Material in Head of Metal Wood Club Broken Away from Shell.**

4-2/2 ***Playing Characteristics of Club Changed While Play Suspended; Error Discovered Before Play Resumed.**

4-2/4 ***Applying Saliva to Face of Club** (formerly 4-3/2).

4-3/4 ***Modifying Penalty for Holing Short Putt with Club whose Playing Characteristics Changed Other Than in Normal Course of Play** (formerly 4-2/1.5).

4-3/5 ***Changing Clubs Because of Wet Grips** (formerly 4-4a/1).

4-3/6 ***Replacing Club When Grip Becomes Loose During Round** (formerly 4-4a/2).

4-3/7 **Club Broken While Used As Cane** (formerly 4-4a/3). Answer amended to reflect new interpretation of "damaged in the normal course of play" and to reflect the reorganization of Rule 4 and Appendix II.

4-3/8 ***Player Starting with 13 Clubs Breaks Putter in Anger and Replaces It** (formerly 4-4a/4).

4-3/9 **Club Broken Due to Habit of Hitting Head of Club on Ground** (formerly 4-4a/5). Answer amended to reflect new interpretation of "damaged in the normal course of play" and to reflect the reorganization of Rule 4.

4-3/10 ***Replacement of Club Lost During Round** (formerly 4-4a/6).

4-3/11 ***Replacement of Club Broken on Practice Ground While Play Suspended** (formerly 4-4a/6.5).

9/1 **Incorrect Information on Rules.** Expanded to reflect change to Rule 6-1.

9-2/8 **Player Wins Hole with Wrong Ball; Error Discovered at Next Hole; Opponent Claims Previous Hole.** Answer amended to reflect specific language of Rule 9-2.

11-2/1 **Status of Tee-Markers After First Stroke.** Question amended to reflect specific language of Rule 11-2.

11-2/2 **Tee-Marker Moved By Player.** Expanded to state that a moved tee-marker should be replaced. Example (a) amended to eliminate opportunity to correct error and avoid penalty.

13-2/1 ***Explanation of "Fairly Taking His Stance."**

13-2/4.5 **Divots Replaced and Pressed Down in Area Which Ball Is to Be Dropped.** Amended to reflect change to Rule 13-2.

13-2/6 **Replacing Divot in Divot Hole Behind Ball.** Amended to reflect change to Rule 13-2.

13-2/10 ***Pitch-Mark in Dropping Area Repaired Before Ball Dropped.**

13-2/14.5 ***Branch Broken on Backswing and Swing Discontinued.**

13-2/18 ***Improving Position of Ball by Bending Boundary Fence.**

13-2/21 ***Area of Intended Swing Improved by Repairing Pitch-Mark Made by Ball on Previous Stroke.**

13-2/23 **Shaking Water from Tree Branch Interfering with Backswing.** Answer amended for clarity.

13-2/27 ***Probing Near Ball For Tree Roots or Rocks.**

13-2/34 **Mopping Up Casual Water on Line of Play.** Amended to reflect change to Rule 13-2.

13-2/35 **Removal of Dew or Frost. Amended to reflect change to Rule 13-2.**

13-4/3.5 **Player Uses Cane or Club to Enter or Leave Hazard When Ball Lies in Hazard. Question amended to reflect title.**

14-2/4 ***Caddie Inadvertently Positioned on Extension of Line of Putt Behind Ball** (formerly 16-1f/2).

15/7 **Wrong Ball Played in Belief It Is Provi sional or Second Ball. Answer expanded to address case where second ball played after original ball holed out.**

16-1a/13 **Line of Putt Stepped on Accidentally by Opponent or Fellow-Competitor.** Expanded to clarify that line of putt may be restored if damaged.

18-1/2 **Ball Visible from Tee Disappears or Is Moved While Play Suspended. Amended to reflect change to Rule 6-8d.**

18-1/11 **Ball Moved by Wind or Casual Water While Play Suspended.** Amended to reflect change to Rule 6-8d.

18-2a/15 **Caddie on own Initiative Lifts ball Considering it Unplayable.** Answer expanded to clarify that player is not required to replace the ball if he elects to proceed under Rule 28.

18-2a/21 **Ball moved Accidentally by Player in Playing Wrong Ball in Bunker.** Expanded to clarify case where the nearby ball was not visible before player A plays from the bunker.

20/1 **Club to Be Used in Measuring.** Amended for clarity. Issue of borrowing a club for measuring covered by New Decision 20/2.

20-1/10 **Ball-Marker Moved Off Green by Wind or Casual Water While Play Suspended.** Title amended to reflect question. Answer amended to reflect change to Rule 6-8d.

20-2c/0.5 ***Ball Dropped from Ground Under Repair Area Rolls to Position Where Area Interferes with Stance; Whether Re-Drop Required.**

20-2c/1.5 ***Ball Rolls Towards Hole When Dropped at Spot from Which Previous Stroke Played.**

20-2c/3.5 **Dropped Ball Comes to Rest and Then Rolls Out of Bounds.** Answer amended to reference addition of Note to Rule 20-2.

20-7b/5 **Competitor's Ball Played by Fellow-Competitor; Competitor Substitutes Another Ball at Wrong Place, Plays It and Then Abandons It and Plays Out Original Ball from Right Place.** Question amended for clarity.

20-7b/6 **Competitor Plays Second Ball Under Rule 20-7b; Clarification of "Penalty Strokes Incurred Solely by Playing the Ball Ruled Not to Count."** Amended to reflect change to the Note to Rule 20-7b.

24/5 **Boundary Stakes Having No Significance in Play of Hole Being Played.** Answer expanded to reference Definition of "Out of Bounds."

24-2b/3.5 **Player Unable Physically to Determine Nearest Point of Relief.** Amended to reference the new Definition of "Nearest Point of Relief."

24-2b/4 **Club Used to Determine Nearest Point of**

Relief Not Used for Next Stroke. Amended to reference the new Definition of "Nearest Point of Relief."

24-2b/12 **Ball in Drainpipe Under Course; Entrance to Drainpipe Is Out of Bounds.** Amended to reflect the new format of Rule 24-2c.

24-2c/1 **Ball Lost in Underground Drainpipe.** Amended to reflect change to Rule 24-2c.

25/10 **Ball Lost in Tree in Ground Under Repair.** Amended to reflect change to the Definition of "Ground Under Repair."

25/18 **Hole of Removed Stake Defining Water Hazard.** Amended to reflect change in Rule 25-1b.

25/19.5 **Footprint of Burrowing Animal, Reptile or Bird.** Amended to refer to the New Definition of "Abnormal Ground Conditions."

25-1a/1 **Ball Outside Ground Under Repair Area But Tree Within Area Interferes with Swing.** Amended to reflect change in the Definition of "Ground Under Repair."

25-1a/2 **Casual Water on Putting Green Intervenes Between Ball Off Green and Hole.** Answer amended to reflect change to Rule 13-2.

25-1b/2 **Diagrams Illustrating Nearest Point of Relief.** Amended to reference New Definition of "Nearest Point of Relief."

25-1b/4 **Casual Water Covering Teeing Ground.** Amended for clarity.

25-1b/7 **Ball to Be Dropped in Bunker Dropped Outside Bunker and Rolls into Bunker.** Amended to reference the new Definition of "Nearest Point of Relief" and reflect changes to Rule 25-1.

25-1b/8 ***Player's Options When Bunker Completely Covered by Casual Water.**

25-1b/9 **Player Who Invokes First Option of Rule 25-1b(ii) Then Wishes to Invoke Second Option.** Answer expanded to clarify that the player may also proceed under Rule 28.

25-1b/10 ***Casual Water on Putting Green; Nearest Point of Relief Is Off Green.**

25-1b/10.5 ***Casual Water on Putting Green; Whether Player Entitled to Relief for Intervention If Ball Is on Green and Nearest Point of Relief Is Off Green.**

25-1b/15 ***Measuring Across Ground Under Repair in Obtaining Relief.**

25-1b/16 ***Ball Equidistant from Two Points Which Meet Requirements of Ground Under Repair Rule.**

25-1b/18 ***Crawfish Mound Interferes with Stance or Swing.**

25-1b/19 **Ball Lies on Mound Made by Burrowing Animal; Unreasonable to Play Stroke Due to Bush.** Answer expanded for clarity.

25-1b/20 **Stance Interfered with by Burrowing Animal Hole; Unreasonable to Play Stroke Because of Other Condition.** Answer expanded for clarity.

25-1b/21 **Cast of Burrowing Animal Interferes with Stroke Towards Green; Tree Prevents Such Stroke.** Answer expanded for clarity.

25-1b/26 ***Player Unaware Ball in Water Hazard Takes Relief from Interference by Burrowing Animal Hole.**

26/3 **Unmarked Water Hazard.** Amended for clarity.

27/5 **Player Searching for Ball Mistakes His Ball for Opponent's.** Amended for clarity.

27/7 **Ball Found in Burrowing Animal Hole After Five Minute Search.** Amended for clarity.

27-2b/1 **Continuation of Play with Provisional Ball Without Searching for Original Ball.** Amended to state equity (Rule 1-4) is basis for answer.

27-2b/2 **When Provisional Ball Holed Becomes Ball In Play.** Amended to state that equity (Rule 1-4) is basis for answer.

27-2c/1.5 **Whether Provisional Ball Becomes Ball in Play If Original Ball Lost in Ground Under Repair.** Amended to reflect change to Rule 27-2.

28/13 **After Declaring Ball Unplayable and Lifting It, Player Discovers Ball Was in Ground Under Repair.** Amended to eliminate reference to Rule 9-2 being applicable in match play.

30-3d/2 **Player Wins Hole With Wrong Ball and Partner Picks Up; Error Discovered at Next Hole.** Answer amended to reflect specific language of Rule 9-2.

30-3d/3.5 **Player Plays Partner's Ball; Error Discovered After Opponents Have Played Next Strokes.** Answer amended to reflect specific language of Rule 9-2.

33/1 **Removal of Casual Water on Putting Green by Committee.** Amended to reflect change to Rule 13-2.

33-2a/1 **Exposed Water Pipe Adjacent and Parallel to Boundary Fence Causes Problems; Suggested Procedure.** Amended to reflect change to Rule 24-2.

33-8/4 **Local Rule for Events in Which Motorized Golf Carts Permitted.** Amended for clarity.

Misc./2 **Whether Rakes Should Be Placed In or Outside Bunkers.** Expanded for clarity.

US/33-8/100 **Local Rule for Lateral Water Hazard with Bunker Adjacent.** Amended to clarify that use of the permissible Local Rule is a matter for the Committee to decide.

DECISIONS WITHDRAWN

6-8c/1 **When Ball May Be Cleaned or Substituted After Play Has Been Discontinued.** Clearly covered by amended Rule 6-8d.

6-8c/2 **Player Discontinues Play and Lifts Ball Without Marking Its Position.** Clearly covered by amended Rule 6-8c.

7-1b/5.5 **Competitor Test Surface of Putting Green Between Rounds of 36-Hole Stroke Play Competition on Consecutive Days.** Clearly covered by amended Rule 7-1b.

12-1/4 **Ball in Ground Under Repair Moved During Search; Procedure for Player.** Clearly covered by amended Rule 12-1.

16-1f/1 **Caddie Deliberately Positioned Off Putting Green on Extension of Line of Putt Behind Ball.** Clearly covered by amended Rule 14-2.

20-1/15 **Ball Moved by Ball-Marker Dropped Accidentally by Player.** Clearly covered by new Decision 20-1/15.

24-1/1 **Movable Obstruction Defined.** Covered by new Definition of "Obstruction."

24-2a/2 **Meaning of "Area of His Intended Swing."** Considered unnecessary in view of the elimination of the prohibition on measuring over, through, or under the obstruction when determining the nearest point of relief.

24-2b/3 **Clarification of "Point on the Course Nearest to Where the Ball Lies."** Covered by new Definition of "Nearest Point of

Relief."

24-2b/5 **Clarification of Relief Procedure from Obstruction in Bunker.** Clearly covered by amended Rule 24-2b(ii).

24-2b/13 **Ball Bounces Across Obstruction After Drop.** Considered unnecessary in view of the elimination of the prohibition on measuring over, through, or under the obstruction when determining the nearest point of relief.

25/19 **Burrowing Animal.** Covered by new Definition of "Burrowing Animal."

25/20 **Holes Made by Non-Burrowing Animals.** Covered by new Definition of "Burrowing Animal."

25/22 **Salamander.** Covered by new Definition of "Burrowing Animal."

25-1b/1 **Clarification of "Point on the Course Nearest to Where the Ball Lies."** Covered by new Definition of "Nearest Point of Relief."

25-1b/14 **Crossing Over Obstruction in Obtaining Relief from Ground Under Repair.** Considered unnecessary in view of the elimination of the prohibition on measuring over, through, or under the obstruction when determining the nearest point of relief.

33-2a/5 **Water Hazard Under Repair.** Considered unnecessary in view of the new Note 1 to Rule 25-1b.

33-6/1 **How to Settle Tie in Handicap Match.** Clearly covered in Appendix I.

33-6/2 **How to Settle Tie in Stroke Play.** Clearly covered in Appendix I.

33-8/6 **Local Rule Prohibits Practice During Round on Putting Green of Hole Last Played; Competitor Practices on Last Green After Holing Out.** Clearly covered in Appendix I.

33-8/32 **Local Rule for Aeration Holes.** Covered in Appendix I.

33-8/40 **Local Rule for Environmentally-Sensitive Areas.** Covered in Appendix I.

RE-NUMBERED DECISIONS

4-2/3 **Applying Chalk to Club Face** (formerly

4-3/1)

4-3/12 **Replacing Club for Stroke Play Play-Off** (formerly 4-4a/9)

4-4a/1 **When Club Is Considered Added** (formerly 4-4a/7)

4-4a/2 **Changing Clubs Between Rounds in 36 Hole Match** (formerly 4-4a/8)

4-4a/3 **Competitor Withdraws During Round and Puts His Clubs in Fellow-Competitor's Bag** (formerly 4-4a/10)

4-4a/4 **Partner's Clubs Carried in One Bag** (formerly 4-4a/11)

4-4a/5 **Fellow-Competitor's Club Put in Competitor's Bag by Mistake During Round Used Unintentionally by Competitor** (formerly 4-4a/12)

4-4a/6 **Excess Club Put in Player's Golf Bag After Player has Counted His Clubs at 1st Tee; Error Discovered After Player Has Started Round** (formerly 4-4a/13)

4-4a/7 **Carrying Weighted Training Club** (formerly 4-4a/14)

4-4a/8 **Retrieving Another Player's Lost Club** (formerly 4-4a/15)

4-4a/9 **Clarification of Match Play Penalty** (formerly 4-4a/16)

4-4a/10 **Breach of 14-Club Rule in Stroke Play Discovered at 8th Hole; Where Penalty Strokes Applied** (formerly 4-4a/17)

4-4a/11 **Excess Club Discovered Before Player Plays from 2nd Tee But After Opponent or Fellow-Competitor Has Played** (formerly 4-4a/18)

4-4a/12 **Competitor Who Misplaces Putter Borrows Fellow-Competitor's Putter** (formerly 4-4a/19)

14-2/4 **Caddie Inadvertently Positioned on Extension of Line of Putt Behind Ball** (formerly 16-1f/2)

THE USGA AND YOU

Please call for any of the following:

USGA Publications List

A comprehensive listing of all USGA books, pamphlets and videos, including:

- The Rules of Golf
- Decisions on the Rules of Golf
- Golf Rules In Brief
- USGA Handicap System
- and much, much more

USGA Order Department 1-800-336-4446

Members Guide & Catalogue from Golf House

The ultimate source for U.S. Open and U.S. Women's Open clothing and memorabilia. Includes a full line of USGA Member clothing and gifts. Generous Member discounts.

USGA Catalog 1-800-755-0293

USGA Member Brochure

Information on joining the USGA and showing your support for golf in the United States.

USGA Members Program 1-800-223-0041

THE USGA ON-LINE

Information on all facets of the USGA: Membership, Championships, Green Section, Equipment Standards, USGA Handicap System, The Rules of Golf, Publications & Catalogue

Join us on the Internet at http://www.usga.org